EDWARD VII
and his Jewish Court

EDWARD VII
and his Jewish Court

ANTHONY ALLFREY

Weidenfeld & Nicolson
London

First published in Great Britain in 1991 by
George Weidenfeld & Nicolson,
91 Clapham High Street, London SW4 7TA

British Library Cataloguing in Publication Data
(available on request)
ISBN 0 297 81125 8

Typeset at The Spartan Press Ltd,
Lymington, Hants
Printed and bound in Great Britain by
Butler & Tanner Ltd
Frome and London

Contents

Illustrations

Acknowledgements

I am deeply grateful to Her Majesty the Queen for gracious permission to quote from those letters to which she holds the copyright, and to Lady de Bellaigue, Registrar of the Royal Archives, for her kind and constant assistance at a trying and inconvenient time. I am similarly indebted to Lord Brabourne and the Trustees of Broadlands, to the Trustees of the British Museum, to the Master and Fellows of Trinity College, Cambridge, to Lord Bonham-Carter, as well as to the authors and publishers of the many works on which I have drawn and to the editors of those newspapers and periodicals which have provided sources. I warmly appreciate the rare privilege, accorded by President Turgut Özal, when Prime Minister of Turkey, of access to the Grand Vizier's Archives; and am grateful to Professor Kasim Gülek and his son Mustafa for their perseverance and pains, and to Lady Daunt for providing the key.

Mrs Anne Thorold has again been an indispensable support, trawling and dredging in the past and the present. I would also express my gratitude to Dr Dorothea McEwan for her own researches and translations from the German; to Haham Dr Solomon Gaon and to Mr Kenneth Rose for their advice, and to the late Lord Rothschild for his thoughtfulness.

I owe a separate debt to the following for their generous response to my appeals: Mrs Caroline Agar (National Horseracing Museum), Mr Simon Blundell (Librarian, Reform Club), Mrs Molly Chalk (Broadlands Archives), Miss Diana Chardin (Trinity College Library, Cambridge), Mr C. M. Drukker (Jewish Historical Society), Mr Henry Gillett and Mr John Hodgson (Bank of England Records), Ms Phyllida Melling (Guildhall Library), Miss Josephine Parker and Miss D. J. Mead (Suffolk County Council Archive), Dr Arnold Paucker (Leo Baeck Institute), Mr Michael Richman (Jewish Colonization Association), Ms Maria Rollo (National Maritime Museum), and Mr Robin Harcourt Williams (Hatfield House Archives).

I would also like to add my appreciation of the services of the staff of the British Library, the London Library, the Bodleian, Oxford, and the Public Record Office.

Others to whom I extend my thanks for the time and trouble they have taken over my petty problems are: the late Mr Michael Behrens, Count John de Bendern, the late Marjorie, Countess of Brecknock, Mr Ian Brooks (King Edward VII Hospital for Officers), Lt. Col. A. Crawforth and Miss Griffin (Waddesdon Manor), Mr Frank Griffin (Jockey Club), the late Mr Max Harari, Mrs Elizabeth Ann Haynes, Donald Freiherr von Hirsch, Lord Jessel, the late Sir Philip Magnus, Sir Anthony Meyer MP, the late Mr Stewart Perowne, Prof. P. J. V. Rolo, Dr E. Rosen (Embassy of Israel), Dr Shirley Sherwood, Rear Admiral Charles Weston, and Ms Mariella Wolf. *Mes remerciements*, too, to M. Jean Daubigny (Préfecture de Police, Paris), to Mme Michelle de Saignes (Mairie de St-Cloud) and to Mme Odette Visconti of Beauregard. In Jerusalem, Ms Olga Weiss, an old friend of the late Dr Kurt Grunwald, was most kind and helpful.

My last heartfelt thanks are due to Mr Anthony Blond for his original inspiration; to Mrs Caroline Gordon for piecing together my mutilated manuscript; to my agent, Mr Andrew Lownie, and to Mr David Roberts, Miss Amanda Harting and all at Weidenfeld & Nicolson for their faith and exemplary patience.

The Bischoffsheims and Goldschmidts

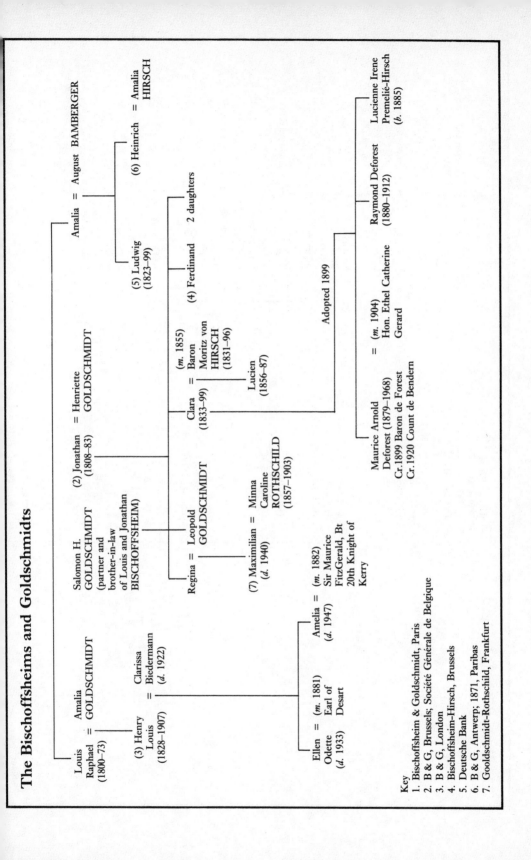

Key
1. Bischoffsheim & Goldschmidt, Paris
2. B & G, Brussels; Société Générale de Belgique
3. B & G, London
4. Bischoffsheim–Hirsch, Brussels
5. Deutsche Bank
6. B & G, Antwerp; 1871, Paribas
7. Goolschmidt–Rothschild, Frankfurt

The Rothschilds (Abridged)

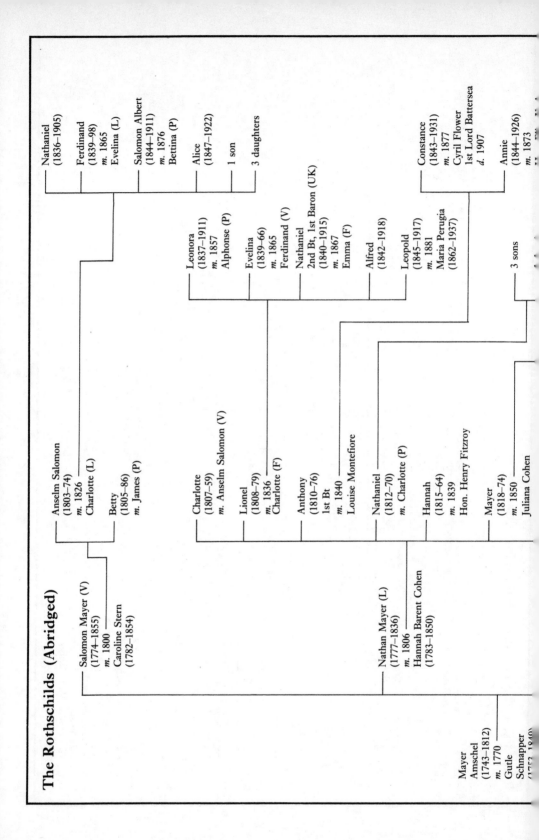

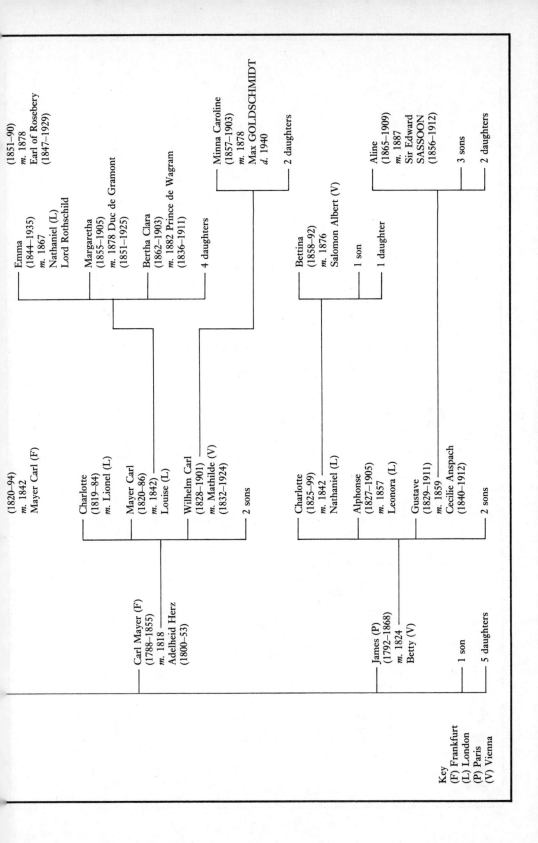

Carl Mayer (F)
(1788–1855)
m. 1818
Adelheid Herz
(1800–53)

Charlotte
(1819–84)
m. Lionel (L)

Mayer Carl
(1820–86)
m. 1842
Louise (L)

Emma
(1844–1935)
m. 1867
Nathaniel (L)
Lord Rothschild
(1820–94)
m. 1842
Mayer Carl (F)

Margaretha
(1855–1905)
m. 1878 Duc de Gramont
(1851–1925)

Bertha Clara
(1862–1903)
m. 1882 Prince de Wagram
(1836–1911)

(1851–90)
m. 1878
Earl of Rosebery
(1847–1929)

Wilhelm Carl
(1828–1901)
m. Mathilde (V)
(1832–1924)

4 daughters

Minna Caroline
(1857–1903)
m. 1878
Max GOLDSCHMIDT
d. 1940

2 sons

2 daughters

James (P)
(1792–1868)
m. 1824
Betty (V)

Charlotte
(1825–99)
m. 1842
Nathaniel (L)

Alphonse
(1827–1905)
m. 1857
Leonora (L)

Bettina
(1858–92)
m. 1876
Salomon Albert (V)

1 son

1 daughter

Gustave
(1829–1911)
m. 1859
Cecilie Anspach
(1840–1912)

Aline
(1865–1909)
m. 1887
Sir Edward
SASSOON
(1856–1912)

3 sons

2 daughters

1 son

5 daughters

2 sons

Key
(F) Frankfurt
(L) London
(P) Paris
(V) Vienna

The Cassels

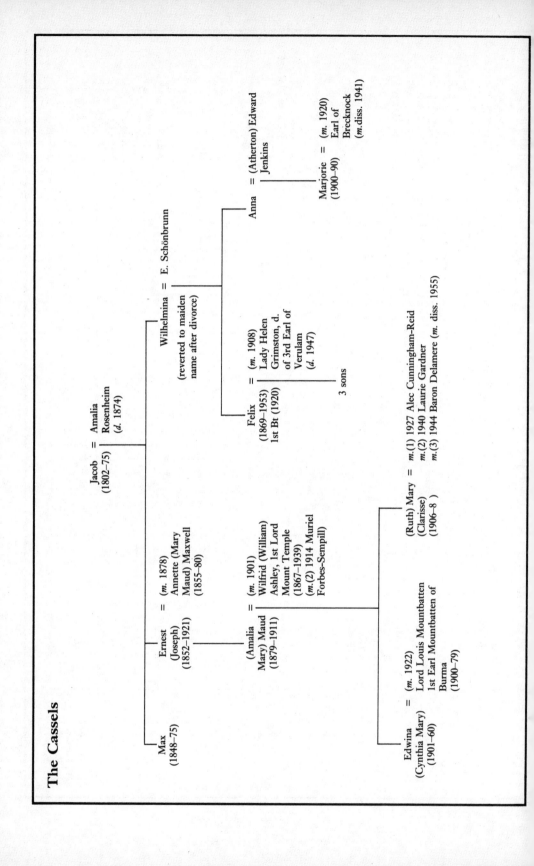

Introduction

Queen Victoria was born four years after the British and Prussian allies checked revolutionary France's pretensions to European hegemony at Waterloo; her eldest son, Albert Edward, died four years before Britain, all but fortuitously tethered to a revanchist France, faced the German empire in Flanders one hundred years later. The mother, who came to the throne at the age of eighteen, reigned for sixty-three years, the last forty in obdurate self-pitying seclusion, with little understanding or sympathy for the unprecedented transformations and turmoils of the age, which is often thought of, erroneously, as a time of serene and secure continuity. The son, once he had set up his own household and taken a wife, had to wait in enforced idleness – he was past fifty before he was allowed a sight of the Prime Minister's reports on Cabinet meetings – until he in turn inherited the throne. Patience was not one of his more evident attributes.

The Edwardian age would never have been the same if its corpulent incarnation had not been blessed with a robust personality. A less spirited psyche must have foundered under the solicitous smothering of the naturally boisterous instincts of childhood and an oppressive rule of unremitting labour prescribed by his father's mentor, the odiously smug Baron Stockmar, whose faith in his own infallibility was only matched by his want of experience and, worse, sense. This harsh regime was founded partly on the morbid fear that young Bertie might take after his mother's Hanoverian uncles (though prim Prince Albert's Coburg forebears, not least his profligate father, were scarcely models of decorum), and partly on the innocent assumption that a rigorous application of learning would iron out any taints of heredity as well as defects of character. The well-meaning and opinionated parents preferred to apply theory rather than to heed lore. To compound these faults of commission, Bertie was shielded from the checks and restraints of what was feared to be the infectious gaiety of his high-born contemporaries. He proved intractable material for such a punishing ordeal. Fortunately, his perversity served to defeat these good intentions. The only remarkable consequence was that he survived with so few scars.

Bertie was judged by one unusually perceptive and sympathetic tutor as 'amiable and affectionate' (though given to teasing his siblings and tormenting the footmen), of a most forgiving disposition with a 'keen perception of right and wrong'. He was loyal and generous. He craved only companionship, approbation and diversion. Unhappily, made painfully aware that he did not match up to his parents' elevated expectations, he had no one to whom he could turn for encouragement, even affection. He reckoned on relief from this oppressive regime when, at the age of seventeen, he was put in the charge of Lord Elgin's brother, Colonel the Hon. Robert Bruce, an austere but kindly Guardsman. His hopes were dashed. Life continued to be just as minutely regulated. The Queen, who confided to her favourite and eldest daughter, Vicky, that she feared Bertie was 'so idle and so weak', instructed Bruce to inculcate 'habits of reflection and self-denial' in the young Prince. Such concepts were unfortunately entirely alien to his easy-going and pleasure-loving nature. His friends were once again chosen for him by his governor, tobacco (ineffectively) prohibited and strict diet sheets composed for him; even his claret was to be watered on hot days, his sherry on cold. (His mother, curiously, laced her claret with whisky and was far more tolerant of habitual drunkenness among her Highland servants than her son.)

Even when, a year later, he was at last able to break free from the immediate confines of the family, he could not escape their cloying care. At Oxford he led a life apart, carefully segregated from his fellow undergraduates by his governor and staff. Within a month the officious Prince Consort descended on him for a visit of inspection; what he found made him 'terribly anxious for the future'. Bruce was urged to make it clear to his charge that 'The only use of Oxford is that it is a place for *study*'. Bertie's demeanour betrayed his frustration: a fleshy face with broody eyes and full, petulant lips above a receding chin was not improved, his mother regretted, by his 'dull, heavy, blasé look'.

His first deliverance from his parents' shadow was offered in the Long Vacation of 1860 by a royal tour of Canada and (at the Queen's insistence, 'incognito') of the United States. A personal triumph, it established his self-confidence, though Prince Albert at once did his disagreeable best to squash such a pretension, telling his son that it was to be seen as a demonstration of loyalty to his mother rather than a tribute to his own qualities.

In the following January the Prince was enrolled at Trinity College, Cambridge. Although still insulated from college life, installed with his governor, now Major-General Bruce, and other attendants some miles outside the town, he made more friends, with increased self-assurance, than he had at Oxford. He even managed, despite being attracted 'almost unconsciously into the company of the idle and frivolous', to draw sufficiently on his charm and good manners to put on a convincing show as an attentive student, if not a scholar.

That same summer, as a special concession, he was permitted to spend two and a half months with the army at the Curragh camp outside Dublin. One night his fellow officers, after a lively evening in the mess, as a prank spirited a young actress, Nellie Clifden, into his quarters. The Prince was not one to forgo such a windfall, but news of his own fall was soon passed by eager tongues to Windsor. His father could not at first bring himself to believe his ears, but his worst fears of his son's character were confirmed. By the end of the same year, Prince Albert succumbed to typhoid and his grief-stricken widow blamed her son, rather than the drains of Windsor Castle, for bringing on his end. She could never look on him again 'without a shudder'.

Even before the unfortunate affair of the Curragh, his parents had been casting about for a bride for the Prince. Marriage was seen as a settling factor, indeed his last chance of redemption. The principal problem was the dearth of Protestant princesses. In this limited field, Princess Alexandra of Denmark was the dark horse. Though Vicky, now married to Crown Prince Frederick of Prussia, had sent her mother glowing reports of Alexandra's beauty, charms and amiability, both parents disapproved of her mother's family, the Hesse-Cassels, for their unpardonable frivolity. Queen Victoria came slowly round to the prospect. No other suitable candidate could anyway be unearthed, and there was the unwelcome risk of the Tsar's snatching the prize from under her nose: it would be dreadful, Vicky wrote, 'if this pearl went to the horrid Russians'. Thus, as much by default as by favour, Bertie's parents were won over, first by photographs, then by Alexandra's person; the groom-to-be himself even found her 'charming and very pretty' – when his opinion was finally sought. Notwithstanding her attractions, the Prince, fearing suddenly to be domesticated and separated from his friends, was only prompted into action by a stern ultimatum from his father. The marriage took place in March 1863, and the whist parties later moved over from the Marlborough Club, which he founded in 1869, to his home at Marlborough House.

Thwarted in his early ambition to take up soldiering, it became evident that there was little likelihood of any offer of any meaningful alternative; the sympathetic efforts of the Prime Minister, William Gladstone, to arrange for him to act in some viceregal capacity in Ireland in the winter and to assume some of the Queen's neglected ceremonial duties in London during the summer were quashed by his mother. The virtual extent of his participation in public life was a seat on two Royal Commissions, on working-class housing and, with what must have seemed to him awful irony, old age pensions. It is little wonder that he sought diversions and was tempted down a profligate path during his tedious and interminable apprenticeship. With no other field in which he was able to assert himself, he developed into a stickler for trivia. Social and sartorial solecisms drove him to distraction; precedence and protocol obsessed him; the correct wear of orders and decorations was as of much moment as the manner of their acquisition. (Most distressingly, the aristocracy was the least heedful of these niceties.)

Though deliberately deprived of any participation or insight into the workings of his mother's government, he had, in the opinion of the radical, and sometime Republican, politician Sir Charles Dilke, 'more sense and more usage of the modern world than the Queen, but less real brain power'; he was nonetheless 'very sharp in a way – the Queen not sharp at all, but she carries heavier metal . . .' Once he had come into his inheritance, he showed none of his mother's dutiful application to official papers, still less when their subjects, home and colonial affairs, bored him; he rarely read a book. He had, however, certain natural aptitudes which did much to rescue the monarchy from the solemn, almost morose (and resented) obscurity into which it had sunk through neglect; they earned him personal popularity at home and exaggerated respect abroad for his statesmanship as the 'Uncle of Europe'. (It was not untypical of the general aura of gloom that overshadowed the middle years of the Queen's reign that the decoration of Westminster Abbey for her Golden Jubilee in 1887 was entrusted to an undertaker.)

Despite the Prince's intellectual limitations, his character, in the eyes of such a shrewd judge as his friend Viscount Esher, 'clothed him with an undisputed authority greater, because far more subtle, than autocratic power'; the mainspring of the spell he cast, though his nephew Kaiser Wilhelm was immune, was his 'power of raising a man in his own estimation'. The Liberal statesman Sir Edward Grey judged him in addition to possess 'a rare, if not unique, power of combining bonhomie and dignity'. This was not an insignificant asset. The Queen's seclusion and the scandals which too often surrounded the heir to the throne – the

Prince was on occasion booed and jeered in the streets and at the theatre – gave rise to widespread republican sentiment. Gladstone, quite unable to prevail on the Queen to modify her ways, confided his anxiety to the Foreign Secretary that Royalty's large fund of goodwill was diminishing and he 'did not see from whence it is to be replenished as matters now go. To speak in rude and general terms, the Queen is invisible and the Prince of Wales is not respected . . .' The Queen feared that Bertie's rackety progress would fan such dangerous emotions and that his excesses, so typical of what she regarded as the 'frivolous, selfish and pleasure-seeking lives' of the upper classes, would damage his reputation in the eyes of the middle and lower classes, thus contributing to a distressing encouragement of 'the spirit of democracy'. Her son countered that she should show herself to her subjects; 'we live in radical times', he warned; she pleaded that the noise of London was bad for her nerves. (The Prince's popularity was restored by loyal scenes of rejoicing over his miraculous recovery from typhoid.)

The resentment bred by the Queen's shrinking from the public stare and shirking her duties led to a general suspicion that she was salting away her annual allowance from Parliament; a pamphlet published anonymously by the Liberal George Otto Trevelyan, *What Does She Do With It?*, sold as well as scurrilous publications exposing the Prince's irregular private life. She had, indeed, through frugal housekeeping over most of the first thirty years of her retirement, managed to put aside £824,000 from an annual Civil List allowance of £385,000. Although ignorant of this harvest, Gladstone supported by *The Times* pressed her to allow the Prince an additional personal allowance for fulfilling her engagements while she immured herself at Windsor and Balmoral. Such a view did not find royal favour. Rumours, meanwhile, continued to circulate concerning Edward's indebtedness; it was assumed he was only kept afloat by loans from obliging quarters.

While society indulged in a public display of unexampled extravagance and ostentation, behind the glittering façade credit was not unusually stretched up to and sometimes beyond the limit (two of Edward's friends ruined themselves in his service). The middle years of the second half of the last century witnessed an insatiable scramble for capital, of which the City of London was the fount, by native promoters and foreign governments in the race to develop the ever more accessible corners of the globe. Feverish speculation, fed by fraudulent prospectuses, was undertaken as a short cut to riches; with few rules, a host of ingenious and colourful swindlers fattened on a seemingly inexhaustible pool of gullible investors. States ancient and modern defaulted periodically on their debts; bubbles burst, markets crashed and banks foundered; worldwide depressions followed. At home, agriculture, which supported the largest single male workforce, at a time when land was still the foundation not only of wealth but of social prestige and political influence, suffered an irreversible crisis. (Estates of 10,000 acres or more made up one-quarter of the land; a little more than 4,000 people owned half of England.) Even Edward's friend the Marquess of Hartington, heir to the Duke of Devonshire who ran Chatsworth and owned chunks of seven counties as well as some in Ireland, was moved at least once to resort to the services of Sam Lewis, the scrupulous and popular money-lender to Society. (On his death in 1901 he was worth £2.5 million, more than twice the fortune of the merchant banker James Stern, who died in the same year.) The Duke himself feared that 'the inexorable necessities of democratic finance' would mark the end of such large estates and the style of living they supported, despite the fact that income tax, from a low of two pence in the pound, only reached a shilling, a rate of 5 per cent, at the turn of the century owing to the demands of the Boer War.

The late Victorian way of life – families were large, dependants numerous – imposed a considerable strain on even the plumpest purses. The landed classes not unusually owned a second substantial country home; a town house, the centre of all entertainment, was required, if even only rented, for the summer season; a hunting box in the Shires was as desirable as a lodge in Scotland with a deer forest and stretch of river, with perhaps a house and racing establishment at Newmarket. With the end of the London season, rounded off with two weeks' yachting at Cowes in July, Society dispersed by special train about the countryside, settling into house parties of anything from ten to half a hundred, with their complement of lady's maids, grooms or loaders, for as long as ten days at a stretch under the same roof; they shot or rode to hounds five or six times a week; for milder spirits, such as the future Conservative leader Arthur Balfour, there were other dissipations – croquet, tennis (invented in the mid-Seventies) and golf, a recent Scottish export (the Prince of Wales boasted a course on his Sandringham estate, as did Lord Rothschild at Tring Manor, where an additional hazard was provided by his heir's wandering emus). This programme lasted until Parliament reopened early in the new year (the land-owning classes still ran the government of the realm).

As the heir to the throne, an enthusiastic host and keen shot, Edward was required to keep his own end up in this exacting regime. He had expensive tastes and onerous obligations, a limited income and no expectations from his mother. He regarded as improper any question of tailoring his tastes to his budget; the pressing need was to maintain, and preferably increase, his income to keep pace with his expenses. Until 1889, when he was in sight of his fiftieth birthday, Edward's income was only a little over £100,000 a year, of which £40,000 was provided by a carping Parliament; the balance represented the remains of the interest, diminishing as fast as he depleted the capital, of the Duchy of Cornwall, the perquisite of the heir to the throne on his coming of age. This was never enough as Prime Ministers of all persuasions, even the thrifty Gladstone, agreed. They were not, however, prepared to go to the House to ask for more money as long as the Prince was the object of rumours about extravagance and debt. Gladstone considered the Queen should disgorge £50,000 a year from her own pocket, especially as she was forever pressing Parliament to grant allowances and dowries to other members of her family who had even fewer responsibilities. As it was, Parliament in 1889 increased his income by a lesser sum – £36,000. Edward as a result remained in debt until a few years before his death, despite the flair and expertise of those who minded his finances.

It was privately assumed, and on occasions publicly reported, that heavy losses at gambling accounted for the Prince's debts, a habit he was popularly reckoned to have caught in foreign parts, notably at Baden and Homburg (in fact he went there to lose weight). The Prince, under some pressure at the time, professed a horror of gambling, though he exempted as harmless those bets on horses or at baccarat for affordable stakes. Playing with men who could generally more easily spare large sums, his losses at the tables were never immoderate. Neither did he wager excessive sums on the Turf. A racing stable with stud was emphatically a rich man's pastime, but fortune, abetted by good management, favoured him. In two consecutive years in the mid-Nineties, he came second in the list of winning owners, and from 1886 until the end of his life he earned over £400,000 in prize money and stud fees. His impulsive generosity ate into this. When, to his huge delight, he won the Grand National, worth just £1,975, in 1900, he lavished £500 on the jockey and half that amount on the head stable lad alone, not forgetting the trainer and his assistant (in the same year his horse Diamond Jubilee carried off the Two Thousand Guineas, the Newmarket Stakes, the Derby, the Eclipse Stakes and the St Leger for a total of almost £28,000). On another occasion, he pressed a gold cigarette case on Margot Tennant, later to marry the future Liberal Prime Minister Asquith, for picking him a winner at Ascot; in a similar vein, he would indulge Lord Burnham, the former Sir Edward Levy-Lawson, with a silver pheasant as 'a recollection of the best day's shooting' he had ever enjoyed. (Paradoxically, his liberality with the Royal Victorian

Order was owed not so much to his 'unholy passion' for decorations as to a sense of economy; at no more than £25, such a bauble came cheaper than a cigarette case from the court jeweller at some £75 or an enamelled ornamental snuffbox from Fabergé at twice that price.)

There was one field in which the Prince, for want of means, was unable to satisfy his generous instincts: philanthropy. (Alexandra's invariable response to a begging letter, to her husband's despair, was a £5 note.) Despite the crass materialism of the age, England was still more than a nominally Christian country; charity was the largest item after food on the family budget of the upper and the increasingly prosperous urban middle classes. (And food was no insignificant expense. The fishmonger's account for Lord Rothschild's household amounted to £5,000 a year, a Minister of the Crown's salary, at a time when smoked salmon cost a shilling per pound.) Once King, but still unsure whether ends would meet, he delegated this pleasure to his friends; among them the Jews were the most responsive, founding charities in his name. He followed their fortunes closely and took a hand in their management.

A further foible of the Prince, and one he did not attempt to deny himself, was a pronounced tenderness for the ladies. In his younger days this was practised, not always discreetly, in Paris, the uncensorious playground for most Victorians deviating from the strict path of marital fidelity. In accordance with the custom of the day, he established casual liaisons with musical comedy stars. In such an intensively competitive arena, an heir to the throne had an edge; his keen rival was the Austrian Crown Prince Rudolf. The more ambitious and comely among them availed themselves of his rank to promote their public careers and in return bestowed fitting favours in private. The Prince later developed a taste for more tangible talent – Sarah Bernhardt and Lillie Langtry, though before she took to the boards. In middle age, overweight but with his vitality unimpaired, he settled down to more lasting attachments. The first such fixture was Daisy Brooke, later Countess of Warwick, an acknowledged 'Beauty' who drew admiring crowds to watch her take her morning ride in Rotten Row or her afternoon drive in the Park. She was wilful, passionate, and an heiress in her own right. When 'My own lovely little Daisy' showed signs of remorse and embraced socialism in his place, though the couple had conspired to convince Princess Alexandra that their affair had latterly been purely platonic, the Prince formed an immediate and final attachment to his hostess at a London dinner party in 1898. The Hon. Mrs George Keppel, at twenty-nine almost half his age, was married to a conspicuously handsome but impecunious army officer, the brother of the Earl of Albemarle, who was presently found employment with the Prince's grocer friend Sir Thomas Lipton. Alice Keppel was vivacious and clever, tactful and discreet; she was never heard to make a malicious remark. If these qualities alone were not enough to endear her to Alexandra, 'the Favourite' was at least tolerated at Sandringham and in consequence at all but a handful of grand houses. She was more appreciated by the court functionaries for her capacity for keeping the sovereign in a good humour, thereby making their life easier. She was indeed reproached by Edward's private secretary, Sir Francis Knollys, for not using her influence in the matter of the company the King insisted on keeping, which was not always to the taste of even the least stuffy courtiers. It is tempting to deride Victorian high society as hypocritical, peopled by complaisant cuckolds and ardent adulterers who preached the virtues of domesticity to their inferiors and could express their public outrage at Richard Strauss's *Salomé* as a salacious and sacrilegious spectacle. There was a strong social compulsion to observe the outward proprieties so as not to compromise the image of their superior fitness to govern, but even more persuasive was the stigma attached to divorce: though allowed by law since 1857, it was regarded as a greater social disgrace than adultery; even innocent parties were ostracized. The widely honoured Lord Hartington lived openly for thirty years with the German-born wife of the Duke of Manchester who had fallen on lean times. She was acknowledged as one of the most powerful women in Society, ambitious and implacable. On Manchester's death, and shortly after Hartington succeeded to the Dukedom of Devonshire, the pair finally married.

When the Prince, aged nineteen, went up to Cambridge, he renewed an old acquaintance – with Charles Carrington, who when at Eton had been approved as a suitable companion for young Bertie at nearby Windsor – and made new friends, notably three brothers, Nathaniel, Alfred and Leopold Rothschild, from a family whose wealth was already the envied subject of rumour and respect. Their father, Baron Lionel, and his brothers were the sons of an immigrant father, Nathan Mayer, founder of the English family's fortune, and had been educated at German universities. The young Rothschilds were by contrast, upbringing and education as English as the Prince (and had as little English blood). Though never much addicted to hunting, Edward followed the Rothschild staghounds in their Buckinghamshire enclave, and the brothers the royal pack around Windsor, only twenty miles away. (Nathaniel, the future first Lord Rothschild, was hunting with the Prince when he was summoned to his father's deathbed.) After a day's hunting with the Rothschild brothers – his appetite before and after the chase was already more admired than his seat on a horse – the Prince was introduced to their uncle, Sir Anthony. (Baron Lionel, head of the London bank since his father's death in 1836, was content to remain in the family's original home, Gunnersbury Park, near Acton.) A jovial, stout Lothario, Sir Anthony had two high-spirited daughters a few years younger than Edward who were both to marry outside the faith. The Prince shot (and danced) with the family, themselves frequent guests at Sandringham, the Prince's place in Norfolk, a short ride from the Wash, which he regarded as his home. Sir Anthony, easy-going and uncensorious, became the Prince's earliest independent financial confidant, free with unobtrusive favours and sound advice. Alfred, extravagant after Edward's own heart, slipped suavely into the Marlborough House set while Leopold shared the Prince's love of the Turf; Nathaniel, brusque and businesslike, preferred the counting house. They were joined in the Prince of Wales's circle by their Austrian brother-in-law, Baron Ferdinand. Such company was welcome, for the Prince was for too much of the time at a loose end. Many of his more orthodox friends took naturally to a career in politics, which entailed long hours of unremunerated toil. Carrington took a seat in the House of Commons within a few years of coming down from Cambridge and moved on to the Upper House on the death of his father; after service there, he, like Hilaire Belloc's lachrymose Lord Lundy, went out to govern New South Wales. Lord Hartington, the Prince's senior by eight years, was already a Member of Parliament before the Prince went up to Cambridge, and by 1863 had begun a long and distinguished ministerial progress.

In 1875, the year before Sir Anthony Rothschild died, the Prince of Wales, aged thirty-five, took off for India, where he encountered the exotic tribe of Sassoon, the 'Rothschilds of the East'. Sephardic merchants who had been established in Baghdad for generations, they had chosen to exchange the increasing lawlessness on the periphery of the crumbling Ottoman Empire for the security and commercial opportunities of the British Raj in India; with the opening of the Suez Canal, their eminence in the East had been recognized with a knighthood and the freedom of the City of London. Sir Albert Abdullah Sassoon endeared himself to the Prince with his lavish entertainment in Bombay. His half-brothers, Arthur and Reuben, were already ensconced in London and, seduced by the picture they painted of the foggier fleshpots, he soon followed them. These nabobs, with their spicey flavour of the Orient, were accepted with amused, if sometimes malicious, tolerance by Society (no opprobrium attached to their profitable sideline in the opium trade). Bald, swarthy Arthur and his beautiful wife, Louise, whose sister married Leopold Rothschild, provided, with disinterested devotion and neglect of their family's own affairs, grouse and stags in Scotland and an informal retreat in the ensured privacy of Brighton. Brother Reuben, whose simple pleasure it was to give the most appreciated presents to the Prince, became one of his most constant companions until gout slowed him down. Sir Albert's son, named Edward Albert in honour of the Prince, married a French Rothschild, Aline, after whom the Prince, returning the honour, named his trim new racing yacht.

When the Prince of Wales was a little short of his half-century, Parliament had voted him a small but still welcome increase in his allowance, but word went around that he was again in desperate financial straits. Succour was at hand. Baron Maurice de Hirsch was a third-generation Bavarian 'Court Jew', a prickly, caustic, cheeseparing and sometimes comical character, ten years older than Edward; he was also the most daring entrepreneur of the age and a prince of philanthropy. His obsessive social ambitions were in no way dimmed by the persistent snubs to which he was subjected: in Vienna, despite his huge estates and the lavish sums he contributed to good works, he was never received at Court; in Paris, where he threw large sums at lost royalist causes, he was never admitted to the most select clubs. Hirsch had secured his introduction to Edward a few years before by way of a loan to the Austrian Emperor's heir, Rudolf, an unstable philanderer. In 1890, after a flurry of meetings with the Prince of Wales in Paris, where his hotel was ringed by money-lenders, Hirsch settled his more urgent needs. (The French police suspected that the Rothschilds had obliged.) Hirsch, assured of an heir to a throne as social sponsor in place of the late Crown Prince Rudolf, followed Edward across the Channel. He set himself up in style in London, rented a shoot not far from Sandringham, bought a house in Newmarket and all but netted the future Margot Asquith as daughter-in-law. He enjoyed a phenomenal success on the Turf, devoting the proceeds without deduction of expenses to the London hospitals. Only Buckingham Palace remained resolutely barred to him, to the chagrin of both Hirsch and his patron. The Prince made ample amends for his mother's slight. He accepted an invitation for himself and a party of English friends, among them the Arthur Sassoons, to stay and shoot with Hirsch in Hungary, under the eyes of the scandalized Austrian court.

Baron Hirsch had served an apprenticeship in banking in Brussels, marrying the senior partner's daughter. He was nearing forty when he snatched the concession from the Turkish government to finance, construct and operate the first railway through the turbulent Balkans to Constantinople, the route of the Orient Express, an adventure of 'cunning, force, robbery and deceit'. It was also profitable; Hirsch amassed one of the greatest private fortunes in history.

He spent the last six years of his life, while he basked luxuriantly in the royal favour, giving most of his fortune away to settle Jewish victims of the Eastern European pogroms in North America and on large slices of the Argentine. The Baron did not believe in unproductive charity. His philanthropy, over which he exercised jealous control, was planned to provide the colonists with the land and implements to make them self-supporting and enable them ultimately to earn sufficient to repay their debts. (He was not so fortunate in practice.)

Hirsch's widow, having lost her only son, adopted her menfolk's illegitimate offspring, securing Austrian titles for the two boys, a reward which she earned through her own beneficence. The elder, Baron de Forest, inherited all of his father's rebarbative character and radical opinions with enough of his money. Educated in England, he became a Liberal Member of Parliament, a crony of Winston Churchill, and the *bête noire* of Edward's son King George V.

Baron Hirsch succumbed to apoplexy four years before his Prince took up the crown. Two months after his death in April 1896, two owners, markedly similar in appearance, faced each other in the paddock at Epsom before the Derby. The Prince, whose Persimmon won the race, was introduced to Hirsch's protégé and executor, a fellow German-Jewish financier, Ernest Cassel. There were affairs of mutual moment to arrange arising out of Hirsch's estate and Cassel was commanded to appear at Sandringham. From that meeting there developed one of the closest, and strangest, relationships of the King's reign and last years.

Cassel had left Cologne almost thirty years before to settle in England. Although a self-made man who had left school at the age of fourteen, he shared Hirsch's banking credentials. He had laid the foundations of his fortune in Sweden and, in partnership with the Wall Street banker Jacob Schiff, in North American and Mexican railroads. Shortly after his meeting with the Prince, he transferred his attentions to Egypt, where Evelyn Baring, the future Lord Cromer, was struggling to animate the economy. Cassel financed the construction of the Aswan dam on the Nile, the largest civil engineering project the world had yet witnessed, which the Rothschilds had turned down; he set up a National Bank and fostered agriculture on the newly irrigated delta lands. Later, at the urgent prompting of the British government, he founded another National Bank in Turkey and set about trying to secure a stake for Britain in the Berlin-to-Baghdad Railway, a projection of Hirsch's line. Despite Whitehall's concern to reinforce the country's declining commercial and political presence in the Ottoman Empire, the Treasury refused to countenance any guarantees in case of loss or default on any of the commitments in which he was encouraged to risk his money. (The Rothschilds, who would not act without such surety, were regarded by Cassel as over-timid, a view with which a delighted Treasury sympathized.) The same politicans and diplomats who had urged him on, recoiling from an outburst of anti-German sentiment in the press or fearing French recriminations for infringing the spirit of the recent Entente Cordiale, cheerfully left him in the lurch to salvage what he could from the mess of their making. He diligently shared the news of these triumphs and frustrations with King Edward, who respected him as the 'cleverest head in England' (he did wonders also for the royal portfolio).

At home Cassel played the leading role in the construction of the Central London underground railway, from which the Rothschilds again, though with some cause, shrank. More fruitfully he sired, this time hand in hand with Lord Rothschild, the string of acquisitions out of which grew Vickers, the foremost armaments manufacturer of the age and the Allies' main arsenal in the Great War.

A loner, forgoing partners and corporate ties, his success derived from his judgement of risks, and in this he proved himself again and again more shrewdly audacious than established merchant banks. A practical and resourceful visionary, he left each country in which he alighted richer by far than he found it. He was trusted to a rare degree by civil servants and politicians of all parties; discreet and dependable, he acquired a unique position as the wealthiest and most powerful financier of the Edwardian era.

Useful as Cassel made himself to the King (and Mrs Keppel), and fascinated as the King was to observe the exercise of raw power through the purse, a genuine and warm attachment grew up between these two men of such dissimilar temperament, to the puzzlement of those around the court. This friendship represented for Cassel the only real pleasure, amounting almost to happiness, that his wealth brought him. Though he was a man of innate kindness, a sympathetic contemporary discerned in him a 'strange and barren inhumanity'. Lacking any social graces and of an unforgiving nature, his bluntness caused offence. However scornful of convention, he indulged in those trappings he considered appropriate to his riches and rank, membership of the Privy Council, a knighthood. He acquired a string of properties, a racing stable, and Brook House in Park Lane, which he transformed over three years with the aid of eight hundred tons of marble into the embodiment of vulgar opulence. He filled his houses with anything which was sufficiently expensive and of certified excellence; two portraits, of Cassel and King, pointedly graced his hall in London. Lacking 'any innate sense of sympathy for suffering', he gave generously, mainly to hospitals and medical research.

When the King fell fatally ill in May 1910, Cassel, who had hurried home from Egypt by chartered steamer with his ailing only daughter, received his last summons to Buckingham Palace. 'I am very seedy,' Edward told his friend, 'but I wanted to see you.' That night the King died. By his bedside was discovered an envelope, left by his last visitor, stuffed with a fortune in banknotes. Cassel, a widower of long standing, lost his daughter in the following year and he retired two years short of his sixtieth birthday, a lonely and saddened man. He retained a recently acquired partnership in the bankers S. Japhet & Company and devoted himself to his two granddaughters, the eldest of whom, Edwina, was named after her godfather Edward VII.

Cassel's sense of grief and isolation was deepened by the degenerating relations between the country of his birth and that of his adoption. He set out to reconcile their differences with the support of his friend Winston Churchill at the Admiralty and in concert with the Kaiser's 'Court Jew' Albert Ballin, head of the Hamburg–Amerika shipping line. These efforts culminated in the Haldane mission to Berlin, a final fruitless attempt to moderate the naval arms race. After its failure Cassel sadly resigned himself to the inevitability of war. Despite his premonitions, the outbreak of hostilities took him by surprise, trapped in the Swiss Alps with Sir Felix Semon, a Jew from Danzig and the late King's doctor; it was only with difficulty that Cassel could raise the fare for their return to London. Although he protested his patriotism in a letter to *The Times*, he was a victim of war hysteria on account of his birth. After returning from a mission to America led by his friend Rufus Isaacs – Lord Reading, the Lord Chief Justice – which had negotiated the $500 million Allied war loan, an attempt was made to remove him from the Privy Council. He retired to Bournemouth for the duration of the war, an embittered man, 'a pathetic figure, a sermon on the vanity of great wealth'. Emerging in the early days of peace, he was roundly snubbed by King Edward's former friends. He died alone at his desk in Park Lane in 1921, never knowing that within a year his granddaughter Edwina would marry Queen Victoria's great-grandson, Lord Louis Mountbatten. To general surprise, he was buried according to the rites of the Roman Catholic Church. (His wife, who had died after a bare three years of marriage, earnestly solicited Cassel to adopt her faith; his conversion only came to light twenty years later when he took the oath for the Privy Council.) He left an estate valued at over £7 million, greater than that of the three

Rothschild brothers combined, having already given away more than £2 million in his lifetime.

Sir Ernest Cassel was the last of the new breed of financiers, mainly of Jewish and mostly of German origin, who played such a pre-eminent part in English social, political and economic life of the Edwardian age, a position they owed to the unprejudiced, if not disinterested, patronage of King Edward. None contributed more to the fruitful flow of capital and diffusion of trade at a time when the industrial strength of Great Britain was ebbing; few contributed as much to the giddy social whirl or to the delectation of their Prince and King. Without them the short-lived, exotic, agitated and often anxious Edwardian era would never have achieved its full flavour and texture.

1

Rothschilds: Breaking Down the Barriers

The French Revolution, begetter of some good and more evil, so much idealism and often idiocy, granted for the first time equal civil and political rights to Jews living under the tricolour although the practice often fell short of the promise. Simultaneously, Prussia's capital, Berlin, was witness to the golden age of Jewish culture. That idyll ended with Prussia's defeat on the battlefield of Jena-Auerstadt. Paradoxically, the revolutionary armies rampaging through Europe during the first decade and a half of the nineteenth century offering emancipation also spawned amongst their vanquished adversaries – the seed of that militant nationalism from which discrimination and prejudice on grounds of race rather than religion – modern-style anti-Semitism – would periodically burgeon and breed in the second half of the same century. The blight's symptoms varied: pan-Slav fanaticism in Holy Russia, infatuation with the *Herrenvolk* in the new-born German Empire, naked chauvinism in France.

Across the Channel a more stable and tolerant climate did not favour such fiercely partisan passions. Anti-Semitism was largely latent; it was considered bad form to give it open expression. George Orwell considered that, until the rise the Nazi Germany, anti-Semitism was not an evil but a silly and venial aspect of social snobbery. A similar stigma was attached to 'Trade'. Kaiser Wilhelm II, despite his own fondness for rich men, would comment caustically about his uncle's habit of 'going yachting with his grocer', Sir Thomas Lipton, otherwise known as 'Tom Tea', who had risen from a Glasgow slum, and he infuriated the Prince of Wales by refusing to receive Sir Thomas; yet Wilhelm found the Jewish financier Sir Ernest Cassel acceptable company.

Such overt discrimination as existed in British law was of a religious nature, touching equally all who did not conform to the rites of the

Established Church. It did not much affect the lives of the main body of Jews, some 35,000 strong in 1850, concentrated in London.

The readmission of the Jews to England after a break of 350 years had come about under Cromwell without any formal enactment. After their expulsion at the end of the thirteenth century their place as money-lenders was taken by Lombard pawnbrokers, a dodge to circumvent the prohibition on Christians charging interest on money lent. The Puritan 'capitalist' ethic extolled the virtues of industry and enterprise; profit, if earned by honest labour, was a means to a commendable end; thrift provided the capital necessary to serve trade.

Sensing the decline of the Dutch trading empire, the Sephardic Jews of Amsterdam led the way to London in the wake of their capital, some £1 million in ready money. Privileges were tacitly extended, freedom of worship was tolerated. These privileges acquired legal status under Charles II. Jews later became staunch upholders of the Hanoverian (and Protestant) succession – they were not uninfluenced by their major shareholding in the National Debt. In foreign wars as in the 'Forty-Five', they shored up the pound and financed the military campaigns, acting as army contractors and paymasters. Solomon de Medina, who had superintended Marlborough's commissariat, was the first Jew to be knighted, in 1700.

These early Sephardim differed little in culture, dress and manners from their hosts; they were wealthy merchants, and welcome. They planted themselves firmly in the City, where twelve 'Jew brokers' were the only operators licensed to practise in the open-air Royal Exchange* without being Freemen of the City of London, a privilege which was not extended, to their just indignation, to alien Protestants.

In Regency England attitudes to Jews were shaped by an unlikely influence: the ring. Such prize-fighters as Daniel Mendoza, champion of England, 'Dutch Sam' Elias, who trained on gin, and Abe Belasco not only became popular idols but were patronized by bucks with the future King George IV at their head. Indeed, Queen Victoria's wicked uncles, for all their frank immoderation, were refreshingly free of any prejudice. They entered into Jewish community life with their accustomed zest; the Duke of Sussex built up a superb Hebrew library and was patron of the Jewish Hospital; with his brothers Cumberland and Cambridge he attended synagogue with Abraham Goldsmid, friend of Nelson and benefactor of Lady Hamilton; kindly Cambridge persuaded his fellow

---

*This imposing building, in which the wealthiest denizens of the City dodged behind pillars, clutching their bills of exchange, to escape the wind and rain, was only glassed over in 1883 at the insistence of Samuel Montagu, first Baron Swaythling.

peers, against their natural inclination, to lift the last obstacle to Jews' election to municipal office.

With the path to Parliament barred, conversion was the key to promotion. A handful of Jews had early embraced Christianity (more properly the Church of England) in order to enter the House of Commons. The first Member of Parliament of wholly Jewish blood, Sir Manasseh Massey Lopes, took his seat in 1802. He was followed by Ralph Bernal, chairman of House committees for twenty years, who was succeeded by his son, the wit Bernal Osborne, whose daughter married the Duke of St Albans; David Ricardo, stock-jobber and political economist; and Benjamin Disraeli, whose father, having quarrelled with his synagogue over his refusal to pay a £40 fine, retaliated by having him baptized before his bar mitzvah.

The repeal of the religious Test Acts in 1828 would have opened up the way for all non-Anglicans, had not an officious bishop insisted on the formula 'on the true faith of a Christian' in the revised oath; an amendment moved by Lord Holland that Jews be allowed to omit these words was defeated. The following year, prodded by revolt in Ireland, the Duke of Wellington's ministry conceded the emancipation of the Catholics. Jews (and atheists) were alone now excluded from the precinct of supreme power (women had not yet developed such vaulting ambitions).

Four years later, a Quaker, Joseph Pease, was permitted to make an affirmation in place of the oath out of consideration for his sectarian scruples, and the first of many Bills to allow professing Jews to become Members of Parliament passed the Lower House but was wrecked in the Upper, the fate of Bill after Bill for most of the next quarter of a century. (Remarkably enough, the English Rothschilds entertained the notion of suborning the Lords by offering Prince Albert, already in their debt, a douceur of £15,000 to 'work the Court party'. The money was to be paid over only when the Bill lifting the restriction on Jews was passed. Perhaps for the sake of discretion, the 'loan' was to come from the French Rothschilds, but they blew cold on the scheme when revolution broke out in Paris in 1848, which dethroned another royal debtor.)

Much of the running in these long years was made by the amiable and attractive Sir David Salomons. Blessed with the means – he was a founder director of the Westminster Bank – and an open hand, he joined in the battle with a will, marking up a series of 'firsts' for his race: sheriff, magistrate, deputy lieutenant, alderman and eventually Lord Mayor of London.

After Salomons had fêted Victor Emmanuel, King of Sardinia and future King of Italy, with the usual pomp and ceremony at Guildhall, a

High Church dignitary, so *The Times* reported, remarked to the Prince Consort, 'Thank goodness, Your Royal Highness, we've got a *gentleman* in the civic chair at last.' 'Yes, my lord,' replied Prince Albert, 'but you had to go beyond the pale of Christianity to find him.'

Westminster itself remained the last bastion of discrimination. There was a neck-and-neck race for first place through the forbidden doors by two quite different characters, the more impatient and assertive Alderman Salomons and the self-effacing but persistent Baron Lionel de Rothschild – as he liked to be known. The first was prepared to push the door, the other, conscious of the respect due him as head of the London house of Rothschild, was content to wear down resistance.

Rothschild was first off the mark in securing a seat; he was returned for the City of London in 1847 as a Liberal. He had boasted to the electors that 'as the representative of the most wealthy, the most important, the most intelligent constituency in the world, I shall not be refused admission to Parliament on account of any form of words whatsoever.' However, when faced with the oath, he faltered and resigned his seat. At this point he was overtaken by Salomons who, having fought three unsuccessful elections, was returned for Greenwich in 1851 with a pledge to take his seat. Sworn in on his insistence on the Old Testament, he omitted the offensive words of the oath, ending, 'So help me God'. Ordered by the Speaker to remove himself, he complied. Three days later, to the consternation of the Commons, he was back, voted in three divisions and delivered his maiden speech to a House in uproar. When he finished speaking he elected to retire again, 'provided that just sufficient force be used to make me feel that I am acting under coercion'. The Serjeant-at-Arms obliged with a tap on the shoulder as the Prime Minister, Lord John Russell, was complimenting Salomons on his address. The Greenwich electors, no doubt preferring solid representation to sturdy resolution, dropped him the following year, only to return him at the first opportunity after the last battle had been won. It was at this delicate stage that the Board of Deputies of British Jews ejected, with ill-timed intolerance, the dissident members of the Reform Synagogue from their midst. The orthodox hierarchy had not only played little part in the struggle, but had no qualms about lining up behind the Christian opponents of emancipation.

Rothschild, meanwhile, having accepted the Chiltern Hundreds as a graceful exit after his initial rebuff in Parliament, was re-elected four times by the more resilient voters of the City to the increasing embarrassment of the government. It was under Lord Derby's minority ministry that Lord Lucan – a foe of emancipation but an old hand at the tactical retreat – proposed a face-saving formula to the House of Lords on the vexed question of the oath. Thus the Baron, aged fifty, finally took his seat in the House in 1858 under the approving eye of his old friend Benjamin Disraeli, Chancellor of the Exchequer, twenty-five years after the first Jewish *député* had been admitted to the French Chamber. (Lionel's younger brother Mayer Rothschild followed him into the House one year later.) The new Member, having proved his point, held his peace for the next fifteen years without interruption until, righteously opposing Gladstone's proposed abolition of income tax, he lost his seat in 1874.

By the late 1860s there were already six practising Jewish Members of Parliament, Liberals all; and by the beginning of the next decade, they had provided a Solicitor-General, a Master of the Rolls and a Privy Councillor. Not all members of their own faith relished this advancement. The *Jewish Chronicle* feared that the political passions aroused by the perception of a 'Jewish lobby' would be visited on the heads of the less fortunate and more vulnerable Jews.

It was Lord Shaftesbury, a supporter, with Wilberforce, of the London Society for Promoting Christianity among the Jews, who urged Gladstone, four years after Jews had won their right to take their seat in the House of Commons, that it 'would be a glorious day for the House of Lords when that grand old Hebrew [the towering patriarch Sir Moses Montefiore] were enrolled in the lists of the hereditary legislators of England'.

The time was not ripe.

Montefiore had received a baronetcy in 1846, and his nephew Lionel Rothschild had been offered one at the same time. Lionel had refused, although his brother Anthony had implored him, 'If you don't like it for yourself, accept it for one of us; these things are always better to be had when one can . . .' Now, ten years since Lionel had entered and graced Westminster in silence, Gladstone strongly recommended him for a peerage, partly from fear he might be lost to the Liberals through his friendship with Disraeli. This time Queen Victoria was not ripe. 'To make a *Jew a peer*,' she convulsively underscored to her Lord-in-Waiting, Lord Granville, 'is a step she *could not* consent to,' though she did not object to a '*Jew* baronet'. Granville conceded that the notion of such a step was 'startling' but pressed it at the Prime Minister's prompting on the grounds that 'he represents a class whose influence is great by their wealth, their intelligence, their literary connections. It may be wise to attach them to the aristocracy rather than drive them into the democratic camp.' The Queen would still not budge.

More than fifteen years passed before Lionel's son, Nathaniel, by then the head of the London house of Rothschild, figured in Gladstone's Dissolution Honours of 1885 and took his place in the Lords as the first Jewish peer. Prudence still played its part. Reginald Brett, the future Viscount Esher, suggested to the Chief Whip that 'some special civility' be shown to him. He was 'not a very robust Liberal but I suppose there is not much object in letting him drift, and still less in driving him over to the Tories'. By this time the Queen had had time to 'overcome the strong scruples she entertained' and, according to Gladstone's secretary, now 'made little or no difficulty'.

Times, too, had changed. Early Victorian society had been 'a very select sheepfold, fenced round by quick-set hedges'. Now new money was overhauling old landed wealth, although the more fortunate magnates had been able profitably to replace their depressed agricultural rents with coal mining and urban property developments. Society, though still meriting a capital 'S', had become adulterated. The shift was accelerated by the arrival of foreign-made fortunes, first South African – the Randlords of 'Jewhannesburg' – and then American.

Snobbery still exercised some temporary check, often excluding the first and even the second generation. The established parvenus themselves reinforced this prejudice. The newer *nouveaux riches* 'would do themselves little harm if they tumbled off their family tree', according to the Princess Murat, the half-American granddaughter of Napoleon's marshal, son of an innkeeper who was finally shot by his Neapolitan subjects as a general nuisance; she herself married Antoine de Noailles, Duc de Mouchy, the bearer of one of the most illustrious names in France.

The conditions of association were not too onerous. Initiation was eased by hiring a full establishment of experienced staff, while gentlewomen offered their services at fees befitting their rank to chaperon the latest arrivals through the shoals of the system. A rash of books on etiquette appeared in the last two decades of the century to cater for this demand. The seductions of society, with its privileges and rewards, offered a powerful incentive to conform.

Nathaniel Rothschild's elevation to the peerage has been hailed as the last milestone on the road to Jewish emancipation. His religion was incidental; he owed his barony to his eminence in the City. The same Westminster 'class of '85' was likewise adorned by the new Lord Revelstoke, the former Edward Charles Baring, head of the only finance house to rival Rothschilds.

Prior to 1885 a man from the dizziest peaks of commerce or industry ennobled in recognition of his services was a rare bird; from that date the number leapt prodigiously, accounting for never less than 15 per cent, and up to as much as 30 per cent, of all new creations. (There was also a practical need to restock the Liberal ranks in the Lords, thinned by the desertion of the Unionists over Irish Home Rule.) Within ten years Lord Rothschild had been joined on the red benches by co-religionists (and fellow Frankfurters by origin), disguised under anodyne Anglo-Saxon styles, such as Wandsworth (Sydney James Stern, another banker) and Pirbright (Henry de Worms, a Rothschild relation and recent Under-Secretary of State for the Colonies).

Paradoxically, riches secured readier access to society in aristocratic England than in republican America. James Bryce, a constant visitor and a future ambassador to the United States, observed that there, 'if his private character be bad, if he be mean or openly immoral, or personally vulgar, or dishonest, the best society may keep its doors closed against him. In England great wealth, skilfully employed, will more readily force these doors open.'

Such facility was not widely welcomed by those behind the door. 'Certainly *money* is a vulgar thing, and money is what rules us now,' lamented a dowager of the old school. 'What right have such people to force themselves into our society?' Such thrusters were condemned as exponents of materialism and that budding bogey, cosmopolitanism. 'Conspicuous consumption', a phenomenon first identified in the last year of the century, aggravated the frustrations of a more venerable and discreet culture. Perversely, materialism and cosmopolitanism were the very qualities that commended themselves in one august (and notably philistine) quarter: Marlborough House and its annexe, the Marlborough Club.

Despite his strict regard for the social graces, Disraeli's improbable, plump Prince Hal – or 'fat, vulgar, dreadful Edward' according to the more prosaic and less partisan Henry James – was, strangely, a lot less particular about the society that he not only tolerated but encouraged to collect about him.

The Marlborough House set, a centre of reaction against the gloom of the court proper, was a curious and incongruous collection of patricians, plutocrats and parvenus, professional beauties and lax ladies, the 'fashionable bad set and betting people', and a cluster of tradesmen.

Prince von Bülow, whose span of office as German Chancellor coincided with Edward's reign, later observed that the King had 'a marked predilection for very rich people'. With this taste it was not unnatural that he should have been drawn to the company of Jews, many of whom also happened to be very rich indeed. He possessed in addition one positive virtue: he was refreshingly free of racial and religious prejudice. 'Because a man has a black face and a different religion from our own,' he remarked in India with typical bluntness, 'there is no reason why he should be treated as a brute.'

The Duke of York, the future King George V, expressed dislike of the 'moneyed associates' around his father, while Sir William Harcourt, recently Chancellor of the Exchequer, confided to the Treasury's Sir Edward Hamilton that he 'could not but feel that the Prince of Wales with all his many other qualities, had more to answer than anyone else for giving money that tremendous social power which it now possesses'.

The attitude of the Marlborough House set to the Prince's Jewish friends was ambivalent. 'We resented the introduction of the Jews into the social set of the Prince of Wales,' wrote Daisy Brooke, Countess of Warwick, 'not because we disliked them ... but because they had brains and understood finance. As a class we did not like brains. As for money, our only understanding of it lay in the spending, not the making of it.'

The Queen had more general reservations. 'If you ever become King,' she had warned her son thirty-odd years before the event, 'you will find all these friends *most* inconvenient, and you will have to break with them *all*.' Although it was a venerable tradition, to which the Hanoverians were no exception, for heirs to the throne to pick their friends principally to vex their parents and drop them once this need was past, King Edward, admittedly over the age when old habits are easy to change, nevertheless remained faithful.

The Prince was moved to embrace this company by an evenly balanced mix of inclination and self-interest. Starved of companionship and affection from his earliest youth, he sought sunny approbation as a counterweight to his mother's moralizing. He found these less inhibited circles more obliging in this respect than the general run of sobersided Society which regarded royalty as rather a bore, a view the reclusive Queen did nothing to dispel. And excluded from taking any part in affairs of state during his mother's lifetime, the Prince found refuge from ennui in expensive diversions suited to his rank but out of reach of his pocket. His Jewish friends, generously endowed with the means, were more than happy to devote these without stint to his entertainment, an example few others could afford, or were inclined, to follow.

A Jewish historian recognized, furthermore, that Edward was equipped with pronounced business instincts. Prevented from putting these into practice, he was able instead to indulge them vicariously among his Jewish friends, merchant adventurers and financiers. As they regally extended –

or sternly withheld – great sums to suppliant states, he was given a teasing glimpse of raw power exercised through the purse. 'All you tell me regarding financial matters,' he wrote to his friend Sir Ernest Cassel towards the end of his life, 'greatly interests me.'

He was himself nagged by need. The Queen's Keeper of the Privy Purse, Sir Charles Phipps, discerned in the young Prince a radical defect in his character 'which makes it impossible for him to deny himself anything that he desires'. Though the traditional courtiers might preach economy, money management was outside their competence. His rich friends were not only able and willing to entertain him royally; they were forthcoming with advice and assistance. They arranged discreet mortgages, loans which the lenders had no intention of calling in; they nursed the privy purse and portfolio; they provided generously for charities which caught his interest; they did not flinch from sharing the burden of such demanding guests as the Shah of Persia.

When he came of age the Prince discovered that he had inherited an income of some £60,000 a year from the Duchy of Cornwall, the traditional perquisite of the heir apparent. As the income had been allowed to accumulate he came into a capital sum of almost £600,000. His London abode, Christopher Wren's Marlborough House, had been assigned to him on his nineteenth birthday. The government had since spent £60,000 on essential renovations, to which the Prince had added a further £100,000 for furniture, fittings and desirable appurtenances to suit his station. (The Privy Purse shamelessly pleaded the Queen's poverty to extort from him a contribution of £10,000 towards Prince Albert's mausoleum at Frogmore to which his widow would repair to offer up prayers for her heir's redemption.) This still left him enough for the compulsory country seat. He made an offer of £220,000 for a run-down estate at Sandringham in Norfolk which its absentee landlord, Lord Palmerston's dissolute stepson, was pleased to accept. The house itself was small, shabby and entirely unsuitable; in Lady Macclesfield's opinion, it would have been 'difficult to find a more ugly or desolate-looking place'. The 7,000 acres brought in rents of £6,000 a year and, though wretched hunting country, supported a quantity of smaller edible game. The Prince's income was now reduced to some £65,000 a year on which to keep a surrogate court. This might be more than a sufficiency for a commoner but paled into virtual insolvency beside the rent-rolls of the terrritorial magnates with whom he rubbed shoulders. The Duke of Devonshire enjoyed rents of £180,000 a year from as many acres; the Duke of Sutherland, with over 1,350,000 bleaker acres, jogged along on rents of £140,000, and was still considered by the Queen not to 'live as *a*

Duke ought'. The ageing Prime Minister, Lord Palmerston, and his Chancellor of the Exchequer, Gladstone, were indeed sympathetic to the Prince's plight, considering that he ought not to have less than £100,000 a year, although Sir Charles Phipps warned the Chancellor that 'even with that he will be unable to do much that will be expected of him'. Penny-pinching Parliament agreed only to provide him with £40,000 with £10,000 for the penniless and recklessly generous Princess as 'pin-money'. ('Thank God', King Edward later exclaimed, 'the Crown Jewels are in the Tower, otherwise the Queen would have auctioned them all off for her charities.')

Just two years after the Prince's marriage, his Comptroller, Sir William Knollys, approached the Palace to ask whether the Queen would object to her son applying to Gladstone for an increase in his annuity. 'As long as capital lasts,' Knollys pointed out, 'of course the Prince of Wales could get on without going to the country. In private life this would be thought an improvident course, and to use it as an argument on the present occasion would be almost to offer a premium on extravagance.' The Prince was indeed already committed to this undesirable course: he was only able to manage more or less comfortably by meeting the excess of expenditure, to the tune of £20,000 a year, out of capital. Gladstone held firmly to the opinion that the Queen herself, whose fortune Lytton Strachey estimated at an immense £5 million, had a duty to help out. The Queen, as usual, disagreed with Gladstone.

In 1870 the Prince embarked on the massive reconstruction of Sandringham House in the Elizabethan style, and improvements to the estate, to which he added 4,000 neighbouring acres. All these developments swallowed up another £80,000 over the years. Four years later rumours began to circulate in the press that the Prince was £600,000 in debt and was only kept afloat by the brothers Rothschild. Indeed, if he had been regularly drawing on capital, his inheritance must have been running dry and his income correspondingly diminished. Disraeli showed more understanding on taking office, but was reluctant to tackle Parliament on the issue. Reassured that there were no debts, he counselled the Prince's advisers to carry on with the sale of capital 'in the interim'. The interim was to prove interminable.

The Queen adamantly declined to loosen her purse strings, the government continued to equivocate, the Prince's pocket drained, time passed. With the return of Gladstone, Francis Knollys, who had taken over from his father as the Prince's Private Secretary in 1870, confided to Lady Spencer that 'the question of the Prince of Wales's debts could not be postponed much longer. That will be an awkward matter for the government to deal with. It is sure to raise a very strong feeling against the Queen who (it will be thought and not unfairly thought) should have made some allowance to HRH in consideration of the extra expenses which fell upon him by reason of her seclusion.' No money was forthcoming. It was only in 1889 that the Prime Minister, Lord Salisbury, whose family did not take the heir to the throne too seriously, set up a Select Committee to consider his finances. The outcome was an award of a further £36,000 a year and a capital sum of £60,000 to provide for his five children. This relieved some of the immediate strain, but by then the Prince was touching fifty and it was not unnaturally assumed that he had been able to keep afloat only by borrowing from friends – and from others.

His financial needs were sometimes distressingly modest. An Oxford Street dealer in silver and porcelain recalled a gentleman presenting himself with a piece of jewellery for sale. His asking price was £100. The dealer, surveying the object and its owner, protested that it was worth much more and insisted on paying £500. He contended that he had not recognized his client as the Prince of Wales, though his friends doubted this. Certainly his honesty (or discretion) was requited. The dealer's name was Joseph Joel Duveen. Through this casual contact, he went on to collect as patrons the Prince's two friends Lord Esher and Sir Ernest Cassel; he was called on to embellish the royal residences on Edward's accession and won a knighthood for himself. From another friend of the Prince's, Horace Farquhar, later Master of the Household, Duveen was given, in the courtier's practical dual capacity as head of Parr's Bank, an open credit of £1,200,000 at a time when Joseph Joel's son, the future Lord Duveen of Millbank, was making his début in Old Masters.

The Duveens were by origin Dutch Jews. Joseph Joel's father was a blacksmith, his mother a collector of delft. When her eldest son was twenty-three she packed him off to England with as much of her treasure as he could carry. Once his stock was exhausted, he resorted to travelling in lard. Within a year he married the daughter of a Hull pawnbroker and moved to London, founding in 1879 Duveen Brothers, offering furniture and *objets de vertu*, in partnership with his brother Henry, who had chosen New York as a marketplace. When Joseph Joel died towards the end of Edward VII's reign, he left an estate valued at some £1.5 million, much of it in cash, and on Henry's death, Joseph Joel's eldest son, Joseph, acquired control of the business, in which most of his many brothers were gainfully employed in London, Paris and New York. Art dealer extraordinary, and benefactor in his turn, Joseph Duveen, knighted himself by Edward VII's son before progressing to a baronetcy and finally a barony, employed his flair and effrontery to build up some of the greatest

American art collections, pandering to the acquisitive instincts of free-spending millionaires such as Frick, Carnegie, Huntington and Mellon, whom he converted to his inflationary philosophy: 'When you pay high for the priceless, you're getting it cheap.'

For some of the older generation, and by no means the least intolerant, Sandringham was 'not at all a nice young Court'. The host, however, was invariably 'gracious and agreeable' and the atmosphere informal. Disraeli and Gladstone were alike (but separately) charmed. The company reflected that shift in society which the Prince encouraged. In the early 1870s the Bishop of Peterborough found the company there 'a curious mixture: two Jews, Sir Anthony de Rothschild and his daughter; an ex-Jew, Disraeli; a Roman Catholic, Colonel Higgins; an Italian Duchess, who is an Englishwoman, and her daughter, brought up a Roman Catholic and now turning Protestant; a set of young lords and a bishop'.

It was through Sir Anthony's three nephews, Lionel's sons, that the Prince of Wales was introduced into the Rothschild circle at Cambridge in 1861. (At Cambridge, the religious 'test', abolished three years before, had had to be taken only on proceeding to a degree, while at Oxford it was applied before matriculation.) Nathaniel, the future first (English) baron, had been preceded by his uncle Mayer at Trinity (the college did not enforce compulsory chapel attendance). Although Nathaniel hunted with the University draghounds based on Trinity – he found it '*absolutely* necessary to take 2 hours at *least* of violent exercise per diem' – Queen Victoria would have been reassured rather than dismayed that her son kept such company. She took a sour view of high society; it was, in her view, '*repulsive*, vulgar, bad and frivolous *in every way*' and doubtless the young Rothschilds were seen as a steadier influence that the unbridled young bloods of the aristocracy. Their grandfather, Nathan Mayer, had been banker to her father, the Duke of Kent, and her uncle, Leopold of Saxe-Coburg-Gotha. This latter connection had brought the meddlesome Baron Stockmar into the Rothschild orbit; through him the family acted as banker to the Queen and Prince Albert in Germany, and the Rothschild courier carried all her confidential correspondence to that country – a 'perfectly *safe* and very quick' service, in her opinion. Nathaniel, ever an outspoken and presumptuous critic, was not impressed with the Prince, whom he found fond of riddles and strong cigars: 'His remarks were commonplace and slow, [he] will I suppose eventually settle down into a well-disciplined German Prince' – that was certainly his mother's dearest wish – 'with all the narrow views of his father's family. He is excessively polite and that is certainly his redeeming quality' – polite enough to request the author of this censure for his photograph.

Nathaniel, who showed no knack for mathematics, foreseeing failure, did not return to Cambridge for the Tripos. His brother Alfred, at King's, was by nature closer to the Prince; even Nathaniel's mother concluded that he lacked 'cordiality and frankness' and was 'reserved and shy, and not generous', while his younger brother was expansive and enjoyably extravagant. He was also a precocious hypochondriac and, concerned lest his studies should interfere with the care of his health, prudently gave them up. Leopold, also at King's, scraped through with a bare Third.

The dynast, Mayer Amschel Rothschild of Frankfurt, who made his début as a dealer in coins and medals, founded the family's fortune on the back of the Margrave of Hesse, the richest man in Europe at the end of the eighteenth century. The Margrave hired out his subjects as mercenaries, not just singly but in battalions; to his Hanoverian cousin he rented over 20,000 stalwarts for £3 million to squash the American colonial rebels. During the revolutionary wars in Europe, he entrusted a part of his personal treasure, over a quarter of a million pounds, to the safe hands (and service) of Rothschild. Every little German state had its bank, and each such institution issued paper which was valueless beyond the borders. Mayer Amschel's sons took up their stations in the nerve centres – Frankfurt itself, Paris, Vienna, Naples and, the hub of the action, London – and the family's bills became immediately convertible in the major currencies. They thus established the first supranational banking empire; their progeny in turn, to refresh their kinship (and to ensure that the dowries remained in the family), married mostly first cousins.

The third son, blue-eyed, red-headed, bull-necked Nathan Mayer, chose England. He established himself, with some £20,000 for capital, in Manchester in his early twenties, dealing in cotton and smuggling contraband goods through the Continental blockade. Moving to London in 1804, he graduated as paymaster to Wellington, gathering in the final stages of the war French gold and silver coins, with the aid of his younger brother James in Paris, to keep the Allied armies in the field. When peace returned, the clan collectively contributed towards putting together the pieces of a devastated Europe. They secured a share, after some menacing manipulation of the market, in the French war indemnity and the Prussian reconstruction loans, propped up Metternich's reactionary rule in Vienna (the brothers were created Austrian barons), managed a £12 million loan for the British government and lent prodigally to Louis XVIII and George IV. In 1825 they bailed out the Bank of England, which, faced with a run on its reserves after a string of bank failures, was on the point of suspending payments. By one Friday it was down to its last 60,000 sovereigns (the mint could coin no more than £200,000 a week);

on the Saturday in was saved by an injection of £300,000 of specie which twenty-five Rothschild couriers had procured from as far afield as Russia and Turkey. The lion's share of the profits of these operations fell to 'NM' in London: at the time of Waterloo the total Rothschild capital was £136,000, of which Nathan Mayer's share came to £90,000; three years later the pool had risen to £1,772,000, of which half a million was set down to Nathan. He remained 'a guttural Frankfurter' to the end of his days (he died in 1836, poisoned by a carbuncle), but if he was 'uncouth, uncultured, ungainly' he was not unsuccessful. He left £1,350,000 and a prescription for his children: 'I wish them to give mind, and soul, and heart, and body, and everything to business; that is the way to be happy.'

His eldest son, Lionel, who had married his Frankfurt first cousin, Charlotte, inherited the business at New Court, N. M. Rothschild & Sons, at the age of twenty-eight, and reigned for forty-three years. He at once applied for royal permission to reactivate the Austrian title his father had scorned, and posthumously re-ennobled him on his mother's tombstone. Lionel's brother Anthony (known as Billy), though he had seen the family's railroad – the Chemin de Fer du Nord – through its teething problems, took a back seat at the bank; a third, Nathaniel, crippled by a hunting accident, married into the French family and moved across the Channel; the youngest, Mayer or 'Muffy' was more interested in his racing stud. One sister, Charlotte, married the Austrian Anselm, another, Louise, Mayer Karl of Frankfurt; two of her daughters married Agénor, Duc de Gramont, and Alexander, Prince de Wagram. (The former was cut out of her father's will for taking her husband's religion; Gramont, much distressed, threatened to sue, but her sisters averted such an unseemly action by alloting her their share of their inheritance.) Lionel's other sister, Hannah, disgraced herself by marrying out of the faith, and in her husband's church; her French uncle, James, lamented, 'She robbed our whole family of its pride,' to which her brother Nathaniel more reasonably protested, 'all she did was to marry a Christian in a Christian country.'

Banking was the riskiest of Victorian professions. The Rothschild recipe for success was great daring matched by great caution. They throve on this simple, if seemingly paradoxical, saw. Not all their rivals observed the qualification; hundreds of banking houses went to the wall in the periodic panics that upset the markets; even the mighty Barings came close to it. During Lionel's rule, the bank brought out eighteen loans for governments at home and overseas, then the staple of merchant banking; they raised £8 million for the Irish famine loan, waiving their profits, and £5 million for the government's expenses in the Crimea. (Lionel's only rival, Thomas Baring, recently appointed agent for the Russian Treasury, felt reluctantly obliged to decline a participation in a similar Russian war loan, though he had moved the Imperial deposit at the Bank of England out of harm's way. He was denounced by Lord Palmerston, who at the same time congratulated the Queen on her good fortune in having the Rothschilds behind her.) Rothschilds, influenced by their large holdings in Southern cotton, only badly misjudged the American Civil War and surrendered their place in the market after the Union's victory.

The year after Lionel lost his Parliamentary seat, he accorded a favour to his friend Disraeli which allowed the Prime Minister to pull off a major personal coup against strong opposition in the Cabinet – the acquisition by the government in 1875 of the Khedive Ishmael's shares in the Suez Canal, opened six years before, which had twice been turned down by the faint-hearted Foreign Office. The debt-ridden Khedive was negotiating with two French groups when the news reached Disraeli, Sunday supping with Lionel, that his shares were on the market. Secrecy and speed were essential. Lionel, according to the fittingly dramatic account composed by Disraeli's private secretary, reached his decision to put up the £4 million in the time he took to munch a muscatel grape. It has been suggested that Disraeli was already under some obligation to the Rothschilds, and the terms – $2\frac{1}{2}$ per cent commission plus interest, a profit of over £150,000 – were hotly criticized. Though Dizzy was indeed a close family friend, giving away most of the Rothschild girls in marriage, Lionel thought him a humbug, an opinion shared by his eldest son as an undergraduate. Nathaniel later came to revere him, a devotion heightened by his increasing disillusion with Gladstone, and Alfred harboured him when he was finally voted out of Downing Street. Nathaniel's wife, Emma, was capable of cooler appraisal: 'Though very eloquent,' she wrote to her mother-in-law on the subject of the author's preface to *Endymion*, 'I think the great man pays himself too many compliments & does not mince matters as regards his own merits.'

The baronetcy Lionel had spurned went instead to his younger brother, genial, stout Sir Anthony. He preferred the country to New Court. The Prince of Wales came to shoot his pheasants at Aston Clinton, just outside the Vale of Aylesbury. This was a rambling and unpretentious home, altogether more the conventional English country house than the usual Rothschild piles which were rising round it; Mary, Gladstone's daughter, found it 'snug and homelike', not qualities which recommended themselves to Lady Rothschild. Sir Anthony and his family in their turn became frequent visitors at Sandringham and the grander houses round about. At Lord Leicester's Holkham Hall the Rothschild girls noticed that the Royal Highnesses 'like nothing so much as a romp';

their father danced the Lancers with the Princess while the Prince waltzed with the daughters. In this informal fashion the talk predictably turned to money, which Sir Anthony, in endearingly outdated slang, referred to as 'tin'. Himself a free-spending gamester, he tackled the root of the Prince's problem by raising his investment income and was able, blessed with 'the kindest heart and most generous nature', to make up any short-term deficiencies by discreet advances. At his death, the Queen wrote to remind her son: 'You will be very sorry for poor Sir Anthony Rothschild who was so very kind and loyal and so fond of you and a very good man.'

The company at Aston Clinton was as curious and eclectic as that at Sandringham, though romps were rarer. Sir Anthony's wife, Louise Montefiore, plain and insecure, was of a literary turn of mind, though the Prince was thoughtfully spared such regulars as Tennyson, Browning and Matthew Arnold. The usual politicans and Protestant prelates were put up. A more surprising guest was the future Tsar Alexander III, who was married to the Princess of Wales's sister. The Russian party was accompanied by the Prince's brother Alfred ('Affie'), Duke of Edinburgh, who was engaged to the Tsarevich's sister. His equerry, the Hon. Eliot Yorke, had earlier the same year married one of Sir Anthony's two daughters, Annie, which at the time, in spite of the Queen's congratulations, had caused the family 'agitation and pain'. Yorke's father, Lord Harwicke, was not the only one of the Prince's friends to have ruined himself in the race to meet the excessive demands of providing for his entertainment. His son, before he had repaired his fortunes through a happy but tragically short marriage, had reputedly been reduced to making ends meet by presenting, for a consideration of £60,000, a rich Russian commoner to his employer's future father-in-law, the Tsar.

Despite this easy-going intercourse, it was not universally accepted as either proper or desirable. Shortly after the Prince's marriage, an anxious Sir William Knollys had consulted his fellow courtier Lord Spencer on the wisdom of accepting an invitation from the Rothschilds. Spencer's advice was that 'If the Prince went to a ball there, a great outcry would arise in the fine world, and I confess I think the world would for once have reason on their side, for I think the Prince ought not to accept any invitation, he ought only to visit those of undoubted position in Society. The Rothschilds are very worthy people but they especially hold their position from wealth and perhaps the accidental beauty of the first daughter they brought out. Other members of Society would complain of the Prince going to that house in preference to their own. I should be very sorry if the Prince and Princess accepted their hospitality.' The Prince had his own ideas. Over twenty-five years later, when he pressed the appointment of Nathaniel, by then Lord Rothschild, as Lord Lieutenant of Buckinghamshire, he felt it necessary to excuse his action to their mutual Cambridge friend and Nathaniel's neighbour, Lord Carrington: 'It would have been strange ten years ago, but times change. He is a good fellow and man of business, and he and his family own half the County!' Though he may have felt some entitlement to the sinecure – his father had held it – there was no personal animus in Carrington's objection; when Nathaniel had taken his seat in the House of Lords four years before, Charlie Carrington had come forward as one of his two supporters.

When Sir Anthony died in 1876, the baronetcy passed to his eldest nephew, Nathaniel (Lionel's eldest son), who also succeeded as the head of the London house on his father's death three years later. Natty may have been a good fellow in the eyes of the Prince, but his personality was not such as to give unqualified pleasure. He more closely resembled his grandfather Nathan Mayer, whose scarcely ingratiating manner he inherited. (One German prince with proportionate pretensions came to pay his court to the banker. 'Take a chair,' NM offered, remaining bent over his books. 'I am afraid', replied the other, unused to such lack of ceremony, 'that you did not hear who I am,' and he enlightened him. 'Well, well,' rejoined his host, 'take two chairs.')

Nathaniel himself was rated, by those whose pomposity he had punctured, one of the rudest men in England – his friend Lord Randolph Churchill was another – and yet, gruff, blunt and intolerant of opposition, he could still inspire surprising affection. Many years later, the coolly aloof Arthur Balfour admitted that 'To me Natty's death is a greater blow than most people would suppose. I was really fond of him: really admired that self-contained and somewhat joyless character . . . utterly indifferent to worldly pomps and vanities . . . he was perfectly simple.' Preferring the counting house to the court, Nathaniel avoided the pomps by thankfully abandoning the chore of keeping up the Prince of Wales's spirits to his younger brothers, Alfred, a seasoned habitué of the Marlborough House set, and Leopold, and his cousin Ferdinand, the more so as his wife, Emma, a Frankfurt Rothschild, was deemed strait-laced even by the standards of the day (she thought, though, that Queen Victoria overdid it).

Mr Alfred, as he was known (Nathaniel's brothers considerately dropped the title Baron when Natty was elevated to the English peerage in 1885), was a bird of quite another feather. Blond (beside his brothers), slim, exquisite and a poseur,[*] he shed his beard for elaborate Dundreary

---

[*]Max Beerbohm captioned one of his caricatures: 'A quiet evening in Seymour Place. Doctors consulting whether Mr Alfred may, or may not, take a second praline before bedtime.'

whiskers. A bachelor, he had no family to restrain his self-indulgence. He was frivolously eccentric, often indiscreet. A contemporary ascribed to him a 'good heart but a mean and miserable mind'. With a gentle manner, he combined a sometimes waspish wit: 'All Emma's children must have been conceived under protest,' he remarked of his sister-in-law. His liberality was legendary, but haphazard and often whimsical. Supercilious with his social inferiors, he yet demonstrated almost excessive consideration for his staff. A connoisseur and patron of art – Lady Dorothy Nevill, one of the leading Society hostesses of the day, reckoned him the finest amateur judge in England of eighteenth-century French furniture, porcelain and paintings – he was an energetic and exemplary Trustee of the National Gallery and Wallace Collection; yet his garish taste in architecture and decoration was execrable even by Victoran standards. He would produce Liszt, Rubinstein and Melba – a family favourite – for his famous London parties; he was part-owner of the Gaiety Theatre, and at home in the country would entertain his guests with performing animals from his private circus. Although at best a dutiful banker, he was appointed the first Jewish director of the Bank of England in 1868, a position he held for twenty-one years until one day, overcome by curiosity, he stole a peep at the account of an art dealer who had recently sold him an expensive painting. Deeming the profit 'out of all proportion to convention or decency', he was quite unable to resist sharing the news of this injustice over the dinner table, and the subsequent outcry obliged him to plead his usual ill-health and resign.

Leopold Rothschild was less complex. He was credited with 'a positive greed for doing good' and, though more assiduous in his attendance at New Court, was a familiar and popular figure on the Turf. 'All his life,' Lord Rosebery wrote after his death, 'he was encompassed by love and gratitude, the universal tribute to his great heart.'

There was a final fourth-generation Rothschild who made up the royal circle, Ferdinand, the son of Lionel's sister Charlotte who married the Viennese Rothschild, Baron Anselm. On the death of his mother, herself homesick and lonely amidst the alien Austrian corn – she returned to London to give birth – he moved to England in 1860. Six years later he married Lionel's daughter, Evelina, who died in childbirth at the end of the following year. Ferdie was a fastidious, willowy, rather forlorn character – a 'dear old duck' in his wife's eyes – whom the German-born Lady Walpurga Paget deemed 'effete', unable to 'eat, sleep or do anything simply, like other mortals'. A bountiful benefactor – he built a hundred-bed children's hospital in Southwark in memory of his wife – he is reported to have promised £2,000 to anyone who could suggest a useful way of spending his money. He hit on the solution to this problem himself. With his father's death in 1874 he could afford to embark on the most flamboyant of all the Rothschilds' country residences, Waddesdon Manor in Buckinghamshire, and when that had been topped out and stocked up with appropriate treasures he turned to politics.

Ferdie's wedding reception had been combined with the house-warming of his father-in-law's London mansion. Lionel had bought 147 and 148 Piccadilly, which he demolished to make way for a grim-fronted building in the institutional style overshadowing Apsley House. It groaned under the weight of white and coloured marble staircases, columns and arches, an excess of ornament, satin curtains embroidered with river goddesses, gold and scarlet plush. Nathaniel inherited this on his father's death, and his brothers set about the demanding task of trying to outdo him around the corner, Leopold at 5 Hamilton Place, Alfred at 1 Seymour Place, which was redeemed by four Gainsboroughs, a Romney and a Reynolds. Alfred had bought the house from another of the Prince's friends who ruined himself in his service, Christopher Sykes, the fawning courtier and butt of the most painful royal 'practical' jokes, thus allowing him to indulge for a while longer his unaffordable extravagance. (Alfred was only trumped by his friend Barney Barnato, the little Whitechapel Jew born Isaacs, who went out to South Africa with a circus troupe and made his fortune in diamonds. Advised by his nephew to take advantage of Alfred's experience in building, he replied, 'I don't need his help. Why, his house would go into my hall!') Ferdinand took up residence at 142 Piccadilly; his sister Alice, who had joined him from Vienna after his wife's death, moved in next door. Down the road at 107, Baron Mayer lived in Nathan Mayer's (and the Couttses') old home. This part of Piccadilly came predictably to be known as 'Rothschild Row'.

However grand their town houses, it was unthinkable that gentlemen should not also have their country seats, as much for the status as the sport, although the Rothschilds, with the exception of Sir Anthony and Alfred, shared a genuine passion for the chase. The family had already established their pack of staghounds (they found the foxes of the Old Berkeley capricious) in hired kennels at Tring in Buckinghamshire. There they proceeded to carve out an enclave of over 15,000 almost contiguous acres that came to eclipse even Rothschild Row in London. Baron Mayer, Lionel's third brother, acquired an estate at Mentmore and set up his stud nearby, becoming in a short time a popular and highly successful owner; having won the Oaks once, in 1871 – the 'Baron's year' – he took the Derby, the One Thousand Guineas, the Oaks again, the St Leger and the Cesarewitch, a feat never since equalled. He also shared the family fashion for collecting; it was cheaper, he reckoned, to buy antique French furniture than to patronize the Prince's friend Sir John Blundell Maple's emporium in Tottenham Court Road. He picked up on his travels such prizes as Rubens's monumental chimneypiece from his Antwerp house, pieces of Marie Antoinette's furniture and outsize items from the Doge's Palace in Venice as well as a remarkable collection of Mazarin's tapestries, paintings and French porcelain. When he married in 1850, he set about providing a suitable home for his cumbrous collection and called in Joseph Paxton, the Duke of Devonshire's former gardener and the architect of the recently completed Crystal Palace. The result was in an approximate Jacobean style, though much play was predictably made with plate glass. 'I don't believe', wrote Lady Eastlake, 'that the Medici were ever so lodged in the height of their glory.'

A more frequent visitor to Mentmore, family friend and fellow race-horse owner, was Archibald Primrose, fifth Earl of Rosebery. A romance sprang up between him and the Baron's only child, Hannah, an over-ripe and senuous beauty with, in the quaint description of the blue stocking Lady Eastlake, 'a kind of Semiramis profile'. Henry James less charitably described her as 'large, fat, ugly, good-natured, sensible and kind'. She had been shockingly over-indulged as a child and became, on her parents' early death, one of the greatest heiresses of the age: she disposed of around £2 million, including Mentmore and its 5,000 acres. She was in addition eminently devout and suffered a severe moral wrench at the prospect of taking a Christian husband. Rosebery's mother, the Duchess of Cleveland, was as strongly disinclined, expressing her sentiments 'with force' on the subject. The *Jewish Chronicle* agreed with her, predicting the 'most poignant grief' at the mixed marriage. Hannah overcame her scruples, accepted Rosebery's hand and clung to her faith; the Duchess, accepting the inevitable, penned a 'not altogether ungracious' letter to her son. The couple were married in March 1878 in a civil ceremony at the Workhouse (more politely, the Boardroom of the Guardians) in Mount Street, Mayfair, followed by a church service. The Prince of Wales attended with the Queen's cousin and friend of old Nathan Mayer, the Duke of Cambridge. Disraeli gave the bride away in the marked absence of the bride's male Rothschild relations. Family loyalty soon asserted itself and Hannah's cousins once more made themselves at home at Mentmore. Alfred Rothschild and Rosebery staged 'absurd historical tableaux' with Mary Gladstone, but when charades – a family failing – encroached on their host's nocturnal political compositions, he, surveying the company with his 'curious cod-fish blue eyes', would break up the party with the cry, 'To your tents, O Israel.' (However, though his chaff was often abrasive, he would counter any disparaging remark with, 'You should not say that to me. I am Jewish.')

Nathaniel, who had represented Aylesbury in Parliament since 1865, played the model landlord at Tring Park with its 4,000 acres – 200 of them deer park – which his father had bought in 1872 for £230,000; he rebuilt the estate cottages, some 400, and instituted an embryo welfare state. The consensus – though Emma found it a 'fairyland' – was that he made a hash of the alterations and enlargements to the original Wren manor, whereas the interior and furnishing presented 'a weird and wonderful mixture of the very beautiful and immensely ugly'. (Curiously, the cultivated Arthur Balfour expressed surprise that he should have refaced it 'with *old* red bricks to please the aesthetes'.) His brothers had likewise inherited land in the neighbourhood, Leopold at Ascott, near Wing, 'a beautiful and glorified old manor house', according to Sir Algernon West, Gladstone's secretary. West had less opinion of Alfred's neighbouring Halton, on which he embarked in 1881, describing it as 'an exaggerated nightmare of gorgeousness and senseless and ill-applied magnificence', though he admitted that when lit up and full of well-dressed people it appeared quite tolerable. Fifteen years later, Sir Edward Hamilton, an intimate of the three brothers, considered that 'there is a wonderful brightness about it. But the decorations are sadly overdone, and one's eyes long to rest on something which is not all gilt and gold'; one peculiarity he remarked was that neither fruit nor flowers were grown on the spot, but brought down from London.

Ferdinand meanwhile had bought nearby Lodge Hill and some 1,000 acres from the Duke of Marlborough where, on a bleak and desolate site, he began building, putting together over the next fifteen years, a pastiche of whichever French châteaux caught the imagination of the architect. Tons of Bath stone were carried halfway up the hill by a specially constructed steam tramway and then hauled to the top by teams of Percherons imported from Normandy. The result of such an expenditure of money and long labour did not please everyone. Mary Gladstone, accompanying her father on a visit, perhaps to persuade his host to fill the seat in the Commons vacated by Nathaniel, felt 'oppressed with the extreme gorgeousness and luxury'. Ferdinand's sister Alice moved into Eythrope Priory four miles down the road, though she slept and dined every night at Waddesdon as she had persuaded herself that the dank Thamesside air did not suit her.

Not the least of these magnates' attractions for the Prince was the care they took with their cuisine. He had been allowed one licence at Oxford – the addition of an accomplished chef to his household to enable him to entertain, so his parents hoped, academic worthies. Brought up in the austere milieu of the family on the homely cheer of Brown Windsor soup, he developed an immediate and immoderate taste for the rarer delights of the table. His appetite was delicately described by his official biographer as that of one who 'never toyed with his food', an understatement on the scale of his girth. He was both a gourmet and an inveterate gourmandizer, guzzling daily huge amounts of rich fare at an indigestible speed and with palpable relish. He would gulp oysters by the dozen to lay the foundations for a square meal; he was equally at home with boned quail or snipe stuffed with foie gras as with Yorkshire pudding. All was washed down with a jug of pink champagne. This self-indulgence was increasingly evident as he added over seven inches to his waistline while waiting for a vacancy on the throne; only five feet seven inches in height, he measured one inch under four feet around the middle and turned the scales at over 200 pounds in his early thirties.

Foreign bankers and the *nouveaux riches* were almost the only hosts to pay much regard to their tables. For the rest of Society, formal functions were catered for by Mr Gunter with results that were as drearily predictable and familiar as the company. For homely occasions, 'Cook' relied on the staple provided by such regular whole-column advertisers in *The Times* as Crosse & Blackwell, Purveyors to the Queen of tinned curries, and Lea & Perrins Original and Genuine Worcestershire Sauce (Beware of Imitations). (Mr Perrin himself made a substantial fortune from this dependence, rising into the ranks of the plutocracy in his turn.) By contrast, the Rothschilds, in the view of the Prince's mistress, Daisy Brooke, later Countess of Warwick, 'undoubtedly gave the best dinner parties in London and they established a taste for the refinements of luxury. They had the best chefs and bottomless purses.' After dining with Lionel Rothschild, Thomas Babington Macaulay absconded with the menu to pass around among his friends. 'Surely this,' he wrote, 'is the land flowing with milk and honey. I do not believe Solomon in all his glory ever dined on *Ortolans farcis à la Talleyrand*. I may observe in passing that the little birds were accompanied by some Johannisberg which was beyond all praise.' Lionel's sons outshone him. But while such a diet did not disturb the Prince, his hosts paid the price in dyspepsia. Though Alfred made a hobby of his health, Natty's malaise was authentic. A young guest would often, to his astonishment, be placed on his right hand. Lord Rothschild would ask him to describe the taste of each dish. 'Ah, yes, I know exactly,' his host would mournfully reply, taking a bite of biscuit and a sip of milk. (He would, however, when he saw his chance, sink to subterfuge. Emma, on remonstrating with the chef, was informed that his

Lordship himself had given instructions for foie gras to be slipped into the game pies.)

The Rothschild fraternity offered another, more serious attraction for the Prince. Their own cosmopolitan outlook and upbringing, as well as the large family network, were put at the disposal of the grateful heir to the throne. Their intelligence service was unequalled; they were usually the first with the news from abroad before it reached the Foreign Office or Fleet Street (Alfred received the report of Russia's naval disaster at Tsushima two days before confirmation arrived at the Japanese mission in London). It had also long been the custom for the family to correspond daily on those public affairs relevant to the financial operations in which they shared the risks and split the profits, although the radical Sir Charles Dilke, then Under-Secretary for Foreign Affairs, who was shown such messages by Alfred, was not impressed by their insight; they seemed to him 'extraordinarily uninteresting'. Foreign affairs was the field of especial interest to the Prince, who was left out in the cold by the Queen despite the sympathy of her ministers and his own remonstrance. He was denied official sight of Cabinet papers and Foreign Office despatches until he was over fifty years of age. The Prince felt this neglect most keenly, the more so as he discovered that Disraeli had entrusted his younger brother, Prince Leopold, with a key to the Cabinet boxes. He confided to Francis Knollys that he was 'not of the slightest use to the Queen; that everything he says or suggests is pooh-poohed'. The Queen's jealousy of her prerogatives was partly responsible, but she also, with some justice, doubted his discretion and his 'fitness for high functions of State'. She was not alone in this. The few carefully selected papers that came his way had first to be screened and approved by the Queen, which entailed long delays. The Foreign Office was most reluctant to part with any information; forever dilatory in sending its boxes round to the Prince, it was particularly slow whenever there was any action, or threat of action, overseas, so that the telegrams were often weeks old.

While Disraeli was in office, confident of the strength of his position with the Queen in the event of the Prince's tongue wagging, he fed him with 'titbits of Cabinet secrets'. Knollys informed Edward Hamilton, then Gladstone's secretary, of this irregular practice in the hope that his chief might maintain it. (The Prince had always enjoyed a more relaxed relationship with the staid Liberal leader than with his flashy predecessor; indeed, he went out of his way to show Gladstone small personal kindnesses to compensate for his mother's abrupt discourtesy and, throughout his later life, sent him a 'magnificent supply' of game from the Sandringham larder.) Gladstone sympathized, but would not agree to do so without the Queen's gracious permission. The Queen flatly refused to credit that her favourite could have been guilty of such impropriety behind her back and refused her *bête noire*'s request which he pressed as a 'very judicious and desirable' course. He decided instead to 'exercise a judicious indiscretion'. The Prince was more fortunate when Lord Rosebery took over the Foreign Office during Gladstone's third ministry. They were already on such intimate terms that Francis Knollys had once even asked Rosebery whether he would lend the Prince his bachelor home in Berkeley Square for entertaining his 'actress friends'. (Rosebery was unaccommodating; he declined the honour on the grounds that there was not enough room in the house.) Now, on his own responsibility, he passed copies of the Foreign Office secret despatches to the Prince, a custom that Lord Salisbury continued on taking over the premiership.

Lord Esher, the *éminence grise* of the Edwardian court, considered that *amour propre* could account for the Prince's insistence on his right to receive official documents, and that from the time he had set up his own household he was aware of everything that was going on, very often more than the Queen herself. No one, he judged, 'was better and more completely informed of the trend of public affairs . . . The Prince not only heard the Government case, but he was taken into confidence by the leaders of the Opposition as well . . . He was speedily the best informed man in the Kingdom.' It was all the easier for the Prince to manage this easy intimacy with politicans of all shades at those small dinner parties 'to meet HRH the Prince of Wales' under a Rothschild roof in town or country.

When Lord Spencer had cautioned William Knollys about the inadvisability of the Prince venturing under a Rothschild roof, he had remarked that they held their position from wealth and the 'accidental beauty' of their first daughter. This was Natty's elder sister, Leonora, otherwise known as Laury, an almond-eyed belle with 'the sweet complexion of a tea rose' (and a keen sense of humour), who in 1857 married her first cousin once removed, Baron Alphonse de Rothschild of Paris. The Prince enjoyed a mild flirtation with Laury, soliciting her photograph through Alfred and returning in exchange not one but two of himself. Her roots did not take in French soil: her sister Evelina enthused, 'She will be an Englishwoman wherever she is. Quite right!' The Baron for his part was in no danger of ever becoming an Anglophile. Both English and French Rothschilds, indeed, inherited the national chauvinism of their adopted countries. Whenever she could manage it, Laury returned for some real sport to Buckinghamshire, where her heart remained and where she was interred at her request.

Alphonse's father, James, the youngest of Mayer Amschel's five sons, had had his envious eye on Mentmore and, determined not to be outdone by his nephew, pressed Paxton into service on his own account with an instruction to produce a Mentmore for him – only more of it – on his 7,500 acre estate twenty-five kilometres east of Paris. The result, Ferrières, was, predictably, a 'somptueuse demeure' surrounded by a 'parc à l'anglais' which 'accentuates the intimate liaison of edifice and nature'. It reminded the poet and traveller Wilfrid Scawen Blunt more of 'a monstrous Pall Mall club decorated in the most outrageous Louis-Philippe taste . . . horribly overdone'. Bismarck more succinctly likened the effect of the priceless bric-à-brac to an overturned chest of drawers.

On the promotion of the president-prince Louis Napoleon in 1848, the French Rothschilds had been elbowed out of favour by the machinations of the Finance Minister, Achille Fould, a converted Jew, in association with the Péreire brothers, Sephardic bankers from Bordeaux, in a calculated attempt to break their grip on the markets. (The Péreires had even, in pursuit of their vendetta, acquired all the land round Ferrières in order to block the Rothschilds' design to extend their domain.) It was only in 1862, once the Rothschilds had broken the presumption of the Péreires' Crédit Mobilier, that Napoleon, then Emperor and veering wildly between absolutism and liberalism to catch the prevailing public mood, sought a rapprochement, inviting himself in style to Ferrières. Six years later, 'le grand Baron' died after pulling off his long-thwarted ambition – the purchase of Château Lafite (his English nephew and son-in-law Nathaniel, son of Nathan Mayer, snapped up Château Mouton). His sons, Alphonse and his younger brother Gustave, were at once thrown into the deep end of the choppy pool of *Realpolitik* – the secret offer of the throne of Spain to a Hohenzollern.

When the news broke on 5 July 1870, the French reacted with hysterical outrage and the Emperor fired protests at Europe's other capitals. London he left to the Rothschilds. Sick and tired and without allies, he was nonetheless spoiling for a fight as keenly as Bismarck. Alphonse was under no illusion about the inevitable consequences of a war against the formidable Prussian war-machine which had so recently and swiftly humbled Austria. It is, on this assumption, probable that he purposefully distorted the Emperor's protest into an appeal for support from the British government. His telegram was decoded by Natty in London, who hastened to the Prime Minister. Gladstone, about to leave for an audience with the Queen at Windsor, offered his visitor a seat in the carriage taking him to the station. Rothschild spelt out the situation and vehemently urged action. Gladstone prevaricated and Natty took his case to the leader of the Opposition, Disraeli. Gladstone did, after reflection, make a *démarche* to Madrid and Berlin, and on 12 July the new Foreign Secretary, Lord Granville, was able to inform his chief that he had heard through the Rothschilds that the Hohenzollern candidacy had been withdrawn. But Napoleon, egged on by the Empress Eugénie,* declared war on Prussia one week later. For the first time in their history, the Rothschilds found themselves not just divided by national animosities but on different sides in an armed conflict. Alphonse never forgave the English for not having, as he saw it, forced Bismarck to back down.

Six weeks later, the unhappy Emperor laid down his own and his armies' arms at Sedan. The King of Prussia made straight for Ferrières, where he set up his headquarters and his camp bed for the siege of Paris. 'Kings couldn't afford this,' Wilhelm exclaimed, peering admiringly round. Strict respect for the absent owner's property was prescribed by royal decree. This was not so strictly observed after his departure. Bismarck, who had been a guest of the house in sunnier times, was irked to find that he was obliged to pay for his wine from the Rothschild cellars and forbidden to practise on the pheasants. Unable to resist such sport, he was reported by the steward. Shortly afterwards, a letter from the encircled capital by the regular postal service – balloon or pigeon – was brought down by the enemy and drawn to Bismarck's attention. It read: 'Rothschild told me yesterday that they [the Prussians] were not satisfied with his pheasants at Ferrières, but had threatened to beat his steward because the pheasants did not fly about filled with truffles.' During the subsequent pourparlers over the French reparations, Baron James, to punish such presumptuous poaching, refused, despite being rudely reminded of his origins, to address Bismarck in German, an affront exacerbated by his excruciatingly accented French; to Gerson von Bleichröder, the Chancellor's banker, he spoke in Yiddish, which had to be translated for his incensed master. In London the Rothschilds rallied; they headed the famine relief organization and set about underwriting the war indemnity, issuing with Barings some £240 million in stock. This had such a wholesome effect on the profits that Lionel proposed that the four houses, London, Paris, Vienna and Frankfurt – Naples had put up the shutters – should each withdraw £700,000 from the partnership's capital.

Three years after this unpleasantness, the Prince of Wales met Alphonse de Rothschild and his English brother-in-law, Nathaniel, at a lavish entertainment laid on for him at the home of the Duc de La

---

*Eugénie de Montijo was supposedly the illegitimate daughter of the fourth Earl of Clarendon, diplomat and statesman; Napoleon, less plausibly, was reputed to be the adulterine son of a Dutch Jew, Verhuel.

Rochefoucauld-Bisaccia near Rambouillet, to the considerable anxiety of his mother as the Duke had just been dismissed as French Ambassador in London for having pushed the claim of the Comte de Paris to the vacant throne.

Under the new-born Republic, French society was a veritable minefield for the uninitiated or the unwary. The Republican government ruled with the reluctant acquiescence of the monarchist majority in the Assembly. The latter were themselves rancorously divided between the inflexible legitimists represented by the mystic Comte de Chambord, and the Orleanists in the person of the Comte de Paris, grandson of King Louis-Philippe. That the Prince of Wales was able to bridge these gulfs and remain on respected and cordial terms with Republicans, Bonapartists and Royalists was due to his tact and great charm, which Henry Ponsonby, the Queen's private secretary and a frequent critic of her son, considered 'amounted to genius'.

On all his many later trips to France, the Prince was certain of a welcome with the Rothschilds, Alphonse and Laury at Talleyrand's former palace in the Faubourg St Honoré, and Gustave in the Avenue Marigny. (A few years later the Prince named a new 216-ton racing yacht *Aline*, after Gustave's daughter.) The Prince was more fortunate than Bismarck with the sport at Ferrières. For privileged English guests, such as the Prince's fascinating and high-spirited mistress, Daisy Brooke, Natty would send over the Channel a draft of foxhounds from his pack at Tring. As the foreign foxes were no more dependable than their cousins in Buckingham, a drag would be laid on, the scent ending for the dogs in a vast pile of food concealed under a wild boar skin, and for the guests a 'magnificent déjeuner' in a chalet in the woods. The rest of the time was spent shooting pheasants, 'flirtations – French style – and cards'. The birds themselves were so fat that they rarely rose higher than a man's head, making the battues distinctly hazardous for guns and beaters.

Another favourite companion of the Prince was Charles Haas, the model for Marcel Proust's Swann, who used to say that he was 'the only Jew ever to be accepted by Parisian society without being immensely rich'. (He was still very comfortably off.) His gallant record in the Franco-Prussian War had earned him an entrée to the exclusive Jockey Club. A cultured rake and wit, he was invited by the Comtesse Mélanie de Portalès, a beauty left over from the Second Empire, to join her box at the opera. Her particular affectation was for talking throughout the performance. 'Yes, I'd love to come,' Haas murmured. 'I've never heard you in *Faust*.'

Although his mother had hoped to 'germanize' him at an earlier age, the Prince felt himself, according to one observer, 'most thoroughly at home with Jews and the French, of all the alien [sic] nationalities'. Wilfried Scawen Blunt estimated that 'His little Bohemian tastes made him beloved in Paris, and he had enough of the "grand seigneur" to carry it off. He did not affect to be virtuous, and all sorts of publicans and sinners found their place at his table. He was essentially a cosmopolitan, and without racial prejudice, and he cared as much for popularity abroad as at home. This made him anxious to compose international quarrels.' Little inclined to hypocrisy, the Parisians respected his privacy with amused tolerance and responded to his natural charm and evident attachment, simply but sincerely expressed, to their country; and the Princess's well-advertised antipathy to Prussia can have done little harm to his image.

If Paris took the Prince of Wales to its heart, he opened his arms to Parisiennes.

In 1867, when the Prince was over for the opening of the Exhibition while the Princess was convalescing in London from a bout of rheumatic fever, Sir William Knollys received 'very unsatisfactory accounts' of his behaviour, going to 'supper after the opera with some of the female Paris notorieties etc. etc.'. Five years later Knollys confided his opinion to the Queen that Paris was 'the most dangerous place in Europe, and it would be well if it were never revisited'. (His son, Francis, shared the Prince's liberal tastes, as the Queen feared. Accompanying him to Vienna in April 1873, he consorted with a local doxy before hearing that 'almost all the ladies of the town were reported to be poxed'. He confessed to his friend Lord Rosebery that he was 'in a horrible fright'.) The etceteras left a lot unsaid. The French police were more exactly informed. They had watched the Prince, when he had not managed to lose them, keeping trysts in the Jardin des Plantes and spending the evenings, and not infrequently much of the nights, with mixed beauties – *les grandes horizontales* – of various nationalities in many of the capital's hotels and visiting his favourite brothel, Le Chabanais. He became acquainted with the captivating Liverpudlian courtesan, Catherine 'Skittles' Walters, whom Lord Hartington set up in Mayfair with a house and £2,000 a year. And fortunately Knollys had not heard that the Duc de Gramont, married to Lionel Rothschild's niece, had introduced the Prince to a still more accomplished lady, the passionate consumptive Giulia Beneni, known professionally as La Barucci, who immodestly described herself as 'the greatest whore in the world'. She had been carefully coached on the behaviour expected of her, above all on the Prince's nice regard for punctuality even on such unceremonious occasions. In the event she was still three-quarters of an hour late arriving in a private room at the Maison d'Or. 'Your Royal Highness,' said her sponsor, 'may I present the most unpunctual woman in France?' Whereupon, as La Barucci curtsied, she dropped her skirts. The Duke remonstrated. 'But you told me to be on my best behaviour to His Royal Highness,' she retorted. 'I showed him the best I have, and it was free.' At the Moulin Rouge in Montmartre, the celebrated La Goulue, the energetic exponent of the new risqué 'quadrille excentrique' – or cancan– shouted out, 'Allo, Wales! Tu paies la champagne?' He launched Liane de Pougy, later Princess Ghika, at the Folies Bergères. 'Sire,' she implored, 'tonight I make my début. Deign to appear and applaud me and I am made.' Whether or not he restricted himself to applause, she was duly made.

All this was good, if not clean, fun and, though rumours might fly around, the sordid details never reached those august ears in Buckingham Palace. But one dalliance at this time was not so discreetly conducted. Its object was for the first time coupled in print with his name in *The Times*. Hortense Schneider was not properly a courtesan but was generous, particularly to royalty, to such a fault that she became known as 'le passage des princes'. The Prince did not harm her reputation. She made another name for herself in *opéra bouffe*, and in the year of the Prince's visit to the Paris Exhibition, she was appearing in the lead in Offenbach's *La Belle Hélène*. The Prince was over-assiduous in the court he paid her, attending on her in her box at the theatre, visiting her backstage and being seen with her in restaurants. Later, at Baden-Baden, the Prince's companion, Lord Carrington, relieved him of her, and was subsequently, if not consequently, proposed by Edward for the Viceroyalty of India.

The Prince's interest in the performing arts (and artistes) was reawakened by a more serious talent. Sarah Bernhardt in 1874 was making her reputation in the Comédie Française in Racine's *Phèdre*. Of illegitimate Franco-Dutch Jewish descent, she had been baptized at the age of twelve and brought up in a convent. Bernhardt did not conform to the contemporary ideal of beauty, nor did she pander to fashion in the shape of accentuated bustles and wasp-waists. Slim, almost gaunt by the standards of the day, she favoured free-flowing drapery in a provocatively bohemian style; her face was unfashionably brightly coloured, her tufts of frizzy curls were dyed and her eyes emphasized with kohl to give her that smouldering look, which fired the Prince. Edward, even though he was conducting a heated affair simultaneously with Lillie Langtry, forgot his prejudice in favour of convention and decorum in dress to fall under her spell both off and even on stage: on one occasion, he took a lie-down part, the overweight corpse of the heroine's murdered lover in Sardou's *Fédora* at the Vaudeville, while Sarah wept over him inconsolably. When she came to London in 1879 for a famous season at Alfred de Rothschild's Gaiety Theatre, the Prince took her up and intimated that he would be pleased for her to be received in Society. He set the style himself by entertaining her at Marlborough House. Society might not like it, but hostesses were obliged to comply if they were to compete successfully for the Prince's presence. Lady Frederick Cavendish peevishly described the Divine Sarah as 'a woman of notorious, shameless character . . . Not content with being run after on the stage, this woman is asked to respectable people's houses to act, and even to luncheon and dinner; and all the world goes. It is an outrageous scandal!'

When Bernhardt returned to London two years later, the Prince persuaded Ferdinand de Rothschild to give a midnight supper party so that the sexagenarian Duc d'Aumâle could meet her. The occasion was not a sparkling success. 'All the other ladies present were English ladies,' wrote a fellow guest, Sir Charles Dilke, 'who had been invited at the distinct request of the Prince of Wales. It was one thing to get them to go, and another to get them to talk when they were there; and the result was that, as they would not talk to Sarah Bernhardt, and the Duc d'Aumâle was deaf and disinclined to make conversation on his own account, nobody talked at all, and an absolute reign of the most dismal silence ensued.'

The French connection was not all frivolity. The Prince was back again in 1878 to attend the inaugural ceremonies of another exhibition. The timing was not propitious. The French were incensed at the Turks' ceding of Cyprus to England under the Treaty of Berlin, interpreting this as a threat pointed at Egypt, which they considered a French preserve. Lord Salisbury, the Foreign Secretary, had warned the Prince that he risked a rough reception. He was not put off by the prospect. The Parisian crowds were won over by his cheerful acknowledgement of the mocking salutes of 'Vive la République'. He reinforced this good impression in a speech at a banquet a few days later in which he expressed his conviction in his guttural English and fluent French that the Entente Cordiale between the two countries was 'one not likely to change'. England, the British Ambassador was able to report, 'is very popular here at this moment . . . and the Prince of Wales's visit has been the principal cause of this.'

The abrupt thaw had been fostered in an unlooked-for quarter. Léon Gambetta, a Genoese Jew by descent, a radical Republican by choice, had emerged as the hero of the war against Prussia, escaping from Paris by balloon to proclaim the Republic and to rally national resistance. Although excluded from office by the envy and intrigues of lesser men who feared him as a tribune of the people, he towered above his colleagues in the Chamber and remained one of the most influential men in the country through the force of his oratory and pen. He was also ill-favoured (he had lost an eye in a childhood accident) and sloppy in his dress – not qualities which might have been expected to recommend him to the Prince. All Paris watched with curiosity (and the British Ambassador with concern) as the unlikely couple came together over a 'merry supper' at the Café Anglais. Gambetta, indeed, at once struck the Prince as 'so vulgar in his manner and so careless of his appearance . . . Then we talked. Gambetta expounded his ideas and his plans; and the captivating charm of his eloquence made me forget the physical repulsion with which he inspired me: I was "carried away" in my turn, like the others.' The Prince's own charm almost converted Gambetta to monarchism. The two thereafter continued to meet frequently and in the most friendly fashion until the Frenchman's accidental death four years later after a brief term in office. Edward was delighted to receive from Lord Salisbury an all too rare and appreciative recognition: 'The crisis had been one of no little delicacy; and, if the leaders of French opinion had definitely turned against us, a disagreeable and even hazardous condition of estrangement between the two countries might have grown up . . . Your Royal Highness's influence over M. Gambetta, and the skill with which that influence has been exercised, have averted a danger that was not inconsiderable.' There is little doubt that if Gambetta had survived, he would have proved more amenable to collaboration than confrontation in Egypt and thus eliminated so much subsequent friction.

The Prince's visits to France were part of what became a regular pattern. Protocol insisted that he travel incognito as the Earl of Chester or the Duke of Lancaster, though he was, of course, recognized wherever he went without the least hindrance or inconvenience. Each March his programme was arranged to allow him a week or so in Paris en route for the Riviera. He might stay five weeks in Cannes or Nice, often living on board his yacht which had been sent ahead. Later, as monarch, he cultivated Biarritz for some weeks before embarking on a Mediterranean cruise. When on an official visit, he would travel *en prince* with a train of thirty servants in addition to his personal suite, but *en garçon* he would take just two equerries, his doctor, two valets and two footmen. This allowed him to live the kind of congenial and informal life that would have been impossible, or at least inadvisable, in his own capital.

2

Sassoons: Baghdad to Belgravia

Despite the demands of his private life, the Prince was still chafing at the want of any more meaningful employment. (He had just been promoted field marshal, but this only kept his tailor temporarily occupied.) As some consolation, he conceived a plan which he kept from his wife, his mother and her government, to descend on the gorgeous East – at government expense. Once his plans were far enough advanced to be disclosed, he won his mother's conditional consent on the false representation that the project had been entirely approved by her ministers. But the expedition would have to be mounted in such a style that he could meet the Indian princes – and match their costly offerings – on equal terms. There was bickering over the bill, to which he could not, and his mother would not, contribute. 'Where is the money to come from?' asked Disraeli. 'He has not a shilling; she will not give him one.' The same question was put more shrilly by the popular press and radical mob orators throughout the country, who saw no reason why the public should be expected to pay for the Prince's pleasures in 'pig-sticking and women'. Disraeli overrode such petty objections and persuaded the House of Commons to contribute £52,000 for Admiralty transport and £60,500 for personal expenses, to which the government of India would add a further £100,000. The Prince (and even *The Times*) thought he had been shabbily treated, but, although he talked 'big' among his 'creatures' of his intention of 'spending, if requisite, a million, and all that', he was reconciled by the Prime Minister to making do. (In the event, he did not exceed his budget; and those princely gifts which exceeded sense or reason, such as the six gold cannon, worth £40,000 apiece, presented to him by the twelve-year-old Gaekwar of Baroda, were discreetly returned.)

The Queen, who had insisted that the Princess of Wales be left behind (the Prince had never suggested otherwise, for which Alexandra '*never* would', she wrote, 'forget or forgive him'), next insisted on taking all the arrangements in hand, and attempted to interfere with the choice of his travelling companions. The Prince, in a huff, rushed round to Downing Street and 'manifested extraordinary excitement'. Disraeli advised the Queen to give ground.

The party eventually set off in October 1875 in low spirits, 'more like a party of monks than anything else', Lord Carrington reported to his mother. Not even a visit to the theatre in the French capital relieved the gloom. At Brindisi they embarked on the converted troopship *Serapis* with two frigates and the royal yacht *Osborne* in attendance. The Prince's personal suite numbered eighteen, with a retinue of thirty-odd servants, among them three chefs and the Duke of Sutherland's piper. The expedition also included an artist, a botanist, a zoologist (and taxidermist), a 'clerk of great merit' from the India Office (one Isaacson) and the Prince's French poodle.

A month later, the *Serapis* was welcomed in Bombay by the thunder of a salute of guns from a dozen British warships and by the Viceroy, Lord Northbrook, attended by some seventy Indian princes in gold tunics glittering with jewels. More surprisingly, the Prince's calvalcade was given a spontaneous and rapturous reception by the local population waving banners with such fond slogans as 'Tell Mama We're Happy'. There were two absentees – the merchant princes Sir Albert and Elias Sassoon, who were praying in the synagogue on the anniversary of their father's death. To excuse himself for any lapse of respect for the living, Sir Albert entertained the Prince in oriental (and strictly kosher) splendour at his marble mansion Sans Souci on Malabar Hill, overlooking the bay, and to mark his public spirit commissioned for the city a ten-foot equestrian statue (at £1,000 the foot) of the Prince as a paunchy hussar. (He had previously commemorated the Prince Consort in a similar fashion, though on a smaller and less expensive scale, and had marked his patriotic piety by naming his own son Edward Albert, after the Prince of Wales.)

Since the death of his father ten years before, Sir Albert was the head of the great eastern trading empire of David Sassoon & Sons. On this occasion he was presuming on a prior acquaintance with the Prince. With the opening of the Suez Canal, the Sassoon pre-eminence in Bombay and points further east had been formally recognized by the award of the Freedom of the City of London and a knighthood for Albert in 1872. On his way to collect these honours, he had put in an appearance at a State ball at Buckingham Palace for that awkward guest the Shah of Persia, Nasr-ed-Din, who had been known to make an offer for a lady-in-waiting. The Queen, who detested the potentate as much as his habits (although he addressed her respectfully as 'My Auspicious Sister of Sublime Nature'), absented herself. Her son, who rarely otherwise saw eye to eye with his mother, was only too happy to leave the Shah to his fellow oriental Albert.

Albert Abdullah's father, David Sassoon, had arrived in Bombay from Baghdad. Babylonia had constituted the second homeland of the Jews from the time of their exile under Nebuchadrezzar in the sixth century BC. The first of the family of whom there is firm evidence is Sason ben Saleh, born in Baghdad in 1750, who could then trace his direct line back through five generations. From ancient times, the acknowledged leader of the Jewish merchant community, known reverently as the 'Prince of the Captivity', had enjoyed a mutually satisfactory and privileged position as banker and tax collector for the local pasha, now a subordinate of the Turkish Sultan. For centuries the Jews had experienced a prosperous peace under a benevolent Islam. But Baghdad, overrun by successive waves of conquerors, was by then a crumbling and gutted shell of its former splendour. As its fortunes declined, so the often capricious demands of the local governor became more difficult to support, and when these exceeded the means of the community, the tyrant resorted to persecution and pillage. Sheikh Sason, who led his charges for thirty-eight years, bore the brunt of his displeasure until at last his eldest surviving son, David, taken as hostage, escaped with empty pockets and fled with his old father to the Persian Gulf trading port, and seat of the British Residency, at Bushire. Here he was shortly joined by his ten-year-old son, Albert Abdullah. But there were richer pastures still another step ahead. The Honourable East India Company had lost its monopoly of the India trade fifteen years before. Father and son, after Sheik Sason's death, made for Bombay and opened shop in 1832 with £1,000 advanced on the security of the family's reputation, one year before John Company lost its monopoly over the China trade.

For more than thirty years while he headed the house in India, David clung to his old ways and insisted his family did likewise, at least under his eye. They continued richly robed and turbaned; Hebrew and Arabic remained their natural tongues, Persian for commerce. The firm's letter-head and cheques were printed in Hebrew and English as a concession, although the patriarch, who was naturalized in 1853, never mastered a word of the English language. The basis of their wealth was cotton and opium and, after the cession of the Chinese ports following the First Opium War, real estate as the family spread eastwards.

The commerce in opium attracted less opprobrium in the nineteenth century than it does today. Laudanum, opium in alcoholic suspension, was cheaper (a penny for 30 grains) than gin and was freely available at every grocery store (the Pharmaceutical Society did not corner the market until early in the present century). It was taken as a panacea for everything from migraine and gastric disorders to the fashionable 'vapours'. China had continued to resist its import even after losing the first war, but there still remained a profitable traffic in smuggling through Hong Kong; the drug was a convenient medium of exchange for the tea and silk coming out of China. After 1859 and a further war, China was forced to legalize the trade. Even before this, David's second son, Elias, had made Shanghai his base, and within a few years the family were established along the whole China coast and were among the first into Japan after that country's barriers had been breached.

The Sassoons were rarely speculators or innovators. They pursued a cautious policy of 'wait and see'. When the first cotton mills opened in Bombay in the early 1850s, they waited and traded in Lancashire's manufactures. They became shippers without incurring the risk of ship-owning; they became brokers and bankers, commission agents and warehousemen. In the period of feverish demand for Indian cotton by Lancashire mills during the American Civil War, a horde of speculators made a fortune one day and lost it the next. The family's fortune on the eve of the war was already solid enough to resist wild temptation. The end of the war set off a slump, the price of cotton lost two-thirds of its scarcity value, the Bank of Bombay collapsed. David Sassoon & Sons' prudence ensured that they were among the very few to emerge in a more powerful position; with their capital reserves so carefully nursed they could now snap up commercial property in a depressed market and confirm themselves as merchant princes of the first rank throughout the East. Indeed, their worth was such that during the Mutiny they had offered to furnish a Jewish Legion to serve against the rebellious sepoys and bought heavily into government stock while others sold in a panic. It was the only occasion that the patriarch, to advertise their loyalty, approved the wearing of Western dress.

David Sassoon gave away some £100,000 to charity in his lifetime, to establish schools for boys and girls, including an industrial training institution for juvenile delinquents, and hospitals in Bombay and Poona. Sir Bartle Frere, Governor of Bombay, held him up as an example of sound sense: 'there are many who can do as you have done, in sending a son to an English school and college there to learn not only what English gentlemen know, but what they feel and think on subjects of more permanent interest and importance than how the wealth of modern commerce is accumulated and distributed.' Such enlightenment would prove fatal to the future prosperity of the business.

When David died in 1864, he was worth some £5 million. He left eight sons – thirty-five years separated the oldest and youngest – by his two wives. The eldest, Albert Abdullah, lacked his father's strict piety and devotion to business and divided his time more agreeably between social and civic affairs and the office. He joined the Bombay Legislative Council, requesting his colleagues there and at his clubs to overlook the Abdullah and address him henceforth as straight Albert. He was rewarded with the Star of India, which he celebrated with a ball at Sans Souci. The local *Gazette* congratulated him on the absence of 'natives', an omission which was hailed as an indication of the family's 'evident wish to ally themselves with English society'. (This attitude towards Indians, at best condescending, aroused the Prince's indignation on his tour of India in 1875, and he forcefully protested to both his mother and Lord Salisbury. The Queen, created in the same year Empress of India by that wily old flatterer Disraeli, was sympathetic. Instructions came from London that this attitude must be corrected. This rap on the knuckles was resented in some intractable circles and was set down, so Salisbury wryly observed, to the 'malign influence' of the Prince.) Albert had given another even grander ball in 1872 to welcome the new Viceroy, Lord Northbrook, one of the Baring banking clan, before dashing off for his first taste of London.

Since the late 1850s the family had been represented at Leadenhall Street, a less important outpost at that time than Shanghai or Hong Kong, by Albert's eldest half-brother, Sassoon David Sassoon, grandfather of Siegfried. A wispy and scholarly dreamer, he settled at Ashley Park in Surrey and devoted himself to Hebrew literature, but after less than ten years in the country he suddenly dropped dead. His younger brother, Reuben, aged thirty-two, who had assiduously kept a royal scrapbook since the Prince of Wales's marriage, at once offered to fill the gap. Reuben, flashily foppish despite his squat build, set up house in Lancaster Gate near Hyde Park. He soon exchanged this for a new corner house at 1 Belgrave Square which possessed all the appurtenances of a gentleman's residence – a conservatory packed with potted plants, a billiard-cum-smoking room and a well-stocked cellar, leaving no space for the horses and carriages, which had to be lifted to the stables on the roof. As a dusky nabob, studded with outsize pearls, flashing diamonds on his fingers, he cut a fine, or at least remarkable, figure in Society, insinuating his way to the card tables in the Marlborough Club and to the notice of the Prince.

Reuben's brother Arthur Abraham, younger by five years, had already had an early taste of London, having been sent over at the age of fifteen and confided to the care of Hermann Adler, the son (and successor) of the Chief Rabbi. He had served his apprenticeship under Reuben in Hong Kong – he was one of the original board members of the Hong Kong and Shanghai Bank – where he had shed his turban and robes and the Abraham. He had probably offered himself as escort to Albert when he went to collect his honours in the Empire's capital, and was delayed by a pretty face, that of Eugénie Louise, daughter of the Chevalier Achille Perugia of Trieste. They were married in 1873. It was unthinkable that such a lustrous pearl should be buried in Bombay, so Arthur happily settled in at Albert Gate. Louise, with her dash of Latin temperament and charmingly accented English, her magnolia complexion and chestnut curls, magnificent diamonds and French chef, became one of the most brilliant hostesses of the age in contrast to Reuben's stout and retiring wife. Louise was, in the view of the often caustic Margot Asquith, 'one of the most delightful women I have known'. The object of this accolade slipped gracefully into the social round with her swarthy, balding spouse by her side. Hannah Rothschild (later Countess of Rosebery) fell under her spell, as did her cousin Leopold, who protested he would never marry until or unless he found a bride 'as beautiful and accomplished as Mrs Arthur Sassoon'. Chance contrived that Louise's younger sister Marie should be visiting them in London. Though more than fifteen years younger than Leopold, she possessed many of her sister's qualities; if there was one fault it was her lack of enthusiasm for horse and hound. Hannah cajoled her into taking riding lessons and, once safely in the saddle, she was casually introduced to Leopold at a Buckingham meet by Anthony de Rothschild's daughter Constance. Leopold, smitten, proudly showed off his stables and offered to mount her. The Prince of Wales attended the wedding ceremony at the Central Synagogue in January 1881.

Albert, each post painfully reminding him of all he was missing in the foggier fleshpots, pined for London in his turn. But as the senior Sassoon, there was the business to be minded. His wife, too, her shaven head unbecomingly bewigged, pleaded ill-health to avoid accompanying him abroad. Albert did not insist, and Louise therefore generously offered her services as hostess while Reuben was instructed to cast around for a suitable pied-à-terre where Albert might just snatch a few months a year; the house he found, 25 Kensington Gore, was far too grand to be left under wraps for the remaining months. The choice of successor for the Bombay business had been made more difficult by the defection of

Albert's brother Elias some years before to set up a rival Sassoon empire. There remained, however, the younger brother of Reuben and Arthur, Aaron Solomon, fittingly serious and devout, who, twenty-three years younger than Albert, was married to Albert's granddaughter. Solomon was recalled from China and put in charge of the main operation under three absentee senior partners. Albert's undiminished attachment to the Crown was reflected in the interior trappings of his new house: the Queen-Empress glowered down from a tapestry over the fireplace in the dining room, which was panelled with inlaid ivory and ebony salvaged from the Prince's British pavilion at the Paris Exhibition; six further immense tapestries rather incongruously featured scenes from *The Merry Wives of Windsor*.

The oriental exoticism of the Sassoons spared them that censure or ridicule that their ostentation invited. They had dropped fully armed with their riches and reputation into the lap of Society, and they were embraced as colourful nabobs for whom the Queen herself had a fondness, with a distinct Imperial aura and the assurance of their ancient lineage. Though a desperate rhymester in the *Pink 'Un* might mock Albert as 'that Indian auriferous coon', the family escaped much of the snobbery and prejudice that still persisted in some quarters towards the new rich, native or immigrant, Jewish or Gentile. Potentates and ministers plenipotentiary from India, China and the Levant came to London to pay their respects to the merchant princes who comfortably straddled two worlds, East and West; British envoys on their way to take up posts in the Orient sought their counsel. The Sultan of Zanzibar, in London to seek closer ties with the Crown, was entertained in Kensington Gore and borne down to Albert's retreat in Brighton.

The family lost no time in establishing their own colony by the sea: the radical Henry Labouchère described Brighton as 'a sea-coast town, three miles long and three yards broad, with a Sassoon at each end and one in the middle'. Albert was in Eastern Terrace, Kemptown; Reuben and Arthur patriotically and respectively in Queen's and King's Gardens, Hove. They were joined by Sassoon David Sassoon's waspish widow – she referred to the Rothschilds as 'the hairy-heeled ones' – who was slightly disapproved of because of her determination that her sons should not sink into commerce that was already ineluctably slipping through the brothers' fingers.

The three Sassoons sidled casually and imperceptibly into royal favour. Reuben and Arthur were familiar faces at the Marlborough Club and at a variety of race meetings in company with Leopold Rothschild. This nodding acquaintance took some years to ripen before they joined the retinue of intimates. Albert made a sparkling début with a ball at Kensington Gore for which the hall had been transformed into a grotto with water lilies, dripping ferns and splashing fountains. The Prince of Wales, reminded of the hospitality he had received at Sans Souci five years before and the uniformed bronze likeness now resting outside Bombay's town hall, was induced to attend and was regaled with a spread to his liverish liking. That same summer Edward and Alexandra, after opening the Children's Hospital in Brighton, were persuaded to take lunch in Eastern Terrace. The modest six-course *casse-croûte* was almost spoilt by the security arrangements: an anonymous letter had been received threatening to bomb the premises. The Prince, not easily put off his meal, scoffed, 'My dear Sir Albert, this is the 21st of July, not the 1st of April!'

Reuben shared with the Prince an addiction for the Turf and the card table (they shared other appetites: Reuben, an observer remarked, 'never opened his mouth, except to put food into it'). He combined a commendable knowledge of bloodstock with a good head for figures. His renown was such that, after Edward's accession, the conversation turning at lunch to the formation of a new government, the Duke of Abercorn proposed that nothing would please the King better than to have Reuben as Chancellor of the Exchequer under Esher as Prime Minister.

Giving gave him much innocent pleasure. He reported to his sister-in-law Louise from Sandringham in November 1887: 'This morning being the Prince's birthday, he received many presents, among them my cigarette case, and there were five other similar cases, but mine was more appreciated as being uncommon.' He had spent most of the previous August with the Prince at Bad Homburg, a ritual penance to provide temporary relief of the royal weight, hosting huge picnics. He wrote to Arthur, laid low at home, that 'HRH thanked me over and over again for the treats I gave him'. Though Reuben was the least congruous (and wealthy) figure in the royal circle, his name figured more frequently in the visitors' book at Sandringham than any other save that of the Prince's friend 'Harty-Tarty', Lord Hartington. Yet there were limits. The Prince would tolerate an unusual degree of familiarity, but it was prudent not to presume too closely on his forbearance. He was observed once, when 'the impudent Semite' playfully put his arm round his neck, to push Reuben so violently away from him going down stairs that he fell and bruised himself badly.

Although the London business was proportionately overstocked with the three brothers (and senior partners), their attention to their trade was divided by these distractions. Albert and Reuben were most sparing of their time, arriving at the office around eleven to sign letters or to dabble in opium if the price were right: 'We thought we might as well buy a small lot and make a little money.' They would then put up the shutters before lunch, and sally forth to Sandown on a 'special' with the Prince of Wales and Lord Rosebery or Leopold Rothschild for a flutter of another kind.

Sassoon–Rothschild family ties were soon more securely knotted. Sir Albert's only surviving son and heir, Edward, married, in October 1887, Aline, the daughter of Baron Gustave de Rothschild of Paris (and nine years later, Albert's granddaughter Louise Gubbay married the Baroness Gustave's nephew). At two removes from the Baghdad souk, the injurious consequence of climate and culture had wrought its effect, diluting the stern piety and single-minded commitment to trade in this English scion of the house of Sassoon. Slim and spruce, Edward was credited with a nonchalant good nature; he took most naturally to flogging the river and gunning the grouse at Tulchan Lodge, the Speyside estate his father had rented from the Dowager Lady Seafield, and finally settled for a relaxed political career.[*] Aline was of a more refined taste and intellect; a talented artist, she was esteemed by Bernard Berenson, who advised her on her acquisitions, as 'the noblest of the Rothschilds'. Albert, approaching seventy, was delighted at this happy solution and such a splendid match was suitably celebrated. The Chief Rabbi of France officiated while the choir of the Paris Opéra sang to the multitude. The Prince of Wales sent a rather florid tribute, a silver basin and ewer depicting Hercules gracefully succumbing to a nymph. The newlyweds moved into Kensington Gore and Albert gratefully retreated to Brighton to nurse his asthma and bronchitis.

Two years later in the summer of 1889 the Prince of Wales urgently called on his friends to help share an unwelcome load. The Shah of Persia was due to return for a second State visit. Nasr-ed-Din had mellowed – he even stooped to retrieve the cherry stones he spat on the Windsor Castle carpet – though it was believed that he had had his masseur bowstrung for incompetence and the body buried in the grounds at Buckingham Palace. Albert, although by now shaky on his legs, rallied to the royal support as became the ruler of a lesser oriental empire. He

---

[*]He sat as Member of Parliament for the Hythe and Folkestone Division from 1899. The seat had previously been held by Mayer Rothschild for fifteen years, a seemingly curious choice of constituency. Nathan Mayer had acquired Burmarsh Farm near Hythe for the substantial sum of £8,750, undoubtedly to serve as a base for his carrier pigeons as well as stables for the saddle-horses of his couriers who, requiring craft and crews at any hour and in all weathers to cross the Channel, were a source of steady and generous employment in nearby Folkestone.

attended Brighton's Kempton Park races with the Prince, patiently commentating and interpreting for their Persian guest. The Roseberys threw a dinner in London, and next day Albert piloted the Shah down to Halton for lunch with Alfred Rothschild and on to Ferdinand at Waddesdon for the night. The Shah was on his best behaviour, but the strain was telling. The Prince of Wales had gratefully abandoned his guest to such trusty hands and had sent in his place his two sons, Albert Victor, Duke of Clarence, and Prince George, with the old Duke of Cambridge. The Shah, nettled at such neglect, took to his room in a sulk and was only tempted down to dinner by the promise of a notable conjurer Ferdie had provided. (The Shah may also have been disappointed that his host had put away the most valuable of his treasures in order to restrict the losses arising from the potentate's acquisitiveness.) With his good humour restored by the prestidigitation, the Shah pressed his host for an introduction to one of the more lustrous stars of the company. 'You are the most beautiful woman I have seen since I have been in England,' he told her. 'I must take you home with me.' 'But, Your Majesty,' she respectfully replied, 'I am married.' 'Well,' answered the accommodating Shah, 'bring your husband along. When we get to Tehran I will take care of him.'

As the climax to the tour, Albert took over the Empire Theatre, where the glittering company was entertained to a full-course supper (the unsuspecting guest of honour had already dined privately in his rooms at Buckingham Palace) and, when the lights finally went down at 1.30 a.m., to a *ballet divertissement* well out of reach of the King of Kings. Albert, giving his guest ten years and now wilting, had not seen the last of him. The Shah descended on Brighton for a long weekend. A banquet at Eastern Terrace was rounded off the following morning in the Turkish baths. Emerging refreshed and beaming, the Defender of the Faith, noticing some lady bathers on the beach, intimated rather loudly that it would satisfy the imperial pleasure to see them disrobe completely. While the objects of his admiration fled in confusion, it was left to Albert to excuse their prudery.

Albert's attachment to the Shah was not solely altruistic. Persia lay squarely in the sphere of interest of both David Sassoon & Sons and the British Empire; it was the buffer between British India and the expansive Russian Empire. Indeed, the reason the Shah had been fêted so effusively in England was that he had already been royally entertained in Russia. Political stability in Persia and British ascendancy were together to be assured by a straightforward expedient. The means were defined succinctly by a later British Minister: 'Persia is a corrupt constituency in which the seat is to be won by the holder of the longest, or, rather, the most lavish purse.'

The financial arm of this design was the Imperial Bank of Persia. In 1872 Baron Julius de Reuter,* born Israel Beer Josaphat in Kassel, who had created the eponymous newspaper telegraph service twenty years before, had won from the Shah a formidable concession – the monopoly of all mineral rights and public works over the whole region for a period of seventy years. Nothing came of this except that the Baron lost his £40,000 caution money. Two months after the Shah's most recent visit to London the Imperial Bank was incorporated, inheriting Reuter's rights. A Royal Charter was granted by the British government to encourage public subscriptions. This was successful; the subscription list totalled seven times the required capital issue of £2 million. The founders with Reuter (who recovered his caution money) were David Sassoon & Sons, Glyn Mills and J. Henry Schroder. This promotion had been plotted by the British Minister in Tehran, Sir Henry Drummond Wolff, and the Imperial Bank's monopoly was strenuously defended by the Foreign Office against all comers. Minerals, however, proved doggedly elusive and the volatile nature of the country's management did not recommend itself to private investment. Eventually the failure of this policy of keeping the Persian government afloat lest it fall into another's pocket obliged the British to reach a *modus vivendi* with Russia, which in turn led to the entente of 1907.

Sir Albert was created the first Baronet of Kensington Gore for his part in this venture the following year. He died in 1896, six months after the Shah was assassinated in a Tehran mosque, possibly as the result of the sale of another monopoly – tobacco – which popular discontent forced him to revoke. Albert's personal estate was valued at £385,000, but he had already provided for his son (and new chairman) Edward. After his father's death, the new baronet gave up Kensington Gore and acquired a Renaissance-style palace at 25 Park Lane, with an unusual history. It had been put up by the megalomaniac cockney Barney Barnato, in order to cast the Rothschilds into the shade, and was an exceptional example of excess. The house boasted a marble staircase, four flights high, top-lit by a glass dome, as well as the usual conservatory and winter garden, a vast ballroom and no less than two billiard rooms, with central heating throughout. It was topped by a series of marble figures ensconced on the roof which were variously rumoured to represent the owner's petrified

---

*Reuter had declined a Foreign Office suggestion that he might contribute towards the cost of the Shah's visit to England. When reminded of the Sassoons' generosity, he replied, 'I do not care . . . the Sassoons are snops. I am not a snop.' He gave £5,000 nonetheless.

shareholders, unlucky bookmakers or, though less likely, the Twelve Apostles (Edward Sassoon presented them to Brighton town council). Barnato had planned a huge house-warming for the night of the Diamond Jubilee in the summer of 1897 but, returning from South Africa, was lost overboard. He had been recently suffering from a distressing delirium, with visions of banknotes crumbling to dust.

The family firm's fortunes, if they had not also sunk, had been sliding slowly since the Sassoons' arrival in London some forty years before in pursuit of the high life. The traffic in opium was condemned in the House of Commons in 1891, although long before that the Chinese had come to terms with it; obliged by the powers to allow its entry into their territory, they had sensibly decided to grow their own crop and tax the imports. After Solomon's death in 1894, the Bombay office, the core of the operation, was run by his energetic but single-handed widow, Flora. The family's ranks were thinning, their initiative flagging.

The Shah was seen off by his relieved hosts at the end of July, to be dropped off at Cherbourg by the *Victoria and Albert*. Sir Henry Drummond Wolff waited until the autumn before taking the long over-land trail to resume his post in the Persian capital. Pausing in Vienna, he was entertained by an old acquaintance, 'the celebrated Baron de Hirsch', who had just disposed of his Balkan Railway to Constantinople. The two men made good company. The guest, with a fund of 'whimsical quips' and 'a certain flippant cynicism', was notoriously Rabelaisian in his conversa-tion; he was said to have been the only person to have presumed to tell Lord Salisbury an improper story. Yet in one important respect they were at odds. Drummond Wolff, grandson of the second Earl of Orford and of the Rabbi David Wolff of Halle, was reticent about his roots. Hirsch typically expressed an interest in the condition of his co-religionists in Persia; Drummond Wolff offhandedly 'undertook, if possible, to amelio-rate their position'. Despising his patronym, he had adopted his middle name, which had been given him in honour of his father's friend Henry Drummond, sectarian crusader and founder of the chair of Political Economy at Oxford as well as the Irvingite Church. His father, Dr Joseph Wolff, had enjoyed a rich and irrepressibly eccentric career – to the mortification of the son. The German rabbi's heir had become such a promising convert to Catholicism at the age of seventeen that he had been presented to Pope Pius VII, who had reinstituted the Inquisition in 1814 (it was abolished in 1821). He was entrusted to the Collegio Romano and the Collegio di Propaganda for his further education but was summarily excommunicated two years later for 'publicly uttering erroneous opinions'. Repairing north, with spirit intact, he declared himself a member of the Church of England and resumed his study of oriental tongues at Cambridge. Equipped with a formidable arsenal of ancient and modern languages, he set off on a hunt to preach to the Jewish communities of Egypt, Mesopotamia, the Crimea, Afghanistan and India. He was more appreciated in London salons. He found himself one day, a lion of Society, seated at dinner next to Lady Georgiana Walpole, 'a mature spinster of no great personal attractions'. When she dropped her fork, Wolff gallantly stooped to retrieve it, giving her leg at the same time a playful pinch. This made an impression. Ever impulsive, he next called on her brother, the Earl of Orford, to request the lady's hand, rounding off his prospects with an immodest declaration: 'I may add that I come of the blood of Abraham, Isaac and Jacob.' 'Oh,' replied the Earl somewhat ungraciously, 'you had better take her, but I fear our family can offer you nothing like that.'

No sooner married, Wolff took off again. In Khorasan he was taken prisoner and enslaved – prudently he had left Lady Georgiana at home – until delivered by a Persian prince, Abbas Mirza, younger son of the Shah. Undaunted, he travelled on to Bukhara, home to a large Jewish community (and a more extensive slave market). He entered arrayed in a surplice and college cap, reciting from the Book of Common Prayer from muleback. Happily unfamiliar with the nature of the rantings of this quaintly robed figure, the fanatical natives took him for a madman and left him to pursue his path in peace. He continued south, spreading the Word in his original way from Kabul to Calcutta and, emerging unscathed, retired to the living of a parish near Huddersfield. His style must have been as puzzling to the folk of the West Riding as to the unconverted; his sermons had 'no order, method, sequence, argument nor arrangement' and he would break off in the middle to sing a Hebrew song. As there was no worthy challenge in preaching to the converted, he returned to Bukhara to offer the inhabitants a second chance of redemption. Many thought him vain and credulous, but no one denied his courage. He ventured to Bukhara a third time in 1843 to enquire into the fate of two British emissaries who had disappeared in the previous year. Wolff did not share their fate – imprisonment and execution at the hands of the local amir – and finally settled for domesticity in a Somerset vicarage. There he published his journals, saying of well-known public figures 'A sad liar' and 'This man is an ass', and lapsing into the third person, 'The Lord said unto Wolff', an excess he excused by describing himself as 'an enthusiast, drunk with the love of God'. His son, of a less robust spirit, was supposed to have bought up all the copies of his father's book.

This colourful character's son trod a more orthodox path. He had, according to a diplomat's wife, 'not a scrap of morals or belief of any kind, all this having been exhausted by his father ... there was in him something of a cheap angel and a German professor'. This did not disqualify him for the Foreign Office, but, aged forty-four, he exchanged diplomacy for a seat in the House of Commons, which he held for a little over ten years.

During Gladstone's second administration, Drummond Wolff, with Lord Randolph Churchill, was the instigator of one of the more discreditable Parliamentary episodes – the exclusion of the elected radical atheist Charles Bradlaugh from the House. More than twenty years after professing Jews had been granted the right to affirm their allegiance in place of the Christian oath, Bradlaugh's opponents now pretended to deny this right to avowed atheists on the grounds that any oath of an 'infidel' was invalid. Indulged by a pusillanimous Speaker, this demeaning debate dragged on for five years before Bradlaugh secured his seat. The two principal protagonists of discrimination combined with Sir John Gorst – the founder of the modern Conservative party apparatus – and A. J. Balfour, an unlikely gadfly, to form the Fourth Party to ginger up their own apathetic party leaders. Drummond Wolff's last political adventure was the creation of the Primrose League in 1883. Named after what was mistakenly believed to be Disraeli's favourite flower, the intent was to forge the late Prime Minister's 'Two Nations' into one by sandwiching the urban middle classes between the upper and lower crusts of aristocrats and artisans in a broadly based popular front. The Portsmouth electors were unimpressed, unseating Drummond Wolff the year before Bradlaugh slipped into his seat in the Commons in 1886. He returned to diplomacy and after his term in Tehran held the embassy in Madrid for nine years until his retirement, serving as a link in King Edward's grapevine.

Sir Henry Drummond Wolff had been fortunate to find his host in Vienna. Though an Austrian subject by adoption, Hirsch never felt at home in that convivial capital. The pervasive social prejudice was uncongenial to a man of such ambition; even the Jewish banking elite would not accept him at his own valuation. Overt anti-Semitism, or any other expression of a nationalist leaning, was rigorously suppressed as too apt to aggravate tensions within the combustible conglomeration of races. Vienna had long been the magnet for Jews escaping the oppressive conditions to the east; they comprised some 10 per cent of the city's heterogeneous population, forming a prosperous bourgeoisie fizzing with intellectual and artistic vitality. Unlike other ethnic constituents of the

Austrian Empire, they gave their allegiance to the Emperor and to German culture and language, of which Yiddish was a dialect. But, behind the *Gemütlichkeit*, the giddy waltzes and dashing hussars, Austrian society was rigidly stratified, noted for its 'good form' and exquisite manners. The court itself was a close society, repressive and resistant. In the sombre halls of the Hofburg, the hidebound courtiers shared a single interest in stifling ritual, precedence and protocol; stolid Franz Joseph's spirited Bavarian Empress had already fled despairingly from the gloom. (Hirsch was said to be the illegitimate son of the dim and ineffectual disfigured Emperor Ferdinand I, Franz Joseph's uncle; if Hirsch did not foster this rumour himself, neither did he discountenance it, a serious misjudgement of the character of the court.)

Few managed to cross the social barriers. The Rothschilds, Austrian barons and for so long the crutch of the Empire's shaky finances, had been no exception. As late as 1886 Baron Nathaniel von Rothschild only obtained the much-coveted entrance to the Schwarzenburg Palace by the expedient loan of his band at some charity for which Prince Schwarzenburg had lent his ballroom, and that despite the fact that the Schwarzenburgs had been colleagues of the Rothschilds for some thirty years in their investment banking arm, the Kreditanstalt. The Emperor, too, attended and, on this occasion, 'some Jews, to whom it gave a glimpse of society'. It was only in the following year that Nathaniel's younger brother Albert, who headed the Viennese bank, was graciously awarded the sought-after style *Hoffähig*, or 'courtworthy'. *Hoffähigkeit* bred haughtiness. Nathaniel, to whom under the sponsorship of Princess Pauline Metternich, the 'Notre Dame de Zion' of Viennese society, all salon doors were open, kept his own closed to other, less honoured Jews.

Rothschild was a solitary exeption, and it had taken the family three-quarters of a century of perseverance to achieve such acknowledgement. And yet in the fifty years following the Congress of Vienna which presided over the demolition of Bonaparte's empire, they had achieved an astonishing ascendancy, securely anchored in the lee of the all-powerful Chancellor Prince von Metternich in a fascinating partnership of power-broking and money-lending. During the first half of the nineteenth century, Jews in Austria had few rights. They could own neither land nor property; they were barred from government service and from most professions; their movement was restricted and they required special permission to marry; foreign Jews were not tolerated without a temporary residence permit. But the Rothschilds themselves were greatly in demand in a continent devastated by war and starved of capital. Salomon, the modest and obliging second son of Mayer Amschel, was tempted to devote some of his attention to the needs of the Empire from his station in Frankfurt.

Granted right of residence in Vienna by special favour of the Emperor, he was nonetheless unable to acquire a home there. He was reduced to taking the best suite in the city's most exclusive hotel, Zum Römischen Kaiser. As the demands of the State multiplied, he took more rooms to accommodate his family until finally his *hôtel* became entirely *particulier*. The brothers had already, after some opposition, been elevated to the humblest rung of the nobility – the right to add 'von' to their name; a dissenting privy councillor argued that as mere businessmen motivated by profit rather than loyalty, they would be amply rewarded by a gold snuffbox with the Imperial monogram in diamonds. (This no doubt was seen to be unnecessarily extravagant.) Five years later all five brothers were made hereditary barons of the Empire. It was another twenty years before Salomon was able to make another, more substantial breach in restrictive practices. In order to service the Rothschild railway, the Nordbahn – Austria's, and indeed Continental Europe's, first major line – he was granted a special exemption to acquire ironworks and coal mines. In the same year, 1842, he was made a citizen of Vienna, which entitled him to own property within the city boundaries. He at once bought his home, the former hotel, and revived an earlier claim to join the landed interest. Salomon had reassured Chancellor Metternich that his ambition was not to achieve still greater prestige; it was to provide insurance and a legacy. The family had been made uncomfortably aware that their wealth, great as it was, consisted almost entirely of paper securities in their safes; although they might manage the markets, there were too many unforesee-able factors outside their control, as the July Revolution in Paris in 1830 had demonstrated. Salomon did not forsake his less fortunate fellows; for each exceptional exemption he won, he whittled away at the remaining disabilities for the Empire's Jews, relief which was conceded more reluctantly, only partially and belatedly. Having earned his right to own property in the capital, this was extended by gracious dispensation to the countryside. He supplied himself with several immense estates and no less than two castles, one, in the fashionable Gothic style, at Schillersdorf just over the Austrian border in Prussia. He became overnight one of the most substantial landowners in the Empire, and certainly a model, if mostly absentee, landlord.

While Metternich leant heavily on Salomon for the boundless demands of the Treasury, their relationship was not solely founded on pragmatic expedience. A close and lasting personal friendship developed between the two Rhinelanders, the autocrat born at Coblenz, and the diplomatic Salomon born at Frankfurt. This was cemented when Metternich took for his third wife the glamorous Countess Mélanie Zichy-Ferraris; her family was wantonly extravagant and it fell to Salomon to arrange a suitable settlement which won the gratitude and affection of groom and bride. A frequent guest at the Römischen Kaiser, she admired the magnificent antiques of 'our dear Salomon' but thought his safe 'undoubtedly the most beautiful part of the house. It contains twelve lovely millions. It made me feel quite melancholy.'

The Frankfurt Five, with their feet in the leading financial centres of Europe, enjoyed in mid-century a virtual monopoly of state loans to the larger and lesser Powers. Their partnership transcended national boundaries, and it was in their interest as much as their inclination to remain objectively outside and above politics. They were, however, subject to the political restraints of their host states, and they were unavoidably drawn into the arena of national antagonism. At home the Rothschild-in-residence was obliged through his exposure to risk to defend the value of government bonds, and even expected to sustain the market through intervention at any time of slump brought on by agricultural depression or sudden loss of confidence in railway specula- tion. During their lifetime, the brothers' loyalty to the house was decisive and overrode any wider considerations; their father's exhortation was strictly observed: 'All the brothers shall stand together in everything; all shall be responsible for the actions of each other.' The unique power of their combined purse allowed them to restrain more wilful national adventures and to preserve the peacefully prosperous status quo in Europe.

For the first half of the century, Salomon had undoubtedly the most difficult task in holding the ring. His master's declared ideal for Europe was 'authority, order and peace'. This was interpreted in practice as unrepentant despotism at home and the repression of all constitutional aspirations abroad. The price of such a condition was men and money. It was Salomon who had to decide where to draw the line: when to indulge Metternich's authoritarian urges, when to restrain them with despairing hints (or thinly veiled threats) of the resulting harm to the credit of the State. Salomon importuned Metternich for some recognition of the family's services; Nathan Mayer and James were appointed honorary (unpaid) Austrian Consuls-General in London and Paris respectively; Salomon's son was later granted the same honour in Frankfurt. One benefit of this appointment was the privilege of the diplomatic bag. Perfectly aware that Metternich kept a strict eye on such correspondence, they used this for their own purposes while continuing to rely on their own more secure, and faster, service for their confidential dealings.

For all their vaunted intelligence service, the Rothschild prescience was fallible, though the whole of Europe was surprised by the suddenness of the explosions of 1848. Their Parisian client Louis-Philippe was the first to go, *le roi bourgeois* fleeing his capital as 'Mr Smith' to suitably suburban refuge in London. The value of mere paper tumbled, and Baron James had to be bailed out by his London nephew to meet his most pressing obligations. The following month it was Metternich's turn. The departing Chancellor had to send to Salomon for relief; he left Vienna in disguise with 1,000 of his friend's ducats in his pocket for his more urgent expenses and a letter of credit on the family. Salomon, holed up in his hotel, survived his patron by six months. 'If the devil fetches me,' Metternich had warned him, 'he will fetch you too!' Salomon summoned his secretary, who had fled the capital, to his rescue. That worthy hired a dairy cart complete with churns as a passport through the barricades. The books, cash and securities were packed and confided to the charge of the National Bank. The Baron, seventy-five years old and his mind at ease, skipped out of the city, never to return. He retired to his château at Suresnes, near St Cloud, only to find that ransacked and burnt by the French mob. His only son, Anselm, married to Lionel's sister Charlotte, took up the relay in Vienna four weeks after order had been restored.

The Rothschilds, because of their remarkable buoyancy even in the mill-race of revolution, were still collectively the cock of the walk. But they had lost a previous and most precious asset, the ultimate sanction to ensure the preservation of peace: the mere threat to turn off the tap of their treasury. War was a needless and often costly disruption of their main business. (An exception might be made in a special case; the English and French houses gave gladly for the sake of blacking the Tsar's eye in the Crimea.) Now they found that the sharp edge of their political cutting power had been blunted by competition; there were simply so many alternative sources of finance that they could be ignored with increasing impunity.

In 1863 the family had succeeded in restraining Napoleon III from intervening in support of the Poles in their struggle against Russian oppression. 'The peace of the world', wrote Disraeli, 'has on this occasion been preserved not by statesmen but by capitalists.' In the previous year when Gerson von Bleichröder, Bismarck's banker and a Rothschild associate, requested a loan from Baron James, he was turned down; the family was perfectly aware that Prussia harboured designs on Anselm's Austria. 'It is a principle of our House', James pointed out, 'not to advance any money for war and even if it is not in our power to prevent war, then our minds at least can be easy that we have not contributed to it.' Such mild moralizing, and even more direct remonstration, was no longer sufficient to curb the Prussian juggernaut. The Rothschilds had lost the ear of the men that mattered in Paris and Vienna; in Berlin they had never secured it. Indeed, Mayer and Wilhelm, who had taken over Frankfurt on the death of their father, the Neapolitan Carl, had so closely identified themselves with Prussia's ambitions that it led to the first fissure in the family solidarity. They forfeited the full and complete confidence of their relations and partners, a delicate predicament given the unique Rothschild marriage maze: Mayer and Wilhelm were respectively Lionel's brother-in-law and Anselm's son-in-law. Frustrated at his unaccustomed impotence in preventing Berlin and Vienna coming to blows, Baron James could only retort by petulantly refusing to honour a cheque for a trifling 5,000 francs issued by the Austrian Ambassador in Paris, the son of their old friend Metternich.

James, the last of the founder's sons, was spared, by two years, France's humiliation at Sedan. (The lives of father and son spanned an extraordinary century and a quarter. Mayer Amschel celebrated his twenty-fifth birthday in the year the first Napoleon was born.) James's nephew Anselm died six years later.

Anselm's wife, Charlotte, had died fifteen years before. It was the inevitable lot of those Rothschild women who made arranged marriages that they suffered displacement and resettlement; Charlotte had been as miserable in Frankfurt, which she made her centre, as her namesake, her brother Lionel's Neapolitan wife, had been in England (she prayed to receive her reward in heaven). Anselm was an unregenerate philistine; he acquired his treasure, mostly portable trinkets, by the gramme. Charlotte, blessed with some artistic sense, kept one of the rare salons in Frankfurt, which was frequented by Rossini, Mendelssohn, Liszt and Schumann while her grandmother, Mayer Amschel's old widow, continued living in the family house in the ghetto until she died four years short of her century in 1849. Charlotte's three sons developed into notable art collectors even by the voracious standards of the family, and her daughter Mathilde, who stayed on to marry a Frankfurt Rothschild, was an exceptionally proficient musician, a star pupil of Chopin as a girl, and afterwards a dedicated cigar smoker. Her second son, Ferdinand, had moved to England the year after her death; her eldest surviving son, yet another Nathaniel, an amiable and amenable bachelor tied to the Turf, had been passed over by his father, who had confided the Viennese bank to the aloof and austere Salomon Albert,* married to a French cousin, the daughter of James's son Alphonse. Both brothers who remained in Vienna were infected with the family building virus; Albert's gaudily gilded pile was dubbed the Albert Memorial by his equally immoderate English cousins; Nathaniel competed hotly with his brother Ferdinand to accumulate an incomparable collection of Louis XIV, XV and XVI furniture for his rival pile. They ran the gamut of giving in the family tradition, providing for the public weal a general hospital, an orphanage, institutes for the blind and the deaf-mute and a neurological clinic; Nathaniel planted and presented to the city of Vienna the Hohe Warte botanical gardens. They also enjoyed their grandfather's landed estates complete with philanthropic infrastructure; even their tenants' churches were maintained at their expense.

There was one conspicuous exception to the strict propriety of the claustrophobic Habsburg court, the heir apparent himself. A minor littérateur, Crown Prince Rudolf was also an accomplished libertine. The Prince of Wales had first met him in Vienna in 1869. Even though this had been a private visit, the social and sporting round had had to defer to etiquette, those courtesy calls on members of the Habsburg family which 'as there are 27 Archdukes now at Vienna', complained the wife of the British Ambassador, 'was hard work' to fit into one week. The Prince developed an avuncular affection for the young scapegrace; the improvident pair shared a similar affection for the begetters of wealth. When Rudolf first visited London in 1878, Ferdinand Rothschild threw a ball for him; when the Prince of Wales attended Rudolf's marriage to the Belgian Princess Stéphanie three years later, he put up at a hotel in the Austrian capital so that he could meet the Rothschilds without embarrassing his official hosts (the Rothschilds were not yet 'court-worthy').

In Nathaniel von Rothschild's most intimate circle was a socially ambitious young beauty, Baroness Marie Vetsera. In 1888 she became the mistress of the Crown Prince. The Prince of Wales later ascertained that Rudolf, hoping to marry her, had written to the Pope for permission to divorce his wife and that the disobliging Holy Father had forwarded the letter to the Emperor. After a bitter scene, the unsympathetic Franz Joseph, dedicated to joyless duty, ordered his son to cast off his paramour. Three months after the Prince of Wales and Rudolf had sought out bear in Romania and chamois in Styria in order to avoid the Kaiser, who was in

---

*Lord Rothschild later wrote to Alphonse, following a dispute over Ferdinand's will, that 'If the policy which he [Salbert, as he was known] pursues in Vienna is at all similar to his conduct towards his relatives of late the only thing I can say is, "I am astonished there is so little anti-semitic feeling in Vienna".'

Vienna on a State visit, Edward learnt that his friend had shot his mistress at his shooting lodge at Mayerling before turning his gun on himself. The news reached the capital by the Nordbahn railway's telegraph and, such as was its nature, was delivered personally to the chairman in Vienna. It fell to Albert von Rothschild to carry the tidings to the palace.

Just nine years later the destinies of Habsburg and Rothschild tragically recrossed. In September 1898 Rudolf's mother, the restless and melancholic Empress Elizabeth, staying at Geneva, spent the day at the lakeside villa of her friend Baroness Adolf von Rothschild, Albert's sister Julie. A creature of black moods and sudden impulses, she found unaccustomed peace in the enchanted gardens with tame miniature porcupines from Java and exotic birds, and in the massive conservatories arranged by country and climate. As she left her hotel next morning to catch a steamer, an Italian anarchist rushed at her and, unable to afford a stiletto, stabbed her through the heart with a homemade dagger.

Rudolf had died deeply in debt, yet nonetheless shortly before his death had managed to afford a present of 60,000 gulden for a house for a longer-serving love, Mizzi Kaspar, to whom he penned an affectionate note of farewell before setting off for Mayerling. He was only able to perfect this last service as a result of a loan of 100,000 gulden – a little more than £10,000 – which he had received at the beginning of the month from Baron Maurice de Hirsch. This was his reward for a small favour he had undertaken to perform for Hirsch the previous month: at a shoot outside Paris he had introduced the financier to his friend the Prince of Wales.

For a man of Hirsch's obsessive social ambitions an heir to a throne was a most desirable object. He had lost one but gained another, and the cost, however considerable, was acceptable. He lost little time in attaching himself to the Prince. His presence was, as it happened, most crucial; the Prince's financial embarrassments were more than usually insistent. Hirsch was not the only one to be aware of this want. The rumours attracted swarms of touts around the hotels the Prince frequented. The British Ambasssador in Paris, Lord Lytton, received an anonymous tip that Edward was negotiating for a £40,000 loan from a money-lender (and newspaper proprietor), Collard; the sum would be put up by a champagne merchant in exchange for royal endorsement of his product. The French police, to whom Lytton confidentially applied, reported that the affair had fallen through after lengthy negotiations six months before as the terms were too severe, and that the Rothschilds had instead furnished the francs. Lord Lytton was sceptical. He informed Lord Salisbury that 'if there be any truth in this information, it was probably Hirsch and not Rothschild, who advanced the money'. He was undoubtedly correct.

If such relief was at hand, there were certain preparations to be made. In the spring of the next year, during the Prince's regular southern odyssey, there was a sudden flurry of activity. The Prince arranged to confer with Hirsch on his return to Paris from Berlin, where he had called on Bismarck, dropped as Chancellor five days earlier by the Kaiser.

On 1 April 1890, Hirsch duly waited on the Prince at his hotel, the Bristol, around tea-time; on the following day the Prince lunched at Hirsch's sumptuous home in the Rue de l'Elysée before leaving for Cannes. Two weeks later, the Prince again saw Hirsch twice in Paris on his way home from the Riviera. Hirsch was launched and, following in the wake of his new debtor-patron, scurried across the Channel to celebrate the Season. No intimation of the extent of this debt emerged until after the death of the Prince's benefactor six years later. Within days, rumours of Edward's obligations found their way into print. The influential *Westminster Gazette* regretfully ('for the sake of His Royal Highness') published a denial with the 'utmost confidence' that the Prince had inherited £1 million from Hirsch. Five years later, no less an authority than Paul Cambon, French Ambassador in London, informed his Foreign Minister that Hirsch had advanced the Prince at least 15 million francs (£600,000 at the then rate of exchange, the equivalent in modern terms of more than £15 million) for which his sister the Empress Frederick had stood surety. (He would certainly have seen her on his visit to Berlin before negotiating with Hirsch.) The Kaiser, in London for his uncle's coronation, had tried to settle the matter, his mother having died four days before. Cambon was of the opinion that the English Rothschilds had taken over the guarantee. It is more likely that Hirsch, in a verbal or written instruction to his wife and executor, had waived the debt.

3

Türkenhirsch: A Bavarian in the Balkans

Moritz Freiherr von Hirsch auf Gereuth, to give him his proud and proper style, was the third generation of a better than well-to-do family of Bavarian court bankers. The post was a plum, privileged and prestigious, in which Jews had maintained a monopoly long after the Christian interdict of usury was abandoned. The Hofbankier collected commissions from his patron and, as army contractor and tax collector, the odium of the public.

By the end of the nineteenth century, Bavaria had supplied many of the most noted Jewish financiers on Wall Street, who had emigrated between the eruptions of 1830 and 1848, the period of Hirsch's adolescence. Hirsch, with the prospect of inheritance, determined to stay and try his fortune in Europe.

The founder of the family's prosperity was the Baron's grandfather Jacob, born in 1765. He first entered the public record in 1803 when he acquired at public auction a property in Würzburg, midway between Frankfurt and Nuremberg, the Ebracher Hof, for 8,400 florins – some £2,000 – on behalf of his father Kurfürstliche Schutzjude* Moses Hirsch. It was a bold stroke at that time, even though Bavaria was then in alliance with revolutionary France, for a Jew to bid for property, but as at two previous auctions the bidding had reached only a little more than half Jacob's offer, the authorities seemingly waived any objection.

Jacob was the salaried agent of Prince Löwenstein-Wertheim and court banker to the Grand Duke of Württemberg and is credited with having raised and maintained at his own expense a company of infantry during the Napoleonic wars, mostly fighting the Austrians on the side of the French until, with fine timing, they joined the Allies in 1813. His services

---

*'Jew protected by the ruler'.

for such 'loyalty and attachment' won him two notable privileges: the right to freedom of movement and domicile within the kingdom of Bavaria, and the right to own land. Three months after Napoleon's final fall, Jacob Hirsch bought the manor of Gereuth with which went the feudal right to hold courts of justice on the domain. As these could be administered only by members of the nobility, 'Court Banker and Wholesaler' Jacob Hirsch declared his readiness to assume his responsibilities as landowner and to join its ranks. As proof of his fitness, he produced a list of his assets valued at a respectable £70,000 – the modern equivalent of a multi-millionaire. It was agreed that, quoting Austrian precedents, his trade was not incompatible with the possession of a title and, his request granted, he was freed from all Jewish disabilities. The reward, this time for his 'selfless devotion, zeal and prudence', was promotion to a hereditary knighthood. He was granted the punning arms of an extinct Bavarian title, his crest a *Hirsch*, or stag.

Soon after his elevation, Jacob von Hirsch moved to Munich, leaving his elder son, Joel Jacob, to carry on the business at Würzburg, and taking with him his younger son, Joseph. There then began another battle to have their privileges formally recognized by the bureaucracy, which bred an addiction to litigation his grandson would inherit; they took a claim for exemption from *Schutzgeld*, protection money of some pound or two a year, up to the Court of Appeal – and lost. Jacob procured a local manor and estate for himself at Planegg near Munich. When he died on Christmas Eve 1841, he left no fewer than sixteen estates as well as the town houses in Munich and Würzburg.

Lacking the family solidarity of the Rothschilds, each branch of the house went its own way on the founder's death. The Würzburger Joel Jacob was the more energetic and enterprising. He mechanized his estates, added a refinery to his sugar-beet plantation at Rottersdorf which his father had bought for a song from the Franciscans when the State was threatening to confiscate their lands, and broke the Dutch monopoly on the Bavarian timber trade. In 1835 he set up, with the neighbouring Rothschilds as majority shareholders, one of the first mortgage banks.

In Munich Joseph had been appointed court banker by Ludwig I and was confirmed in that post by his eccentric successor. Even after the creation of the Bavarian State Bank, the court bankers – Joseph's only rival was the converted Jew Eichthal, born Seligmann – preserved their position by charging only their real expenses for pedestrian transactions, transfer and the like, reserving their commissions for more serious business; the new bank, objecting, was told it would only be considered if it undercut such charges. In 1869, having endowed the State with a generous portion of philanthropy and public works, he applied for and was granted a barony. Then, preferring the pleasures of a gentleman farmer at Planegg, he passed the charge of the bank over to his son Emil. It is probable, too, that Joseph lacked his father's and brother's business sense; it was believed that old Jacob, in an attempt to preserve his fortune, had instructed the family stockbrokers always to reverse his younger son's orders. Joseph died in 1885 at the age of eighty, leaving nine children, compared to his more industrious brother Joel Jacob's seventeen.

Maurice de Hirsch, as he was later and better known, was born in Munich on 9 December 1831, Joseph's third child and second son (his elder brother died aged fifteen). His mother was a member of the well-connected Frankfurt banking family of Wertheimer, and saw to it that her son received a fittingly orthodox education – religious instruction and little else. (Chaim Weizmann, first President of Israel, recalled that an 'enlightened' teacher smuggled into his school a Hebrew textbook on natural science and chemistry, a 'proceeding not without risk, for discovery would have entailed immediate dismissal'.) This served only to cultivate an aversion to formal religion. After his bar mitzvah, at the age of thirteen, Maurice was sent to Brussels for a more catholic education. This in turn served to breed in him a lifelong distrust of academic attainment. Four years later, the novice cynic returned to Munich, where legend describes him as cutting his teeth on speculation in commodities from copper to cattle. Whether his personality was too abrasive for his placid parent, he was soon packed back to Brussels and apprenticed to the banking house of Bischoffsheim & Goldschmidt. There, in 1855, Hirsch married Clara, the daughter of Senator (and senior partner) Jonathan Bischoffsheim and a Goldschmidt mother.

The Bischoffsheims and Goldschmidts, distantly related to Hirsch's mother, were another capable clan which from the middle up until the last quarter of the nineteenth century almost equalled the Rothschilds in the variety and extent of their operations, though lagging well behind them in circumspection. They were heavily involved in American railways, on which they burned their fingers in the great crash of 1857; they were partial to South American loans, of which too many defaulted. But out of their ashes rose some of the great Belgian and French banks.

The Senator's elder brother Louis Raphael, a banker of Antwerp, began the partnership by marrying a Goldschmidt, daughter of a Frankfurt banker. In 1848, he transferred his operations to Paris at a time when many established bankers were leaving or at least locking up; a few years earlier his son Henry had opened a London office. Jonathan Bischoffsheim, Hirsch's future father-in-law, who also married a

Goldschmidt, set up in Brussels shortly after the Belgians had rid themselves of the House of Orange, becoming one of the architects of the sudden and dramatic industrialization of that country; he acted as financial adviser to the new King Leopold (a Saxe-Coburg), he helped out the Treasury, handled the funds of the Liberal Party and became a steel and railway magnate in his own right. His other daughter, Regina, married another Goldschmidt, and their son Max married Minna Caroline, the daughter of Wilhelm Rothschild of Frankfurt. Although neither Wilhelm Carl nor his brother had sons, there was no suggestion that Max, a mere son-in-law, should inherit the senior Rothschild house; liquidation was preferred to a break with family tradition. Max instead borrowed their name, operating his own bank as Goldschmidt-Rothschild. For most of its life, this had but one major account – in the name of Maurice de Hirsch.

After his marriage, considering perhaps that his talents were not sufficiently honoured by the immediate offer of a partnership at Bischoffsheim & Goldschmidt, Hirsch returned with his bride to Munich, where their only child, Lucien, was born in 1856. Two years later they moved back to Brussels and Hirsch took Belgian nationality. Hirsch was never made a partner. Despite being now related by birth and marriage to both branches of the bank, he seems to have operated very much on the periphery. This may simply have been the choice of a self-reliant and unconventional spirit, though it has been suggested that it was the result of the partners' fears of his excessive daring and enterprise. It is true that some of his early speculations were thought to have resulted in heavy losses, even jeopardizing his wife's dowry. (This was estimated at an implausible 20 million francs, or £800,000, many times the standard Rothschild hand-outs – the recipients of which complained that they were mostly made up of sickly South American railway shares.) But the partners themselves were not averse to an incautious flutter. Ludwig Bamberger, whose younger brother Heinrich married Hirsch's sister Amalia, recounted that both his Bischoffsheim uncles in Paris and Brussels, while conservative with credit, nevertheless fell an easy prey to the investment lures of unscrupulous operators. When Bamberger remonstrated, Bischoffsheim retorted, 'Do you think Rothschild will come to me with business propositions?'

Hirsch is popularly supposed to have launched himself on the strength of an inheritance of a considerable fortune from his grandfather and father. This is unrealistic. His grandfather, who had died many years before Hirsch was married, had divided his estate between two sons and had left twenty-six grandchildren; and Hirsch's father lived until well after Hirsch had made his own fortune. It is reasonable to suppose that he took a settlement in return for renouncing his claim to any share in the family bank. The only certainty is that he prospered, and speedily. Within four years of returning to Brussels he had set up his own bank in partnership with his brother-in-law, Ferdinand Bischoffsheim, who, more gifted as a bon viveur than a banker, faded gracefully from the picture, leaving just his valuable name as a comfort to creditors. A Dutch diplomat's wife wrote that she remembered Hirsch already in that same year 'as a very rich man and a real gentleman'. Unless she was blinded by his undoubted gallantry, this is intimation of an astonishing ascent.

It was at this stage in his career that the ambitious and energetic Hirsch fell in with a strange bed-fellow, a Belgian adventurer by the name of André Langrand-Dumonceau. A modest bank clerk with a vision of marrying piety with profit, Langrand-Dumonceau's original idea was to exploit the sentiment and savings of ardent Catholics to 'christianize' capital. A man of wilful optimism, his empire mushroomed into a jumble of real estate, mortgage and insurance companies which survived twelve years. When the paper-chain snapped, the founder – created a Papal count by Pius IX – fled to Brazil and, after a delay over the setting up of an inquiry which caused a political scandal, was sentenced in his absence to fifteen years' penal servitude for fraudulent practices. (He died thirty years later in Rome.) His former collaborators escaped all indictment. Despite his pious design, there was hardly a name among the *haute banque juive* which was not tempted to collude with one or other of Langrand-Dumonceau's ventures. Hirsch had his doubts. 'He is sceptical of you,' wrote one of the Belgian's collaborators, 'he believes you won't stop living with illusions. He thinks you have a lively imagination, and an optimism that does not know obstacles.' Hirsch, confident he could harness and bridle such an errant disposition, took his chance. Langrand-Dumonceau himself had been urged by his mentor, Edouard Mercier, a former Belgian Minister of Finance, to collaborate with Hirsch: 'It is good to have a Croesus behind you.' There is no evidence to indicate how Hirsch, then in his late twenties, had achieved this status on his own account: his credit was undoubtedly inflated by the Bischoffsheim background.

The first joint venture of Hirsch and Langrand-Dumonceau was the foundation of a Viennese insurance company, Der Anker, in 1858. The Baron, with his family associates, acquired one-third of the shares and took his seat on the board. The next summer the pair, with Hirsch's father-in-law, Jonathan Bischoffsheim, and their kinsman Heinrich Bamberger, combined to form a holding company, the Association Générale d'Assurances. (Hirsch, joint managing director in charge of finance and internal administration, kept the company's books at his home.) Perhaps chafing at such restraint, Langrand-Dumonceau five years later set up the Banque de Crédit Foncier et Industriel with himself as sole manager, and absorbed the Association Générale with profit to the original shareholders. Having scoured the European capitals for savings, he next turned his attention to London.

Pointing to the 'brilliant results' of its progenitors, which could be verified by 'authentic documents', the International Land Credit Company was incorporated in 1864 under the umbrella of recently extended limited liability; the directors included Lord Robert Cecil, MP (later third Marquess of Salisbury and Prime Minister), and former Belgian ministers of Foreign Affairs, the Interior, Finance and Justice. This impressive array, combined with the aura of the London market, ensured that of the first issue of shares totalling £6 million, £5 million had already been taken up abroad. But even this injection of capital was not sufficient to save the parent Crédit Foncier, which by the end of the 1860s had lost its entire capital through paying exaggerated prices for estates in Hungary and Spain destined to be sold off in lots of smallholdings. Hirsch, consulted by a now chastened Langrand-Dumonceau, advocated radical steps to avert catastrophe but was understandably wary of accepting an offer to preside over the decline of the empire. (The demise of the International Land Credit Company caused great excitement in London, which had not fully recovered its nerve after the spectacular collapse of the Quaker bill-brokers Overend, Gurney & Co. in 1866. Fortunately for the prospects of the future Prime Minister, Sir Henry Drummond Wolff, appointed by Parliament to oversee the interests of the British shareholders, could not discover any evidence of unlawful conduct; such schemes, he reflected sorrowfully – his own promotions did not all prosper – often failed in inexperienced hands.)

Langrand-Dumonceau had not completely parted company with Hirsch when he set up his Crédit Foncier. The Baron continued to undertake his banking operations and share-dealings, some underhand, some above board. When a Papal loan was floated in 1864, the Belgian was obliged to use the Baron's bank to place it in Paris and Brussels as the faithful were disobligingly loath to dig into their pockets even in such an irreproachable cause. And the previous year, the two had come together to constitute the Société Générale de Commerce of Amsterdam. This had joined in the creation of the International Land Credit Company and additionally acquired concessions to operate railways in Holland, Belgium and the Balkans.

By 1860 the rail networks of Britain, France and Germany were virtually complete while large-scale construction was only just getting under way in Russia and Austria-Hungary; the Balkans, where Russian and Austrian ambitions clashed, were largely untouched by progress. Hirsch, whose father had founded the East Bavarian Railways with the Frankfurt Rothschilds, already managed the line from Moscow to Riazan, some 100 miles south-east. By 1868 he had acquired, with Bischoffsheim backing, the concession for the East Hungarian Railway; associated with him was the Anglo-Austrian Bank, set up five years before by a British consortium led by Glyn Mills. Within twelve months, the cracks in Langrand-Dumonceau's edifice could no longer be papered over with fresh prospectuses, and out of the ruins Hirsch, under the nose of the greatest contractors and financiers, mysteriously produced a concession which would make him the pre-eminent railroad baron of the age. He most probably retrieved this asset from the wasted remains of Langrand-Dumonceau's portfolio through the Anglo-Austrian Bank, a major creditor. By this coup he engaged to link Vienna in the European heartland to Constantinople, the Ottoman Empire's capital on the Bosphorus, a distance of over 1,000 miles for a crow and the longest single track yet laid anywhere in the world. The history of their great endeavour, which would occupy him for the best part of twenty years and earn him a corresponding fortune, was, according to a less than admiring German nationalist, one of 'cunning, force, robbery and deceit'. But then, as a defendant pleaded some years later in a case involving the British-built Lemberg (later Lvov) to Czernowitz railway in law-abiding Galicia, 'Railways are not built by morality sermons.' (The jury accepted this: he was acquitted.)

The Orient Railway – 'the pivot', in the opinion of *The Times*, 'upon which the politics of Eastern Europe turned for fifteen years' – was both a prodigious feat and a courageous undertaking. Once the track left the security of Austria-Hungary, it entered the Balkans, Turkey-in-Europe, a wild and unwelcoming terra mostly incognita. What little was known was not reassuring. It was the scene of intermittent nationalist insurrection and savage repression. The disparate Christian races, when not cutting Muslims' throats, cut each other's with an equal will; banditry and extortion were an accepted way of life, local administration was corrupt or apathetic. The Balkans were, too, the stage for Great Power struggles, often simmering, occasionally boiling over: the only common aim was to confine hostilities to that unhappy region. Russia aggressively exploited every opportunity – and when such was missing, created her own – to exacerbate racial and religious rivalries in order to advance her own ambition: control, or even ownership, of Constantinople with a warm-water outlet for her ships from the Black Sea into the Mediterranean. Austria, encouraged by Bismarck to find compensation for her losses in Italy and her humiliation in a Greater Germany, had other conflicting acquisitive aspirations. Britain was determined to keep the 'Sick Man' on his feet to avert any threat to communications with India. Turkey itself, awarded a side-seat at the Concert of Europe at the close of the Crimean War, had half-heartedly consented to introduce reforms; their implementation was undermined by profligate and despotic sultans, masters of procrastination and dissimulation. No railway contractor, hoping to cut his way through these obstacles, could escape embroilment.

The dream of a land route to the East preceded – and survived – the opening of the shortened sea route through the Suez Canal. At the close of the war in the Crimea, Lord Palmerston had advocated a rail link with India through Constantinople by way of the Persian Gulf, thus anticipating by half a century the Baghdad Railway. The archaeologist Henry Layard, a man of many talents, had, while attached to the British Embassy at Constantinople, revived this prospect. Foreign promoters hurried to offer their services in bridging the Balkans, but the Turks, intent on dividing in order better to rule their turbulent territory, were wary. The Péreire brothers' Crédit Mobilier sniffed around for a chance, founding the Imperial Ottoman Bank in 1861 as a declaration of their interest. A few years later, the rival Austrian railways, the Rothschilds' Südbahn (which they had added to their Nordbahn) and the Péreires' State Railway, extended their different lines up to the edge of the Ottoman domains and proposed to carry them on, but their time limit expired before they could agree on a common route. The few modest experiments in rail transport in Turkish territory were not auspicious. Langrand-Dumonceau, financed by the Bischoffsheims and Hirsch, had already built a line from Ruse in Bulgaria to the Black Sea at Varna to catch the grain trade (it had caught cold instead). The most successful line in Turkey proper, British built and owned, a mere fifty-mile link from Smyrna inland to Aidin begun in 1858, took ten years to complete, and a further twenty before dividends began to be paid out of earnings.

In 1867 the Sultan Abdul Aziz visited Vienna with his Grand Vizier, Fuad Pasha. The Austrians had a paramount political and commercial interest in sponsoring a rail link to the East to promote their own trade and balk the Russians. It was the former Saxon diplomat, now Austrian Foreign Minister and Chancellor, the liberal Count von Beust, who persuaded the Sultan to take the plunge. On Beust's recommendation, so it is said – the few records available are unclear or contradictory – a concession was granted on 31 May 1868 to an associate company of the Langrand-Dumonceau empire. The Belgian promoter's front man in Vienna was Count Zichy, a director of the associated Der Anker. (Five months before the concession was granted, his plans for the railway were leaked to the British Embassy, which was closely watching developments in the Balkans.) Zichy later complained that Hirsch never recompensed him for his preparatory work.

Langrand may have regarded his concession as a tradeable asset. He had anyway more pressing worries and failed to attract the finance to embark on his scheme or any bold spirit take it off his hands, although he boasted in his sanguine fashion to Hirsch of having had 'wonderful' offers. He defaulted and the concession was cancelled on 12 April 1869. Just five days later a new agreement was reached by Daoud Pasha, the Minister of Public Works, with Baron Hirsch in Vienna (and confirmed by imperial firman on 7 October of the same year). Hirsch was said to have enjoyed the support of the Austrian government – he was reputed 'to hold Count Beust in his hand' – and had reassuringly undertaken to share the operation of the railway with the Rothschilds' Südbahn or the Crédit Mobilier's State Railway. Hirsch had already reputedly won Péreire's assent to this arrangement in Paris; this is curious, unless the latter was hoping to make a comeback, as he had recently been driven from the management of Crédit Mobilier as a condition of aid for survival by the Banque de France. In any event, this was vetoed by the railway's president in Vienna, Baron Wodianer. (The grandson of an old-clothes merchant, the Baron, having changed his faith, shunned all intercourse with Jews despite the fact that his appearance and accent betrayed his origins.) 'I have a house in the heart of Vienna,' he is said to have ponderously rebuked Hirsch. 'You want to build one in a distant suburb and suggest that we should be equal partners in that joint property!'

Although Serbia, an autonomous principality under the Turkish flag, had been pressing hard in Vienna to have the railway cross its territory, both Turkey and Austria preferred, for political reasons, to route it through more mountainous Bosnia. The single-track line was planned to run from Constantinople to Adrianople (present-day Edirne) to Philippopolis (Plovdiv) in Eastern Rumelia (appropriated by Bulgaria before the railway was complete) and on to Sofia; it would then enter Serbia before continuing to Sarajevo in Bosnia, finally to join up with the Südbahn in Austria. This was the project; the path was not followed so simply. Four spurs were also anticipated: one from Adrianople to the Aegean at Dede-Agach (Alexandroupolis); another to the Black Sea; a third north through Serbia to pass Belgrade and connect with the

Austrian State Railway; and a last, longer link south through Skopje to Salonica. Construction of a total of over 2,000 kilometres of track was confidently anticipated to take from five to seven years. The concession, with commendable confidence in the immutability of empires, was granted for one year short of a century.

The concessionaire, responsible for construction and operation, was to receive from the Turkish government, the Porte, an annual subsidy of 14,000 francs (£560) for each complete kilometre throughout the duration of the concession; and an annual rental of 8,000 francs (£320) per kilometre from the operating company, a total representing 10 per cent of the estimated cost of construction per kilometre. The Porte would, of course, share in the eventual profits.

Having been rebuffed by the Austrian State Railway, Hirsch courted the Südbahn with the object of leasing it the operation of his line. This was agreed, and then repudiated by the Südbahn under pressure from Baron Anselm von Rothschild in Vienna; whether this was from prudence – the three British railway companies in Turkey had just published a warning that the Porte was years in arrears with its subsidies – or a personal prejudice against a perceived parvenu, is not known. Hirsch, who had not wished to devote his life to the running of a railway, was now nonetheless obliged to set up his own operating company. He contrived this in January 1870, with its headquarters in Paris. In revenge Hirsch recruited one of the founders of the Südbahn, the Frenchman Paulin Talabot, as chairman; among his fellow directors were Edward Blount, who became chairman of the Société Générale of Paris that same year, and Count Kinsky, a co-founder of the Anglo-Austrian Bank. Hirsch still needed a track. A construction company, to which he assigned his concession, was next formed. Each company, operation and construction, was capitalized at £2 million, of which one quarter was paid up. Hirsch took the chair and continued his poaching of Rothschild luminaries, among them the Südbahn's chief engineer as director-general, and its renowned architect, Wilhelm von Pressel.

The principal concern of the concessionaire before he laid his first rail was how to ensure the prompt payment of the construction subsidy by the Turkish government. The country's financial health was fast deteriorating. As expenditure rose, remaining revenues were mortgaged as security for new loans to cover the deficits. London, Paris and Brussels were awash with Turkish bonds, traded at heavy discounts. Hirsch devised a novel form of finance, lottery bonds at a low rate of interest – 3 per cent, two points below the usual Ottoman rate – redeemable at par over ninety-nine years. There was to be a bi-monthly draw, three of the winning tickets earning prizes as high as 600,000 francs (£24,000). This speculative paper was to become famous (and suddenly infamous) as 'Türkenlose'.

The Baron – 'Türkenhirsch' as he came to be known – put together an impressive underwriting syndicate led by the Société Générale. The Turkish government issued Hirsch with 1,980,000 bonds of a nominal value of 400 francs, which were credited to him at 128.50 francs, a little over 32 per cent of par. The Austrian Finance Minister at first refused to allow these to be introduced on the Vienna Bourse, but was overruled by Chancellor Beust. (It was later alleged that he had received 800,000 francs for this favour. He was, indeed, suddenly and surprisingly dismissed by Franz Joseph in 1871; he himself protested that he was ignorant of the true reason for this.)

In March 1870, Hirsch sold to his syndicate the first series of 750,000 bonds at 155 francs, which were offered to the public at 180 francs. The timing was propitious. Europe was enjoying one of its great boom periods based upon a great surge of international investment. Hirsch tapped it. The issue, backed by spectacular publicity and a glowing prospectus, was a tremendous success throughout Europe, notwithstanding that subscriptions were not accepted in London and Paris. A not insignificant reason for their popularity was the impression encouraged by the promoters that the bonds were debentures. They were not: there was no lien on the line; there was no security other than the Porte's promise to pay to the construction company an annual subvention of 28 million francs – just over £1 million – for ninety-nine years.

In September 1872 the remaining 1,230,000 bonds were offered through the same syndicate. The price, reflecting market conditions, was set lower: 150 francs to the syndicate, 170 to the public. It was too late. The Franco-Prussian War had come and gone like summer lightning, leaving the Continental money markets stretched with the loser's war indemnity. Three South American states had defaulted; in the following year they would be joined by Spain, while Bolivia, Guatamala and Uruguay suspended payments on their debts. The promotion mania which had swept Europe crumpled, panic rattled Vienna and the German markets – the 'Krach' of '73. The bank rate in London hit an unprecedented 9 per cent. Hirsch's lottery bonds were an inevitable casualty. By the summer of 1873, more than half of the Türkenlose was still sticking to the underwriters' hands. The price in Paris was down to 130 francs; in Vienna, from a peak of 183, they tumbled to 115.

Although some of the underwriters had suffered, the one person unaffected by the vicissitudes of the market was Baron Hirsch himself. As concessionaire he had £14 million of working capital in his pocket for construction; the Baron as banker had netted a profit on the Türkenlose of almost £2 million. An intriguing aspect of these bonds to emerge later was that a suspiciously high proportion of the larger lottery prizes was surprisingly never collected.

The Baron's life was, however, not quite free of cares. Construction had begun with little delay from the eastern seaboard: from Adrianople spurs ran to Constantinople and down to the Aegean at Dede-Agach, and from Skopje down to Salonica. By the time the second bond issue was offered, 387 kilometres were already in operation, 100 approaching readiness and a further 660 under construction. He was well up to schedule. But a long tunnel lay ahead which would derail him. In September 1871 the reform-minded Grand Vizier Ali Pasha had died. The Sultan, freed of all restraint, now indulged his natural propensity for despotism and unbridled extravagance. One of his mother's favourites was the Russian Ambassador, Count Nikolai Ignatiev, 'Turkey's evil genius' ('C'est mon métier', he pleaded in justification). He was now free to pursue his country's aim of weakening Turkey and loosening her ties with the West. Ignatiev planned to abort Hirsch's concession and open up a way to the East through Romania to Russia. He persuaded Abdul Aziz to appoint as Ali's successor Mahmud Nedim Pasha, subsequently dubbed Mahmudoff for his sympathies. Mahmud obligingly made an attempt to repudiate Hirsch's contract. This failed, but the concession was never-theless revised. The construction company was demoted to mere contractor to the Ottoman government, and its responsibility was limited to little more line than was already in operation or under construction, in all 1,280 kilometres. The routes through Serbia and Bosnia were to be abandoned, and from Adrianople a new line was to be driven north, aiming to link with Romania's rail system. The concessionaire's agree-ment with the operating company was taken over by the Turks. Acting as Hirsch's mediator with the Porte was Ralph Anstruther Earle, borrowed from the board of his East Hungarian Railway, a former diplomat and Member of Parliament. As a young attaché he had passed confidential information to Disraeli, then Leader of the Opposition, and when Disraeli became Chancellor of the Exchequer he appointed Earle his private secretary. It was whispered that Earle profited in Throgmorton Street from what he picked up in Downing Street. Certainly, when he was replaced, he was forbidden access to the office by his successor. Earle managed at least a minor compensation for Hirsch, a ninety-nine-year timber concession over 900 square kilometres of forest in the Rhodope mountains at Bellova, where the line now ended. Even lumbering presented special problems in the Balkans; the overseer, later carried off by Bulgar bandits, had to be rescued with a £6,000 ransom.

Hirsch was the victim of this political machination but, it was suggested, was not too unhappy to accept *force majeure*; it relieved him of the most costly and difficult section of the line through the rugged ranges of Bosnia. But his only alternative would have been to throw in his hand, and in that case he would have been pursued by the Porte for restitution of the unused portion of the construction costs. For there was one curious aspect to the settlement: he retained the balance of the Türkenlose. He was now quit of over 1,000 kilometres of construction, for which he held some £5 million. *The Times*, which was sympathetic to Hirsch and defended him against the grosser libels of his critics, presumed that he shared this kitty with the Porte; the Sultan's share was believed to have been £350,000, Mahmud's £400,000; Ignatiev was also credited with a reward. But in order to disguise the political nature of the retrenchment, the Turks and Russians put it about that Hirsch, having already made his profit out of half his original concession, had paid a heavy premium to escape further obligations. Some years later a German newspaper published letters from Hirsch which, if genuine, established that he had also provided Daoud, the original Minister of Public Works, with the customary douceur, either to support his application for the concession or to overlook a certain cutting of corners in the course of construction. Certainly Daoud, from being a poor man, became suddenly rich; he died in safe exile abroad.

The high moral tone of Hirsch's critics was humbug. There was no contemporary illusion about the ethics of the marketplace; though there was tacit agreement on what were unacceptable practices, 'secret commissions' did not yet attract the attention of the law even in Britain. A revealing instance of the pragmatism on the part of no less an institution than the Treasury was evident twenty years later. Sir Edward Hamilton, then Assistant Permanent Secretary, and a regular guest of the Rothschilds, was engaged in converting the Turkish Loan of 1855, issued by the Rothschilds under a British government guarantee. The Turks had to be brought to agree to the terms. 'I have got the Chancellor of the Exchequer to admit', Hamilton confided to his diary, 'that nothing can be done without a handsome commission or in other words Backshish [*sic*] for use in ministerial circles at the Porte.' This was to be provided 'without having direct attention called to it by financing the new loan ourselves' and by arranging for the Savings Bank to take the guaranteed stock at a premium of 1½ per cent which would be diverted to the Turks. The Chancellor, Sir Michael Hicks Beach, had second thoughts. The

Turkish Ambassador, as a result, was 'very much exercised and put out' and made a 'piteous appeal' to the Prime Minister, Lord Salisbury. 'He evidently fears recall,' wrote Hamilton, 'not to say being put out of the way.' The Chancellor finally relented and the loan went through on the wish expressed that the 'Porte behaves well during the next six months'. In such conditions the difference between a commission (payment for a favour received) and a bribe (payment in expectation of a favour, honours included) was too fine to be regularly observed by politicians, financiers or businessmen dealing in actualities.

Mahmud himself fell out of favour during the next year. He was succeeded by Midhat Pasha, the only surviving sincerely progressive minister. He at once traced this peculation on the part of his predecessor. Mahmud, confident he was in good company, confessed to his offence before a court of inquiry. Midhat insisted on restitution. This was going too far. The Sultan, concerned where this zeal might end, dismissed him, and recalled Mahmud.

The depression of 1873 had perforce ended the Ottoman habit of borrowing to cover the interest payments and the deficit. In 1875 Ignatiev, his Embassy's banker having disembarrassed himself of Turkish bonds in the previous week, persuaded Mahmud to declare a moratorium on the Porte's £200 million of debt. The Western Powers promptly declared Turkey bankrupt and appointed an international commission to act for foreign bond-holders. There was no such protection for bearers of Türkenlose; they made an attempt to hold Hirsch personally responsible before a Viennese court, but failed. The Grand Vizier officially opened the main Constantinople–Bellova line in July 1873 – Hirsch was represented by his brother James, whom the Sultan decorated – and by December of the next year Türkenhirsch had completed his commitments under the revised concession. The Turks, however, had not commissioned any further construction themselves, so that Hirsch was left with two long tracks with spurs, operating in isolation and ending in the air. Starved of funds with which to pay the subsidies, let alone new building costs, the Turks attempted a diversion by claiming the track was defective. A technical committee, packed by the Porte's placemen, argued that an additional 30 per cent of the original construction cost would have to be spent to put it into working order. A rival panel of European engineers appointed by the railway refuted this, and its decision was evidently upheld by impartial experts delegated by the British government to which the frustrated Turks had hopefully turned.

Meanwhile Turkey, cut off from all further credit, turned for relief to taxation, still levied in kind by rapacious tax-farmers. The resentful Serbs at once revolted. The Great Powers, concerned to localize the trouble, bestirred themselves. The three Kaisers' club – Germany, Austria-Hungary and Russia – proposed reforms. This unwelcome intrusion sparked Turkish nationalist reaction. Midhat Pasha was recalled. He responded in May 1876 by forcing the abdication of Abdul Aziz, who committed suicide with a pair of scissors within the week; he was replaced by his nephew Murad, who was declared irredeemably insane within three months and was succeeded by his brother Abdul Hamid, who would earn himself the title Abdul the Damned.

His throne was scarcely warm when Serbia declared war on Turkey. Her army, though largely officered by Russians with a force of volunteers in support, was still no match for the underrated Turks. Bulgarian revolutionary guerrillas, agitated by Russia to harass the enemy lines of communication, took the field; in reprisal the Turks unleashed their armed irregulars, the rightly feared Bashi Bazouks. The inevitable excesses, trumpeted to such electoral advantage by Gladstone – his *The Bulgarian Atrocities and the Question of the East* sold 40,000 copies in a few days – had the effect of alienating British sympathy for the Turk as an underdog. Disraeli, hoping simultaneously to avert the disintegration of the Ottoman Empire and to satisfy the national aspirations of its subject races, convened a conference in Constantinople. Midhat Pasha, misjudging the strength of British backing, refused to accept the Powers' reforms, and the new Sultan, an adroit schemer, trumped their proposals by producing a new constitution drawn up by Midhat. The conference, its teeth drawn, dragged on aimlessly until it disbanded – whereupon, two weeks later, Abdul Hamid abruptly dismissed and banished Midhat.* Russia, having exhausted its stores of cats' paws, declared war on Turkey herself. Turkish arms, valiantly and, at times, even effectively wielded, were overborne. With both armies at their last gasp, the Turks held the invader at Adrianople. Britain, with public opinion warming to the brave and beaten Turk, awoke to this looming threat to the straits and paraded the fleet. An armistice was at once arranged, and in March 1878 Russia imposed its terms on Turkey at San Stefano. The architect was Count Ignatiev, who, having achieved his object, overreached himself. Russia was required to renegotiate terms with the other Powers at the Congress of Berlin that summer.

While Gladstone was moralizing on the hustings of the intemperance

---

*Midhat Pasha was lured back to Turkey by the promise of a free pardon, arrested and charged with the murder of Sultan Abdul Aziz, condemned, reprieved at the insistence of the British government, and exiled to Arabia, where he was subsequently strangled. His head was sent back to Abdul Hamid in a box labelled 'Japanese ivories'.

of the Bashi Bazouks, Baron Hirsch mobilized his reservoirs of energy to remedy as far as lay in his powers and purse the sufferings of the victims, Jew and Gentile, civilian and soldier. He recruited as his man in the field a local bank manager and chairman of the Alliance Israélite Universelle's Constantinople committee, the Chevalier Emmanuel Felix Veneziani. Aided by his two brothers, he roamed the afflicted areas armed with just a blank cheque; he opened a 200-bed field dressing station in Sofia, a 400-bed hospital in Adrianople and provided food, clothing and bedding for the relief of all refugees. While the war was still raging, Hirsch, a practical and pragmatic philanthropist, even made a gift of £40,000 to the Tsarina for war charities. The fighting over, Hirsch and his team looked after the rehabilitation of the Jewish population which had fled before the Russian advance. His efforts earned him the public appreciation of the people of Bulgaria and the Sultan's personal salaams, while in Constantinople the Jewish hierarchy decreed that all male children born that year be named after him.

These distractions had understandably done nothing to encourage Turkey to complete the rail network in the Balkans. And now the problem was further complicated by the Berlin accords which recognized the formal independence of Serbia, Montenegro and Romania; Bulgaria was redivided into two parts, Bulgaria proper, a dependent principality under Russian sway, and Eastern Rumelia, an autonomous Turkish province under a Christian governor; Bosnia and Herzegovina were handed over to Austrian administration under the Turkish flag. But the greater part of the failure to continue the track had been due to the Turks' endemic inertia. A Belgian traveller a few years later came upon vestiges of the railway which had been started ten years before to link Sofia with the Bellova–Constantinople line: 'in the ravines were the piles of half-finished bridges, or stones lying on the ground, also embankments and cuttings furrowed by the rains, even some rails buried under the weeds and shrubs. It is a lamentable history which shows plainly the impotence of Turkish rule and the causes which have hindered reform.'

The revoking of Hirsch's concession had adversely affected Austria's interest. It was still cut off from the Balkan heartland, which could now be served more conveniently from the coast on Hirsch's shortened lines. Almost half of the Turkish trade was in British hands, with the advantage of cheap sea freights. Hirsch was blamed for these and other ills by an increasingly vociferous German nationalist lobby, his methods maligned and his motives misrepresented. He was accused of having commenced construction at the cheapest end, that is, from the coast inland, and at having connived with the Turks over the truncation of the network. It was even claimed in retrospect that he had protected the British merchants' monopoly as a favour for his 'intimacy' with the Prince of Wales (they had not yet met). His detractors' real grievance was that the bulk of the Türkenlose, on which the interest payments had been frozen, was held in Vienna and Berlin. In fact the British Ambassador in Constantinople had strongly seconded his Austrian colleague's pressure on the Porte to complete their lines, and a paper promise to do so had been issued. A manager of the Crédit Lyonnais – a sub-contractor in the Türkenlose underwriting syndicate – writing to a colleague in the Turkish capital, noted that Hirsch 'is always busy trying to find money for Turkey to continue the railway construction' – and this at a time of acute disorder in the Balkans. Indeed, he would seem to have been so surprisingly successful that he informed the government in Vienna that he was ready to continue the lines in the direction of Austria without any financial support from the Turks. Angling for Austrian endorsement, he transferred the seat of his operating company from Paris to Vienna in the year of the Congress of Berlin, naturalised himself and distributed charity to advertise his presence. But his concession was now at risk from the new division of the Balkans. He held it from the Porte, but Turkey's writ no longer ran in the northern territories: would the successor states respect his rights? Russia's pretensions in the Balkans, staked out too flagrantly in the treaty of San Stefano, had been balked at Berlin, where they had counted on better things than the even-handed honest broking of Chancellor Bismarck. Again it was alleged that Hirsch owed these favourable revisions to the influence of the indebted Prince of Wales (they had still not met) over the English envoys, Disraeli and Salisbury. (It was the former's performance at Berlin that earned Bismarck's admiring 'Der alte Jude, das ist ein Mann'.) Hirsch certainly put in an appearance at the Congress and solicited Count Andrássy, Beust's Magyar successor, for his support. But newly independent and assertive Serbia refused the Chancellor's request to allow Hirsch to complete the rail connection.

Andrássy countered such obduracy by inserting into the final protocol of the treaty the obligation on Serbia, Bulgaria and Turkey to confirm Hirsch's concession and to complete those parts of the railway which lay in their territories as far as the Austro-Hungarian border.

Predators now scrambled to usurp and appropriate Hirsch's former rights. The Austrian State Railway, previously so dismissive of Hirsch as an upstart, was poised to branch out south to Serbia and east to Romania. By 1876 it had reached the Black Sea, but its request to construct a connection to Belgrade in Serbia was rejected by the Hungarian government which, relishing home rule, did not welcome a foreign company with mostly French capital under Austrian jurisdiction. Hirsch had no further chance; his application for a concession for a rival route down the Danube was turned down in 1878. The Austrian State Railway then considered a new scheme to take a line to Constantinople further east through Romania to Ruse on the Bulgarian border. This was strongly backed by the French government, fearful that any extension of the track from Salonica would prejudice the trade of their own Mediterranean ports. This, too, was unavailing.

A newcomer now emerged: Paul Eugène Bontoux, a railman who had won his spurs in France, then with the Austrian State Railway and most recently with the Rothschild Südbahn. On falling out with the family, he borrowed a leaf from Langrand-Dumonceau's book and organized in Paris the Union Générale, a Catholic bank, so as to free the market once again from the stranglehold of Jew, Protestant and Freemason. This prejudice, reinforced with a message of goodwill from the Pope, sufficed to separate the pious successfully from their savings, and thus emboldened he extended his holy war on the Rothschilds to Vienna. With the moral support of the new opportunist Chancellor Taaffe, a childhood crony of the Emperor Franz Joseph, he founded the 'Imperially and Royally Privileged' Länderbank. Bontoux opened negotiations direct with Belgrade for a concession to build those railway lines for which Serbia had been made responsible. He was again backed by Taaffe, who advised the Serbian government to disregard Hirsch's rights under the original concession. At this point, in 1881, the lines got even more strangely crossed. The Banque de Paris et des Pays Bas, which had arisen out of a merger with Bischoffsheim & Goldschmidt and was directed by Hirsch's brother-in-law, Heinrich Bamberger, allied itself to the Austrian State Railway to resurrect the alternative route to Constantinople through Romania, a more attractive prospect because it caught the trade of the Danube delta. This interest at least pricked the Serbs into taking counteraction from which Bontoux benefited. He won the contract for the construction of the line down from Belgrade to connect with Constantinople in the east and Salonica in the south. The presumptuous Bontoux, however, was being quietly stalked by his former employers, the Rothschilds, who were acquiring scattered holdings of the Union Générale's shares. Judging that he had now over-extended himself, they dumped the lot in one blow over the New Year of 1882; between 5 and 20 January, the shares fell by 2,090 points from a high of 3,050. There was panic in Vienna, the Bourse in Paris closed its doors. Alfred Rothschild set about insuring the family against recriminations should the ripples reach the London Stock Exchange. He took care to advise Sir Charles

Dilke, Under-Secretary for Foreign Affairs, that his cousin Alphonse had been approached by Bontoux to bail out the Union Générale. Alphonse, Alfred reported, had decided that he would not help unless he had very strong, purely financial, reasons for it. This, as Dilke, unaware of the background, commented innocently, 'was indeed to be expected'. In the same month, Bontoux expressed a wish to meet Hirsch, first in Paris and then in Rome, presumably with a similar proposal and perhaps an offer of a stake in the Serbian concession as a carrot. The meeting never came off. Another French banking syndicate, under the leadership of a board member of Hirsch's own operating company and an occasional associate of the Bischoffsheims, took over the contract for the Serbian railway. After the collapse of his bank, Bontoux was arrested and after a long-drawn-out trial was condemned to five years in prison; he received the news on the safe side of the Pyrenees, electing to remain in Spain for the duration of the sentence. Throughout his ordeal and after, he made himself out to be the innocent victim of manipulation by others. Given the Union Générale's *raison d'être*, these could only be members of a 'Jewish conspiracy'; the furore acted as bellows on the embers of anti-Semitism, which persisted at an uncomfortable temperature in France for twenty years. In the immediate aftermath Hirsch, quite unfairly, collected the odium.

The railway line was progressing fitfully. Bulgaria and Turkey still dragged their feet. Only in May 1883 did the reluctantly interested parties meet in Vienna to sign an ultimate agreement to complete the network. It took a further two years of political prodding before the Turks could be brought to contract for the construction in Eastern Rumelia of a link between Bellova and the Serbian frontier – a mere 46 kilometres – and a longer line connecting the Salonica-Skopje section also with Serbia. Hirsch, now reduced to tendering for his proper concession, lost out to a French group whose bid was one-third higher (perhaps owing to an unusual oversight in neglecting unmentionable expenses). The operation of the line went to an associate of the Ottoman Bank. Hirsch protested, but it was five years before an arbitration award restored the operation to him; the construction was already completed.

There still remained one last substantial section, some 100 kilometres through Bulgaria. Russia had never renounced its designs to thwart the western connection and instead divert the track through Romania towards Russia. Bulgaria was a virtual Russian vassal, but the Bulgars, so recently emancipated from the Sultan, were disinclined to exchange that bondage for another under the Tsar. They stalled and prevaricated until they could no longer avoid a decision – and then they neatly outwitted the

Russians, whose contractors were already confidently in place. The Russian consulting engineer at the Public Works Department had set an onerous specification at a low estimate which, after it had discouraged the opposition, would be suitably revised. The Bulgarians quietly put together a local syndicate whose bid, guaranteed by the National Bank, undercut the Russians. This was submitted at the last hour and accepted overnight before it could be countered.

Russia's principal agents, who had agitated so vainly for two years on behalf of their government, were an unusual pair. Baron Horace de Günzburg, descended from a Bavarian Jewish family whose fortune had been founded on the sale of vodka to the troops in the Crimea, was one of St Petersburg's leading bankers. His daughter Louise at this time married Joseph, the son of the late Sassoon David Sassoon of Ashley Park, Surrey. He himself was soon to be recuited by Baron Hirsch to mitigate the miserable conditions of his less fortunate co-religionists in Russia. The other, Samuel Poliakoff, a former plasterer from Kiev, developed into one of Russia's greatest road and rail entrepreneurs. He had extended Hirsch's Moscow–Riazan Railway and in 1880 had married his daughter Zenaide to Hirsch's brother James. He had also founded the Moscow Agricultural Bank, and the fanatical Procurator of the Holy Synod, Pobedonostsev, had even offered him the Finance Ministry – on condition that he would convert to (Russian) Orthodoxy.

There was yet another Balkan imbroglio in the offing. As the rails were approaching Bulgaria from the south through Eastern Rumelia, that province revolted against Turkish rule in September 1885 and opted for union with its northern neighbour. This was a reversion to the 'Big Bulgaria' which Russia had tried to impose at San Stefano and which the other Powers had redivided at Berlin. Now the positions had changed. Russia was opposed to unification on the grounds that an anti-Russian clique had the upper hand in Sofia. Britain and Austria supported the merger for the same reason. Turkey mobilized but, its revenues under the strict control of the Ottoman Debt Commission, did not have the means to take the field. Hirsch, foreseeing further loss of line, came to its rescue. He advanced £1 million out of the accumulated rental due from the operating company which had been withheld since the Turks' failure to honour the contract to complete construction. (This led to a thaw in relations and a readjustment of the terms in Hirsch's favour.) Before Turkey could move, the unsavoury self-proclaimed King Milan of Serbia invaded Bulgaria, and was trounced. The Great Powers recognized a *fait accompli*, Turkey lost Eastern Rumelia, Bulgaria grabbed its railway. On 12 August 1888, twenty years after the signing of the concession, the first train steamed out of Vienna bound for Constantinople, which cut the previous land and sea journey of between four and a half and seven days to forty hours.

There was recurring criticism of construction. It was remarked that the line looped about in a meandering fashion. The object was reputedly to avoid the cost of tunnels and to collect increased subventions on the additional kilometres; although Constantinople was barely 150 kilometres from Adrianople by road, the rail covered almost 200 kilometres. However, the Turks, who had approved the route and were never slow to find fault if it was to their advantage, were not known to have complained about this peculiarity. One inconvenience which impressed itself more unfavourably on passengers was that the stations were often located at some distance from even the main cities they were designed to serve. There was logic to this. Not only did the Turkish government save on compensation for compulsory purchase, but isolated stations (and their telegraph) were more easily defended in the case of the occasional insurrection. Hirsch was also accused of not paying the locally indentured labour employed on the literal donkey-work of earth-moving; it is more probable that the wages, paid to the government, stuck to the fingers of venal officials at the Ministry of Public Works. Such was the case with the owners of the tenements which had had to be demolished to make way for the approaches to the terminus at Constantinople. The compensation, paid by the railway to the Porte, never percolated down to the dispossessed. Hirsch referred such complaints to the government, but when they reached his wife's ears Clara paid the claimants out of her own purse.

There were indeed enduring differences between both parties, and while the troubles in Bulgaria were still brewing, arbitration was set up. The Sultan had turned down Hirsch's nominees, the French and then the Austrian ambassadors, but they both agreed on the American Minister, Oscar Straus,[*] a Bavarian Jew by origin. But Straus, although he had his Secretary of State's consent, was wary: 'Any transaction with the Turkish government involving money was open to suspicion of improper methods and bribery. Had I as arbitrator made a decision unfavourable to the Turkish government, I should certainly have fallen under such suspicion.' Instead, in 1886, two jurymen were chosen by each party and the casting vote was held by the German Liberal jurist and historian, Professor Rudolf von Gneist. The arbitration dragged on for two years. Hirsch's critics waited hopefully, expecting an award of 'hundreds of millions' of

[*]Straus was the first Jew to be appointed to a cabinet post in America, as Secretary of Commerce and Industry in 1906, by President Theodore Roosevelt.

francs against him. They were surprised and disappointed. Turkey had claimed for repayment, including interest, of 60 million francs – something short of £2.5 million – one-third of which comprised the track rental due from 1872 which Hirsch had retained on the grounds that the government had not met its own obligations under the revised concession. The company had counterclaims. Under the final award the payment to the Porte was reduced to a net 14.5 million francs, a bagatelle. Gneist made it clear in a letter to Hirsch that this would have been even less if his hands had not been tied by the articles of arbitration. He paid Hirsch an unusual and unexpected tribute: 'I may proceed on the assumption that in the matter of this greatly complicated affair the question of honour is of deepest concern to you, for it is a fine trait in the nature of man that, progressively with his acquisition of wealth, his regard for the importance of his good name increases. It became a source of great satisfaction to see that in a matter of great responsibility and in a time of bitter prejudice, I was enabled in my award repeatedly to emphasize the probity of your course . . .'

Following twenty years of frustration, all remaining contentious matters were now settled. There is evidence that the affair ended even on an amicable note. Hirsch received from the Sultan the Grand Cordon of the Osmanje Order, the highest award for foreigners. Rumour soon put it about that courtiers had been bribed to persuade the Sultan to make this gesture: he was said to detest Hirsch and had once all but had him arrested and 'put away', as the Sultan's Ambassador in London feared would be his own fate. Though Abdul Hamid was easily displeased, Hirsch was no mere expendable entrepreneur but honorary Belgian Consul-General in Constantinople, and this course would have been judged a trifle high-handed even for the Commander of the Faithful. Nevertheless Hirsch, so it was said, taking no risks, took refuge instead on board an Austrian steamer until the Sultan's temper improved.

Once the last of these loose ends had been knotted, Hirsch set about ridding himself of the railway which it had never been his intention to manage. It was plausibly reported that his old rival the Austrian State Railway was interested in acquiring his stake, but he had not forgotten their patronizing slight when he had been a débutant railwayman. It came to the ears of Austrian diplomats that he had already been tempted by the Russians, who coveted his holdings as a means to continue their squeeze on the Bulgarians. Hirsch instead, in April 1890, disposed of his controlling stake in the railway to a group led by the Deutsche Bank, co-founded by Ludwig Bamberger, whose brother Heinrich, married to Hirsch's sister, headed Paribas. The new proprietor was to carry the track through Anatolia and on to Baghdad, an enterprise which would cause as much international heartburn as Hirsch's Orient Railway.

Speculation and wild surmise continued to exercise the minds of the multitude of the curious, then and thereafter, on the question of the extent of Hirsch's profit from his railway. The Türkenlose had brought him a first fortune of around £2 million as a banker, and a working capital of £14 million for the construction of 2,000 kilometres of railway. Under the revised concession, this had been reduced to 1,280 kilometres, the easiest and thus the cheapest portion of line, which had most reasonably not cost him more than £7.5 million. There is no means of even approximately estimating the likely level of the traditional douceurs he had distributed along the way, but on the assumption that he had been able to contain these within a figure of 10 per cent of his working capital, he would still have shown an overall profit of around £8 million. On the operation, profits aside, if he had retained the rental for ten years, he would have had about £4 million in hand, out of which he had advanced the Turks £1 million for their attempt to retain sovereignty over Eastern Rumelia, and had now had to repay them a further half-million under the arbitration award. A contemporary and colleague, one of the bright young men Hirsch attracted, put his profit at between £6.5 and £6.75 million, but this would seem too modest; the *Jewish Chronicle* reckoned a figure of nearer £10 million, something in the region of £300 million in present-day values. Although these profits constituted the backbone of his wealth, he had managed to double this fortune during the same period. The exact means remain a mystery: he had a hand in Hungarian and Russian railways; he was reportedly engaged in the large-scale manufacture of sugar from beet in France, where agricultural subsidies made it most profitable; he was thought to have bought up immense quantities of depreciated metal at the time of the copper crash, and he indubitably discovered other profitable uses for his savings. (Among his more evident interests was a brasserie near the Paris Opéra, which sold the family's Bavarian beer. He was nonplussed when his manager, having made a modest fortune, intimated that he wished to retire. 'What,' was Hirsch's shocked reaction, 'he does not want to make another million?')

To his natural talent was harnessed inexhaustible energy and industry – his normal working day began at 5 a.m.; he ascribed his own success to his mastery of detail – and to economy in small things. (Coming on him haggling with a cabby over sixpence in the pouring rain, a German diplomat, Baron Eckardstein, urged him to pay up and come in out of the wet before he was laid up for weeks. 'That's all very well,' replied Hirsch, 'but I have my principles.')

Single-handed he had coaxed and contrived, bullied and bribed to beat a path through Balkan intrigues, bloody racial and religious rivalries and one major war. As the midwife, executor and principal beneficiary, Hirsch offered a solitary target for all the censure surrounding the project. This was partly political, partly personal. It had less to do with alleged improprieties than with nationalist prejudices, nourished by chauvinism, and with it anti-Semitism, and reflecting the conflicting ambitions in the peculiar conditions of the decaying Ottoman Empire. At the best of times, as an Austrian obituarist remarked, 'public opinion on the rapid accumulation of fortunes is never flattering', whereas the decade in which Hirsch operated suffered an unusual share of misfortune. There had been first the burden on the market of the French war indemnity to Prussia, followed by the depressions of 1873 and 1882, while the holders of Türkenlose themselves went without their interest for six years with no certainty they would ever see their savings again. Single-minded and persistent, the Baron had also trodden on a bunch of traditional toes along his path, and his blunt and caustic manner had ruffled some fine feathers. There were not a few among even his compeers who hoped that the presumption of 'this little banker from Brussels' would trip him up. Widely viewed as 'a foolhardy promoter', he had engaged himself in an enterprise which no one before him had the courage to tackle and in which he encountered obstacles which no one could have foreseen. He had to reckon with his clients, the Turks, dilatory, evasive, corrupt and for much of the time bankrupt, torn between the desire to enjoy the financial fruits of modernization and the fear of its political effects. Of the two most concerned outside Powers, he faced the obstruction of Russia and only the sporadic support of Austria.

The sale of the railway marked his retirement. Although approaching sixty, he was influenced in this decision by a personal tragedy. He had previously lost his only daughter in infancy; his father had died in 1885, and two years later his only son, Lucien, died of pneumonia in Paris at the age of thirty-one. 'My son I have lost,' he replied to a letter of condolence in untypically grandiloquent fashion, 'but not my heir: humanity is my heir.' Faithful to his promise, he dedicated himself for the remaining nine years of his life to philanthropy – and to social diversion. His secretary testified that he applied himself additionally to three other abiding passions: blood sports, law suits and evasion of income tax and estate duty, which he considered unjust. But if he fought to guard his fortune from governments' grasp, he spent at the same time as much energy and obstinacy in dispensing it to the benefit of the oppressed as he had in acquiring it.

Baron de Hirsch was already a legend before he shed the Orient Railway. Chaim Weizmann recalled four pictures that hung in his parents' home in Pinsk in the Pale of Settlement: the medieval sage Maimonides, the Wailing Wall in Jerusalem, Anton Chekhov, grandson of a serf who portrayed the predicament of the 'little man', and the philanthropist Baron de Hirsch. His wealth too was legendary. Estimates of his fortune ranged from £15 million to £30 million; his estate in England alone was valued at £1,372,000. (The first Duke of Westminster, the richest man in England, was reputed to be worth £14 million in 1894.) The amounts he gave away or bequeathed in his lifetime can be more accurately assessed. That humanity was indeed his heir was no empty boast; among his contemporaries, his benefactions were probably only surpassed by the Scottish ironmaster Andrew Carnegie. (King Edward visited Carnegie at his home, Skibo Castle in Scotland. The great philanthropist insisted on reciting a poem which had been written in celebration of his birthday. It began with invocations to various monarchs and President Roosevelt. '"Hail fat Edward" – that's you sir,' Carnegie thoughtfully explained.) Hirsch's friend Oscar Straus judged that his gifts exceeded $100 million, or £20 million at the then rate of exchange; and his widow Clara spent £3 million on charity during the three years she survived her husband, and left bequests totalling a further £2 million. Though he might cavil at the least wastage, Hirsch did not spare any expense on himself, his houses and estates or on his royal patron, the Prince of Wales, and his friends. In the view of Lady Randolph Churchill, who cultivated the company of the well-to-do, Hirsch, despite his excessive economy, was still one of the few millionaires who 'knew thoroughly how to enjoy life'.

While his munificence was too manifest to deny, his detractors could and did question his motives. These were imputed posthumously to pangs of conscience and overweening social ambition; it was said he wished to bury his unsavoury reputation under a shower of prodigious philanthropy. Hirsch, a realist to his boots, would have been the last man to accept that he had any reason for remorse. Without conceit, he would have felt nothing but satisfaction that he had acquired the means to gratify his aspirations. The Austrian Rothschilds gave with cool calculation to grease the wheels of goodwill with the government, a few thousand crowns here to celebrate the Emperor's safe return to his capital, a few tens of thousands there to celebrate a royal marriage or anniversary in expectation of some future favour. Hirsch had no favours to expect from the Austro-Hungarian government, and curried none. On the contrary he insisted, in the matter of philanthropy, on his own manner and means in the face, more often than not, of the obdurate opposition of the secular and religious authorities. He did not spend his way into high society to placate his critics, as was suggested, but to please himself; a hobby he could afford to indulge with philosophic cynicism: he had learnt the price of every man in a hard school. His craving for crowns and coronets certainly verged on the comic but, while revelling in the glamour and glitter of high society, he had a clear appreciation of the hollowness of its pomp and pretension. 'You see all these people,' he told his son, watching the bearers of some of the proudest names in France mounting his famous staircase in Paris. 'In twenty years, they will all be our in-laws or our concierges.'

Although the sum of his benefaction was unparalleled in Europe, more significant still was his practical approach to philanthropy. Straightforward charity, except in special cases to alleviate immediate distress, he scorned, regarding it as self-defeating because it bred an addiction to alms with a consequent loss of incentive and independence. There was no sentiment in his philanthropy. He preached and practised a doctrine, not universally appreciated by the recipients, of industry, thrift and self-improvement. In short, he dedicated himself to implement what that other railwayman Samuel Smiles had advocated so successfully thirty years before: self-help.

But his travels in the Balkans had opened his eyes to a more urgent and basic need. 'During my repeated and extended visits to Turkey,' he wrote to the Paris-based Alliance Israélite Universelle in 1873, 'I have been painfully impressed by the misery and ignorance in which the Jewish masses live in that Empire . . .' – their plight worsened when the Cross superseded the Crescent – 'progress had bypassed them . . . and only the education and training of the young generation can remedy this dismal situation.' He forthwith offered the Alliance a fund of one million gold francs for schools and vocational training on the spot in the Balkans or abroad. (He had foreseen the need for skilled and semi-skilled labour from the beginning of his rail laying and 'thus . . . built schools as he built railway stations'.) This was such a novelty that it met with the stiff resistance of the ultra-conservative leaders of the important Jewish colony of Salonica, who did not relish the introduction of such fanciful, if not frankly dangerous, innovations to adulterate their religious curriculum. Hirsch continued to subsidize these schools until in 1882 he undertook to cover all the Alliance's annual deficits, and in 1889 set up an endowment of a further 10 million francs.

The situation of the 700,000 Jews in the furthest and poorest eastern provinces of Austria-Hungary, Galicia and Bukovina, was little better: the majority were steeped in ignorance and degradation worse even than that of their brethren in the neighbouring Polish provinces of Russia. Here too Hirsch busied himself bringing light into a dark corner, here too he ran up against entrenched prejudices. He consecrated some half a million pounds to set up the Baron Hirsch Foundation to create an embryo welfare state for all, irrespective of creed: primary schools and recreation grounds with books, food and clothing for poor pupils; commercial, technical and agricultural schools and interest-free loans to artisans and farmers. Although special provision was laid down for religious instruction of Jews and Christians, it took three years of wearing down the opposition of the Catholic and Jewish hierarchies before the government would give its assent to the scheme. Hirsch declared his aims to the great Viennese preacher and scholar Dr Adolph Jellinek: it would afford him the liveliest satisfaction if the 'Judisch-Deutsch jargon' were to disappear and if the Jews were to abandon all customs, unconnected with religion, which unnecessarily divided them from their Christian fellow countrymen; all that he desired was that they should receive the requisite culture and vocational training to enable them to earn their living by the work of their hands. Such loosening of racial and religious ties in pursuit of assimilation was anathema to the strictly orthodox. The authorities finally bowed to his persistence. Fifty-odd assorted schools were established, and after Hirsch's death his widow topped up the Foundation's funds with another £350,000. His care for the Emperor's subjects did not end there. He created a fund, the income of which, some £12,000 a year, went to assist those tradesmen in Vienna and Budapest who had fallen on hard times, to help set them on their feet (ruined gamblers on the Bourse were specifically excluded), and similar funds were set up in Cracow and Lemberg (Lvov). He donated a further £300,000 of which the income was distributed among the Hungarian poor without regard to religion. (Open-handed as he was, he deplored the least waste. After a great fire at Tokay, he sent his secretary to Vienna with over £4,000 for the immediate relief of the homeless, and a caution to take a fiacre not at the railway station, but from a rank nearby: he would save fourpence.)

When Baron Hirsch at last received Imperial approval for his Galician Foundation in 1891, he was a world away – lording it near Thetford, where he had rented 10,000 acres of some of the finest shooting in the country. At nearby Sandringham, the first engagement noted in the owner's diary on 1 January that same year read: 'Left Sandringham to shoot with Baron Hirsch at Wretham Hall, Norfolk.' To those in the know, as a later biographer recorded, the Prince of Wales had found, like the destitute of Austria-Hungary, a financial safety net.

4

Dangerous Liaisons

The acting East Anglian squire found his new life much more congenial than life in Vienna. Hirsch had inherited from his father a barony and a comfortable competence, and by his own exertions had added to that to become one of the richest men in the world. And yet 'great as he had become', wrote one later Jewish historian who would have met many people who had known the Baron, 'he had not been able to get rid of many human weaknesses which . . . at times made him look petty and comical'. Notable among these peculiarities was his misleading habit of behaving like the least and most recent *nouveau riche*; he took a perverse pleasure in shocking his compeers, made worse by a bitter and sardonic humour. By dint of patience and persistence the senior Austrian Rothschild, Baron Albert, had recently been pronounced 'court-worthy' by a special act of grace and, jealous of its honour, the family was not inclined to share the favour of its promotion. Albert's English mother had herself found the Austrian atmosphere oppressive, and two of her other children, Ferdinand and Alice, had already fled to England. Hirsch saw no cause to show them any deference. Although possessed of prickly racial pride, he was scornful on the subject of his rich co-religionists; he considered that while they might dutifully give their tithe to charity, they avoided all direct personal involvement in remedying the plight of the oppressed. His political views, which 'inclined to the sturdy radicalism of the self-made man', were not designed to ensure his popularity either. ('I agree with every word he said,' he once told his companion after listening to a Socialist orator holding forth at Hyde Park's Speakers' Corner. 'I will talk to him.') It is little wonder that this original and rebarbative character was shown the cold shoulder by even his peers, who were every bit as hidebound as the Habsburgs.

He lay under another, still less savoury cloud. On Christmas Eve 1882, the Austrian Ambassador in Paris, Count Wimpffen, had committed suicide. His mother was a Sina, one of the big three Jewish banking families of Vienna. It was known that Wimpffen had left a note for Hirsch, a request, it seems, to take care of his family and remove them from Paris. Certain newspapers in Germany and Vienna perverted this, publishing a letter in which Wimpffen purportedly accused Hirsch of having bribed him, although Hirsch's motives were not explained. This revived rumours about his activities in the Balkans. There is no evidence that Hirsch himself took any action publicly to deny the allegation; the slur lingered on, and it was only when the canard was reprinted in a Viennese paper eight years later that the Austrian authorities compelled the paper to publish an admission that the letter was a forgery.

For these reasons, although his railway operations had been centred on Vienna since 1878, Hirsch had never settled down there himself. Instead he had spread outside the capital in style. In 1885 he had bought for £230,000 from an Ypsilanti princess the twelfth-century castle of Eichhorn and its 20,000 hectares. (Built on a mountain crag near Brno, it was the only stronghold to have withstood the Swedes in the Thirty Years War.) And on the sandy plain of the Hungarian Marches he had transformed the manor of St Johann into a 'shooting palace' (the Prince of Wales, however, found it 'unpretentious'), linking it with a ten-mile-long road to the outside world. It was here he enjoyed his triumph over conservative Viennese society.

If Vienna society and Hirsch shared a mutual aversion, in London he was considered to have an amiable nature and polished manners, at least where it mattered most, and the Prince of Wales let it be known that where he went, Hirsch went too. Not all His Royal Highness's courtiers were convinced; Sir Francis Knollys confided to Sir Henry Ponsonby, the Queen's secretary, that the Prince looked on Hirsch as a personal friend, adding in parenthesis that 'whether he is a good one or not is another question'. And it was no disadvantage that a certain raciness about him proclaimed the sportsman – and, moreover, the provider of spectacular sport. He at once made a splash.

An early caller was a journalist, Lucien Wolf, who arrived with a preconceived prejudice, expecting to confront a poseur. He was disappointed. The previously spritely figure was now portly but still robust. He carried his sixty-odd years (and his millions) lightly. There was a twinkle in his close-set, black-button eyes. The huge longhorn moustache with the dandified waxed ends was iron-grey, his hair thinning over his crown. And though less distinguished looking than in his portraits, he was infinitely more genial. Wolf found him exceedingly unabashedly Jewish both in manner and conversation. Theodor Herzl, the apostle of Zionism, found him 'on the whole a pleasant, intelligent, simple, natural man – vain *par exemple!*'

Hirsch had another entrée into society: his wife's cousin, the banker Henry Bischoffsheim. He had been settled for some twenty years in London with his wife, Clarissa Biedermann of Vienna, in sumptuous style at 75 South Audley Street, the former home of the Earls of Bute, which he had turned into 'a Versailles in miniature'. With cautious contortions of the neck the visitor could admire Tiepolo's 'Allegory of Venus and Time' on the ceiling of the blue drawing room, hung with hand-painted satin of the same colour; in the black drawing room the furniture was curiously upholstered in matching satin. Henry Bischoffsheim's 'sanguine and energetic temperament' had lured him into too many uncertain, and often unfortunate, adventures and the London bank had gone into decline in the mid-Seventies. But the 'Bishs', as they were known, were still popular figures around London, favourites even of Queen Victoria. They were soon to celebrate their golden wedding with a gift of £100,000 to charity. Their two daughters, thoroughly acclimatized, had married some years before the fourth Earl of Desart and Sir Maurice FitzGerald, twentieth Knight of Kerry.

Hirsch had established himself in a palatial pied-à-terre for the Season a little further south – Bath House, in Piccadilly, overlooking Green Park, which he acquired from the daughter-in-law of another great railway contractor, Thomas Brassey. And to his already formidable collection of property, in Moravia, Hungary, Paris and Versailles, he added Grafton House at Newmarket in order to be better positioned to grab the sport of kings by the tail.

It was in the spring of the previous year, 1890, that the Prince and the Baron had stitched together a satisfactory support system during that spate of tête-à-têtes in Paris. Hirsch could now take his place in English Society by royal appointment. By way of some modest payment of interest the Prince had graciously accepted an invitation to visit his benefactor in Hungary. Once news of this engagement leaked out, the Austrian Ambassador threw up his hands: the Baron, he expostulated, was not received at the Emperor's court. (The Prince was himself '*dreadfully* annoyed' when his mother refused to extend her hospitality to his protégé for a State concert at Buckingham Palace.) He arrived in Vienna on 5 October 1890, with his loader and dogs; among his other companions were Horace Farquhar, banker, Member of Parliament and future Master of the Household, Lady Randolph Churchill, and Arthur and the delectable Louise Sassoon. After laying a wreath next morning on Crown

Prince Rudolf's tomb, the Prince gave a luncheon party at the Grand Hotel for his brother-in-law King George I of Greece and Hirsch. (The Grand served as Hirsch's headquarters when he was forced to put up in the capital, but he avoided eating there himself as, in his own personal opinion, he 'couldn't afford it'.) Hirsch then whisked his guests off by special train to St Johann, while 'the Austrian archdukes gasped'. (This was not solely anti-Semitism. The royal dynasties were inclined to look down their noses at each other: the Habsburgs regarded the Coburgs as upstarts, while Queen Victoria considered the Austrian Archdukes 'worthless'.)

'Life at St Johann', wrote Lady Randolph Churchill, a frequent visitor, 'was simple and healthy.' After breakfast a fleet of victorias paraded to drive those so inclined to the scene of slaughter, the postilions in hussar-like blue jackets, Hessian boots and shiny high-crowned hats. The battue then began. Six hundred beaters set off in a circle of some seven miles in circumference, directed by a head keeper sounding his bugle from a high tower. The guns, rarely more than ten, were spread over a three-acre site in butts walled in, for their neighbours' safety, with fir branches. Jennie Churchill remembered one sportsman who, as the huge coveys sped overhead, called out to them in his excitement, 'For heaven's sake, stop! O, do wait a moment.' After five days' sport, the Prince sent his son, Prince George, his score, 'which will indeed amaze you – I never saw so much game in my life.' The party spent ten days in this strenuous fashion and shot nearly 20,000 head of partridge, pheasants and big blue hares. 'This certainly beats everything on record,' Edward again wrote to his son, 'and will quite spoil me for any shooting at home.' If the Prince of Wales stinted himself, other guests might remain for as much as six weeks, shooting every day. The Duke of Portland noted that quite moderate shots, like Lord de Grey and Harry Stonor, became very good indeed, simply from persistent practice with Hirsch. Jennie Churchill's brother-in-law, the luckless speculator Moreton Frewen – 'Mortal Ruin' to his unfortunate partners – made a game attempt to touch the Prince of Wales's new friend to help him establish a corner in silver. He received in reply an offer through his wife, Clara Jerome, to come and shoot with the Baron. Bitterly disappointed, he reproached her that he did not 'like your Jews, truth to tell . . . I don't like all these rich vulgar people, and I would sooner break stones than have any dealings with Natt. Rothschild. His co-religionists are worse!' (The fare was another problem, and he did not have a clean shirt to his name.) Confident, however, of his silver tongue, he relented, but returned empty-handed, leaving his wife with the injunction, 'Cultivate Old H———,' and insufficient money with which to tip the servants.

At St Johann the Prince's few Austrian and Hungarian fellow guests, were congenial though not aristocratic, and it was doubtless with the best intentions that he attempted to improve his host's standing with his neighbours. A former host of the Prince's, the Hungarian Count Tassilo Festetics, responded with an invitation which pointedly excluded Hirsch. The Prince, who fiercely resented any affront to his friends from whatever quarter, refused it. 'I should be glad to receive you on any other occasion,' retorted the Count, 'but not when coming from that Jew's.' (Festetics, married to the daughter of the Dowager Duchess of Hamilton, herself the daughter of the reigning Grand Duke of Baden, was later forgiven and decorated with the Royal Victorian Order.)

Baron Hirsch's first taste of the English Turf was acquired at second hand from his son – rather strangely, since Lucien, according to his father, preferred collecting coins to horses. (On Lucien's death his racing stud was sold and the proceeds were distributed by his father among a number of charities.) Egged on by Edward, in 1890 the Prince's racing manager, Lord Marcus Beresford, bought for Hirsch the yearling La Flèche at the Royal Stud's Hampton Court sale for 5,500 guineas, a record price that caused the auctioneer to call for 'Three cheers for Baron Hirsch and success to the Royal Stud'. A chronicler scoffed, 'We do like to see people spend money, and if we think they are spending it rather foolishly, why, we cheer the louder!' (La Flèche won £34,700 in prize money in her career and was sold for 12,600 guineas at Hirsch's death, a record for a brood mare.) Unbeaten as a two-year-old, she went on to carry the Baron's colours – citron jacket with turquoise cap – to victory in a rare treble in 1892: the One Thousand Guineas, the Oaks and the St Leger, and all her other races as a three-year-old, save the Derby, in which she was badly ridden. Hirsch persuaded the Prince to follow his example and move his horses from John Porter at Highclere, who had saddled more Derby winners than any other trainer, to Richard Marsh at Newmarket. Twelve months later Hirsch returned to Porter with an offer to buy his stables for £20,000, pay him a salary of £1,000 as his trainer and place £100,000 at his absolute disposal for the purchase of bloodstock. Porter regretfully declined out of loyalty to other, older patrons. Despite his successes, however, the Baron's eye for horseflesh was suspect. Proudly he showed the Prince and the Duchess of Devonshire round the new quarters. His new horse's name had not yet been placed on the wall of her box, and the German-born Duchess maliciously asked Hirsch to put a name to the animal. He was unable to do so, even though La Flèche had unmistakable characteristics. Hirsch had another hopeful, Matchbox. Beaten also in the Derby, he started as 6–4 odds-on favourite for the Paris

Grand Prix in 1894. All the very best sporting people in France were, *The Times* assured its readers, very anxious that an English horse should win so that the race might retain its international character. 'I will not go so far as to say that this sentiment was not in any way modified when it was learned that Matchbox had become the property of a German.' Matchbox was beaten at the post by a short head. The Prince was equally unfortunate in losing £596, the largest recorded bet he ever placed on a horse for a win. He repaid the amount three days later to Colonel Paget, an equerry who kept his game and turf books. He was philosophical: 'Hirsch is certainly not in luck. But sending Matchbox over was always rather hazardous. However, he may have been beaten by a better horse. The Baron bears his disappointment with great fortitude, and it was far better for him not to make objections for possible foul riding.'

There were others less fortunate who might have felt the loss more keenly. Although it was not widely known, the Baron 'raced', as he liked to say, 'for the London hospitals'. They received all his winnings on the Turf without any deductions for expenses. In 1891 these amounted to only £7,000, but in his golden year they reached £35,000. In 1893, however, his colours were not so successful and, thinking the prize money of £7,500 a sad and undeserved disappointment for charity, he doubled it. Hirsch distributed his bounty through George Herring, who began his remarkable career, it was said, as a carver in a boiled beef shop in Ludgate Hill before advancing to the status of a turf commission agent of strict integrity. From bookmaking he went on to make a mysterious million and more in the City in association with Henry Bischoffsheim. A neighbour of the Rothschilds in Hamilton Place, he remained a cheerful cockney: 'Come 'ungry', he would urge friends invited to dine.

Jewish institutions were, with few exceptions, less favoured. The Baron invariably replied to their persistent applications, often made through friends he would normally have liked to oblige, that he was not disposed to relieve the Jewish community in Britain of any of its proper obligations.

It would have been out of character for Hirsch to make any attempt to recover some of his racing expenses by wagers on his runners, however well fancied. He shared none of his royal patron's delight in 'the glorious uncertainties of the Turf' and neither did he relish a role as the plaything of Fortune. After entertaining the Prince to dinner at Monte Carlo, Hirsch accompanied the party to the Casino, where he had reserved a special roulette table. Hirsch took his seat but placed such small bets, five-franc pieces, at most one gold louis, in such evident trepidation and with trembling hand that one of the guests chaffed him. 'It's not on account of the five francs,' Hirsch reassured him, 'but for fear that playing might be the beginning of my going downhill. For no fortune, not even mine, is big enough to last if the devil of gambling once gets hold of one.'

Another of the Prince's hangers-on who had observed Hirsch at Marienbad noted that he was 'by nature distrustful and ungenerous'. No doubt such a pinchpenny and pessimistic view of humanity was occasionally justified, but once at least he suffered a deception. Nellie Melba had been playing heavily with atrocious luck at the same tables at Monte Carlo until she ran out of funds. She spotted a potential saviour standing nearby. 'Baron Hirsch,' she accosted him, 'I want to throw good money after bad but I haven't got any. Will you lend me a thousand francs?' The diva was a lady who was used to having her slightest whim indulged, and Hirsch's unenthusiastic response surprised her. Instead of diving into his pocket 'as most of one's friends would have done', he pulled a face, hesitated and only after a considerable display of reluctance finally produced the desired funds. Melba did not let such ungraciousness disturb her peace of mind, but next day sent him a cheque with her sincere thanks. Two days later a small packet arrived at her hotel. She opened it to discover a charming diamond gewgaw. 'Dear Madame Melba,' Hirsch wrote, 'you are the first woman who has ever paid me back money which she has borrowed. I am so touched that I have taken the liberty of sending you the enclosed little brooch, which I hope you will accept as a token of my admiration.' She did not disappoint the Baron with any churlish display of self-denial.

Hirsch's racing successes and royal patronage won him membership of the Turf Club. He was not so fortunate in Paris where, after being 'pilled' for a club – the same story is told both of the elite Jockey Club and the scarcely less prestigious Cercle de la Rue Royale – he responded, as he boasted to Margot Tennant (later Asquith), by buying the premises and evicting the members. (In the case of the Jockey Club he is credited with having replaced the members with his horses. It is curious that Edouard Drumont, remembered chiefly as an anti-Semitic author and agitator, conceded that 'There is more intellectual energy, will and tenacity of purpose in the least Jew of Galicia than in the entire Jockey Club'.) Margot Tennant had been impressed. 'You must be very rich,' she artlessly surmised. Hirsch asked with some surprise where she lived that she had not heard of him. In spite of her unworldiness, he had been impressed with her sangfroid when, at a dinner at the Bischoffsheims', a glass of iced champagne had been spilled down the front of her gown and she had stoically concealed her chilled discomfort from the company. They met next in Paris. Hirsch and his wife invited her to dinner, he gave Margot his box at the opera and supplied a mount for her to ride in the

Bois de Boulogne. He then boldly proposed a tête-à-tête dinner in a private room at the Café Anglais. He came to the point at once, engaging in a strange surrogate courtship. Did she have any idea why he had invited her? he enquired.

'I haven't the slightest idea!'

'Because I want you to marry my son Lucien. He is quite unlike me, he is very respectable and hates money; he likes books and collects manuscripts and other things and is highly educated.'

'Your son is the man with the beard, who wears glasses and collects coins, isn't he?'

'Quite so! You talked to him the other day at our house. But he has a charming disposition and has been a good son; and I am quite sure that, if you would take a little trouble, he would be devoted to you and make you an excellent husband: he does not like Society, or racing, or any of the things that I care for.'

'Poor man! I don't suppose he would even care much for me! I hate coins!'

'Oh, but you would widen his interests! He is shy and I want him to make a good marriage; and above all he must marry an Englishwoman.'

Her host revealed his concern that some designing girl might marry Lucien for his money.

'Over here I suppose that sort of thing might happen,' Margot replied. 'I don't believe it would in England.'

'How can you say such a thing to me? London Society cares more for money than any other in the world, as I know to my cost! You may take it from me that a young man who will be as rich as Lucien can marry almost any girl he likes.'

'I doubt it! English girls don't marry for money!'

'Nonsense, my dear! They are like other people; it is only the young that can afford to despise money!'

The Baron reproached Margot for her frivolous attitude. Surely she would not like to be a poor man's wife and live in the suburbs – would she not hate to be dowdy and obscure? Margot, resorting to defensive banter, warned him she might be just the sort of adventuress he dreaded most; far from widening his son's interests, she might 'keep him busy with his coins while I went about everywhere, enjoying myself and spending all your money.'

Hirsch, after admitting that he had another candidate in mind, Lady Katie Lambton, the Earl of Durham's sister, enquired whether Miss Tennant's affections were seriously engaged in another quarter. As he continued to press this unwelcome line, she retorted hotly, 'I only hope that Mr Lucien is not as curious as you are, or I should have a very poor time; there is nothing I should hate as much as a jealous husband.'

'I don't believe you,' Hirsch replied. 'If it's tiresome to have a jealous husband, it must be humiliating to have one who is not.'

In the face of his persistence, she was forced to tell him directly that she was the last girl in the world to suit his son. She was undoubtedly correct: Hirsch was intent on saddling his son with more than he could, or would wished to, have handled. (Arthur Balfour, quizzed by someone who had heard he was to marry Margot, replied, 'No, that is not so, I rather think of having a career of my own.')

This was only a short time before Lucien's death. 'What a fool Margot Tennant was not to have married your son!' an acquaintance told Hirsch. 'She would be a rich widow now.'

'No one would die if they married Margot Tennant,' was the gallant response.

Although the Baron affected to despise intellectual pursuits, he nevertheless encouraged Lucien to follow his own bent. He hired for him a professor of history at the Sorbonne. Hirsch's nature, unfortunately, got the better of him. 'Take this cigar,' he advised the worthy teacher, 'you won't smoke anything like it at home, it cost me 25 sous.' The good man stuck it for two weeks.

Baron Hirsch was a Parisian implant of long standing. He had acquired a grand hôtel, a prime site in the heart of the capital, 2 Rue de l'Elysée, which the Duc de Mouchy had vacated. At Chesnay, near Versailles, he had the Château de Beauregard, famous for its elaborate winter gardens. (Spotting some inexpensive melons in a market, he remarked ruefully, 'Mine cost me 500 francs apiece.') There was an ironic affinity to these properties. He built his Parisian *palais* on the site of three houses he bought from the ex-Empress Eugénie for almost £100,000. Beauregard had belonged to the courtesan Harriet Howard. A belle from Brighton, she had been taken up by a wealthy married major in the Household Cavalry who, on her bearing him a son, had settled on her a large fortune in real estate. She then fell in with the aspiring Louis Napoleon in London and had floated him to the presidency on loans secured by mortgages and jewellery. She put down 575,000 francs for Beauregard as a prospective matrimonial home just as Louis Napoleon, now Emperor Napoleon III, publicly announced his betrothal to Eugénie Montijo. Harriet died of cancer at Beauregard in 1865, aged forty-one. It suffered under the occupation of the Prussians in 1870 until Hirsch bought it for 850,000 francs two years later and restored it. (Gustave de Rothschild bought Harriet's Paris house and garden at 14 Rue de Cirque – which conveniently connected with the Luxembourg by a back door – for the site of his own mansion on the corner of the Champs-Elysées and the Avenue Marigny. On his death it was left to his daughter, Mrs Edward Sassoon.) Hirsch, who had 460 acres of his own, leased the shooting rights over the State preserves at Versailles, moving the council to protest that the public was harassed by his armed keepers. As with the Rothschilds at Ferrières, all the game was sold in advance to poulterers, though Hirsch was not known to go to such extremes as the late Baron James de Rothschild, who, knowing guests sometimes managed to elude the vigilance of the keepers, went over their rooms with a retriever while the company was at coffee, and confiscated contraband game.

The *fine fleur* of the French nobility, *ancien* and otherwise, paraded through Baron Hirsch's halls as it had at Compiègne, the centre of the social whirl during the Late Empire. Indeed, their complaisance was the despair of such xenophobic bell-wethers as Edouard Drumont. The Prince de Sagan, a noted pederast and one of the models for Proust's Baron Charlus, did the honours *chez* Hirsch, Drumont sourly noted, where the Comte de Chabot played the role of chamberlain and the Comte de FitzJames, before his marriage, was employed at 5,000 francs a month. Hirsch's social success was attributed with some justice to his grasp of 'le tarif de chaque scrupule et le prix marchand de chaque conscience' (the price of each scruple and the going rate for each conscience).

It is all the more surprising that he should have been accepted, for his probationary years in Paris were marked by more than one scandal. Ten years before Wimpffen's suicide, Hirsch had been embroiled in another *cause célèbre*. Friedrich von Holstein, the future *éminence grise* of the Wilhelmstrasse, had been attached to the German Embassy by a mistrustful Bismarck to keep an eye on his chief, the Jewish-born Count Harry von Arnim. The Ambassador, who had acted as commissioner to settle the final peace treaty with France, was suspected of coveting the Chancellor's chair and of pursuing a defiantly independent policy. Bismarck felt safer with France under a Republican regime; Arnim favoured the Royalists who were plotting to overthrow President Thiers. On the latter's resignation in 1873, the Orleanist Duc de Decazes, an intimate of both Arnim and Hirsch, became Foreign Minister in the Duc de Broglie's short-lived ministry. Holstein intercepted a compromising letter from Arnim to Hirsch in Nice. It proved to Bismarck's declared satisfaction that the Ambassador 'had worked the market' with Decazes through Hirsch. Arnim was recalled to Berlin early in 1874 and, notwithstanding his misdemeanour, was designated envoy to Constantinople. This was a step down from Paris, but Hirsch was eager for him to accept; he would reward him financially for his intercession with the Porte. Four months later it was discovered that a quantity of State papers were missing from the Paris Embassy. Arnim was arrested in October and tried. He was, however, acquitted of all but one offence and received a light three months' sentence. He then underwent a new trial for treason on account of the publication of an anonymous but impolitic pamphlet disparaging his master and monarch and this time was condemned to five years. He chose exile in Switzerland.

The incriminating letter was not produced in court. Did such a document ever exist? A more plausible candidate for the role imputed to Arnim was Holstein. A psychopathic intriguer, described by Bismarck as 'the man with the hyena eyes', he was an obsessive daily speculator on the Bourse and was later more than once suspected of being influenced by personal financial considerations in his diplomatic dealings, and before that had contributed to Bismarck's own fall. It is improbable that had any underhand dealings with Arnim been proven, Hirsch would have kept on such good dining and shooting terms with his irreproachably honourable successor, Prince Chlodwig von Hohenlohe.

The collapse of Bontoux's Union Générale eight years after Arnim's disgrace was followed by an industrial slump, the decline of agricultural prices and land values, while phylloxera ravaged the vineyards. One of the fruits that flourished in this sour soil was anti-Semitism, which inspired Edouard Drumont's best-seller (fourteen reprints in twelve months) *La France Juive* in 1886. A sub-editor on a newspaper owned by the Péreire banking brothers, and by a vexatious physiognomical anomaly often taken to be Jewish himself, Drumont set up his own organ, *La Libre Parole* (his business manager was a converted Jew), and an Anti-Semitic League which vowed to fight the 'clandestine and merciless conspiracy' of Jewish finance which 'jeopardizes daily the welfare, honour and security of France'. His notoriety won him a seat in the Chamber of Deputies. Although his diatribe was hailed as the standard textbook on anti-Semitism, its author was even-handed in his denunciation of those he held responsible for what he saw as the corruption of an idyllic, pastoral, feudal France by a cosmopolitan capitalist conspiracy. This embraced the usual bugbears of the Catholic Right: Jews, Freemasons and Protestants – in short, everything that was 'unFrench'. He railed too at the aristocracy – 'la noblesse de cartes de visite' – for having renounced its historic role and prostituted itself before the 'Almanach de Golgotha'. (The *nouveau* Prince de Wagram and the undeniably *ancien* Duc de Gramont were married to Rothschilds.)

This agitation was a by-product of France's humiliation at the hands of the Prussians, and it was doubly unfortunate that many of the more prominent Jews in France were of German origin. At the conclusion of a libel action brought against him, Drumont shouted in court, 'Down with the German Jews! France for Frenchmen!' which his supporters in the gallery reduced to the response 'Down with the Jews!' Herzl attributed French anti-Semitism to hatred of the Rothschilds as much as to Drumont's demogogic talent. They were popularly perceived to have twice profited from France's misfortunes over the war indemnities stemming from the defeats of 1815 and 1870; the Republic's monogram RF was said to stand for Rothschild Frères. Drumont painted a more sympathetic portrait of Baron Hirsch than of the assimilated Rothschild brothers, whose father had never taken French nationality or lost his atrocious accent. Hirsch had 'none of the pride and arrogance of the Rothschilds . . . a cheerful parvenu, he is infinitely more open, more straightforward than the princes of Israel, and, altogether, less ridiculous. He is doubtless impudent, but his impudence is mocking and familiar . . . he happily plays the good-natured one with a touch of banter.' (His good humour, Drumont relates, was only affected by atrocious liver pains.)

Hirsch resurfaced in Paris in the year of the publication of *La France Juive*. The same year saw the rise of a national phenomenon in the improbable person of General Georges Ernest Boulanger. Boulanger – facetiously dubbed Emperor Ernest by the Kaiser – first drew attention to himself at a military review at Longchamps, where he cut an impressive figure as War Minister in full-dress uniform on his prancing black charger, Tunis, quite upstaging the sombrely clad President and other ministers. This performance was made the subject of a popular song which enjoyed immense success in the *café-concerts*. His reputation was enhanced by a shot aimed at him from the Strangers Gallery of the Chamber of Deputies, but lost some of its lustre through his discomfiture in a duel with the President of the Chamber: a precipitate sabreur, he was caught in the neck by the sword of his opponent, an elderly civilian, who was sprawled in a bush on which he had tripped. But in spite of his maladroitness with arms, Boulanger was the darling of the Paris mob, who needed a hero after the defeat of 1870, and the disaffected elements which attributed the corruption of France to the influence of Jewish capitalism. He was also adopted as the incongruous tool of the conflictingly ambitious Bonapartists and Royalists.

The popular support essential for a *coup d'état* was an expensive commodity to secure and retain. The editor of the nationalist newspaper *Le Gaulois*, the converted Jew Arthur Meyer, set about raising a war-chest for the now unemployed general's campaign. Count Münster, the German Ambassador in Paris, informed Berlin that the Rothschilds had hung back when touched by the Orleanists for fighting funds, but that 'Hirsch was not averse to putting a few millions on this card'. Hirsch, in fact, hedged his bets on a Royalist restoration, sharing his favours impartially between the mystic Comte de Chambord a few years before and the Orleanists, represented by the Comte de Paris, grandson of King Louis-Philippe. He is credited with having contributed £100,000 to the total £160,000 collected by the Duchesse d'Uzès for the Royalist Committee. The Orleanists fared less well. The German Foreign Ministry archives suggest that out of the Comte de Paris's contribution of some £32,000 to Boulanger's election fund, Hirsch had put up £20,000. But it may have been at the same time that another Orleanist, the Marquis de Breteuil, the party treasurer and friend of the Prince of Wales, solicited Hirsch's aid. Hirsch listened to his appeal, pulled reflectively at his moustache and at last wrote out a cheque. 'My knees shook under me,' Breteuil reported. 'It was for six million francs [£240,000].' (It was after lunching one day with the Marquis that Hirsch took the young Winston Churchill off on a visit to the Paris morgue, a popular tourist attraction. 'I was much interested', Winston wrote, although he was disappointed to find 'only three Macabres – not a good bag'.)

In January 1889 Boulanger was returned for a Paris seat with a huge majority. When the Foreign Office learned that the Prince of Wales, a friend of the Comte de Paris, was curious to meet Boulanger, a telegram was at once sent to the Embassy pointing out the undesirability of such a step. The Prince, however, discreetly secured an introduction, but 'thought him a poor creature'; neither did he consider there was the least chance of an Orleanist restoration,[*] while the Bonapartists were 'too lazy and unenterprising'. Boulanger wavered and missed his chance. But he still posed a serious threat to the government. Calling his bluff, they let it be known they were about to issue a warrant for his arrest. His nerve broke, he fled to Brussels, was tried for treason and condemned in his absence. Two years later Boulanger shot himself on the grave of his mistress, who had loyally supported him out of her own pocket. On his tombstone was inscribed 'A bientôt Marguerite'. Tunis ended his days between the shafts of a hackney carriage.

Rumours reached London from Paris that the French authorities were considering Hirsch's expulsion for his part in this fiasco. But by this time,

[*]President Thiers was himself dismissive of the Pretender's chances. The Comte de Paris, he judged, 'From a distance . . . looks like a Prussian, from close up like an imbecile.'

1890, Hirsch was frequently seen in the Prince of Wales's company around the capital and his ejection might have been judged too delicate.

Hirsch's predilection for the bluest blood was notorious, and his cash contributions to this preposterous adventure were seen rather as a means to 'open doors hitherto closed to him'. The gift to the Royalist Committee was indeed said to have included the condition of his election to the Cercle de la Rue Royale, a condition unfulfilled and which accordingly cost the uncompromising members the loss of their premises. But the doors of Paris had for the most part been open to him for many years, although his perverse manner must have put up the backs of not a few seigneurs. (He would not resist such raillery as that in answer to a request for aid for the wounded in the Spanish civil wars: 'I would like to give you some thousand-franc notes, but are you sure that this money will go to the Carlists?') Others evidently repaid him in the same coin. On being congratulated on the success of a dinner at his Paris home, he replied, 'Yes, but I swallowed insults with it.'

Hirsch was linked mysteriously with another member of the house of Orleans, Prince Ferdinand of Saxe-Coburg, who, elected to the Bulgarian throne as a young Hungarian army officer in 1887, nursed his country to full independence with shrewd calculation. His mother was the daughter of Louis-Philippe; his father's mother was the only daughter of the fabulously rich, and supposedly Jewish, Hungarian Prince Kohary. But if it were not for King Ferdinand's own admission to Theodor Herzl – 'I was really brought up by Jews; I spent my youth with Baron Hirsch. I am half a Jew, as people often reproach me' – both his roots and his relationship with Hirsch could be dismissed as fanciful supposition. But another near contemporary confirms that Ferdinand was 'a faithful friend' to Hirsch, and *The Times* obituarist stated that Hirsch was on 'intimate terms with Prince Ferdinand, a circumstance which, it is pointed out, led at one time to much speculation'. Unfortunately, the substance of this speculation is nowhere recorded. It is difficult to conceive that the bond was other than personal; by the time Ferdinand came to the throne, Hirsch had no bones left to pick in the Balkans. Hirsch may well have provided financial services to the new ruler; but there were no apparent political advantages in so doing.

Opinion was divided on Ferdinand's appearance. 'He was a typical Orleans . . . every feature of his interesting head disclosed that he was a scion of the French Royal Family,' wrote one whose father had been general manager of the Orient Railway in Constantinople. The veteran *Times* correspondent Sir Valentine Chirol considered that 'his features, and more especially his nose, betrayed his partly Jewish descent'. (The Kaiser dubbed him 'Der Naseferdinand' – the Nose-Ferdinand.) Opinion was, on the other hand, unanimous on the mental qualities of 'Foxy Ferdy'. King Edward admitted that he 'hardly ever felt so uncomfortable in my life as when that fellow got me into the corner . . . He's one of the cleverest men in Europe.' He was eccentric, foppish, always exquisitely bejewelled and bemedalled; his fancy for flowers and blond aides-de-camp was freely indulged, while he still fathered an heir and three siblings on a Bourbon-Parma princess. His irreverent and sardonic humour matched Hirsch's own. Showing off his capital to Alfred Rothschild, from whom he had procured a loan, he enquired, 'Dear Baron, what do you think my subjects are saying as they see us pass?' 'Sire,' replied Alfred smoothly, 'they must surely be saying "There is a sovereign who is congratulating himself on the progress of his people."' 'Not at all, they are saying, "Look at those two old Jews, each of them rubbing his hands because he thinks he has got the better of the other."'

There is one remote link which might have served to bring Hirsch and Ferdinand, thirty years his junior, into contact. Ferdinand's father's marriage had been arranged by his uncle, King Leopold I of the Belgians, one of whose closest friends and advisers was Senator Jonathan Bischoffsheim, Hirsch's father-in-law. There is final proof of a close attachment. News of Hirsch's death reached Ferdinand on an official visit to St Petersburg. *The Times* reported from the Russian capital that Ferdinand cut short his stay and made straight for Paris in order to attend Hirsch's funeral. Once there, he was closeted with the widowed Clara for half an hour before the ceremony. And almost ten years before, his elder brother was mentioned among the mourners at Lucien Hirsch's funeral.

Hirsch and Ferdinand had one identifiable bond. When the former's secretary, Martin Fürth, left his service, he converted to Christianity, joining the Jesuits. It was as a reward for this sacrifice, so Theodor Herzl understood, that he secured a similar post with Ferdinand. It is much more likely that Ferdinand simply accepted a recommendation from Hirsch, with whom Fürth had remained on good terms, than that he wished to accord a favour to the Society of Jesus.

It was doubtless difficult for the world to acknowledge that a disinterested and genuine friendship could have existed between this wily, wordly and not dissimilar pair. Each, the self-appointed entrepreneur and the elected ruler, had against all the odds successfully imposed himself on a distant, turbulent and devious corner of Europe, the

Balkans; each had a mind as sharp as his tongue. And Ferdinand was regarded as an upstart by the Tsar and Kaiser, who were as outraged by his pretensions as the members of the Cercle de la Rue Royale had been with Hirsch.

5

Philanthropy in the Pampas

In the summer of 1894 the Tsarevich, who succeeded his father as Tsar Nicholas II in November, brought his German fiancée, Queen Victoria's grand-daughter, to England. The Prince of Wales invited him to spend two days at Sandringham where he was auctioning a string of his horses. Nicholas, well-meaning, withdrawn, simple-minded with none of the physical presence or assurance of his towering Romanov relations, found the company, as he told his mother, the Princess of Wales's sister, 'rather strange. Most of them were horse dealers, amongst others a Baron Hirsch! The Cousins rather enjoyed the situation and kept teasing me about it; but I tried to keep away as much as possible, and not to talk.' For the shy twenty-six-year-old it must have been an unusual encounter; such company would have received short shrift at Tsarkoe Selo. Hirsch for his part would have had lots to say but, out of respect for his host, must have refrained from bearding the future Tsar of All the Russias about the state of his country, which had been steadily haemorrhaging in its side for the last fifteen years.

The greatest agglomeration of European Jews had been acquired by Russia through the partition of Poland at the end of the eighteenth century; upwards of three million were penned into the western borderland – the Pale of Settlement. Superstitious, inclined to mysticism, mostly speaking only Yiddish, they clung obstinately to their customs; landless, qualified for few trades, obliged to subsist in poverty, they were at the same time execrated by their neighbours as symbols of exploitation, particularly as the hated middlemen in the traffic in alcohol (the government monopoly made the peasant pay for his opiate at 125 per cent above its cost).

In 1855 when Alexander II, the emancipator of the serfs, came to the throne, many of the more onerous restrictions on his Jewish subjects were

eased; merchants able to pay £50 for their release, university graduates –
now eligible for government service – and soldiers whose term had
expired, were let out of the Pale with their families. But universal
conscription, introduced in 1874, set off the first wave of emigration. Six
years later Natty Rothschild confided to Disraeli that he was concerned at
the influx of these aliens who arrived in a state of starvation and 'are
socialists until they become rich'. (He obligingly paid the passages to
Canada of 200 Jewish immigrant families.)

In 1881 the Tsar was blown up by utopian terrorists, who, not
unsurprisingly, counted Jews amongst their number. Alexander's
successor and namesake, the brother-in-law of the Prince of Wales, did
not become heir apparent until the age of twenty. He had received the
perfunctory education considered adequate for a grand duke and had
come under the sway of his tutor, Constantin Pobedonostev, dubbed the
'Black Tsar', a passionate obscurantist, nationalist and reactionary, and
the leader of the ascendant Slavophile party. Russification was thrust
down the throats of the unconforming races of the empire – German
Balts, Finns, Poles, Lithuanians and others. Non-Orthodox Christians
were harassed. The Jews alone were allowed to retain their language, but
they received few other concessions.

Within weeks of the Tsar's assassination, in the fervour surrounding
the Orthodox Easter celebrations, the first pogrom erupted, seemingly
simultaneously and spontaneously, across White Russia down through
the Ukraine and Bessarabia. Thousands of homes and shops were
destroyed, though loss of life was small. Helpless, hopeless and often
homeless, the great tide of refugees surged westward. The immediate
result in Russia was a commercial depression affecting the nation's credit.
Through the early 1870s, the London and Paris Rothschilds, agents for
the Tsar's Treasury, had raised almost £70 million in Russian loans. The
London house now warned the Finance Minister that unless his
government mended its ways the bank would withdraw from another large
loan for which the preliminary contract had already been signed. The
Tsar, piqued at such presumption, ordered overtures to be made to non-
Jewish sources in France, setting the scene for their alliance.

Baron Hirsch reacted to the news of the exodus with his customary
despatch: he sent one million francs to the Alliance Israélite's emergency
fund and two personal representatives, one his former alms agent in the
Balkans, Veneziani, to Brody on the Austrian border, where the refugees
gathered. In all Hirsch's deputies lavished some £200,000 for the
immediate relief of the marooned masses. The pogroms aroused a storm
of protest in the West. In London the Lord Mayor's Mansion House

meeting, to organize sympathy and support for the victims, caught the prevailing feeling, which was spoiling for a fight with Russia. In Paris Victor Hugo set himself at the head of a relief committee, but the Alliance Israélite itself refused to organize any demonstration for fear of provoking an anti-Semitic backlash.

Action was now needed. The most pressing problem was how to handle the flood of Jewish refugees. Western Jewry acted to resettle those who had already fled and to stem the outflow. Hirsch, single-handed, determined to improve the material position of the Jews remaining in the Pale. He activated a scheme similar to the one he had with such difficulty persuaded the Austrian authorities to approve in Galicia. He sent a delegation to St Petersburg to propose the establishment of technical schools, model workshops and agricultural training centres for which he proposed personally to provide the enormous sum of 50 million francs – £2 million.

This reckoning did not precisely coincide with Pobedonostev's strategy. He was prepared to consider only the extremes of conversion or emigration; amelioration of the condition of Russia's Jews did not figure on his agenda. Hirsch, ever accommodating, offered the Procurator of the Holy Synod, a consideration of one million francs to convince him. While Pobedonostev was not too proud to pocket the money, Hirsch, after a year of wrangling, broke off negotiations over the Russians' insistence that they retain control over the administration of the fund, a quite unacceptable risk.

Meanwhile a fresh influx of Jews had arrived at Brody. But indignation and initial sympathy for the victims was wearing thin. Condemning the cause, few had perceived the consequences. Their numbers were still small – no more than 25,000 émigrés reached Galicia in 1882 – but the European Jewish establishment viewed with alarm the prospect of being swamped by swarms of destitute exiles. Respecting the wishes of the great majority of refugees, the Alliance Israélite obligingly proposed to pass them on. But America's quarter of a million Jews entertained similar fears: their Board of Delegates insisted only skilled and unmarried workmen be sent. The Committee at London's Mansion House deemed these terms inadmissible, but the Alliance Israélite in Paris felt obliged to accept them. Predictably, the families of refugees refused to be separated, and towards the close of 1881 the Board of Delegates demanded an end to migration to the United States. As refugees continued to pour into Brody, the Americans relented the following year, expressing a willingness to resettle 10,000 newcomers – if the Europeans would cover the lion's share of the cost, some $1 million. This was never implemented, not from any shortage of funds but for fear that news of such bounty filtering back east would only trigger a further exodus.

The Anglo-French Jewish leaders next determined to stem the flood at source by advertising to the Jews in Russia that they could expect no relief for the first critical six months of residence in the West, while the religious authorities attempted to dissuade the eastern congregations, as pious as they were poor, that far from offering salvation, the West represented a spiritual descent on the strict path of the orthodox. There was now the added danger of Austria resorting to the mass expulsion of all refugees remaining on its territory. Veneziani, representing the Alliance Israélite as well as Hirsch, recommended that those with no trade – that is, the major part – should be sent back to Russia, but it was naturally difficult to persuade them to retrace their steps voluntarily. Their Viennese brethren even considered compelling those they considered 'wild men from the uncivilized East' to return with the assistance of the police. London informed the Alliance Israélite that none of the Brody refugees were acceptable in Britain, and as America refused to accept them 1,000 were repatriated in July 1882. Such treatment was defended by the justification that the Russians represented 'the worst element', that only that section of the Jewish community which perpetually appealed for charity had fled in the first place, and that against the advice of their own leaders. It was decided to do everything possible for the children of these unworthy émigrés, and to spend as little as possible on the parents.

By this time many of the refugees themselves had had enough. Some elected to return to Russia, having suffered more hardship since their flight from the pogroms. By the end of 1882 there were no refugees left in Brody. They were an embarrassment in France, now allied to Russia. A useful flow of trade followed the tricolour. Twelve years later, as a demonstration of national loyalty on the heels of a second wave of persecution in the Pale, prayers were offered in the leading Paris synagogue for the life and continued health of Tsar Alexander III. (It may have been mere lip service; he died ten days later.)

It was, however, towards America that Baron Hirsch looked for some practical solution to the problem of resettlement. The Baron's concern was not to scatter charity but to create communities which were self-supporting, and in 1889 the Alliance Israélite informed the American relief committees that Hirsch was ready to set up a fund to assist Jewish immigrants from Russia and Romania (another black spot), to establish a spread of agricultural and industrial settlements in order to prevent them crowding together in the cities. The Americans raised the old fear that such munificence would simply serve to attract an ever greater number of the destitute. This was indeed Hirsch's intention. It took him two years to break down this resistance, during which time he contributed $10,000 a month to the New York committee to help with short-term relief. His perseverance was eventually rewarded with the foundation of the Baron de Hirsch Fund in 1891 with an initial endowment of $2,400,000, later raised to $4 million. Among the first trustees was his friend from Constantinople, Oscar Straus. In the decade following the first pogroms 650,000 Jews, almost all from eastern Europe, reached Ellis Island. (Among the first generation of immigrants were the founders of the film industry and Hollywood: Louis B. Mayer and the Schenk brothers from Minsk, Schmuel Gelbfisz (later Goldwyn) from Warsaw, Lewis J. Zelenik* from Kiev, the Warner brothers from Krasmaskhilz, Sam Spiegel from Jaroslaw; and Al Jolson from Lithuania and Israel Baline (Irving Berlin) from Siberia.)

Baron Hirsch had so far had to face such cautious responses, and often downright opposition, to his resettlement schemes that he had begun to look around for a promised land of his own elsewhere in the Americas. His interest was aroused by a report forwarded him through the Alliance from a scientific researcher, Dr William Löwenthal, in the Argentine, then among the world's half-dozen richest economies. This country seemed to offer all the ideal conditions for colonization: a small population of around three million, a great deal of land, good climate and soil, and a government, moreover, eager to encourage immigration. Löwenthal pointed out that the $50 million Hirsch had saved in Russia and which was now burning a hole in his pocket would earn sufficient interest to settle 500 families each year on the land. He further commended the scheme by insisting on the eventual repayment of these advances by the settlers once they had established themselves. Hirsch sent out his own fact-finding mission of a British and Belgian engineer under Löwenthal. They returned with a favourable report and carte blanche from the Argentines. After other offers of tracts of land, notably from Egypt and Australia, which produced a squawk of alarm from antipodean Jews, he settled on the Argentine as the country of refuge. He is said to have been encouraged in this by the Prince of Wales.

He next had to tackle as a private citizen a problem which must have daunted any diplomatic mission – the orderly emigration of Jews from

---

*Lewis J. Selznick, as he was better known, sent Tsar Nicholas a cable on his dethronement: 'When I was a poor boy in Kiev some of your policemen were not kind to me . . . Stop I came to America and prospered Stop Now hear with regret you are out of a job . . . Stop Feel no ill will . . . If you will come to New York can give you fine position acting in pictures Stop Salary no object Stop Reply my expense Stop.'

Russia itself. In 1891, following a disastrous harvest, with thousands of people starving to death in the countryside or eating their frozen neighbours, the Tsar's government arbitrarily expelled thousands of Jewish artisans from Moscow and other towns. The fear of worse to come set off another exodus to the West. Although it was theoretically still illegal to leave Russia without a passport, a further 140,000 Jews fled Mother Russia in the following year. Hirsch chose as his ambassador an English journalist of the Radical Right, Arnold White. It has been deemed strange that a man with suspected anti-Semitic sentiments should have been picked for this delicate mission. This is a narrowly selective judgement. He campaigned hard for restriction on immigration into Britain, and it happened that such immigration was predominantly Jewish. To White, as to Lord Rosebery, the immigrants were 'undesirable aliens' suspected, not altogether without justice, of importing subversive dogma in their baggage, and there is no reason to believe he would have felt less strongly if they had instead been Orthodox Russians. He sniped at 'international capitalists', and these again happened to be mostly Jewish (and also Liberals, thus doubly damned). But he deplored popular outbursts of anti-Semitism and did not spare any member of his own party who fell below his own standards of public morality. Hirsch, indeed, was the epitome of one of his favourite bugaboos – 'cosmopolitan finance'. Such credentials commended themselves to the Russians, and White proved to be an inspired choice as a disinterested intermediary. It is noteworthy that eighteen months after Hirsch's death, White was still active in trying to 'work out' a solution for Russia's Jews with the British Ambassador in St Petersburg.

In May 1891 Arnold White, accompanied by an official of the local Jewish community who could speak the 'jargon', David Feinberg, set off on a great sweep through the Pale of Settlement, west to Minsk, down to Kiev and on south to Odessa. He was armed with letters of introduction and recommendation from Pobedonostev. White's first surprise was the unexpected opposition of the leaders of the weathy and privileged Jewish community in St Petersburg,* who were hostile to the emigration of their brethren on principle (and remained so even after their co-operation had been enlisted to expedite it). He was to find the Tsar's ministers more accommodating. White was well primed with the run-of-the-mill prejudices of St Petersburg, where he had so often heard the 'typical Jew' described as a 'compound of thief, usurer and pimp'; Pobedonostev had personally warned him, 'The Jew is a parasite.' White also expected that

---

*A measure of the degree of toleration their affluence had earned them is reflected in the performance in St Petersburg in 1912 of Saint-Saëns *Samson and Delilah* – in Hebrew – before the city's Jewish upper crust.

his companion would be often insulted on their travels, but this only occurred once, in Kiev, where Feinberg was ordered to leave the hotel on the grounds of his religion. 'I am bound to say', White wrote to Hirsch, 'that even on that occasion a visit to the Governor soon put matters right.' He judged the physique of the poor town dwellers largely inadequate for the hard labour of colonization; no more than 20 per cent were fit for the task. By contrast the 30,000 settlers at Kherson on the Black Sea plain were 'marked by all the characteristics of a peasantry of the highest character'. He discovered qualities in the Jew which 'more than compensate for his poverty in muscle . . . an astonishing capacity to sustain exertion for lengthy periods of time impossible to the stolid beer-drinking Englishman or equally self-indulgent Russ'. He praised the 'high moral tone of the average Jew', who was in general abstemious, a good family man, not addicted to the use of filthy or blasphemous language, patient and industrious. Sharing the Baron's belief in the regenerative powers of the soil, White considered the Jew could be 'moralized by sunshine and sweat'. ('Nihilism', he remarked, 'comes from empty stomachs and University training.' Hirsch would have nodded vigorous agreement.) In short, White enthused, 'if courage – moral courage – hope, patience, temperance are fine qualities, then the Jews are a fine people,' and would make successful colonists.

This encomium, perhaps unforeseen, bred false hopes and expectations. After he had reported to the Baron in Paris, White returned to St Petersburg in September to try to secure the 'public and cordial assistance' of the Tsar's government without which orderly emigration could never be organized. It might be thought that the Tsar would have been concerned at losing such potentially valuable subjects, but to him the Jews were irredeemable heretics, disloyal and ungrateful to boot. Even his more liberal-minded ministers had a more practical preoccupation: they were convinced that the ranks of the revolutionaries were half staffed by Jews (Chaim Weizmann considered this an understatement). As it was, White found the government co-operative and prepared not only to turn a blind eye to emigration but actively to support it: the costly passport system was modified, would-be emigrants were exempted from conscription, transport to the frontier was to be provided, and permission was granted to set up local committees inside Russia to vet the applicants and arrange their departure. It is certain that Arnold White, in order to win over the government, had painted an unrealistically rosy picture of the benefits that would flow from such generosity. The ministry was clearly persuaded that emigration would rid Russia of 20,000 Jews each year in the early stages, rising to 100,000 a year thereafter. Pobedonostev was enchanted with the sum: three and a half million Jews would leave over the next twenty-five years – that is, if he had known it, until the eve of the Revolution. (Unfortunately, the sump was more than sufficient to supply eager recruits from the growing Jewish proletariat and intelligentsia for the Jewish Marxist 'Bund' and the Social Democratic Labour Party, the architects of the real revolution.) Pobedonostev had overlooked one calculation: the conjugal couch. Some two million out of a Jewish populaton of five million – three-quarters of the worldwide reservoir – may have left Russia in the thirty-odd years from the first pogrom up to the outbreak of the First World War. The exodus had no effect in reducing their numbers. Nevertheless this carrot was effective in opening the door for their release. Hirsch personally appointed the members of the central committee which would oversee the scheme from St Petersburg; among them were the brothers Baron David and Horace Günzburg, who had played so hard for the Bulgarian section of the Orient Railway, and Baron Jacob Poliakoff, another banker, whose niece was married to Hirsch's brother James.

Baron Hirsch was perhaps surprised by the speed and ease with which his emissary had overcome Russian resistance, for there was one element of his scheme still missing. There was as yet nowhere for the emigrants to go. While White was haggling in Russia, Hirsch was creating the apparatus in London. Fully intending that a philanthropic venture of this magnitude should be run on proper business lines, he chose the form of a limited liability company, registering the Jewish Colonization Association in London in September 1891, in its time the greatest charitable trust in the world. The authorized capital was £2 million issued in 20,000 shares of £100 each. Hirsch subscribed for 19,993 of these. The Baron had up till then been dealing directly with the most autocratic, reactionary and capricious regime as a private individual. He now sought to enlist godfathers for his pet by invoking the association of international Jewry as a reassurance and guarantee for the Russian government. He issued one share each to the seven other signatories of the memorandum and articles of association. He thus brought in leaders of the Anglo-Jewish Association, the Paris-based Alliance Israélite, Lord Rothschild as President of the United Synagogue, and Ernest Cassel, Hirsch's representative in London. N. M. Rothschild & Sons was appointed bankers. This was just a first taste of Hirsch's munificence. The following year he donated a further £7 million to the Jewish Colonization Association, a total more than twice the annual budget for the Russian Imperial Navy. (With his strong views on the morality of all taxation, Hirsch must have been nettled in 1894 by Sir William Harcourt's introduction, in defiance of the hostility of the Prime Minister, Lord Rosebery, of the first consolidated death duties on estates; the Association found itself liable within two years to the top rate of tax at eight per cent.) Hirsch divested himself of a parcel of his shares as a gift to the Anglo-Jewish Association and the Alliance Israélite, though he was careful to retain the voting rights for life. His remaining shares he bequeathed in his will to the Jewish communities of Frankfurt, Brussels and Berlin; the over-proud burghers of Vienna were passed over.

The way was now open for Hirsch to colonize the Argentine. The sheer wealth of means at his disposal aroused the envy of other philanthropic organizations and the opposition of the fledgling Zionist movement; Chaim Weizmann likened any deflection from Palestine as a goal to 'a form of idolatry'. There were misunderstandings and mismanagement which bred disenchantment and vituperation. The Baron suffered his own share of disappointments, but these did not deflect him: he took the reins more tightly in his hands and applied a touch of the spur. He expected no thanks and was not disappointed. His ambition was quite up to his generosity. He envisaged at one time snapping up an entire province of the Argentine and even floating it off as a separate Jewish State.

While Arnold White was still talent-scouting in the Pale of Settlement, Dr Löwenthal had been packed back to the Argentine with a commission to acquire land, put up houses and provide equipment and livestock to furnish plough-power and food. Löwenthal already had two small embryo settlements, one 300 kilometres south-west of Buenos Aires, the other in the remote north in Sante Fé province, but he was thwarted in his attempts to extend these – the Baron thought the price of land too high. And before White had come to an agreement with the Russians, before Hirsch had set up his Association, 775 immigrants were on their way with another 4,000 expected on their heels. Nothing had been done to prepare for their arrival. Löwenthal sent frantic messages to stem the flow, which was partly prompted by his own over-optimistic reports, but as yet there was no one to heed him. To add to his problems another large party of Jews, stranded in Constantinople on its way to Palestine, was heading instead for the Argentine. The first two shiploads of Russians landed at Buenos Aires to a cold welcome. A portion of the local Jewish community, hostile to immigration, spread rumours among the newcomers that the food handed out to them was not kosher and that they were to be sold into slavery. (Some, in fact, of the indigenous Jews were themselves prominent in the white slave trade, for which Buenos Aires was a flourishing centre.) When the refugees arrived at their settlement after a twelve-hour train journey with only dry biscuits for sustenance – followed by, for the men, a tramp on foot through a violent thunderstorm – they found nothing but an old warehouse, sufficient shelter for the women and children only. Their supervisor, an Italian Jew converted to Christianity, could neither understand them nor make himself understood. It was not long before the new arrivals rioted and the police had to be called in to quell them. This was very much a pattern of what was to follow over the years.

Worse was to come. The first crop of the northern colony was destroyed by locusts. The settlers, unable to work their own land because of lack of implements, hired their Christian neighbours to sow their seed. Hirsch, only partially informed and totally ignorant of local conditions, flew into a rage at this news. Löwenthal was commanded to ensure that all the colonists worked fifteen hours a day for seven days a week, and to expel all those who could not stand the pace. Löwenthal demurred, foreseeing that this would have a disastrous effect on world opinion, already sceptical where it was not downright hostile. (Furthermore, there was a practical deterrent: by the terms of the agreement White had reached with the Russian government, an indemnity was payable for each returning emigrant.) Hirsch lost faith, or patience, and sacked Löwenthal in November 1891. He died three years later, a broken and frustrated man, at the age of forty-four. Until the Baron's own death five years later, no fewer than six chief administrators, sometimes in double harness, came and went. He had by now come to appreciate, as he told the *Jewish Chronicle*, that 'my difficulty here is not in money, but in men. I am in want of directors for this company.' (He was as determined as ever to run it with all the authority of president and principal shareholder.) 'Men who have the necessary moral and mental capacity for grappling with the work of so complex and difficult a nature are not easily obtained. I am looking for them.'

Meanwhile pressure to emigrate was still building up in the Pale. Hirsch felt impelled to issue a sternly patriarchal proclamation to the Jews of Russia, exhorting them to be patient, and as the heirs of their fathers who had suffered so much for centuries to 'bear this inheritance yet awhile with equal resignation'. But by 1893 the worst of the rush was over, not least because of the dire reports coming from the Argentine and the hostility of the leading Hebrew paper in St Petersburg.

The Baron had high hopes of his next choice of administrator, who had been personally recommended by the Prince of Wales as a man who could stiffen the sinews of the recalcitrant colonists. Colonel Albert Goldsmid was a remarkable man from a remarkable family. His father, a converted Jew, had been a distinguished Indian civil servant, a member of the Bombay, and then the Viceroy's, Council. His uncle, a major-general, had come out of retirement and was even then organizing Sir Garnet Wolseley's intelligence service in the successful Egyptian campaign. Goldsmid, seemingly ignorant of his Jewish origins until his father's death, had converted back to the old faith at the age of twenty-four with his wife and children, taking the name of Michael. He had recently served as Deputy Quartermaster-General and was now granted furlough by the War Office. A Zionist at heart, he looked on the Argentine experiment as a 'nursing ground' for Palestine, a notion he presumably concealed from his employer. His task was defined by Hirsch: to impose discipline, to send back any who shirked work or were not content with a bare diet, and to treat cases of mass insubordination with mass expulsion.

The new taskmaster arrived in Buenos Aires on the eve of Passover 1892 and at once issued a minatory message in the name of 'Michael' –the Archangel who favoured the stick over the carrot – 'of the people of Israel, called Lt. Col. Albert Eduard Wilhelmsohn Goldsmid'. The substance was clear: 'obey with a glad heart those set in authority over you', and to choose 'between boundless salvation and boundless misery'. He reinforced this admonition with an impressive entrance. Welcomed by the curious settlers, for whom the sight of a military uniform was not naturally reassuring, flanked by elders and rabbis bearing scrolls of the Torah, the colonel drove through their ranks in full-dress uniform seated in a landau drawn by white horses. He greeted the settlers in Hebrew, ending with an exhortation in Yiddish: 'Our idea is great! We will begin with the A of Argentine and end with the Z of Zion.' (His efforts to make himself understood were appreciated; too many of the other administrators and overseers, educated in the Alliance Israélites francophone schools in the Near East, could not communicate with their charges.)

Goldsmid did manage in a quartermasterly fashion to introduce some promised discipline, economy and reforms, cutting back on the Association's local management, which had multiplied at a faster rate than those it was there to serve. But he was too peremptory with his patron, demanding not unreasonably that decisions be taken in Buenos Aires (by himself) rather than in Paris (by the Baron). He resigned after fifteen months, founded the Jewish Lads' Brigade and in a few years saw active service as the 6th Division's chief of staff during the Boer War. His mission had attracted the attention of the Foreign Office. The British Vice-Consul in Buenos Aires produced a full, thorough but somewhat optimistic paper on the experiment which, he considered, had 'succeeded beyond all expectation', not an opinion shared by the promoter.

Fault was not all on one side. Only a tiny proportion, some 2 per cent, of the Russian Jewish émigrés had any farming experience; the greater part were small traders, shoemakers and tailors, with little aptitude and less enthusiasm for the hard and solitary life on the pampas. The average colonist, in Arnold White's view, was 'keenly sensible of his rights, and not over sensitive to his duties'. This awkward dissonance was now exacerbated. The Jewish Colonization Association was a commercial, albeit non-profit-making, enterprise in keeping with the Baron's puritan philosophy of philanthropy. In 1894 he felt the time had come after three years of grace and favour to enforce the settlers' contracts. A typical family's debt – for transport, maintenance, livestock, seed and his land, some 185 acres a family on average – was between £270 and £300. The farmers were now called on to repay this in twelve annual instalments with a charge of 5 per cent for interest. There were in addition stringent conditions of tenure and usage; if broken, the property would revert to the Association. To many, grown accustomed to seemingly limitless bounty, this came as a most unpleasant shock. The timing also was unfortunate. There were simultaneously disputes over the marketing of grain and the surplus, if any, the colonists were allowed to retain for their own use. The next harvest failed: frost followed by a heatwave accounted for the southern colony's crops; in the north rains flattened the wheat; there was drought elsewhere. And at this moment the administrators indelicately chose to announce that the settlers would be expected to bear the cost of harvesting a disappointing crop without any assistance from the Association. Open rebellion broke out, the colonists calling on the police and provincial governments to protect them from their own administration. The Buenos Aires newspapers took the part of the colonists. The Association thereupon moderated its conditions. This incensed Hirsch who, thousands of miles away, wanted the ringleaders punished; indeed, he had it in mind to set an example by sending all the settlers back to Russia. He relented, however, and suitable concessions were made. The anti-Semitic newspapers in Russia dwelled delightedly on these misfortunes, but they also provided fuel for the many vocal critics of the venture among Jews themselves. The abuse continued long after the founder's death. Ill-advisedly, the Association felt no need to placate opinion and remained magisterially aloof, complacent in the independence its ample funds allowed it. But whatever Hirsch's private doubts, even despair, he kept up a brave front in public, insisting that the Argentine colonies would yet be the home of hundreds of thousands of Russian Jews.

Unless he was singularly misinformed, the Baron was whistling to keep up his spirits. By 1895 the Association owned over 470,000 acres, of which barely 10 per cent were cultivated. These supported only 1,222 families, and by the next year this figure had dropped to 910 families, or 6,757 persons all told. One in ten of the immigrants was unsuitable – unwilling or incapable – and was 'got rid of, root and branch' without ado. (Their travel expenses, though, were paid by the Association, most of them making for the United States.) Many wished themselves back in Russia where conditions, if more uncertain, were less demanding; others were discouraged by the poor crops. Much of the land was inferior; the Baron had refused to pay Löwenthal's price for the richer land on the grounds that the settlers would never be able to afford to repay the Association. (It is evident that he continued to be as severe on himself as on the administrators of his philanthropy. Lady Augusta Fane, dining at the Amphitryon Club in Albemarle Street, just around the corner from Bath House, encountered an elderly lady 'who looked like a German hausfrau' with her husband, who was arguing loudly with the waiter and complaining bitterly over the price of chips on his bill. The haggler was Hirsch.) Too often the Baron's physiocratic notions did not, in the harsh light of experience, match the settlers' own ambitions. Only half of all the families brought to the Argentine stayed on the farm. The children, after attending the Jewish colonies' schools, flocked to the towns and universities, followed by their elderly parents. As one of the colonists commented, 'We have sown wheat and harvested doctors.'

There was, too, a contradiction. Hirsch envisaged the establishment of semi-autonomous, self-governing entities in an alien state. The Argentine government was averse, for social and political reasons, to such self-contained and self-perpetuating colonies in its midst. The goals Hirsch had set himself were unattainable. He never lost faith in his ideal, only in its agents. To David Feinberg, secretary of the Association's St Petersburg central committee, he sadly confessed that he had lost confidence in the directors and the colonists themselves. He had never visited the settlements, or even the Argentine, and, perhaps imagining his firm hand could still salvage something from the wreckage of his great dream, he planned 'to charter a first-class British ship' to take a hundred newspaper correspondents with him to show off his achievement. He died before the plan could be realized. After his death the Association, forever dogged by controversy and criticism, Jewish especially, spread its work to Russia itself, to Brazil, Canada and the United States and, lastly, to Palestine.

One of the party Hirsch had hoped to carry across the South Atlantic with him to admire his colonies was Theodor Herzl, the father of Zionism. The year before, Herzl had covered the Dreyfus trial in Paris for his paper, the Vienna *Neue Freie Presse*. He had witnessed the popular frenzy whipped up by Drumont and his like; he had witnessed the degradation of the disgraced but dignified staff officer who, before crowds of conscripts, had intoned, 'Vive la France! Je jure que je suis innocent,' while the mob behind the railings of the Ecole Militaire bayed for his blood. He had been shocked that such scenes were possible in 'republican, modern, civilized France, a hundred years after the Declaration of the Rights of Man'. Others shared his incredulity and dismay. After Dreyfus's later retrial, at which he was again found guilty but pardoned, Queen Victoria, thanking the British Ambassador in Paris for informing her of the 'monstrous judgement on the unfortunate Jewish victim', gave out that she would 'not go to France this year' (she had never had the intention of setting foot in foreign parts); more positively, a Strand chop-house keeper advertised his outrage by putting in his window a notice, 'No French beans will be served in this establishment.' French anti-Semitism was given a rest, and paranoia distracted, by Albion's perfidy at Fashoda and Gallic delight at its discomfiture at the hands of *les braves* Boers. Queen Victoria and her son succeeded the Rothschilds as the principal butts for scurrilous caricature, so that even the ardently Francophile Prince of Wales felt obliged to cancel his annual visit to Paris in 1900 because of the 'filthy abuse' of his mother and to miss the inauguration of the International Exhibition for fear of being publicly insulted.

Herzl went back to his room and sat down to draft his plans for *Der Judenstaat*, a national homeland for the Jews. This concept was anathema to the prosperous Jewish gentry of Central and Western Europe; a Jewish state offering Jewish nationality, in place of mere philanthropic settlements, offended their every instinct and raised an uncomfortable question mark over their own identity and loyalty. To counter such a subversive notion, the London Rothschilds financed the League of British Jews and shut their doors to the architect of Zionism. (Ironically, it was to the second Lord Rothschild that A. J. Balfour, as Foreign Secretary in the wartime coalition, addressed his Declaration; it was left to Edwin Montagu, son of the devout Jew Lord Swaythling, to wage a bitter rearguard action as Secretary for India in the interest of the Empire's Muslim subjects.)

Herzl now wrote to Hirsch out of the blue, requesting 'a Jewish-political conversation'. Hirsch replied, telling him first to put his ideas on paper and mark the envelope 'Personal'. Herzl was a difficult personality – self-conscious and naive, swinging between optimism and sulky despair. Intemperately tactless, he had an unfortunate habit, for a proselytizing preacher, of haranguing his listeners.

He did not go out of his way to ingratiate himself with the great philanthropist: the Association, he wrote, was 'as generous as it is mistaken, and as costly as futile'. Hirsch, perhaps both irritated and amused by this presumption, nonetheless agreed to see him in Paris on 2 June 1895.

Herzl was as sensitive about himself as he was insensitive to the feelings of others. 'When I am dealing with famous or well-known people,' he acknowledged, 'I often become ridiculous through embarrassment.' He dressed himself for this rendezvous with discreet care; he had purposely broken in a new pair of gloves the day before so that they would still look new, but not fresh from the shop; yet 'Rich people must not be shown too much deference' was another of his maxims. Herzl was prolix, Hirsch patient; his guest had asked for an hour on the ground that 'I need that amount of time merely to indicate how much I have to say'. They had the same views on philanthropy: it was mistaken. 'You breed beggars . . . ,' Herzl said, preaching to the converted, ' . . . it debases the character of our people.' 'You are quite right,' agreed Hirsch. Herzl scolded Hirsch for having before anything else built a house 'of uncertain fame' in the Argentine; instead, his first duty must be to raise the general moral level of the people before emigration could be considered. Hirsch responded vigorously: 'No, no, no! I do not want to raise the general level. All of our misfortunes come from the fact that the Jews want to climb too high. We have too many brains. My intention is to restrain the Jews from pushing ahead. They shouldn't make too much progress. All of the hatred against us stems from this.' He admitted that all had not begun well in the Argentine: 'True, at first some worthless fellows were sent over, whom I would gladly have tossed into the sea . . .' There was no great meeting of minds. 'You have such visionary notions,' Hirsch said despairingly. He must have been eyeing nervously the bundle of notes in Herzl's hand, some twenty pages of them, but Herzl was not more than a quarter of the way through when he rose to leave. 'I will go to the German Kaiser,' he admonished Hirsch, 'and he will understand me, for he has been trained to judge big things.' Hirsch's eyes twinkled. Herzl interpreted this as respect for his daring and drive.

As they made for the door, Hirsch asked, 'Where will you get the money? Rothschild will subscribe 500 francs.' (He was wrong. Herzl did not get as much.)

'The money? I will raise a Jewish national loan of 10 million marks [£500,000].'

'Fantasy! The rich Jews will give you nothing. Rich people are worthless; they care nothing for the sufferings of the poor.'

'You talk like a socialist, Baron Hirsch.'

'I am one. I am perfectly willing to hand over everything, provided the others do likewise.'

Herzl returned once more to the breach the next day. 'At the utmost,' he upbraided Hirsch, 'you can stem the course of evolution for a brief moment, and then the whirlwind will sweep you away . . . Are you aware that you pursue a ghastly reactionary policy? Fortunately your resources are insufficient . . . Your intentions are good,' he conceded as a condescending if reluctant afterthought. 'Would you like to make a wager with me? I shall raise a national Jewish loan. Will you obligate yourself to contribute 50 million marks when I shall have raised the first 100 million?' – a tenfold increase on his original projection. Hirsch made no reply to this challenge, but Herzl showed himself equally persistent, though more peevish. He wrote again on 18 June admitting that as the Jews were not yet desperate enough to listen to him, he was demoralized and was throwing in his hand. He did, however, propose a solution: to weld all the secondary Jewish banks into a 'formidable money-power' to fight the Rothschilds, 'to pull them in with us, or pull them down – then over and across'. Although he was personally done with Zionism as a practical proposition, 'I cling to the theory of it and cherish it.'

This time Hirsh did reply, two weeks later. Herzl imagined that his interest had been engaged by the fate he had conjured up for the Rothschilds and that this had 'struck home'. But Hirsch, doubtless moved by the underlying sincerity and unquenchable faith of this Austrian journalist with no political experience, answered that he would be delighted to see him again but that he had not in any way modified his views. Indeed, it is impossible not to be touched by Herzl's great spirit allied so inconveniently to his prickly ego, trying so hard to impress. 'I was greatly annoyed', Herzl rebuked Hirsch on 5 July, 'that you did not reply at once to the letter I wrote to you after our conversation.' Now, the self-appointed shepherd disappointed in his flock, he decided that he would still do something *for* the Jews, but not *with* them. He repeated that he would take his problems to the Kaiser. He was even worried that his reputation might be tarnished if his letter by an unlucky accident fell into other hands and he should be thought to be cadging: 'It's damnably compromising to write to rich people.' But now, he told himself, after receiving a chillier reception elsewhere on his rounds, 'If this man goes along with me, we may really change our times.'

Time passed. Herzl was immersed in his plans for the first Zionist Congress in Basel. His tract on the *Judenstaat* had been published; he had sent copies to everyone but Hirsch. Then on 21 April 1896 he wrote to

Max Nordau, doctor, author and Zionist ally of Herzl, to request him to sound out Hirsch over the prospect of 'a few millions' for a settlement in Palestine – 'and we will be able to spend something for baksheesh in Turkey'. The following afternoon, one hour after he had posted this letter, the news of Hirsch's death reached him. 'Perhaps I did not know the right of way of handling Hirsch . . . ,' he later said regretfully. 'For I always believed that I would still win [him] over to the scheme.'

This was wishful thinking. Years before, they might have found common ground; their views were closer than either man realized. Herzl, unlike the later Zionists, was not wedded irrevocably to the creation of a Jewish homeland in Palestine; he found only the 'powerful legend' of the Holy Land in its favour, and he was later prepared to accept a British offer of a tract of East Africa for an autonomous Jewish settlement. The Alliance Israélite was opposed to sending destitute refugees to an impoverished land, believing that this would only produce more beggars. Hirsch's agent Veneziani had indeed begun to distribute aid to one or two early colonies of Jews in Palestine, but Hirsch put a stop to this when he heard that the French Baron Edmond de Rothschild was engaged in similar activities. (Rothschild insisted on anonymity so as to shield the family name from such an unpopular course. He was as hard a taskmaster and as ruthless a disciplinarian as Hirsch in the Argentine.) Hirsch also had practical and political reasons for preferring South America. There was a real and pressing problem to resolve which could not wait on the political process of coming to terms with the Sultan. There was also the further threat that the Ottoman Empire itself might fall into the hands of the Russians, a cruelly ironic fate for any newly settled Russian Jewish refugees in Palestine. This was not a remote possibility at that moment. The current feeling against Turkey in England, the only Power which might have felt impelled to intervene, was such that 'no government would venture', in the opinion of Edward Hamilton at the Treasury, 'to move a ship or a soldier to prevent [Russia] occupying the Bosphorus'. Hirsch had been prepared seriously to consider alternative sites for his colonies in the Americas or Australia, but he had satisfied himself, after consideration and examination, that Argentina was a superior prospect. He was now too deeply involved to withdraw, and his resources, as Herzl had so obligingly reminded him, were not without limits. Herzl, motivated only a year or more previously by the chance of the Dreyfus trial, was too late. But as a tribute to Hirsch, he always reckoned that the day of his visit to the Rue de l'Elysée marked the inauguration of his Zionist movement.

Baron Hirsch had sold his shoot at St Johann in Hungary the year before for £300,000 to his fellow Bavarian, and now German Chancellor,

Prince Hohenlohe. The reason for the sale, it was said, was Hirsch's reluctance to pay the annual indemnity of some £4,000 to his peasant neighbours for the damage his deer caused to their crops. He had bought in its place the 88,000-acre estate of Ogyalla in Hungary. Here he had started to build the Château Gereuth (named after the estate in Bavaria from which the family had taken its title) where he hoped to entertain in the coming season the Prince of Wales and the French President, Félix Faure (a genial *mondain* who a short time later died in the Elysée in the arms of his horrified mistress). Hirsch was staying with a friend near the estate where he could keep an easy eye on the progress of what he admitted was his folly. On the morning of 20 April 1896 he was found dead in his bed by his valet, the victim of an attack of apoplexy. He was sixty-four.

His widow, Clara, was named in his will as his 'universal heiress' except for a number of special bequests; should she decline, his whole estate was to pass to the Jewish Colonization Association. He also left one million francs to be divided equally between Jewish and interdenominational charities in Vienna where, as an Austrian citizen, his will was to have been proven. There had been a surge of anti-Semitism in the capital in the year before Hirsch's death. Dr Karl Lüger, a personable demagogue and Christian Socialist, had been elected mayor, although ratification was delayed by the authorities for two years. Jews, who accounted for some 10 per cent of the capital's heterogeneous population, were banned, with Social Democrats, from the city administration, notwithstanding that he counted Jewish trade unionists among his closest associates and his party admitted converted Jews to membership ('I myself decide who is a Jew,' he proclaimed). Nationalist clubs decreed that their members should not fight duels with Jews, who were unworthy of bearing arms. The government did its best to cool tempers, dissolving student societies which passed anti-Semitic resolutions, but Lüger held on to the Rathaus for ten years and enjoyed the doubtful distinction of being direct in line to a later and more dangerous Austrian-born demagogue, who saluted him in *Mein Kampf* as 'the greatest German Mayor of all time'. In the year of Lüger's election, Hirsch, in a codicil to his will, had substituted the Brno courts for those of Vienna, despite the complicated international ramifications of his affairs, and Moravian charities for Viennese. One family responsibility preoccupied him. He left 'before all others' one million francs to his adopted eleven-year-old daughter, Luciena Premelie Hirsch, presumed to be his studious son Lucien's by-blow by the Hungarian singer Irene Premelić. (Luciena was born in the year before Hirsch had proposed his son as a suitable husband to Margot Tennant.)

He appointed as her guardian Clara's brother-in-law, Georges Montefiore-Levi, a Belgian senator, whose wife was placed in charge of Luciena's education and upbringing. Her mother or any of her maternal relations were strictly forbidden to interfere in any way, and every measure was to be taken to ensure that Luciena was prevented from laying her hands on the capital during her life. But the Baron had left two other little legacies to his wife who were not mentioned in his will.

The Viennese newspapers noted that Hirsch had been seen accompanied by two teenage boys whose mother was believed to be Anglo-Saxon. They went by the name of Maurice Arnold and Raymond de Forest-Bischoffsheim. This would have aroused little curiosity were it not for the Baron's obsessively secretive nature. He was generally believed to be the father, but the identity of the mother remained a mystery. There were few clues; both boys had been born in Paris, were the legal wards of Altgraf Franz zu Salm-Reiffenscheidt, a colleague from Hirsch's railway days, and later qualified for American citizenship. The *Semi-Gotha*, which purported to chart the family trees of those of Jewish blood, claimed that the boys hailed from the old French aristocractic family of de Forrestier. According to Hirsch family legend, the two were the products of such a shocking mésalliance that the greatest secrecy had to be preserved to conceal the mother's identity, and an obliging American couple handsomely stood in as putative parents, and were generously paid for the loan of their identity before discreetly disappearing. (The boys were described on their birth certificates as the legitimate children of Edward Deforest, rentier of New York, and his wife Juliette.) This intriguing and romantic story has never been proven; the Conde de Barcelona, son of King Alfonso XIII of Spain, lent it some credence by once telling Maurice Arnold's son, 'We have something in common, we are both Habsburgs', but would not elaborate. Hirsch's Austrian descendants believe in a more prosaic and plebeian origin. A Miss Deforest, an American art student in Paris, was set up in her own establishment by the Baron who kept his identity to himself and Miss Deforest on short commons. Walking once on the Champs-Elysées, she spotted her parsimonious protector driving past in a spanking equipage. Her companion revealed his true name and fortune. Furious at the deception, she took her offspring round to the Rue de l'Elysée and dumped them on the doorstep, never to see them or their father again.

Three years after Hirsch's death, in failing health herself and having lost her own son, Clara, in an act deserving a citation for selflessness, adopted all three little bastards so as 'not to die childless'. She then petitioned the Imperial court to have her husband's barony transferred to the progeny of her menfolk's liaisons. Raymond, the younger boy, was sickly; Maurice Arnold, then aged twenty, had been educated at Eton and had recently come down from Christ Church, Oxford. They had independent means and Clara left them each £200,000 as a bonus in her will. As it was a Bavarian title and other members of the family were still flourishing there, she was persuaded to change her petition for the creation of an Austrian barony; since the boys were Americans and republican, there was no need for any official authority, the United States certainly seeing in this ennoblement 'a special act of the very highest graciousness for these two citizens'. The application was supported by the Minister of the Interior and was granted by Franz Joseph. It was assumed that this favour was given as a reward for waiving Crown Prince Rudolf's old debt, but Minister Thun cited Clara's great munificence as justification. These 'extraordinarily rich and, in Austrian circumstances, really rare acts of charity' – she had given away something just short of £500,000 over the last two years – had been rewarded with the Hungarian Order of Elizabeth, First Class.

Barely a month after Clara had won over the Emperor to her 'heart's desire', she died in Paris on 1 April 1899. To the end she had continued to cherish her husband's charitable institutions, even those 'he may not have remembered in his will', such as the young Deforest-Bischoffsheims. She had added $15 million for Jewish and general charities and in her own will left a further $10 million to a collection of other good causes throughout Austria-Hungary as well as in Paris, New York and Jerusalem. (Herzl wrote ungraciously and untruthfully to Jacob Schiff, one of the trustees of the late Baron's American Foundation, deploring the activities and unhelpfulness of the Jewish Colonization Association, and sneering, 'Hirsch's relatives now at least have the satisfaction of knowing that the poor Jews too didn't get anything of his money.') Clara had also set up a foundation to provide convalescent and maternity beds in Munich, Hirsch's home town. The city fathers honoured this gift by naming a street Hirsch-Gereuth Strasse. (This street disappeared in the course of redevelopment in 1935, but there was a happy postscript: in 1945 another street, the former Julius Schreck Strasse, named after the SS Brigadier and Hitler's driver, was renamed Klara von Hirsch-Gereuth Strasse.)

No other memorial was put up to honour the name and prodigious bounty of this remarkable couple, though New Yorkers considered one. Jacob Schiff gave his reason for holding himself aloof from the appeal for contributions: from his personal acquaintance with the Baron and Baroness de Hirsch, he wrote to the *New York Times*, he did not hesitate to say that nothing could have been further from their minds than to be commemorated in stone and iron, that if the ideals and endeavours embodied in their foundations could not 'secure honour and permanency to their memory, no words or monuments could do this.'

Of Clara's adopted children, Luciena won her independence by securing the hand of her own banker in marriage. Raymond died in 1912, aged thirty-two. His brother, by then Baron de Forest, became a naturalized British subject four years after his father's death and received royal assent to continue the use of his title; he dropped his father's forename and never acknowledged his Jewish roots. That same year he joined the Prince of Wales' Militia; he served on the London County Council and saw active service in the Great War as a temporary Lieutenant Commander in the RNVR; and for seven years he held a London seat as a Liberal Member of Parliament. He remained a close friend of Winston Churchill, whom he had met with Baron Hirsch at Newmarket and in Paris, but his character was not as amiable as his nickname 'Tuty' suggested. Having inherited all of his father's radicalism, together with some of his wealth, the combination earned him a great measure of dislike and distrust which he did nothing to dispel.

6

Cassel: American Apprenticeship

The Prince of Wales noted Baron Hirsch's death in his diary without even a perfunctory expression of regret. Perhaps his social pretentions had palled; perhaps, as the radical wit Henry Labouchère suggested, he had tired of the unremitting regime of *parfait au Hirsch* at Marlborough House. By happy chance there was a remount at hand: the Prince had come on another and ultimate financial safety net in the solid shape of the late Baron's executor. Ernest Cassel, ten years younger than the Prince, was armed with complete knowledge of the Baron's affairs and intentions and, enjoying Hirsch's unlimited confidence, had absolute discretion in managing his estate. The transition was effected smoothly. Cassel and the Prince nodded in the paddock at the Derby in the year of Hirsch's death and were introduced by Lord Willoughby de Broke. (The Prince's horse Persimmon won, Cassel's was unplaced.) In December Cassel was commanded to appear at Sandringham.

The Nineties for the Prince were as much endlessly frustrating as naughty. Now in his mid-fifties, he regarded with something less than equanimity the unbridled antics of his nephews on the thrones of Russia and Germany, while he still struggled in leading reins; Nicholas he deemed 'weak as water', Wilhelm 'a political "enfant terrible"'. The Prince was fobbed off with the fancy uniforms of those foreign regiments of which he was allowed by his mother to accept the honorary colonelcy: 'Visit Emperor and present myself in new uniform . . . 10.15,' the Prince, in St Petersburg for the funeral of Tsar Alexander, recorded in his diary. (One of his suite, Lord Carrington, ushered into the Prince's apartments, was astonished to be faced with 'a fat man in a huge shaggy greatcoat looking like a giant polar bear. It was the Prince of Wales!!' fitting himself out in the uniform of the 27th Dragoon Regiment of Kiev.) Over the past seven years the Prince had enjoyed an increment of £36,000 a year from a reluctant Parliament. He had a successful season on the Turf in 1896, and the following year he was placed second in the list of winning owners, with earnings of almost £44,000. But he was still only able to make ends meet by eating into his capital, and that larder was fast dwindling. At the same time he had renounced yacht racing, which owed much to his patronage and had so enhanced his own popularity. The competitive Kaiser had appeared at Cowes with a bigger and better version of the Prince's own *Britannia* by the same designer. Unable to afford to compete, Edward sold his racing yacht to the inventor of Bovril, John Lawson-Johnston, after failing to persuade Boni de Castellane to take it off his hands for £10,000. (Boni was running through his wife's fortune – or that of her father, the American millionaire Jay Gould – creating a pink marble folly in Paris fashioned after the Petit Trianon. 'You need to be used to it, if you're going to handle all that money,' warned Baron Alphonse de Rothschild.)

Queen Victoria was a comparatively robust seventy-seven-year-old and was herself occasionally reminded by her comptrollers of the need for strict economy. Unlike Edward she considered it edifying to deny herself small pleasures: 'she thought to economize by having fewer different kinds of bread at breakfast!' she confessed to a lady-in-waiting. Such supreme self-sacrifice did not commend itself to her son.

Baron Hirsch is generally considered to have waived the Prince's debts in a verbal or written instruction to Cassel. This would have been a handsome quittance, but unfortunately the exact arrangements must remain a subject for conjecture. Hirsch left instructions for his own personal papers to be destroyed, and his executor had himself a negative attitude to prying posterity: he later told the Viennese journalist Sigmund Münz that although King Edward 'had written him important letters', he 'would have regarded it as a breach of trust not to have burned the majority of them . . . that all the accounts of the late King would contain lacunae which he alone could fill, but he did not feel that authorship was in his line, and certainly felt no obligation to complete the next generation's knowledge of history'. Edward's own papers were minutely weeded by the faithful Francis Knollys after his death, and even if such delicate matters were ever committed to paper, no correspondence between Cassel and the Prince survives from this early period. Just the tip, however, of a possible iceberg may be discerned in one minor and discreet property transaction. Hirsch had acquired Grafton House (otherwise known as the King's House) in the High Street of Newmarket, opposite the Jockey Club. Whether or not he left some wish regarding its disposal, Cassel pressed it on the Prince, though the gift was not at once taken up. It was only three months after Queen Victoria's death that the new King thanked Cassel for the 'renewal of your offer regarding Grafton House which sounds most tempting'. It was accepted though never occupied by Edward, who stayed on his frequent visits to Newmarket at Cassel's own place, Moulton Paddocks.

Of the seven luminaries of Anglo-French Jewry who were allotted one share each in Hirsch's Jewish Colonization Association, Ernest Cassel, though undoubtedly well past his first-million milestone, was very much the minnow. Indeed, he never joined the Jewish hierarchy, remaining all his life an outsider and loner – 'a partner', he explained, 'is a man who can commit you to things and I don't mean ever to be committed to anyone'. Twenty years Hirsch's junior, Cassel shared a common background with his mentor: an apprenticeship with the Bischoffsheims and a fascination with railways. They were each indifferent to the animosity and envy of the society to which they so tirelessly aspired, but while the Baron affected the blatant parvenu, Cassel, a truly self-made man, effaced all trace of it. In other respects, too, their temperaments were seemingly incompatible: Cassel was a dour, graceless and humourless character and did not in the least share Hirsch's preoccupation with the plight of his fellow Jews. The Baron, spry, jaunty, gave offence with his mocking banter, Cassel by his uncompromisingly blunt tongue. On the other hand, this very stolidity preserved him from any presumption: 'he had not had his head turned', the Treasury's Sir Edward Hamilton considered, 'or given himself airs or adopted any snobbish tendencies'. But beneath this forbidding and taciturn exterior, Hirsch had at once discerned Cassel's financial acumen. He took up the younger man in the early 1880s and promised him that 'whenever he wanted to do something big on his own account he would support him financially to the fullest extent'. With such an endorsement Cassel soon became a power, and over some three decades built up one of the most impressive fortunes in England and established himself as one of the most influential all-rounders, at home as much in the City as in Whitehall. He devoted his business career to amassing wealth and after his retirement was brought to admit, 'You know, money does not make for happiness.' Even while still in pursuit of it, he took little pleasure in the things it could provide. Social life was for him a means, not an end: he indulged dutifully in the high life, seeing it only as an obligation he owed to his position and wealth. As one who knew him wrote, he had 'something of that strange and barren inhumanity which is not rare among those whose abilities have long and exclusively been devoted to the acquisition of wealth', this ambition once achieved, life loses its savour and a 'curious impotence to experience pleasure results'. Yet despite this unpromising soil, their friendship was King Edward's warmest and most intimate attachment (excluding the opposite sex), perhaps of his life, certainly of his later years, and provided for Cassel the only real pleasure amounting almost to happiness that his wealth ever bought him.

If Ernest Cassel's brooding character was in most respects the antithesis of Hirsch's flamboyant style, any personal affinity with the expansive and boisterous Prince of Wales was surely grotesquely improbable. Cassel was eminently unclubbable – ordinarily a disastrous distinction for anyone hoping to win and hold the gregarious Prince's favour. He was, as painted with the deferential restraint of the obituarist, 'without superfluous urbanity' in contrast to the Prince's easy charm and natural courtesy; he was brusque to those beneath him and unforgiving of any slight or affront. While both men were subject to sudden rages, Edward's good humour quickly reasserted itself, usually in some generous act of contrition, whereas Cassel gave no man a second chance. The seeming incompatibility of their temperaments continued to puzzle those in the royal circle who were witness nonetheless to their incontrovertible friendship. Edward VII's official biographer, Sir Sidney Lee, did not attempt any explanation for this understanding between two men he knew well. He offered it as a simple fact that 'from that day onwards' – their first meeting – they 'were friends for life', and that 'their friendship had further been cemented by the sagacious advice which Cassel was enabled to give the King'. But investment management, however fructuous, does not by itself, gratitude apart, lead inevitably to any degree of intimacy. Sir Edward Hamilton, who respected both men, remarked that Cassel's 'attraction to the King is not self-evident' but for the fact that he 'has always liked to have a rich man at his beck and call', adding mischievously 'and by this means is able to benefit the *Favourite*' – and indeed many other, less intimate acquaintances. An ulterior motive was certainly one element, and not the least, but it does not satisfactorily explain that genuine regard that won the financier grudging recognition as 'Windsor Cassel'.

Mere money and the social position that it could buy meant little to Cassel. It was the power of such assets that he valued, and this fascinated Edward even after he became King: on two occasions at least he encouraged Cassel to keep him in touch with all the financial news, which 'greatly' and 'always interests me'. Solitary and self-contained, with riches beyond the reach of most, Cassel viewed with cynical detachment the scramble of other men for place and position; the Prince surrounded by self-seeking sycophants and suave courtiers, recognized his disinterested honesty and judged him 'the cleverest head in England'. Cassel offered cast-iron personal reliability, loyalty, and incomparable discretion. Perhaps the Prince, disparaged and disregarded by his mother, even saw in this severe and solid figure someone he could respect, who neither preached nor fawned.

Cassel succumbed to the conventional call of the Turf in 1889, the same year that Hirsch was bitten by horse fever. He entered a five-year partnership in a racing stud with the 'Diehard' peer, the eighteenth Lord Willoughby de Broke, and also took a lease on the eighteenth-century mansion, Compton Verney in Warwickshire, where he could contemplate his accounts in a Capability Brown landscape. It was at this period that Cassel and the Prince of Wales came face to face for the first time. They could not have failed to recognize one another, doppelgängers in the substantial flesh, in spite of the fact that Sir Felix Semon, one of Edward's doctors, though conceding the likeness, considered Cassel 'neither striking nor particularly attractive'. He elaborated with professional detachment: 'Of medium height, very thickset, of distinctly Jewish type' – Semon was a German Jew himself – 'with an almost bald head, short full beard, big nose, rather small eyes.' The pair even sounded alike, each with a North German burr. (Max Beerbohm twitted Edward's guttural rendering of the pre-Raphaelite 'Hhwossetti'; the spiteful Frank Harris detected in his strong accent 'an indefinable tang of the Jews'.) 'Skittles', the courtesan who had passed through the hands of Edward, teasing Wilfrid Scawen Blunt with court prattle, related that though Jewish businessmen such as Hirsch and Cassel were Edward's particular friends because they were generous, in the latter's case there was a blood tie: he 'was the illegitimate grandson of Prince Ernst of Saxe-Coburg, King Edward VII's uncle'. (This uncle Ernest would have had to be particularly precocious even for a Coburg; Duke Ernst I, Edward's grandfather, would have been a more plausible candidate and, indeed, was famously profligate. And the old rumour was revived that Prince Albert had been fathered by his mother's Jewish court chamberlain. No evidence, naturally, was ever produced to support this tale, while on the other hand it is impossible to prove a negative to the satisfaction of the sceptical.)

Sonia Keppel, the younger daughter of the King's last mistress, at first experienced difficulty in telling Edward and Cassel apart. She spent many Easters with her mother and 'Kingy' at Cassel's villa at Biarritz. A bashful child, she never dared raise her eyes higher than beard level, so played safe and curtsied to the cigar and rings. Ernest Cassel, too, sported a beard, wore rings and smoked cigars, so, more often than not, he collected a curtsy. Cassel was the more awesome of the two, and she never presumed to race slices of bread and butter, butter side down, along the stripes of his trousers for penny bets, a sport which the King affected to find hugely diverting. Sonia gradually learned through familiarity to distinguish Tweedledum from august Tweedledee: for one thing the latter laughed more easily. Though Cassel may not have been addicted to nursery games, Sonia, like her mother, came 'to rely on him as a living form of gilt-edged security'.

It was in pursuit of such a desirable status that Ernest Joseph Cassel, two months short of his seventeenth birthday, had first arrived in England with a bundle of clothes and a violin, of which little was later heard. The Cassels originated in Cologne. The first of the family of whom there is any record, Joseph, acted as 'Court Jew' to the seventeenth-century Wittelsbach Prince Elector Joseph Clemens, who doubled as Archbishop of Cologne, and whose subsidies from Louis XIV did not match his ambitions or his taste for high living. Joseph's descendant Jacob had three children, of whom Ernest was the youngest, and a small banking business in the same city. A friend and long-time colleague, the banker Saemy Japhet, claimed that Ernest Cassel's early life was happy, yet in his last year, when childhood memories might have been lightened by nostalgia, Cassel remarked to his social secretary, 'I think you must have had a very much happier home than I had when I was young.' His father's cousin, another Jacob, was the founder of a strictly traditional orthodox synagogue to counter the advances of relaxing reformist tendencies, and young Cassel's musical talent was called on to play its part in the service. The repressive religious discipline might well have cast a gloom over the boy, and if his father too was a domestic tyrant in the same mould as his son, this would have made for a joyless home, the atmosphere of which was described by Saemy Japhet as forbiddingly 'wholesome'.

Cassel, so he later stated, was tempted to follow his musical bent; his father, according to another version, offered him an alternative career as a 'professional chess player'. Neither held any certain prospect for an untried teenager, and the family bank yielded only a moderate competence. Instead, at the age of fourteen, he was put out to apprenticeship with a local banking firm, J. W. Eltzbacher, originally of Amsterdam. Two years later he took off. His motive for departure is not known; it was too easily ascribed by hindsight to restless ambition and that tenacity of purpose of which he later showed such proof. Family pressures may have driven him as well. Solicited later by a school friend for a contribution towards a new wing for a Cologne hospital, Cassel agreed to shoulder the whole cost of 200,000 marks on condition that a tablet be put up in honour of his old chiefs at Eltzbacher, whereas he might more naturally have commemorated his parents.

Early in the New Year of 1869 he landed in Liverpool, then the world's richest port, and secured a job with commodity merchants Blessig, Braun & Co., but after a little more than a year he exchanged the Mersey for the Seine, with a clerkship in the Anglo-Egyptian Bank in Paris in April 1870, barely six months after the opening of the Suez Canal. But the outbreak of the Franco-Prussian War in July made his continued presence in the country undesirable. Cassel returned to England and landed on Bischoffsheim & Goldschmidt's doorstep. This was in its way a natural resting place; the mainline Bischoffsheims of Paris owned the Franco-Egyptian Bank in Cairo and had that year raised a £7 million loan for the development of the Nile delta's sugar estate. Edward VII's biographer relates how Cassel applied directly for a vacancy as confidential clerk in a typically terse note:

Dear Sirs,
I apply for the position in your office and refer you to my former chiefs, Messrs. Eltzbacher, Cologne.
Yours sincerely,
Ernst Cassel

Impressed with such succinct self-confidence and weary of the florid and ingratiating style of the period, Henry Bischoffsheim exclaimed, 'That's our man.' The new clerk, not yet twenty, had been at his desk an astonishingly short spell when he was entrusted, on the strength presumably only of his character, with important and delicate missions on behalf of his employers. These were free-lenders, negligent and none too particular, who through cupidity and insouciance had been tempted into some unfortunate undertakings. Within a year of his engagement Cassel was sent out to Constantinople to salvage a piece of their business or, according to another tale, to Nicaragua where American navel teams were surveying a choice of routes for a prospective canal. His dextrous handling of such matters caused him to be remembered twenty-five years later at the Treasury for 'pulling Bischoffsheim "out of the mud"'.

There were other, less controvertible but still more contentious affairs, a legacy of unsavoury loans in Central America worth more than £5.25 million which had been issued by Bischoffsheim in London. In one year, 1872, the Dominican Republic and Costa Rica defaulted; Bischoffsheim was responsible too for the £3.5 million 'Honduras Loan Swindle' of the same year. These were a foretaste of other failures which led to the crash of financial markets in 1873. Once a government had been tempted to borrow – never too difficult a task – the public had to be persuaded to lend. Here the ability to make a market was paramount. All that was needed was enough capital to provide artificial stimulants. Financial journals mushroomed to supply this service.* After the first days following the launch, the proceeds of the loan itself could be used to keep the price buoyant on the Stock Exchange. This was so essential an element that stockbrokers themselves, such as Capel and Cazenove, brought out loans for governments and railways on commission. The borrowers, in the interim before default, used the loan to pay the interest. There was no redress for the bond-holders. When public opinion finally turned against this custom, Sir Henry James, a recent Liberal Attorney General, forced a reluctant government, Disraeli's second ministry, to appoint a Select Committee in 1875 to investigate 'the powerful and unscrupulous financial vultures' in this lucrative loan business. (The members included John Walter, proprietor of *The Times*, whose city editor, and director of the Rothschild São Paulo railway, had retired in disgrace the previous year with a fortune amassed on a modest salary, and 'Baron' Albert Grant, *né* Gottheimer, prior to his own unmasking for fraudulent company promotion.) Barings was the only bank to assure the Committee that it was not involved in rigging the market; Bischoffsheim & Goldschmidt was singled out for special mention with the recommendation that 'a remedy . . . ought to be found in the tribunals of the country'. The matter was quietly dropped, however, though the revelations did much to bring the foreign loan mania to an end.

For a débutant employee of a bank with such a dismal record, it was a delicate initiation. Ernest Cassel gave satisfaction and was proportionately prized. In the year before the Select Committee was set up he was offered promotion to manager and an increase in his salary from £200 to £500. 'You mean £5,000,' he countered. 'Quite so, quite so,' Henry Bischoffsheim hastily confirmed. 'I meant £5,000.' (Cassel later denied he had ever started life as a clerk, as legend had it, on as little as £1 a week, below the recognized poverty line: 'I never got less than £2 a week. I was not so cheap as all that.')

If Cassel's rise was spectacular, he attributed his success to a banal formula: 'Hard work, good information, and then instinct.' His decisions, he claimed, were never made by a conscious process of reasoning. Many others, however, followed a similar recipe, very few with such consistent success. Clearly Cassel's sharp instinct was the key. He had inherited multiple headaches from Bischoffsheim and had much early practice to help him develop his own special remedy, compounded of the elements of poker and chess. His firm was tied into railways, a peculiarly litigious

---

The Times, whose financial pages were regarded as a Rothschild newsletter, was known as the 'Jew's harp'.

branch of investment. After he took over the management, not one of the cases in which the company was involved came to court. In consequence lawyers feared him. He anticipated the precept of his future friend, Albert Ballin: 'Better a lean compromise than a fat lawsuit'.

Cassel's worldly success, however, was offset by family losses. In 1874, the year of his promotion, his mother, Amalia Rosenheim, died; within a year his father and elder brother Max followed her. His sister, Wilhelmina ('Bobbie') Schönbrunn, divorced with two children, Anna and Felix, was summoned to join him in London, where at his demand she reverted to her maiden name. He was already secure enough to award her more than her half-share in their father's modest £4,500 legacy. He was, indeed, by any standards a man of means, earning as much as a minister of the Crown, to which he could add commissions on his successful liquidations and rescue operations and a share in any profits. He was well able to support a wife and all the trappings. (A household managing on a mere £1,000 a year was, in the judgement of Mrs Beeton, able to support an essential male servant, a cook, upper and under housemaid with a nursemaid.) He took for wife Annette Mary Maud, daughter of the late Robert Thompson Maxwell, of Croft House, Croft on the borders of County Durham and the North Riding of Yorkshire. Although the bride was a Catholic, and reputedly a convert at that, the couple were married at Westminster Registry Office on 3 September 1878. Cassel assumed British nationality and settled in Orme Square; though he was just north of the Park, there was a compensating view of Kensington Palace across the Bayswater Road. In the following year a daughter, Amalia Mary Maud, was born, but after only three years of marriage Annette died of consumption. There was an unusual sequel. Almost twenty-five years later, the newly created Sir Ernest Cassel was waiting to be sworn in as a Privy Councillor. The Clerk of the Council, Sir Almeric Fitzroy, had considerately provided the Old Testament and a hat for Cassel to cover his head when taking the oath. Lord Rothschild, another of the postulants, averted an awkward incident by letting Fitzroy into a closely guarded secret. It had been Annette's dying wish that her husband should follow her into the arms of Rome and Cassel was, it was said, hastily baptized on the spot by the priest in attendance. Keeping faithfully to his promise, he took instruction for six months from the Jesuit Father Bernard Vaughan, paradoxically a popular preacher* against the gross materialism of the age of which Ernest Cassel was one of the most prominent pillars. Although he applied himself as sedulously to the

*His sermons, published as *The Sins of Society*, went through fourteen editions.

mysteries as he had to his books, he gave up the attempt at spiritual enlightenment as unprofitable. Not even the Duke of Norfolk, the country's leading Catholic layman, was aware of this cursory conversion: Sir Almeric Fitzroy, with a practical turn of mind, hoped that he would touch Cassel for a contribution towards the cost of completion of Westminster Cathedral.

Before this pious project was as much as a gleam in the eye of Cardinal Vaughan, the brother of Cassel's preceptor, the surgical services of the newly-married Cassel were required in the New World. For such sanguine speculators as the Bischoffsheims, railways held an irresistible attraction. They had previously been engaged in an operation to repair the fortunes of the Atlantic & Great Western, which had been built as a speculative venture to link the Erie Railroad with the Ohio & Mississippi. The Atlantic & Great Western was insolvent as soon as it was completed, but the debt carried by the London banks was so large that it had to be kept afloat. The Erie itself, the first single-rail connection between the Atlantic and the Great Lakes, had been acquired by Jay Gould who, after marketing $5 million of fraudulent shares, plunged the company into one of its recurrent bouts of bankruptcy. Cassel's employers undertook its resuscitation, relying on their young manager's steady hand and strong nerve. Gould was ousted and forced to make restitution; his partner, the former circus hand James Fisk, who specialized in corrupting the state legislature and judiciary, took a more abrupt exit – he was shot dead by a colleague. It was under such conditions that the young Cassel confidently eased himself into the driving seat. The investors were encouraged by Henry Labouchère in *The World*: 'Holders need not despair. We ourselves make them an offer. We have a small room in our humble abode which we should like to paper with Erie shares; we therefore offer to give 2d per lb for all that are sent to us.' Cassel, fortunately, working with the New York bankers Kuhn, Loeb & Company, did better for the shareholders and his masters. He was also dealing on his own account; it is probable that, if he fancied the prospects, he took his commission on the salvage operation in the form of participation in the revived enteprise. Such, certainly, was the case in Scandinavia. Bischoffsheim had large sums locked up in the Swedish Central Railway, one of three separate and rival lines connecting the important iron ore deposits of Grängesberg with the Baltic port of Oxelösund, south of Stockholm. Not only was each line unprofitable, but there was little demand for the poor-grade ore, which contained phosphorus. The breakthrough came in 1878, when Sydney Gilchrist Thomas, a police court clerk and part-time chemist, invented a system to separate off the phosphorus, which enabled cheap steel to be made from inferior ore. Cassel snapped up the rights to this process for Sweden, acquired an interest in the struggling mines and relieved Bischoffsheim of a part of their holding in the unprofitable railway. He had not so far set foot in Sweden. In 1882 he secured a seat on the board of the Swedish Association, a shareholders' pool, and in the following year negotiatd a debt conversion with the local banks. He slowly built up an ascendancy, amidst acrimony from the Swedes, to create Sweden's largest enterprise, incorporating ports and lines, mines and mills – and the foundation of his own fortune; and in the pursuit of personal gain he established the country's capital market and industrial infrastructure.

By 1880, ten years after joining Bischoffsheim & Goldschmidt, he had set aside capital of £150,000; widowed in the same year, with just a small daughter to care for, he devoted himself determinedly to multiplication. Although the pattern of his career was set, it is not easy to fit this into any category. He was not, like Hirsch, a pioneering entrepreneur; he was not a banker proper, nor the head of any great enterprise; he presided over no board and was not even a director of the many companies in which he held such substantial stakes. He had no permanent partners. He was one of a new breed, an economic imperialist, a lone strategist as well as tactician who conducted his campaigns without a general staff or any supporting troops; when he went on holiday, he took his affairs with him. Having cut his teeth in the service of Bischoffsheim, he now had capital of his own to direct. If he was offered a partnership in the bank, he refused it, although remaining on excellent terms with Henry Bischoffsheim. In 1884 he hung up his own plate, retaining a foothold in the Throgmorton Street offices. Jacob Schiff, his partner in the Erie Railroad, may unwittingly have supplied the inspiration. He had written to Cassel the year before to advise him 'that for many reasons we are seeking another brokerage connection in London'. Kuhn, Loeb had many offers every day, but Schiff demanded special qualifications, pointing out that 'it is after all no great feat to execute orders promptly on the Stock Exchange'. Kuhn, Loeb's new agent should be alert, 'understand the American market well (which can easily be learned with a little practice) . . . Their responsibility and credit must be beyond question, so that we can entrust them with large amounts of money,' and they should offer expertise in the money market. This was a mouth-watering prospect. Cassel never became a broker. Instead he and Schiff entered into a tacit partnership for their lifetime, which stimulated Cassel's close involvement in North and Central America.

Jacob Henry Schiff, a native of Frankfurt, where his family had shared the same roof as Mayer Amschel Rothschild – the ship and shield of their names carved in stone over their respective entrances – had taken United States citizenship in 1870. Five years later he had been invited to join Kuhn, Loeb and had married Solomon Loeb's eldest daughter, Therese. In 1885, when his father-in-law, the surviving partner, died, Schiff, aged thirty-eight, picked up the reins and directed the firm until his death in 1920, raising it to a pre-eminence among American private banks matched only by the house of J. Pierpont Morgan.

Cassel first met Schiff in the spring of 1870, and this acquaintance ripened into the closest personal friendship, as well as fruitful partnership, over the following four decades. Some 1,500 letters, mostly in German, exist from Schiff to Cassel in which they share economic, financial and political intelligence laced with family news, evidence of a rare warmth and intimacy; they exchanged visits and Christmas presents (Cassel commissioned a bas-relief by Saint-Gaudens of the two Schiff children), and Schiff's son Mortimer served under Cassel in London. Schiff, a fine-looking man, Cassel's senior by five years, was described by a successor as 'aggressively ambitious, adventurous, opinionated and strong-willed'. In Cassel he found his match. He was, however, more austere in his personal tastes; he did not share Cassel's weakness for cigars and social diversions. Unlike Cassel he was generous with his time, which he devoted to the charities he endowed; he was already treasurer of the American Committee for the Relief of Jews in the Ottoman Empire, in which he had, through Cassel, enlisted Baron Hirsch. Also unlike Cassel, he was deeply religious; one is left to wonder whether he was ever aware of his friend's apostasy. (Indeed, would Hirsch, if he had known of it, have made Cassel a director of his Jewish Colonization Association?)

The families regularly shared holidays. In August 1890 they were exploring the Mer de Glace at Chamonix, Schiff with his wife and two children, Cassel with his sister and her son and daughter, when Schiff's daughter slipped and fell some hundred feet down a crevasse. Cassel was the first to react. He slithered down after Frieda while his sixteen-year-old nephew, Felix, restrained the distraught father. Cassel managed to scramble back to safety with the girl, her shoulder broken. Thereafter, on every anniversary of the mishap, Schiff wrote or telegraphed to his 'Dear, Good Friend' to remind him of a father's gratitude: 'Frieda is standing beside me, saying "Say to Mr Cassel he is the most lovely man in existence".' Cassel, a man who generally inspired little affection, evidently had another side to him of which the world was not usually permitted a glimpse. Five years after their first meeting, Schiff wrote: 'I always feel that you are the most faithful friend I have ever had, and I do not think it necessary . . . to express my feelings for you'; two years later he

Nathan Mayer Rothschild (1777–1836), founder of the English house.

Baron Lionel de Rothschild (1808–79), eldest son of Nathan Mayer. After four attempts, he became the first professing Jew to sit in the House of Commons.

Baron James de Rothschild (1792–1868), youngest of the dynast Mayer Amschel's five sons, founded the Paris house.

Baron Alphonse de Rothschild (1827–1905), son of Baron James and Lionel's first cousin and son-in-law.

Above: King Edward VII (1841–1910). He had to wait sixty years before he ascended the throne on the death of Queen Victoria.

Right: Edward VII with his favourite dog, the terrier Caesar.

Edward VII and his nephew, Wilhelm II (1859–1941), third German Emperor. The Kaiser's naval ambitions caused apprehension in England.

A royal shooting party on the Duke of Devonshire's Chatsworth estate. From left to right: Hon Mrs George Keppel, the King's last mistress; the Prince of Pless, husband of Daisy Cornwallis West whose brother was married to the widowed Lady Randolph Churchill; Lady Gosford, the reputed mistress of Lord Rothschild; Edward VII; Lady Desborough; Earl de Grey; the laryngologist Sir Felix Semon; Arthur Sassoon.

Nathaniel Rothschild (1840–1915), Lionel's son, a 'self-contained and somewhat joyless character', was created first (English) Baron Rothschild in 1885.

Above: Alfred Rothschild (1842–1918), a self-indulgent bachelor, became the first Jewish director of the Bank of England.

Above: The Austrian Baron Ferdinand von Rothschild (1839–98), Lionel's nephew and son-in-law, settled in England after his mother's death.

Leopold Rothschild (1845–1917), a popular figure on the turf. He married Arthur Sassoon's sister-in-law.

Above: The Château de Beauregard near Versailles, acquired by Baron Hirsch in the wake of the Franco-Prussian war. Nothing remains today save the portico.

Right: Ferrières, outside Paris, which Baron James de Rothschild commissioned from Joseph Paxton as a challenge to his nephew Mayer's Mentmore.

Mentmore, Buckinghamshire, built for Mayer Rothschild (1818–74), Lionel's youngest brother, by Joseph Paxton of Crystal Palace fame.

Above left: Reuben Sassoon (1835–1905) shared King Edward's appetite and love of the Turf.

Above right: Sir Albert Abdullah Sassoon (1818–96), whose father fled Baghdad to found a great eastern trading empire in Bombay.

Baron Maurice de Hirsch (1831–96) constructed the first railroad through the Balkans to Constantinople, a history of 'cunning, force, robbery and deceit'.

Sir Ernest Cassel (1852–1921), financed the Aswan dam on the Nile and vitalized the Egyptian economy.

Sir Edward Hamilton (1847–1908), Permanent
Financial Secretary to the Treasury and
intimate of King Edward, the Rothschilds and
Sir Ernest Cassel.

Jacob S. Schiff (1847–1920), senior partner of
Kuhn, Loeb & Company, New York.

wrote: 'Your kindness and friendship really knows no limits,' and in December 1889: 'There is nothing I care so much for as your friendship.'

As soon as Cassel set up on his own account, he sought Schiff's advice on investment opportunities in America. 'I shall answer you', Schiff replied, 'as I should very few others. I am sure you will not hold me responsible for my advice in case it should turn out to have been bad. Good stocks are cheap if one has the patience to stick to them . . . Keep away from all trash though.' The two had collaborated in running the Erie Railroad, from whose board, after a tenure of five years, Schiff now resigned. They pooled their talents to tackle other railroads.

The American capital market was not sufficiently developed to supply all the investment for which the country was crying out. Europe was the lender, the railroads the great borrowers, accounting for 60 per cent of all issues on the New York Stock Exchange. Traffic was seasonal, and freight rates were strictly regulated. In the decade before this redoubtable team took up trains, the track in the United States had almost doubled to just under 95,000 miles in length; during the next thirty years in which they were actively interested, a further 150,000 miles was added. This growth was mostly across the great prairies; the railroads set up the towns, farmer-settlers followed and their harvest was the factor which decided the profitability of the system. During the worldwide crash of 1873, half the railroads ended up in the hands of receivers. In this environment of cut-throat competition Jacob Schiff exerted himself to impose a conservative policy of financial management and investment; he opposed the creation of floating debt for construction, he urged the limitation of cash dividends in order to build up resources and accumulate reserves, prudent aims which did not always suit the more ambitious and avaricious entrepreneurs. During the early 1880s Schiff and Cassel spread themselves, their commitments reading like a roll of honour of the age of steam. They each took a share in the construction of the Canadian Pacific before that ran out of steam and had to be rescued by the Federal government; the year after Schiff retired from the Erie, he advised Cassel to buy into a rival line, the Chicago & Atlantic. Cassel took a slice of a share issue of the Denver & Rio Grande, of which Schiff was a director; three years later Schiff reported that the management, though honest, was incapable; Cassel urged an independent report from an outside inspector which brought about some improvement. They participated in the reorganization of Jay Gould's Texas & Pacific and associated lines which were characterized by 'mismanagement and inefficiency'. From 1883 to 1886 they had associated themselves with the construction of the Texas & St Louis line, although Schiff soon changed his mind, advising

Cassel to dispose of his holdings as he did 'not share at all the rosy opinion ... which apparently prevails everywhere'. In the summer of 1885 Schiff was in Europe on one of his now regular visits; he put his head together with Cassel to try to acquire a sufficient holding of the New York, Ontario & Western to allow them to improve their own control in order to sell it off after they had put it back on its feet. Cassel acted on his own to rearrange the affairs of the Atchison Topeka & Santa Fé. For over a decade from 1884 Schiff and Cassel, though they declined to underwrite the share issues, nursed the fortunes of the Louisville & Nashville with such success that they contemplated adding to it another trunk line, the Baltimore & Ohio. It was one of the select railroad companies to weather the storm in 1893–4, when over 20,000 miles of track fell into the hands of the receivers. Cassel expressed surprise at their good fortune; Schiff put it down to the weather – a cold winter in the South made the waterways impassable. The directors, however, were over-confident about the future, and the ever-cautious Schiff wrote to Cassel: 'I personally can remain on the board only so long as is required by your interests, and, secondly, our own ...' (He hung on, though, for a further two years.) In the same year, 1889, that Schiff joined the board of the Louisville & Nashville, he was recommending the Northern Pacific to Cassel as 'no doubt ... the most promising enterprise on the continent', and they considered raising $13 million worth of bonds for the company. That line too was hit by the crisis of '93, and as a large amount of its shares were held in Europe, Schiff urged Cassel to persuade his friends at the Deutsche Bank to use their influence to reconstruct the company's finances. They planned to force a merger with the Great Northern and thus cut out competitive services and duplicate agencies. Schiff visited Cassel in London to promote this, but the Great Northern was struck by another cyclical panic which temporarily resolved the problem of competition. Kuhn, Loeb in company with Ernest Cassel acted also for the Illinois Central to finance the purchase of the Chesapeake, Ohio & Southwestern, placing $6 million of shares at the height of the alarms of '93, when the rail unions struck through half the states and Federal troops had to be called in to suppress riots in Chicago. They came through the scares and real recessions of the period unscathed. And yet when Lady Randolph Churchill's scapegrace brother-in-law Moreton Frewen tried to interest Cassel in making a large European issue of Pacific Railroad stock, he declined because of his 'shocking experience' of American railways (unless the real reason was Frewen's doleful reputation); the issue, when subsequently floated, was richly rewarding.

Cassel was called upon to mediate in a boardroom feud at the Illinois Central to avoid a rupture with the associated Union Pacific. It was the great battle for the salvation of the Union Pacific, during which Jacob Schiff, always in consultation with Ernest Cassel, established Kuhn, Loeb as a financial force of the premier rank. The first coast-to-coast link had been made possible when the Union Pacific met the Central Pacific at Promontory, Utah, in 1869, a golden spike being driven symbolically into the last joining tie (and, more practically, retrieved). Built with the aid of over-generous grants from the government in land and dollars, it had already suffered from the depredations of Jay Gould when in 1893 the creditors foreclosed. It was rescued from its bankruptcy by the rough, tough Edward H. Harriman, vice-president of the Illinois Central (and father of the suave and polished Averell), with Schiff and Cassel holding the money-bags. Harriman's grand design was to snatch control of the entire American railroad system, and with the profits of a revived Union Pacific he began to acquire connecting and competing lines. Having pocketed the Southern Pacific in 1901, he took on the megalomaniac magnate James J. Hill, backed by J. Pierpont Morgan, in an abortive contest for the Northern Pacific, which resulted only in one of the most serious financial crises ever to hit Wall Street. Even in the rough world of railroaders Harriman's methods excited unusually bitter criticism and earned the censure of the trust-busting President Theodore Roosevelt in 1907. Kuhn, Loeb chose that inopportune moment to underwrite a $75 million conversion of Union Pacific stock and were left with all but $2 million on their hands. Cassel was critical, but Harriman stuck courteously to his armament: 'There is no one in Europe whose approval I would rather have than Sir Ernest's; even, however, to obtain that, I do not concede the correctness of his criticisms.' The damage was repaired next year; $50 million of Union Pacific shares were unloaded in England 'with the energetic and valuable co-operation' of Cassel and his friend John Baring, second Lord Revelstoke. But Harriman was already ailing. Schiff wrote to him from Luxor, where he was cruising with Cassel: 'Here I am, on board of a Nile steamer, thinking of you, while the imposing ruins on the shore remind me of how hollow everything earthly is; how we strive so often for naught; how short a time we live and how long we are then dead . . .' With this reminder ringing in his ears, Harriman died the following year, and the US Supreme Court began to break up his empire, which at the time of his death extended to some 60,000 miles of track.

The Pennsylvania, with its subsidiaries the Long Island and the Philadelphia, Baltimore & Washington railroads, for whom Kuhn, Loeb acted as bankers from as early as 1881, was another railroad which guzzled capital in mouthfuls of never less than $50 million. Cassel was as a matter of course offered a slice. In 1908 Kuhn, Loeb offered one large issue direct to Barings in London, and it was Lord Revelstoke this time who enlisted the aid of Cassel and the Rothschilds; this league was confident enough to dispense with underwriting to the benefit of its own profits. Schiff and Cassel diversified out of railroads into other businesses. They took a joint interest in the American Beet Sugar Company, but before that, in the early Nineties, it was Cassel who spotted another prospect, which he recommended to Daniel Guggenheim, one of the seven sons of old Meyer, who had abandoned his native Swiss embroideries for metal processing. They moved into Anaconda Copper. Jacob Schiff even anticipated the Guggenheims' own ambitions to control the industry: 'We must now both direct every intention to Anaconda . . . which should show brilliant results . . . Especially is this true if a combination of all copper producers can be effected . . . and in the long run that is inevitable.' In 1899 a cartel, the American Smelting & Refining Company, was set up in which the Guggenheims won ascendancy, establishing at the same time an exploration company to gain control of the sources of ore. All these operations were financed by Kuhn, Loeb, with Cassel in its wake emerging as a major stockholder in each of the operations. Together Cassel and Schiff financed the Westinghouse Electric Company, and when that collapsed in 1908 they put the pieces together again.

The friends had long before moved outside the confines of the United States. Bischoffsheim & Goldschmidt, while still the source of Cassel's bread and butter, had headed a $12 million syndicate invested in America whose income had dried up in the aftermath of the crash of '73. Edouard Noetzlin, president of the Banque de Paris et des Pays Bas, in which the Bischoffsheim bank was recently merged, was sent by Cassel to discuss his problems with Schiff, who recommended he look for opportunities in Latin America. Noetzlin undertook the organization of the National Bank of Mexico. Cassel and Schiff soon followed behind him south of the border. From 1885 onwards they took in hand the two chief railroads that ran from Mexico City to the American border, the National and Central, the main market for whose bonds was in London and Berlin. Cassel soon represented a majority shareholding in the Central; important decisions, such as a replacement for a defunct president, would bring him across the Atlantic, but otherwise his interests were overseen by Schiff. By 1892 Schiff hoped that an 'arrangement' could be reached with the various Mexican railroads 'so that a permanent check will be placed upon all unhealthy competition'. In the event it was the government of strongman

Porfirio Díaz which, profiting from the temporarily straitened circumstances of the Central, later forced through a merger with the National, securing a majority of the shares for itself, although Cassel retained a substantial stake.

Cassel is customarily credited with more liberality in the way of loans to the Mexican government itself than he deserved; after a third loan in 1893, his advice supposedly rejected, he never again entered into any business which was in the slightest way connected with Mexico, a decision which worked out to his advantage. The evidence points to a lesser and later commitment. The overheads, too, were not inconsiderable; Bismarck's banker Bleichröder, who had a secret option on Mexican loans, in order to win a competition four years before, had had to disgorge a 'commission' to the Minister of Finance of £300,000, and two Krupp cannons for the government. The country, enjoying a long spell of political stability, was a happy lending ground: Edouard Noetzlin had laid the groundwork for the scrupulous settlement of all foreign debts; it was hugely rich in gold, silver and copper – a principal and profitable source of revenue for the Central Railroad. Cassel did negotiate a first loan in 1893, but six years later the Mexicans approached Kuhn, Loeb direct with an invitation to promote a further loan. Schiff, out of consideration for his friend, declined. 'I have arrived at the only possible conclusion,' he wrote to Cassel, 'namely, that it will not be fair to appear as a competitor in business in which you are already interested, even if you would not mind . . . The question is quite simple, and I am convinced that you would not have acted differently.' But Cassel, though still a minority shareholder in the incorporated National Railroad, does not seem to have extended his interests, while Kuhn, Loeb remained locked in the economy even after the fall, largely provoked by his generous concessions to foreign capitalists, of Porfirio Díaz. Schiff expressed himself philosophically in what may serve as a testament of all latter-day lenders to Latin America: it was 'all very much to be regretted, especially for foreigners who like all of us have material interests in Mexico; but in the last analysis, whoever takes his capital into a foreign country, to gain profit, must be prepared to take the same risks, under the prevailing laws and conditions, as does every inhabitant of the country to which he has entrusted his resources.'

It is impossible to put a figure on the fortune Ernest Cassel earned in these American dealings but, excluding even his Mexican enterprise, he had certainly made himself into a dollar multi-millionaire, a rare enough bird in that age, and among the half-dozen richest rail barons behind Jay Gould, who died unlamented worth a reputed $100 million, Edward

Harriman, James J. Hill and 'Commodore' Cornelius Vanderbilt. And these engaged only part of his attention throughout the period; there were other, concurrent calls on his time and talents nearer home and further afield.

7

Eastern Enterprise

By the late 1880s Ernest Cassel, in his mid-thirties, was already something more than a mere somebody in the City, the capital power-house of the world. Over the next decade his career blossomed and flowered in an extraordinary surge of bustling initiative in which he came to challenge the predominance of the Rothschilds in the money markets. He arranged loans for foreign governments around the globe and, while keeping one eye on his American investments, tightened his grip on Sweden's industrial base; he dabbled in the great gold and diamond discoveries in South Africa and reconstituted Egypt's economy. At home he undertook the construction of the Central London Railway (which became the Central Line of the Underground) after the Rothschilds had refused the risk and, with Lord Rothschild, managed the series of mergers which went to create the arms, ordnance and naval shipbuilding giant of Vickers, which was to prove its mettle as the Allies' main arsenal in the approaching Armageddon, a conflict which Cassel himself hoped to help avert. He achieved this remarkable tally in his established fashion, single-handed, forging tailor-made partnerships for each situation or accepting the risks on his own account with only his reputation for capital.

The economic turbulence of the Nineties was matched with the rise in newly assertive nationalism. Britain was isolated; when faced with bands of intractable Boers, it found itself without an ally and with scarcely a friend. France and Russia, perceived as Britain's hereditary foes, had entered into a *mariage de convenance* which threatened Germany. But France's own qualifications for continued membership of the Great Power club were beginning to be questioned. When in 1898 the Prime Minister Lord Salisbury referred in a speech to 'dying nations', although he probably had the Manchu and Ottoman empires in mind, Paris promptly protested at the imagined innuendo. Germany, a rapidly risen economic power, had achieved such a crushing superiority in manpower that, no longer fearing French revanchism, it had its hands free to meddle in everyone else's quarrels. The Reich was bursting with bottled-up energy and tension. Such belligerence was not the consequence of any sudden rush of blood to the head induced by new-found affluence; in the false spring of 1848 even the Liberal Democrats in the national convention at Frankfurt had emphasized Germany's desire for 'power, power, power'. As the Nineties opened, the young Kaiser, intelligent but excitable and unstable, had confidently removed the restraining hand of Bismarck from the brake. The Chancellor himself chose a different analogy. 'The Kaiser is like a balloon,' he remarked before his dismissal, 'if you don't keep fast hold of the string, you never know where he'll be off to.' The Kaiser had no doubts at all: 'There is only one master in the Reich and that is I,' he boasted. 'I shall tolerate no other.' His subjects enthusiastically endorsed the mystique of might. The newborn Pan-German League, which dreamed of carving a greater Germany out of the heart of Mitteleuropa without regard to national boundaries, distributed shop-window posters affirming 'The world belongs to the Germans.' But despite this challenging rhetoric, despite the critical view of the Kaiser's character by his grandmother Queen Victoria ('a hot-headed conceited and wrong-headed young man') and his uncle Edward, Anglo-German rivalry had not yet given way to outright antagonism. (Lord Revelstoke's son, Maurice Baring, was surprised by the extent of latent Anglophobia, collective than rather particular, among the bourgeoisie and professional classes in Germany. Any public expression of this was received in England with pained surprise – 'in a kind of way the Germans were supposed to be our cousins'.) The Kaiser fancied himself a born leader, and his conversation was peppered with the menace of 'I and my army'. Such bombast might be disregarded; Lord Salisbury considered he was 'not "all there"'. But when, as the decade drew to a close, the Kaiser uttered his fateful dictum 'Our future lies upon the ocean,' he set his country on a collision course with Britain.

Britain's ascendancy in world trade and wealth was also being eroded. The last, booming years of the 1880s ended with a bang that came close to bringing down the whole house. In November 1890 the great firm of Barings, the only rivals to Rothschilds, went on the rocks with liabilities in excess of £20 million arising from over-speculation in Argentina and Uruguay, the most serious crisis since the failure of Overend, Gurney on Black Friday almost twenty-five years before. The government was appalled, but powerless. Lord Salisbury sent for Lord Rothschild, who was by turns sceptical and vengeful. However, second thoughts – and self-interest – and the urging of his cousin Alphonse in Paris to make 'the greatest effort to forestall a catastrophe', prompted him reluctantly to change his tune. It was largely through the intervention of the French Rothschilds that the Bank of France advanced £3 million in gold to the salvage operation cobbled together by the Bank of England over a Friday evening and a Saturday morning. (Ironically, in view of the London Rothschilds' boycott of Russian finance, the Tsar's Finance Minister wrote to congratulate them on their honourable role in succouring their rivals, with whom Russia had some millions on deposit.) The gravity of Barings' predicament had taken even insiders in the City by surprise, though Cassel evidently had wind of it before he was asked for a contribution. Barely two weeks after the danger had passed, Jacob Schiff wrote to him: 'Still pondering intently the abyss before which the financial world stood . . . to my great regret we did not take prompt enough advantage of the hint which you gave us at the right moment.' Three years later the bottom fell out of the British agricultural market, the Australian banking system collapsed and American railways slumped, ushering in a world depression which persisted for four years. Before this Britain almost came to blows with the United States; conflict was only averted by Salisbury's cool diplomacy – and a further ruinous drop in American stock.

Through these tumultuous times Ernest Cassel steered a path for his purse with such unerring success that he could remark in his gracious fashion, when advised that one large London landowner, Sir Richard Sutton, enjoyed an income of £200,000 a year, 'I do not call that rich.' (It is true that Cecil Rhodes for one earned three times as much.)

Before the Nineties had dawned, Cassel had gone into the foreign loan business in association with Carl Meyer, a Hamburger and chief clerk of N. M. Rothschild. In 1888–9 the two men arranged loans for Egypt, Brazil, Argentine and Uruguay. (The profits from this business allowed Cassel to move from north of the Park to join the swells in Grosvenor Square.) They were poaching: the first two countries were the preserve of Rothschilds, the latter two of Barings. Meyer, indeed, developed ideas above his station. Some years later, the Treasury's Sir Edward Hamilton, staying with Natty Rothschild at Tring Park, reported 'considerable excitement in Rothschild circles: latterly, having feathered his nest well, [Meyer] wanted to be less tied; and fully expecting that he could dictate his own terms, he threatened to resign unless his position was improved. Much to his surprise, he was taken at his word; it being thought by the brothers that he was getting a little "too big for his boots".' Before Cassel lost his friend at New Court, he and Meyer had tried their fortune in

China. Cassel, the loner, had only limited success; Meyer in due course providentially picked up a seat on the board of the Hongkong & Shanghai Bank.

In August 1894 Japan went to war with the Celestial Empire over Korea. The colossus collapsed at the first push and was forced to cede Korea, the neighbouring Liaotung peninsula with Port Arthur, and Formosa, as well as to pay a massive indemnity. Such rapacity was countered by three Powers – Germany, France and Russia – who had their own views on fair shares. The victor was commanded to return the Liaotung peninsula, which cost the Chinese an increased indemnity. There was little philanthropy in their concern for China's territorial integrity. The same Powers scrambled to obtain privileges and concessions and, by offering to lend the money – £50 million was now required – to establish their own political influence. Britain's principal concern was for her commercial ascendancy: China constituted the most important market for her largest export, Lancashire cotton. But the British had one trump in Sir Robert Hart, the superintendent of the Imperial Maritime Customs, and thus the controller of virtually the sole collateral for foreign loans. The Chinese turned to Hart for help, he approached the Hongkong & Shanghai Bank, a wartime lender. The bank was able and anxious to undertake the operation, but the sum to be raised was too large for any single market; the bank could answer for only £15 million on its own account. The Foreign Office, indeed, favoured concerted action by the Powers in order to prevent any one gaining exclusive political and commercial advantages. But the other Powers, who had championed a defeated China, were not prepared to let the British carry off the prize and, without their governments' approval and support, the foreign banks would not collaborate. Germany, France and Russia prepared to go to work on their own account, for which they had their eye on the Customs revenues; Britain naturally was determined not to surrender this advantage. There followed, in May 1895, a month of feverish manoeuvring, at best Delphic, at worst deceitful.

The Prime Minister, Lord Rosebery, a melancholic widower disinclined for supreme office (Hannah had died in 1890), sought Lord Rothschild's advice; Natty counselled co-operation between London, Paris and Berlin and, as a bonus, suggested that he might participate with the Hongkong & Shanghai Bank in issuing the British portion of the loan. The bank was indignant at losing official recognition and support; the Germans feared that the Rothschilds in this way would get their hands on the whole operation; the French suspected that Rosebery, whose wife had been Natty's cousin, was intent on feathering the family nest. (The Prime

Minister's fifteen-month tenure was remarkable chiefly for the success of the Rosebery-Rothschild stables in winning the Derby two years running – his Ladas beating Baron Hirsch's Matchbox in 1894 – a unique record which did little to add to his popularity with the nonconformist wing of his own party. The following year was the Prince's turn, his Persimmon beating the odds-on favourite owned by Leopold de Rothschild. Rosebery sourly remarked that everyone would say that the other horses had been pulled.)

The most determinedly predatory Power was China's northern neighbour, which had already been awarded a concession from an ill-considered sense of obligation to take the Trans-Siberian Railway through Manchuria on the shortest direct route to Vladivostok. Russia resolved to reinforce her presence. The government approached the French Rothschilds for the funds; they, no doubt prompted by their English cousins, declined to co-operate without official British approval and participation. News leaked through to the Foreign Office that Russian banks, backed by a government guarantee, had offered £16 million for the first indemnity loan at 4 per cent, two points below a reasonable market rate. As the British Ambassador in St Petersburg reported, Count Witte, the Russian Finance Minister, 'did not conceal his hope that China might fail to meet her engagements punctually in which case Russia would obtain the right of interfering directly in the administration of Chinese finance'. The British and Germans were now prepared to put pressure on the Chinese to refuse the loan or, if afraid to go so far, to procrastinate. The Chinese regretted their commitment, but it was too late to back out. Although the Foreign Office had shown unprecedented support for British interests to secure commercial dominance in China, the government was criticized by *The Times*: 'The nation must do its part as a nation, instead of trusting solely to individual exertion, as in the good old days when Englishmen had enormous foreign markets all to themselves.' That appeal fell on deaf ears. However, this exceptional British exertion did ensure that Chinese assurances were respected and that the two subsequent indemnity loans went to London in association with Berlin. For these the Rothschilds, with Lord Salisbury now back in Downing Street, were not consulted, which they took as a 'great mortification': Edward Hamilton heard that 'in order that there may be an appearance of their being "in it", Natty Rothschild put it about that he had tendered his advice, which was being acted on'.

The Russians again took up the fight three years later over the third indemnity loan with a promise to match the British terms for a last £16 million. They turned 'so bellicose', threatening 'to throw troops across the frontier if the Chinese take our [British] money,' that China, thoroughly cowed, turned down both offers and considered instead an attempt to come to an arrangement with the Japanese to lessen the indemnity. The Cabinet took this as an unwarranted affront and prepared demands for suitable satisfaction. But the following month the Chinese recovered their nerve and awarded the loan, as they had the second, to the Hongkong & Shanghai Bank. The British government had 'after all scored in China over the Russians'. Edward Hamilton congratulated himself, 'for they have practically got all they wanted without incurring any liability in respect of a guaranteed loan'. That may have been the satisfied view from the Treasury, but Hamilton's complacency was soon punctured. A little more than a week later, when the loan was still in the balance, he voiced fears in his diary that Britain was 'being excluded from China totally by Russia and Germany dismembering it to our disadvantage'. That was the view of the Foreign Office and the Board of Trade. Russia, in retaliation for her failure to browbeat the Chinese, seized the Liaotung peninsula, driving a railway down to Port Arthur, which Russia occupied until dislodged by the Japanese in a later war. 'We have bungled, Russia has scored,' lamented Edward Hamilton, relaxing at Ferdinand Rothschild's Waddesdon. Admiral Tirpitz had already grabbed for his Kaiser the main port and hinterland of Shantung province, facing Port Arthur. The French, after a slow start in the scramble, prepared their demands for an exclusive preferential claim on a great swath of the southern provinces adjoining their Indo-China possessions and including the mainland behind Hongkong. Hamilton conceded that this was 'a clever move on their part; because if we remonstrate they will retort that we had declared we wanted no Chinese territory and to taunt us with our high-minded professions'. Lord Rothschild took it so seriously that he anticipated going to war with France in a week or two's time. 'This may be a hopeful sign,' Hamilton consoled himself, 'for his political barometer is generally most correct when it is read upside down.' Britain, though, achieved a lesser but longer-lasting compensation, a ninety-nine year lease on Kowloon, the 'New Territories' backing Hongkong. This sudden proliferation of rival powers with naval pretensions in the China Seas pushed Britain towards an alliance with Japan.

Ernest Cassel was moving in his own mysterious way on the periphery of these tortuous transactions. In the month that Port Arthur had fallen to the Japanese, Jacob Schiff had been approached by a former US Secretary of State to manage a small £1 million loan to China. Schiff turned to Cassel, but four weeks later called it off: 'I am afraid we said more to you than was necessary or justified by the prospects . . . [We] shall only trouble you again after peace is established.' And yet five months later, Cassel raised a £1 million gold loan at 6 per cent which was sanctioned by Imperial Edict just five days after the signing of the peace treaty, that is, after the first indemnity loan had been won by the Franco-Russian combine. Having held out his hand to the Chinese while they were still at war, and clearly losing it, he must have hoped to do better through such a show of confidence. 'The Chinese transaction', Schiff wrote to him, 'has doubtless given you great satisfaction and it is only a pity that the Russians and Frenchmen intervene so that you now control only the smaller and not the larger part.' There is no other existing record of Cassel's part in this. Not the least remarkable presumption is that, unless Edward Hamilton was much mistaken, Cassel spent some time in China to satisfy himself on local conditions at some stage during the fighting. This would have been in character: Reginald Brett, later Viscount Esher, testified that 'he feels obliged to look personally after his interests'. He was evidently not reassured. Robert Hart, on whose Customs revenues the loan was tightly and doubly secured, felt Cassel's terms and unusual demands were exorbitant. 'The Cassel affair is not quite intelligible,' he noted, barely containing his frustration, 'and *I* prefer simply taking the position that the loan is inexpedient.' It had, indeed, been 'knocked on the head three of four times' until Imperial sanction was finally forthcoming, and even then it was the Foreign Office which forced it through.

Although this loan represented some small consolation rather than a minor triumph for British finance and officialdom, Cassel had kept the British presence alive, and his enterprise was appreciated by the Foreign Office, whose trust he retained for the future. The results were to be hugely fruitful in Egypt, largely frustrating in Turkey. Within a few years he was regarded at the Treasury as an old China hand: the Assistant Financial Secretary thought it worthy of interest to note in his diary Cassel's opinion that the occupants of the Legations at Peking, under siege by the Boxers, were alive. His grounds for optimism were purely that an Imperial Edict had said so, and 'such a document is absolutely sacred in his eyes'. (Such simple faith was, indeed, justified.) Six years later the Foreign Secretary, Sir Edward Grey, was prepared to put another Chinese loan in his way, this time for £15 million for trunk railways, after the Chancellor of the Exchequer, Asquith, having consulted Edward Hamilton, had given it as his opinion that Cassel was decidedly the man it would be desirable to consult. The Chinese had made an unusual private approach to the British Legation, insisting on 'close privacy' in order to conclude their 'bargain quietly'. They wished to avoid the Hongkong &

Shanghai Bank or any other concern which had engaged to share business with financial institutions of other countries; they feared the notorious proclivity of those governments to extract further concessions in exchange for approval of loans. Even the Chinese Legation in London was to be kept in the dark. Sir Edward Grey confided the affair to Eldon Gorst, who had previously suffered one break in his career in Egypt through over-close attention to Cassel, as the fly-fishing Foreign Secretary and the Permanent Head of the Foreign Office, Sir Charles Hardinge, did not expect to be in London at such an unseasonable time (it was late August). Cassel was conscious of his own dignity; his holidays, too, were hallowed. Willing as ever to be of service, he could not immediately attend to the matter as he did not plan to leave the Villa Cassel, near Mörel in southern Switzerland, until the end of September; he would then be prepared to send a minion out to China – he was over fifty with a full plate of his own – to negotiate direct with the Chinese.

In fact, Cassel's loan of a mere £1 million was irrelevant to China's pressing requirements, a drop in the China Sea as a contribution to the indemnity. It is more probable that the sum was tied to the procurement of the necessary hardware to continue the fighting and subsequent rearmament.

In the early 1880s, Robert Rintoul Symon, the brother of the vice-president of the Mexican Central Railroad, Cassel's future takeover target, introduced Albert Vickers, a member of the Sheffield steel family, to Hiram Maxim, the American who had perfected and patented a design for a revolutionary weapon, the first truly automatic machine gun. The three men incorporated the Maxim Gun Company in London in 1884 with a paid-up capital of £50,000. Cassel and the future Lord Rothschild took up some 10 per cent apiece. Four years later the two of them pushed through a merger with the larger Nordenfelt Guns & Ammunition Company, acquiring with it the services of Nordenfelt's overseas agent, Basil Zaharoff, who was to become notorious as the 'Merchant of Death'. Cassel and Rothschild were rewarded with shares roughly equal in value to the Vickers family holding. The management, however, was not as effective as its wares, and after successive losses Lord Rothschild put in a protégé, Sigmund Loewe, younger brother of the founder of the celebrated German arms firm Deutsche Waffen, as manager. Within one year he turned the company round to produce a six-figure profit in 1895. The new broom prompted Cassel to make the offer of a loan to China as a hopeful market for the Maxim. In that same summer, the defeated Chinese commander in Korea, Li Hung-Chang, a Krupp client, visited England. Lord Salisbury entertained him at Hatfield, Loewe invited him down to witness a demonstration of tree-felling in his garden with the new 37 mm Maxim, the 'pom-pom'.

Two years later, Cassel, still with Lord Rothschild, masterminded the sale for £1,353,000 of Maxim-Nordenfelt to Vickers, which earlier in the year had acquired the recently renovated Barrow Naval Construction & Armaments Company. The sale was managed by an issue of £1,250,000 of debentures and an increase in Vickers' issued capital to £2,500,000. (Maxim insisted on Cassel's approval of the terms before the completion of the contract.) The two brokers remained major shareholders in the new company, Vickers Sons & Maxim. Rothschild's ambition was to wean the ebullient Admiral 'Jackie' Fisher away from the Royal Navy, where he was then Lord Commissioner and Comptroller, to head a great armament and naval shipbuilding combine to challenge Krupp. When this failed, he took a back seat. Cassel remained on good terms with 'King Fisher', who dashed off to him one of his characteristic notes: 'Next week I shall send you my whole scheme of Naval Reform! It's lovely!!!' (This is undated, but may have referred to his decision to build HMS *Dreadnought*, which consigned the British and foreign navies to obsolescence.) Cassel, as was his way, never sat on the board though he remained a trusted adviser. He insinuated his own protégé, Vincent Caillard, into a directorship. In 1902 Cassel, on joint account with his friend Lord Revelstoke of Barings, undertook to raise £1 million for the company, although Vickers' name was not mentioned in the prospectus; Revelstoke found this association 'one of the pleasantest features of this particular business'. It enabled Vickers to acquire a half-share in the competing armour plate specialists, William Beardmore of Glasgow.

Although Ernest Cassel had carefully eliminated all element of risk in far-off China at the expense of the Customs, at the same time at home he took a hand in a venture of a markedly speculative nature. In 1895 the Electric Traction Company embarked on the construction of the underground Central London Railway from the Bank to Shepherd's Bush, not the first but the most effective electric 'Tube'. The syndicate had been formed five years before, initially with Rothschild backing; this cooled and Cassel became the moving spirit of the railway. He brought in with him Baron Hirsch, then in the last year of his life, and his old employer, Henry Bischoffsheim. He quarried also amongst his recently acquired Court connections to add that polish to the prospectus which was so unaccountably reassuring: the new board of directors was graced by the presence of Lord Colville of Culross, the Princess of Wales's Lord Chamberlain, and Sir Francis Knollys, the Prince's private secretary. A director of the Maxim-Nordenfelt Gun Company, the Hon. Algernon

Mills, managing director of the bankers Glyn Mills, also joined the board. Despite this array, the public was chary: Cassel was also the underwriter, and the company was obliged itself to take up a quarter of the share issue. The line took five years to complete. The Prince attended the official opening with a late luncheon in the generating station at Wood Lane (one unusual guest was Samuel Clemens, better known as that innocent abroad Mark Twain). The Rothschilds' reserve, however, was largely justified. Though a boon to Londoners, the (temporarily) 'Tuppenny Tube' was not an equal source of profit to its promoters, even though the fare was soon raised by 50 per cent for longer journeys, a weighty decision that required one of Cassel's rare appearances round the boardroom table. Cassel later admitted that the more profitable course would have been to let someone else build the line while he bought the land surrounding its westernmost terminal in Shepherd's Bush.

Having set this in train, Cassel switched the points towards Scandinavia. He had prepared the ground by acquiring two years before a large stake in the foreign shareholders' Swedish Association. In June 1896, his signature scarcely dry on a second loan to Uruguay he descended on Stockholm with an associate, Frederic Warburg of the Hamburg banking dynasty, who was Jacob Schiff's son-in-law. The revolutionary treatment of iron ore that Cassel had first introduced had boosted exports some tenfold, and Cassel now determined to consolidate the three competing railways, the mines and the harbour installations at Oxelösund. In need of a native cloak behind which to launch his design, he teamed up with the apprehensive conservative management of one of the larger local banks, the Kreditbolaget, with whom on his return in July he incorporated the Grängesberg Oxelösund Traffic Company with a capital of £995,000. His new partners were in a fix; although they neither liked him – 'The Great Mogul' – nor appreciated his methods, he now held 95 per cent of the shares, still without a seat on the board. They suspected him of pushing up the price to take his profit; whereas, unknown to them (he had had to concede some say in policy), and in order to neutralize their opposition, he sold many of his shares at below the market price to win allies among Sweden's politicians and newspapermen in what became known as 'Cassel's greasing system'. His colleagues were not the only ones to regard him with reserve. His success aroused the concern of such influential native private bankers as the Wallenbergs, who already resented the influence of the 'cosmopolitans', the limited liability banks, Kreditbolaget among them, largely led by Jews with foreign affiliations. The Wallenbergs were interested in promoting the development of a rival clutch of iron ore mines in northern Lapland, for which they hoped to attract local investment. Instead, they soon found the value of their asset being talked down by 'the Englishman'. A few years later Cassel swallowed the competition. 'The right people have not got control,' wrote an outraged K. A. Wallenberg to his brother, 'though the way it all happened has been nothing short of scandalous. The very people who for years had been trying to undermine the whole thing by chatter and gossip and press intrigue' – those recipients of Cassel's grease – 'have now rushed to buy, and paid far more than we thought reasonable. Last year Luorsavaara was supposed a rotten swindle, but now its 1,000 Kr shares are worth 2,800 Kr apiece. And the safety of our country has been preserved because Cassel, the London Jew, directs the companies!' Although it is difficult not to feel some sympathy for the outwitted Wallenberg, as a result of Cassel's tactics more than half the shares of his combine were by then in Swedish hands. Whatever the means, the end was an invigorated and more integrated national economy and an active capital market; this was recognized by the award of the Order of Vasa and, nine years later, the Grand Cross of the Polar Star, to add to his collection. The Wallenbergs themselves aped Cassel's technique of backstairs control and cross-holdings to lay the foundations for what is Europe's largest family empire.

Five years before Cassel's contentious take-over in the tundra, he had focused on a hotter spot where he was to establish his main mint. His initial exposure to the shoal-strewn shallows of Egyptian finance – his apprenticeship at the Anglo-Egyptian Bank in Paris, where he might have remained forever but for the Franco-Prussian War – had been at a time when the building of the Suez Canal had already begun to impose a strain on the public purse. From that time Egypt became a happy hunting ground for unscrupulous usurers bleeding an eager and complaisant Khedive Ismail – the Magnificent or, more properly, the Profligate – on the security of his vast private domains, until his country was mortgaged to the hilt. A shrewd and forceful character, he contrived a subtle system whereby all profits went to sustain his expensive habits (there were 3,000 of them in his harem alone) while the debts were transferred to the state; two-thirds of the country's revenues went to service these. In the year that the young Cassel had joined Bischoffsheim & Goldschmidt in London, the firm had loaned £7 million at 7 per cent to develop the sugar industry on his estates; in 1873 the Bischoffsheim syndicate won a spectacular £32 million state loan at the same rate, which swallowed all that was left of the unsecured revenues. After another two years, Ismail, his pockets once more to let, earned a temporary reprieve by realizing £4 million from the sale of his Suez Canal shares to the British government and by borrowing twice that sum on short term from the Anglo-Egyptian Bank, which had hoped, with the blessing of the French government, to secure the Suez shares for itself. Sadly for his immediate prospects, his overlord, the Turkish Sultan, defaulted without warning in the same year. This rocked Egypt's credit, and the Khedive in turn suspended payments on his debts, incidentally wiping out the Anglo-Egyptian Bank's entire reserves. Prodded by the French, the sheriff's officers moved in to set up the Caisse de la Dette Publique, appropriating half the country's revenues of £10 million to satisfy the foreign, mainly French, bond-holders. An Anglo-French condominium was establshed. Within six months, the Khedive, restless under such restraint, and now reduced to borrowing from Greek and Jewish money-lenders in Alexandria at 30 per cent, countered by dismissing his guardians. The Powers retaliated by persuading the Sultan to depose his spendthrift viceroy in favour of his more amenable son, Tewfik. (Ismail's first intimation of the loss of his throne was a telegram from the Sultan addressed to 'His Highness the former Khedive'.[*]) With the Khedival estates now safely in the care of the Caisse, the Rothschilds injected some oxygen into the economy, issuing the £8.5 million Domain Mortgage Bonds loan at 5 per cent in London and Paris. Strict economy was enforced. This bred nationalist discontent. A political puppet from a fellah family, Arabi Pasha, encouraged by the deposed Khedive with a promise of a wife from his harem, carried out a coup d'état. His proposal to discontinue payments of interest on foreign debt offended even the Liberal government's sense of propriety, and Gladstone tried in vain to induce the other Powers to act jointly against Egypt on behalf of the defrauded bond-holders.

There is a curious postscript to this affair retailed by Wilfrid Scawen Blunt, an ardent and active champion of Egyptian nationalism. Charles Rivers Wilson, the finance minister appointed under the Anglo-French condominium, smarting from his brusque dismissal by the Khedive Ismail, had gone straight to the Rothschilds in Paris and painted an ominous picture of the turn of affairs. The Khedive, he warned, intended to repudiate his debts, sheltering from retribution from the Powers by proclaiming constitutional government. Rivers Wilson succeeded in so thoroughly alarming the Rothschilds that they were moved to use their influence in favour of forcible intervention. Neither Downing Street nor the Quai d'Orsay was moved by the family's entreaties. In 'despair for their millions', they sought the help of Bismarck, who 'ever since his Frankfurt days had extended a certain contemptuous protection to the

[*]His penchant for excessive consumption eventually proved fatal. He died in exile by the Bosphorus in an attempt to down two bottles of champagne in one draught.

great Hebrew house'. The Chancellor, who was always ready to seize any chance to sow dissension between London and Paris, was happy to oblige. He made it known that if they were unable to intervene effectively in the interests of the foreign creditors, Germany would make their cause its own. That settled the matter. Pressure was applied on the Sultan to dismiss Ismail. Arabi was more difficult to remove. Blunt was told that the Rothschilds had offered Arabi £4,000 a year for life if he would quietly decamp. (Many years later Arabi told Blunt that he had never heard of any offer of a pension from the Rothschilds, but the French Consul had proposed to double his pay to £6,000 if he would retire.) It cost a lot more than that to remove him in the end. The crunch came when the Arabists began frantically fortifying Alexandria, where a British and French fleet lay. This was taken as a provocation. The Royal Navy began a bombardment; the French admiral, on the instructions of a new ministry in Paris, sailed away. An army under Sir Garnet Wolseley, sent in to follow up this success, won a resounding victory at Tel-el-Kebir; the Prince of Wales had pleaded vainly with his mother and the Cabinet for permission to serve in the field. France, though invited, again declined to join in the adventure, fearing it was a plot by Bismarck to draw off troops facing the German frontier in readiness for a surprise attack. The French thereby forfeited a role in the reconstruction of Egypt; they did not forgive or forget this hurt for over twenty years. Although the Sultan offered to hand over exclusive control and administration of Egypt to Britain, Gladstone, reluctant to assume the responsibility and expense of running the country, refused. The Prime Minister might have declared a Protectorate, but missed this chance; the British 'found themselves in a position from which they had no desire to advance, but from which it was impossible to retreat'. Instead, Major Evelyn Baring, son of the first Lord Revelstoke, who had earlier served for two years on the international debt commission, was recalled to Egypt in 1883 with a knighthood as British agent and consul-general, effectively ruling under these modest titles for almost a quarter of a century with what an Egyptian historian described as 'arrogant altruism'. Endowed with exceptional qualities of leadership, he was respected or feared, but little liked; aloof and peremptory, he had already earned himself the sobriquet 'Over-Baring'.

His priority, to establish 'a sound financial system before every other consideration', was impossibly compromised from the start. A loan was needed; Baring urged the British government to guarantee it. Gladstone, in his last fatal legacy to Egypt, refused. There was now no choice but to accept the guarantees of the concert of Powers, all six obtaining seats on the Caisse (and a veto on government expenditure). The 1885 loan, for

£9,424,000 was issued in London and Paris by the Rothschilds. It was over the question of these negotiations that Rosebery felt obliged to exclude himself from office. He wrote to Lord Granville, the Foreign Secretary, in November 1884: 'You can guess the extreme delicacy of my relation to that question, for though I am not a member of the House of Rothschild, I am allied to it as closely as possible by kinship and friendship, and I feel therefore strongly the difficulty of entering the Cabinet . . . As to both policy and finance I could probably accept a *fait accompli*; but I do not see how with self-respect I could swallow all the considerations and enter now.' (Once the matter had been decided, he joined the Cabinet four months later as Lord Privy Seal for the final months of Gladstone's second ministry.) In the interval, in order to satisfy Egypt's more urgent needs, Natty Rothschild had advanced £1 million on the security of a note of hand from Granville, a gesture which may have had not a little to do with the bestowal of a peerage in Gladstone's Dissolution Honours.

Lord Salisbury, the new Prime Minister and Foreign Secretary, soon came in his turn 'heartily [to] wish we had never gone into Egypt'. But British tutelage was seen as an essential, if provisional, expedient until such time as a strong and efficient Egyptian government should be established, though the prospect of evacuation was dangled as a pawn to win concessions on the larger board of power politics. Baring, created Lord Cromer in 1892, set about attracting foreign, preferably British, investment, but although Egypt was now solvent and politically stable, British finance was resolutely and exasperatingly wary. 'European capital is certainly coming into the country,' Cromer grumbled in 1895, 'but I am sorry to say that it rarely comes from England.' The need to nurse the budget, now boasting a modest surplus, made Cromer reluctant to endorse the reconquest of the Sudan province, overrun by the Mahdi since the death of Gordon at Khartoum. As the British Parliament would not vote the funds, he well knew where the burden would fall. His ambition was instead to harness the Nile's seasonal floods at Aswan for year-round irrigation (and income). Imperial policy, however – rumours of a French advance towards the Sudan from Equatorial Africa, which it was mistakenly believed would yield them control over the source of the Nile – decided the British government to undertake the expedition. 'The French are mad with rage about it,' the Prince of Wales informed his elder son, 'but as we never do right in their eyes, it is useless paying any attention to their abuse.' Kitchener pushed south along the river bank past Wadi Halfa, laying a railway line in his wake, until he met and smashed the dervishes at Omdurman in September 1898. (Cassel would have been proud to learn that the complement of forty-four Vickers Maxim guns carried by the force accounted for almost a quarter of the 40,000-man opposition with fewer than 500 British casualties.) Before Kitchener had reached Dongola on his march south, the Chancellor of the Exchequer was considering selling some Suez Canal shares to meet the costs; and before he had even faced the Mahdi, the Treasury was proposing to privatize his railway. The quandary was resolved by charging the greater part of the campaign to Egypt, less the sum of £800,000 which Cromer had 'borrowed' from the Caisse and which Russia and France insisted be returned. Although the campaign had been run on a shoestring by the economical Kitchener, this still left £1.5 million, the railway included, to be found in Egypt. Faced also with the additional costs of administering a liberated Sudan, Cromer had not waited for the bad news to be confirmed before casting around for an alternative source of finance for the Aswan dam. He sought the advice of his nephew Lord Revelstoke. Barings, emerging from under a cloud of debt, could and did (but unsuccessfully) apply for the agency for the payment of the interest on the Egyptian loans in London and Paris, but it would have been indelicate to have associated themselves with a public works contract in what would be seen as a family fief. Cromer was directed to the Rothschilds and Ernest Cassel. The former, for twenty years Egypt's financial agents, turned it down after long negotiation. Cassel took it up. (This miscalculation of risk and return caused an estrangement between them. When Cassel gave a small stag-party for the Prince of Wales in 1900, Edward Hamilton remarked that 'in spite of the jealousy with which the Rothschilds regard Cassel, Alfred Rothschild was of the company. It was due to his timidity that the Rothschilds declined' to finance the Nile project.) It was also the year he left the Bischoffsheim roof in the City to set up at 21 Old Street with a modest plate reading 'E. Cassel. First Floor'. He came up with a scheme exactly tailored to the country's requirements: he would assume financial responsibility to the contractors while the Egyptian government would pay only on completion of the dam out of the increased revenue, estimated at £2 million a year, generated by extended irrigation. 'I have never submitted a proposal with more confidence,' Cromer advised Lord Salisbury. Cassel arived in Cairo in 1898 with an unexpected neophyte, Jack Churchill, in his train: 'Mind you try and make Cassel take you to Egypt,' his elder brother Winston had urged him. 'You can't push too much in all things.' He formed the Irrigation Investment Company which commissioned the British contractor Sir John Aird; this was wound up on completion of the dam, its place taken by the trustees, of whom Cassel was one, of the Egyptian

Government Irrigation Trust, whose 4 per cent certificates yielded to Cassel and his partner for the occasion, Algernon Mills, half-yearly payments of £78,613 for the next thirty years. It was one of those felicitous arrangements with which everyone involved was content: as Winston Churchill, who attended the star-studded inauguration aboard Cassel's yacht, crowed, 'they [the government] were offered what was, upon the whole, the best investment in all history.'* Four days after the signing of the contract, Cromer wrote privately to Cassel: 'Let me now express to you how pleased I am that this matter at which we have been working for years has been satisfactorily ended. Of the benefit to the country I entertain no manner of doubt.' One of the greatest civil engineering works ever carried out, it was completed one year ahead of schedule (although at greater cost, £3.5 million against an estimated £2 million) in spite of technical difficulties: the granite foundations of the cataract were found to be rotten. The benefits of what another great proconsul, Lord Milner, considered 'one of the noblest monuments to civil rule in the world' paid for the development of Egypt and the administration of the Sudan, swelled the Treasury and still left a comfortable surplus for the unco-operative Caisse. The boon of water had an electrifying effect on land values. Wilfrid Scawen Blunt, who had bought a walled garden containing the shrine of a Bedouin saint – he had pronounced nationalist rather than religious sympathies – for £40 an acre, sold it within four years of the opening of the dam for a profit of 4,000 per cent.

It would have been uncharacteristic of Cassel if he had not foreseen such a fruitful prospect. Within four months of contracting for the Aswan dam, with Kitchener still battling his way south towards Khartoum, he took another productive initiative, the acquisition of the Khedive's fertile fiefdom.

The Daira Sanieh, some fifth of the cultivable land in Egypt, had been purchased or, less expensively, appropriated by Ismail impartially from his family and fellahin. Pledged as security for every loan he could muster, it had been taken over by the Caisse de la Dette as its sole asset. Once the economy was solvent, the Caisse sought to disembarrass itself of an administrative burden which had shown losses until 1891, and after that only meagre profits. The option for the purchase of the estates for a little under £6.5 million had been acquired by one of the leading local merchant bankers, a Sephardi, Raphael Suares. On the lookout for a suitable substantial partner to share half the huge risk, he approached Cassel. 'I know nothing of this class of business,' Cassel countered

*By an ironic twist of history, the Suez Canal was nationalized within Winston Churchill's lifetime in a reaction to the Anglo-Saxon powers' refusal to finance an updated Aswan dam.

cautiously. 'What do you think it ought to yield?' When Suares replied that he hoped to make about £1 million – a conservative forecast – Cassel was converted. He at once put down a deposit of half a million (which went to pay for part of Kitchener's railway); the balance of the purchase price was to be paid over ten years. Cassel expected to run the estates at a profit while, in the certainty that the sum of the parts was worth more than the whole, simultaneously selling off parcels piecemeal. Six years later, the nominal £1 shares of their limited company – Sir Edward Sassoon also joined the board – were quoted at £108, whereas the disposals realized a total of over £13 million, a profit shared with the government (and the Caisse).

Suares had another ace in his pocket, a concession for a National Bank of Egypt to compete with the French-controlled Ottoman Bank and hopefully to channel investment funds into the country. Suares wished to introduce German capital, from Bismarck's banker Gerson von Bleichröder in particular, but Cassel objected to the preferential premium Suares was prepared to offer. Within days of sealing the deal on the Daira Sanieh company, the decree for the National Bank, now an exclusively Anglo-Egyptian instrument, was signed. Cassel subscribed his own name for half the £1 million initial capital, and invigorated the board of seventeen founder directors, of whom six were local Jewish bankers, with some fresh blood and old friends, among them Carl Meyer, who had by then quit Rothschilds. He next broke new ground, initiating a then unconventional traffic, the poaching of heads from the public service. The first of these transplants, Vincent Caillard, may have come to him on the recommendation of the Treasury in London. Caillard, whose mother was a second cousin of Disraeli, a product like Gordon and Kitchener of the Woolwich military academy, had served as a sapper on various boundary commissions in the Balkans. He had then spent a helpful fourteen years as British commissioner on the Ottoman Public Debt administration in Constantinople, and more recently served as an intelligence officer on Wolseley's staff in the campaign against Arabi Pasha. He was installed by Cassel as a director of the National Bank of Egypt, the Daira Sanieh estates and the Irrigation Investment Company; from there he joined Vickers Sons & Maxim and, a long way off his path, the Mexican Central Railways Securities which Cassel tied up the following year.

Cassel was also exceptionally fortunate in the appointment of one of the two government commissioners to the National Bank, Victor Harari, Director-General of State Accounts at the Ministry of Finance. Educated in France, he was equally at ease in Arabic, English and French and was one of the few members of the Jewish bourgeoisie to be as cordially welcome in both camps, reflected by an unusual double distinction: he became a Pasha and a Knight. In 1906, aged fifty, he retired from government service and joined the board of the National Bank, a directorship he held for an astonishing span of forty years until his death. He acted as Cassel's personal representative in Egypt; together they established the Mortgage Company, with Lord Milner in the chair, and the Wadi Kom Ombo development of 800 square miles of land for cultivation below the Aswan dam. The National Bank set up its own department for agricultural loans. This was hived off as a separate Agricultural Bank at Cromer's suggestion three years later and was financed under Cassel's leadership with an injection of £2 million. In the year of its birth, the Agricultural Bank, as Cassel was delighted to inform the King, had lent £1 million, one-quarter in sums below £20 to smallholders who could otherwise only borrow on the uncertain expectation of their crops. After three years of operation the founder shares, of a nominal £5, rose to £800. If Cassel left Egypt a richer man than he had arrived, he left Egypt unprecedently prosperous. In the last year of the old century he received his recognition and reward as a Knight Commander of the Order of St Michael and St George. ('You know we rejoice', Jacob Schiff wrote to him, 'in all the beautiful and good that comes to you.') But notwithstanding Cromer's sincere appreciation of Cassel's great services, it would have been surprising if there had not been occasional friction between two such strong-willed and single-minded characters. Neither was Cassel any more tactful and conciliatory; even in the gentler setting of the drawing room he was brusque to a degree barely short of offensive. And although he broadly served Cromer's ambition for Egypt, the Agent's notions were not always compatible with Cassel's *raison d'être*. Their differences are difficult to fathom; they were doubtless exaggerated by the tittle-tattle of club and chancery. In 1902, the same year that Cassel had presented a personal cheque of £40,000 to Cromer for travelling eye-clinics to treat the age-old scourge of trachoma, a young diplomat, Horace Rumbold, reported to his father that the financier, then on a visit to Cairo, was intriguing to have Cromer removed, or at least reduced in authority, in order that he might take over the country's finances; he had even, Rumbold alleged, secured King Edward's support with the promise of a share in the spoils. This was an implausible, not to say impracticable, goal, and was a reflection of those dark mutterings in some quarters which imputed sinister motives to the growing intimacy between the King and the Jewish millionaire. Cromer's deposition, however, was very much the wily Khedive's unfaltering object.

The Khedive Tewfik, a biddable nonentity, had died suddenly in 1892 and was succeded by his eighteen-year-old son, Abbas Hilmi, who, as a frequent guest at the court of Franz Joseph – a sovereign who ruled as well as reigned – had acquired autocratic yearnings. He was encouraged by his French tutor, appointed European Secretary in his cabinet, to throw off Cromer's galling yoke, and to this end he encouraged and subsidized the nascent nationalist movement which found a sympathetic home in Paris. Abbas Hilmi had also a venal and acquisitive side to his character. This Cassel did nothing to discourage, although a genuine sympathy seems to have developed between them. Cassel, cutting out Cromer, set himself up as a broker between the Khedive and the King; perhaps the King, so long excluded from State business, rather relished the subterfuge.

Sir Ernest, as he now was, had seen much of Abbas Hilmi over the official opening ceremonies of the Aswan dam, attended by the King's younger brother the Duke of Connaught. He profited from this acquaintance to promote a private visit of the Khedive to London once the King had agreed to receive him. Cassel found his new role of purveyor of courtly banalities demanding; a report to the King of his meeting with the Khedive took him three drafts to polish to his satisfaction (he deleted his original diagnosis that the Egyptian ruler 'fully recognizes that his own and his people's interest demand that he should treat the English with the utmost confidence and give them his full co-operation'). Evidently hoping that Edward's avuncular charm might soften the Khedive's Anglophobia where Cromer's imperious manner had so conspicuously failed, he added a gentle reminder that his guest was 'very susceptible of kind and considerate treatment and . . . resents a brusque and hard manner'. (Edward Hamilton, staying with Cassel in Switzerland, found the Khedive 'a very pleasant, unassuming little man'.) After the Khedive had expressed through Cassel his pleasure at the prospect of a visit, the King gently reminded his friend, 'I should hardly like to encourage him to come till I know if Lord Cromer approves of it.' Lord Cromer had no objection whatever, Cassel assured the King; he had found him 'ill and aged' but 'in an amiable frame of mind'. The King, delighted, cleared the visit with his ministers.

In June 1903 Wilfrid Scawen Blunt noted that Abbas Hilmi was 'staying with the King's millionaire . . . in Grosvenor Square'. (The King had told Cassel that he thought it 'would *look* better' if their visitor accepted his hospitality, though 'I see no reason why you should move out of your house! as frankly he would not bring many people'.) Blunt, the champion of the underdog, was not considered wholly desirable company for the Khedive, who had expressed a wish to see his famous Arab stud at

Crabbet Park. When all the arrangements had been made, the visit was cancelled by telegram at the last minute. His frustrated host was convinced that no less a person than the King – 'for the Khedive would hardly be such a goose as to be frightened by Lord Lansdowne' – had been responsible: the Khedive is 'under Cassel's charge, and Cassel is the King's man'.

It was Blunt again, a glutton for gossip, who picked up rumours of an intrigue, favoured by the King, to retire Cromer and replace him with Eldon Gorst, the financial adviser to the Egyptian government. Gorst's predecessor imputed this 'extraordinary and rather impudent programme' to Gorst himself, who was seen by Cromer's Oriental Secretary as 'a hardened opportunist'. Whatever the substance, if this sort of talk was current at the Agency, a less tolerant and patient man than Lord Cromer would have been irked. He had other reasons for dissatisfaction. Gorst, who had in his gift concessions coveted by Cassel, combined with the financier to encourage the Khedive's extravagances and speculations which Cromer was doing his best to curb. Cromer disapproved of Gorst's intimacy with Cassel as much as the latter's bad influence over the Khedive. The matter came to a head in 1904 when Cassel lent the Khedive £500,000 at the friendly rate of 2½ per cent. Cromer suspected that Gorst had encouraged this and, infuriated by such irresponsibility, insisted on his dismissal. Cassel intervened with the Foreign Secretary, Lord Lansdowne; Gorst was appointed Assistant Under-Secretary of State in London over Cromer's head.

However, it is evident that Cromer bore no grudge, if indeed he gave any credence to the rumours of Cassel's designs. In the year following Sir Ernest's indulgence of the Khedive, Cromer consulted Barings about the sale of a new issue of Egyptian bonds, but shied away from the direct use of their services: he was constantly assailed, he pleaded, by 'a very vigilant, very hostile and utterly unscrupulous opposition', egged on, as he might reasonably have complained, by the newly affluent Khedive. Cromer, however, suggested to his nephew Revelstoke, 'if Cassel likes to associate Baring Brothers and Co. or anyone else in the business, I don't mind. This is his affair . . .' Barings shared in the business, and proconsular propriety was preserved.

In 1907 Cromer finally resigned through ill-health, and was indeed succeeded by Eldon Gorst. It then became the turn of the new Agent, now keeper of the public purse, to suffer the importunate advances of his former accomplice in profligacy. Ronald Storrs, a young orientalist attached to the Agency, heard that Cassel and a colleague were intent on forcing the government to borrow an unwanted and unneeded £2 million in order 'to steady the market'. 'We don't want any,' wrote Storrs, 'but they say we can have it *so* cheap.' Cassel, according to Storrs's flatmate, *The Times* correspondent, retaliated by organizing a press campaign to harass Gorst.

Gorst's earlier intimacy with Abbas Hilmi was one reason for his appointment. He had been instructed by the new Liberal government in London to reverse Cromer's policy and to conciliate rather than cow the Khedive. The latter, who had previously expressed a willingness to be more co-operative, immediately interpreted this as a sign of weakness and unleashed a torrent of anti-British abuse in the local press by his nationalist dupes. King Edward in consequence cooled towards him. He would receive him if he came to London, he advised Cassel, though he would never trust him again. Cassel, by now out of sympathy with the new Agent, continued to cosset the Khedive.

The King had a last, untypically tactless word. Awarding Cromer the Order of Merit, which he had founded early in his reign, he said, 'I am happy to bestow this final honour upon you and all the more so because I hear so good an account of your work in Egypt from my friend Sir Ernest Cassel.' Cromer had devoted almost a quarter of a century to Egypt at no personal profit, so it is hardly surprising that this remark, according to Blunt, raised Cromer's bile. It was, however, most probably a calculated reprisal. Cromer had countered a previous summons by the King by somewhat brusquely suggesting an alternative appointment. 'He seems to take me for the Khedive,' His Majesty had muttered.

The Entente Cordiale of 1904 was the final disappointment to the Khedive's hopes of using the French lever to prise the British out of Egypt. The 'actual determining cause' of this fateful entanglement was, in the eyes of the head of the Foreign Office, Cromer's anxiety for an understanding with France which would allow him a free hand to govern. In exchange France was to be permitted to 'protect' Morocco, a barbarous and precarious feudal conglomerate.[*] The rununciation by France of her claims in the Nile valley was seen in London as a sincere sacrifice; in Paris it was seen as a distressing privation but a prerequisite to engaging Britain's support in pursuit of the national obsession – the recovery of Alsace and Lorraine. After the French and English officials had sat down to negotiate an entente, the Foreign Office called on Cassel to advance a loan to the Moroccan government as a sop to the French; Cassel himself later confirmed that this was founded 'upon considerations mainly political'. The Treasury, as Cassel soon found out, was less quixotic. 'Of

---

[*]Until early this century, the Jewish community in Morocco enjoyed an esteemed and valuable prerogative – the salting of the heads of the Sultan's not infrequent victims for public display.

course he is glad to oblige the Government at home,' Sir Edward Hamilton conceded, but 'he is not very happy about locking up several hundred thousands.' Cassel understood that the loan would at least be guaranteed in return for his favour. The Chancellor, Charles Ritchie, disabused him of this notion; the government could merely undertake to do all in its power to enforce payment against Morocco. Hamilton, a more sternly principled public servant, considered that it had a moral obligation and could not allow him any loss; the government would have to 'go to Parliament to ask them to indemnify the lender and then condone their irregular conduct'. Ritchie proposed to go further and insert a clause expressly repudiating any pecuniary liability. Small wonder, Hamilton reflected, that Cassel should object. Lord Lansdowne, the Foreign Secretary, sent for Hamilton to try to arrange the business. While Cassel was prepared to advance £300,000, Ritchie remained adamant that all liability should be disclaimed. Cassel would not agree. Hamilton thought it 'mainly a difference of words; and I think we ought to find a means of adjusting the difference'. But seven months later, in December 1903, just four months before the Entente Cordiale was proclaimed, Hamilton, who was staying with Cassel, was less buoyant, even though Ritchie had by then been summarily dismissed by Balfour. 'I don't believe he will go with the Moorish loan . . . On the face of it I don't see how a sixpence can be sent.' Some time elapsed before a compromise was reached by Cassel insisting that the money be channelled to a specific purpose over which he could exercise control. In this way was established the National Bank of Morocco, fashioned on his Egyptian model. The new creation was a less spectacular success than its exemplar. The environment was not encouraging. The French chose to consolidate their hold by ensuring their role as principal creditor, to the eventual exclusion of all other lenders, and, by open pressure and bureaucratic obstruction, to monopolize commerce against the strict letter of the Entente. Cassel's compliance may have accounted for his promotion to GCMG in 1905; the following year he received the customary Legion of Honour – and perhaps, as the Grand Mufti informed Wilfrid Scawen Blunt, a more tangible benefit, a land grant of over 100,000 Moroccan acres.

Sir Ernest was called back to the Foreign Office in 1908 by Lansdowne's successor, Sir Edward Grey, and begged to inject another £500,000 into Morocco. Though he must have wondered where this importuning might end, he agreed, but suggested that his fee as a milch cow should be the Grand Cross of the Order of the Bath. There were conventions even in the traffic in honours which such plain speaking flouted. Such subtleties did not much weigh with Cassel. Sir Charles

Hardinge, Permanent Under-Secretary, who had no cause to love Cassel, maliciously related that the King, though none too particular about his own promotions, was displeased; the Foreign Secretary took it 'quite calmly'. It is unclear who put up Cassel for the honour; his name appeared on a list for the Birthday Honours of 1909, handed to Asquith with the King's verbal approval. The Prime Minister had certainly promised Cassel that he should have it, but, having heard no more of the matter, the financier grew impatient. Francis Knollys, after being badgered, informed Asquith's office – Cassel had not yet formally agreed to the loan – that 'he is anxious . . . to have it conferred upon him without loss of time'. True, Grey, a first cousin of Cromer, was unworldly, but the Prime Minister was certainly aware that the Chief Whip was selling honours in exchange for contributions to party funds. Cassel, on the other hand, was being urged to perform a service to the State without any security or guarantee. Any comment may have been caused by the modesty of Cassel's demand; that same year the disreputable and widely detested South African financier J. B. Robinson, no stranger to Sandringham, had earned a baronetcy with a donation of a trifling £30,000 to the Liberals, a creation urged in fulsome terms by the Colonial Under-Secretary, Winston Churchill.

Cassel, at all events, achieved his 'childish desire' the following year.

8

Jews at Court

In 1899 Winston and Jack Churchill were preparing for another expedition further south. Winston had enlisted as a war correspondent to cover the disastrous early stages of the Boer War and had procured for his younger brother, despite one defective eye, a lieutenancy in the South African Light Horse on the stipulation that Cassel, his employer, should agree. Winston always recognized Cassel as 'my father's old friend', but the evidence for this is scant. Cassel inherited from Baron Hirsch a sense of obligation towards Lady Randolph Churchill, whose beauty was matched by warmth and wit. (Never, even in that golden age of diarists, was there the least hint that Cassel indulged in dalliance; he was happy to observe the unwritten convention that he should provide comfort and assistance to the Prince's companions.) Jennie and her sister Clara, married to the reprobate Moreton Frewen, had been frequent guests on Hirsch's Hungarian estate (the attraction for Jennie was the presence of Charles, Count Kinsky). Winston meanwhile had been sent to France, during the Christmas holidays in 1891, to learn the language; he hoped to ride with Hirsch's boys, although, as their English was fluent, his Harrow headmaster felt it would be 'a loss to him to be much with them'. Winston, aged seventeen, had evidently fallen under the spell of Hirsch's reputation, for he upbraided his mother: 'I don't know how to get to see Baron Hirsch. I am afraid you have not written.' A few days later, when the Baron's arrival in Paris was announced, Winston was urged by his old nurse to call on him as soon as he had his new clothes.

In 1892, some three years after Cassel had moved into the Marlborough House orbit, Lord Randolph was on sufficiently close terms with him to tap his goodwill. If Winston again failed his army examination, he considered putting him into business: 'I could get him something very good through Natty [Rothschild] or Horace [Farquhar] or Cassel.' Lord Randolph managed his relationship with Cassel, who had not yet attracted much public notice, more discreetly than that with his old schoolfriend Natty. Randolph Churchill was the stormy petrel of politics; flamboyant, extravagant, rude and quarrelsome, though with undeniable personal charm, he was an uncomfortable colleague. He had a patrician disregard for public opinion and mere money; to others it seemed he owed his success to his insolence. When he became Chancellor of the Exchequer in 1886, Lady Salisbury, informing Herbert Bismarck that many of the Cabinet were dull but could all be trusted, inveighed against Lord Randolph, who 'communicated everything to Natty Rothschild'; she hinted that 'people did not give great financial houses political news for nothing'. (Ironically, Arnold White later castigated her nephew Arthur Balfour, by then in charge of his own Cabinet, for his 'habit of spending his weekends with hosts whose powers in the world of cosmopolitan finance enables them to exercise great influence on the questions of the day'.) After a few months in the Exchequer, Lord Randolph, in a moment of pique, dashed off an impetuous letter of resignation – Alfred Rothschild reproached him for not first consulting the family – and confirmed it to *The Times* before he had a chance to reconsider. Lord Salisbury, greatly relieved, accepted it. Though only thirty-seven, Lord Randolph never held office again. (Eddy Hamilton recorded in his diary that Natty Rothschild and Rosebery agreed that 'no man ever had a better political instinct and a worse political judgement'.) In the same month, Hamilton confided to Lord Rosebery (of all people) that 'trouble might in any case have come from the excessive intimacy of a man occupying the post of Chancellor of the Exchequer with a certain great financial house'. It would be charitable to suppose that Natty helped Randolph to an understanding of 'those damned dots' which so exercised him at the Exchequer.

Jennie's father, Leonard Jerome of New York, was generally but mistakenly believed to have settled an adequate income on the Churchills, whereas money was a permanent problem in the former Chancellor's household. Five years after resigning, Lord Randolph declared himself to be 'done with politics' and took himself off to Mafeking to try instead 'to make a little money for the boys and for ourselves'. Cassel had followed a similar southern path before making up his mind, in his typically cautious fashion, to take a share in the flotation of Julius Wernher's and Alfred Beit's first deep-level gold-mine in the Rand, and on his return Lord Randolph proposed himself to dine to discuss 'Johannesburg affairs'. These, at least for him, did not prosper, and in 1895, after a lingering demented death from syphilis, he left his wife with just a small annuity of £500, debts, two dependent sons and no home of her own. (Shortly after Lord Randolph resigned, Natty Rothschild wrote him a teasingly enigmatic note, written, as usual, in indelible mauve pencil and with a cavalier disregard for conventional punctuation: 'I have sown the seed, the corn is just beginning to grow it depends on yourself if you cultivate it.' It clearly withered. Lord Randolph died indebted to the Rothschilds to the sum of over £65,000, the bulk incurred after he left office.) The doubly distraught widow – her lover, Charles Kinsky, had recently married under family pressure – struggled gamely against these odds. Jennie, as the great showman C. B. Cochran observed, threw money round like water; neither did Winston flinch from drawing on her for financial support. It was Cassel's task to limit the flood. She embraced a literary career; Cassel, with more altruism than expectation of profit, invested in her *Anglo-Saxon Review* (it survived ten issues). In return she provided an entrée to that society which Cassel found more congenial than the solidly male bastion of the Marlborough Club. In 1899 Cassel was present at a dinner Jennie gave for the Prince of Wales, the Duke and Duchess of Devonshire, Cecil Rhodes, Lady Gerard, Lord Hardwicke, the Prince's godson, and the Countess of Warwick.

Within months, Jennie was engaged to a young Guardsman of Winston's age, George Cornwallis-West, another godson of the Prince. (Eddy Hamilton described the new couple as 'the Cornwallis-Wests (Lady Randolph and her boy)'.) A genial sportsman, he was described by a fellow officer as a 'good-looking fellow; bit short on brains'. He was also short of money. Cassel was again called on. George was attracted, so he admitted, to electrical engineering. 'Not the City?' enquired Cassel. George replied that the life of a half-commission man on the Exchange held no allure. Cassel thought for a moment (he was, he admitted to Sir Almeric Fitzroy, a 'man who measures his words'). 'There are many young men of your class', he finally replied, 'who should never go east of Temple Bar. Perhaps you are one of them.' Cassel dutifully found him (unpaid) employment in Glasgow with the contractors for his Central Railway Company. (George took this to be a test of his character.) Five years later George did set up on the Exchange, trading on Jennie's contacts. He called on Leopold de Rothschild at New Court, who received him courteously but evasively. Ushering his guest out, Leo stopped by the cashier's desk, muttered a word into the old man's ear and, slipping something into George's hand, said, 'Here's a little present for you, my dear George, with my best wishes for your future in the City.' George, slow-witted, stuffed it unthinkingly into his pocket, only to discover later a £100 note. His feelings, as he described them, were not unmixed, but, in the spirit in which the gift was intended, he returned it with proper thanks. The same afternoon he received a summons from Lord Rothschild. 'Um,' he opened, 'what was it you came to see Leo about this morning?' George explained his mission. 'I'll take 5,000 Cargo Fleet shares,' responded Natty. 'Goodbye.' With such gruff endorsement George succeeded in placing 50,000 shares within the next fortnight. This success was short-lived. Cassel's assessment was proved correct and the Cornwallis-Wests, largely through George's inability to provide, were divorced in 1913.

On the eve of the Churchill boys' departure for South Africa, Winston was a guest at a farewell dinner Cassel gave at the Carlton Hotel for the Prince and some forty men of the 'ruling generation' in honour of Lord Gerard. (His Lordship, who died in 1902, was the posthumous father-in-law of Baron Hirsch's heir, Baron de Forest. His unfortunate widow was somewhat unusually sued for slander by Forest, who had inherited his father's litigious nature, for alleging that he treated his wife with cruelty. Lord Derby, whose household comptroller was a co-defendant, was subpoenaed but declined to recall the uncharitable words, and the case, for which Forest had retained no fewer than four KCs, was dismissed before lunch.)

The Boer War was the last of the gentlemanly campaigns in which the privileged combatants set off with the insouciance (and all the accoutrements) of those undertaking a combined big-game safari and Grand Tour. At home, by contrast, the conflict provoked a public display of anti-Semitism, born of antagonism to the conspicuous excess of the Randlords, the financiers with the 'Rhine-wine names', who had taken over Park Lane. Both supporters on the radical right and opponents on the Liberal Left discerned behind the cause of war the manipulative hand of 'cosmopolitan capitalism'. Anxious Anglo-Jewry, with the Chief Rabbi and the *Jewish Chronicle* in the van, aligned themselves with the Conservatives and the 'Limps' – the Liberal imperialists such as Rosebery; this patriotic example inspired as many as 2,000 Jews to enlist for service on the veldt. Alfred Rothschild considerately relieved the tedium of George Cornwallis-West's month-long voyage to Cape Town with twenty cases of 1887 Perrier-Jouët for his mess, after arranging the famous Gala Night at Covent Garden, starring Patti and the massed bands of the Household Cavalry and Brigade of Guards, which raised more than £10,000 for war charities. Natty chose to welcome the returning local heroes, the Bucks Yeomanry, to a suitable spread at Tring with veal and ham pie, salmon and champagne jelly, with wine cup and, for the rare abstainer, aerated water – and a silver watch for every man.[*]

Winston returned from South Africa a hero. The author of two books of stirring adventure, he set about turning his experience to profit. Cassel was already caring for his surprising surplus of income when he was further entrusted with £6,000, the greater part of Winston's lecture fees, and later with much of the £8,000 of royalties he received for the biography of his father. He was instructed to 'Feed my sheep'. He fed them, as Churchill later wrote, 'with great prudence. They did not multiply fast but they fattened steadily and none of them ever died. Indeed from year to year they had a few lambs; but they were not numerous enough for me to live upon. I had every year to eat a sheep or two as well; so gradually my flock grew smaller until in a few years it was almost entirely devoured. Nevertheless while it lasted I had no care.' This touching pastoral panegyric owed not a little to wilful wool-gathering. Despite the dwindling flock, Winston still had need to ask his mother to relieve him of burdensome loans and to overdraw with Cassel. Jack was a different sort of problem to his mother. She was anxious for him to return to England. Cassel, she assured him, considered that 'now that the war was almost over, you had done your duty by your country, and that you ought to come home and attend to your business'. A few days later she pleaded, 'You will find Cassel ready to receive you with open arms.' Jack, however, was determined to soldier on for the duration. He later went back into the City, though none of his mentor's financial flair had rubbed off on him.

The British government also had problems in making ends meet. The first talks about ways and means of funding the fighting opened just after some of the worst news of the war reached London. Fresh commanders, ever more troops were required on a scale unprecedented for a Victorian colonial war, and it would cost accordingly – a colossal £200 million (fourteen years later the same sum lasted a bare month of warfare). There was a difference of opinion on how to raise the wind; it was Sir Edward Hamilton's responsibility to bridge that difference. The Treasury (and Ernest Cassel) favoured an exceptional

[*]When his son Walter had been commissioned in the family regiment twelve years before, Natty had presented his company with a Maxim gun, a unique acquisition for the Yeomanry at a time when the military hierarchy scorned such innovations.

short-dated loan; the Rothschilds and the Bank of England preferred another issue of Consols on the ground that it was what the public (and the City) wanted and expected. Cassel believed this would cost the government more in the long run. The Chancellor, Sir Michael Hicks Beach, saw all the protagonists in turn. Whatever the decision, Natty Rothschild and Cassel offered gladly to assist in guaranteeing success for the operation, though Cassel preferred the Rothschilds to take the lead while he would 'work quietly behind the scenes'. Within two weeks the Bank of England came round to the idea of a special £30 million ten-year War Loan, though Natty and Leopold Rothschild still hankered for Consols. The Treasury view prevailed, a decision Cassel was called on to defend in a long letter to *The Times*. The day before the final details were to be decided between the Chancellor and the Bank of England, the 'Rothschilds, Cassel and Schuster* all came this morning to say their last word about the terms of the Loan,' Sir Edward Hamilton recorded, 'and I arranged that none of them should clash and that one should not know that the other had been at the Treasury.' The issue was 'understandably' a great success, over-subscribed by more than ten times. Hamilton congratulated himself that 'I don't think that I could have secured for the Chancellor of the Exchequer better advice than I did'. The loan had also, at the insistence of Hamilton and Cassel, been issued without any government guarantee, despite Natty Rothschild's 'prognostication' that such an omission 'would ensure a "Magersfontein"' (a recent war disaster). (The previous year Hamilton had been staying at The Durdans with Lord Rosebery, his exact contemporary at Eton and Christ Church, and Natty Rothschild, who had 'been making himself very agreeable'. Hamilton, though admiring Natty's 'immense amount of knowledge . . . and a good memory whereby to bring it out', nevertheless considered that he was 'prone to inaccuracy and to exaggeration'.) One-quarter of the applications were for £100 only, 'so,' Hamilton congratulated himself, 'we have got the small guy in, which was just what was wanted'. Cassel, however, still 'thought that we were giving the big folk too much . . . We can easily remedy this.'

The corollary to the immense resources that had had to be called up to prosecute the war was casualties: out of the half a million men in the field, some 8,000 were killed, more than 20,000 wounded, while many died of fever. A new friend of the Prince, Miss Agnes Keyser, at once offered her large house in Grosvenor Crescent, which she shared with her sister Fanny, as a nursing home for officers returning from South Africa, to be

*(Later Sir) Felix Schuster, descendant of Frankfurt bankers who had migrated to London during the Napoleonic Wars; headed the Union Bank, later merged with the National Provincial.

run entirely at her own expense; as, unusually for the time, she had nursing experience, she offered herself as matron. Her father, Charles, was fortunately a wealthy stockbroker, a great-nephew of David Ricardo, the economist and Member of Parliament (after he had dropped his Jewish faith on taking a Quaker wife), and an even more successful speculator. Agnes, then forty-six, a handsome woman with a strong but sympathetic character, had first met the Prince in February 1898, the same month in which he had also formed his attachment with Alice Keppel, so she was spared the heavier attentions of 'Edward the Caresser' (as Henry James called him). They built up a comfortable, uncomplicated relationship; she would remonstrate gently with him over his eating and smoking habits, while simultaneously pandering to his taste for such nursery fare as Irish stew and rice pudding. When the last of her patients had left her after the war, Sister Agnes, as she was respectfully known, considered recovering the full use of her house, but King Edward, as he now was, persuaded her to continue the good work under his patronage. As the inimitable cockney 'Duchess of Jermyn Street', Rosa Lewis of the Cavendish Hotel, put it, Edward 'got his nob friends to dole out'. Twenty-four of them were solicited for £100 a year over ten years for King Edward VII's Hospital for Officers. The King and his son Prince George headed the list; there followed the names of Sir Ernest Cassel, Alfred de Rothschild, old Henry Bischoffsheim, one of the Sassoons, Edward Levy-Lawson, first Baron Burnham, principal proprietor of London's first penny paper, the *Daily Telegraph*, and Sigmund Neumann, Randlord and London banker. In 1904, the hospital moved to Grosvenor Gardens. There was room for twelve officers (those on the retired list were charged 2s. 6d. a day); towards the evening the butler would make the rounds of the patients to take their orders for physic of a cheering as much as a healing nature, which, in those spacious days, was on the establishment. This gracious regime imperilled the hospital's future financial security; the original twenty-four angels were retapped, while Sister Agnes herself sent out an appeal to all serving officers for an individual subscription of five shillings a year, a prototype private health insurance. The results were disappointing, only a third of the hoped-for target of £6,000 being raised. Sister Agnes again dug into her own pocket to make up the difference. An intimate friend of Edward's daughter-in-law Queen Mary, Sister Agnes died a spinster in her ninetieth year.

Among the warriors who rejoined the colours at the outbreak of the South African War was an eligible bachelor and copy-book hero whose good looks reinforced his high opinion of himself. Major Wilfrid Ashley, a grandson of the seventh Earl of Shaftesbury (the great factory reformer, philanthropist and ardent Evangelical), and great-grandson of Lady Palmerston, through whom he inherited the estate of Broadlands in Hampshire, was dry and distant, niggardly and, despite his impeccably liberal lineage, reactionary (after serving as Baldwin's Minister of Transport through the second half of the Twenties, including the General Strike, he was created Baron Mount Temple). He did not see much service in the field, but was more fortunate in London, meeting at the age of thirty-three in the first year of the century that much-sought-after prize, a young, pretty and personable heiress. Maud Cassel had been brought up by her aunt, Mrs 'Bobbie' Cassel, without the benefit of the company of brothers or sisters, while indulged by a doting but dour father who had little time to spare for family life. She had emerged quite unspoilt. Maud was the antithesis of her father, 'a delightful companion', thought her friend the Duchess of Sermoneta, 'with a great sense of humour and joie de vivre . . . very popular' (although she played bridge and poker for rather high stakes); the same friend was ungrudging in her admiration of Maud's 'most exquisite complexion . . . clear hazel eyes and very pretty hands and feet'. She was frail, however, and tended to tire easily. The couple, so seemingly ill-matched, were married in fashionable St George's, Hanover Square, on 4 January 1901, unusually a Friday (the date had been dictated by the Prince of Wales's prior public engagements). The Prince attended with his sister Princess Louise, and his mistress, Mrs George Keppel. Also present were the odd Duke and the American Ambassador. Sir Ernest's present to the bride, a full crown of diamonds, was admired almost as much for its beauty as for its worth; the trousseau was said to have cost another £5,000, a Cabinet minister's salary. In November, Cassel's first granddaughter, Edwina, was born, King Edward standing as godfather.

Just weeks after the wedding, the Prince, advised of his mother's fast-failing health, supped quietly with Agnes Keyser before starting for Osborne at dawn by special train. On 22 January 1901, 'Bertie', rising sixty, most respectfully declining to assume the style of Albert, became King Edward VII. There was immediate speculation, not all of it flattering, on how he would respond to his new responsibilities, and above all whether he would now change his ways and drop his former cronies. Edward Hamilton was benignly indulgent: 'One cannot help feeling glad that the Prince has succeeded to the throne before he is too old. He will I feel sure fill the throne admirably; I feel pretty confident he will be more dignified and if he errs at all it will be on the side of excess of strictness.' Others were less confident. Over thirty years before, William Bagehot in *The English Constitution* had expressed the fear that it was 'worse when [the Prince of Wales] comes to [the throne] old or middle-aged'; he might then be nothing but 'a pleasure-loving lounger, or an active fool', the tool of others, guided by his favourites and corrupted by his mistresses. *The Times*, which had always regarded the Prince's antics with the greatest reserve, impolitely recalled that he had been 'importuned by temptation in its most seductive forms' and that he must often have prayed 'lead us not into temptation' with 'a feeling akin to hopelessness'.

Four months later Hamilton's own high hopes were dashed. One Saturday, after visiting the Bischoffsheims at Stanmore, he returned to London to dine with Cassel, a small party composed of the King and 'the Favourite', the host's sister and her son. 'It shows how easy it is to be out in one's calculations,' Hamilton mourned. 'I quite made up my mind that when He came to the Throne, the King would have such a sense of his own dignity and be so determined to play the part of monarch that He would only dine at exceptional houses . . . But after dining with Cassel of course he can dine anywhere. I regret it much.' Two days later Francis Knollys, the otherwise broadminded private secretary to the King, echoed this lament. He did 'not like at all the King making himself common by dining about here, there and everywhere. But nothing can be done,' he lamented to Hamilton. 'There is nobody who could speak so as to influence him.' Within the month the King dined with Alfred Rothschild. 'This going round everywhere, to anybody, is a thousand pities,' Hamilton confided to his diary, 'and if it gets known by the public it will do him great harm.' (Hamilton, a liberal and kindly man but *plus royalist que le roi*, had a strict notion of kingcraft. He disapproved for the same reasons, though 'sensible of the honour of His coming,' of the King (and Mrs Keppel) dining with him in his rooms at Whitehall Court.) The carping had nothing to do with the company. Hamilton shared the same delights. That year he spent the weekends, on the evidence of his diary, at least once a month on average with the Sassoons in Brighton, the Rothschilds at Tring, Ascott and Gunnersbury, and with the Bischoffsheims at Stanmore; he would meet many of the same faces at Mentmore or Sandringham, while cheerfully dining with Cassel or Alfred Rothschild in London. Two years later Hamilton relented. After the triumphant conclusion of a potentially thorny State visit to Ireland, Hamilton admitted, 'The fact is he always does the right thing . . . partly by intuition and partly because he is a very remarkable man.' Though his character might be restored, the King's long familiar predilections could still surprise and dismay his subjects. 'But why', Eddy Hamilton wondered in the course of a good gossip with 'a most agreeable, charming and clever woman', Lady Gosford, 'should he now prefer to associate with Jews?'

(Lady Gosford might have enlightened him. The Queen's Lady of the Bedchamber, she was generally recognized as Lord Rothschild's mistress.) The rumour that Edward himself had Jewish blood 'through some indiscretion of his father's mother' was still current. Such wonderment was not confined to his own subjects. One year after the Entente Cordiale was sealed, a friend of Hamilton's in Paris was assured by a bus conductor that the King was 'at the moment most popular', but 'Why should he be so continuously surrounded by Jews, who would not be received in Paris?'

The King himself gave a forthright reply to those who were pondering on how he would handle his long-awaited elevation. Expectations had been raised when it was noticed that, visiting Brighton, the King omitted to pay his usual call on the Sassoons. They were soon dashed. Sir Ernest Cassel and Lord Rothschild were inducted into the ranks of the Privy Council. (The King had tried to secure peerages for Cassel and Sir Thomas Lipton, but Lord Salisbury had firmly resisted the royal wish.) They were both awarded Edward's personal Royal Victorian Order, which he was accustomed to lavish to such charming (and economic) effect, Rothschild as a Knight Grand Cross, Cassel as a Knight Commander. A short while later, Hamilton was staying at Sandringham. 'There is nobody here,' he confided to his diary, 'bar Reuben Sassoon, on whom to his great delight the King has bestowed the Victorian Order 4th or 5th class (I don't know the difference).' (Hamilton had been made a KCVO in private.) Arthur Sassoon received the same; his half-brother Sir Albert had died two years previously, two years short of his eightieth birthday, having furnished himself with a magnificent mausoleum on a street corner of Brighton (it was later converted into an air raid shelter). The only other death among the ageing court circle had been Ferdinand Rothschild.

In May 1890, the year after Ferdinand, Natty's cousin and brother-in-law, had put the finishing touch to Waddesdon, the old Queen's curiosity had prevailed on her to break with custom by calling on one of her subjects. The Manor had taken the Baron fifteen years to complete to his entire satisfaction, a labour of love in his eyes, though at the time of creation he already feared that his future home would sadly 'share the same fate of most properties whose owners have no descendants, and fall into decay'. His French architect he had found 'a purist in style' – High Renaissance in this case – 'painstaking, conscientious and of the most scrupulous honesty'. He was on the other hand dilatory and impractical, with the most supreme contempt for internal conveniences – 'he and his numerous family lived huddled together in a small and musty house' (Ferdinand lived alone in over two hundred rooms). It was tedious to have to explain 'the simplest facts about comfortable life – that guests would need dressing rooms and bathrooms, and space for their clothes . . .' Victoria toured the broad, wooded acres – fully-grown trees had been hauled up by teams of as many as sixteen horses to be planted around the bare hilltop – in a contraption resembling a Bath chair drawn by a pony. The only shadow cast over the reception was when Lord Hartington absent-mindedly* shook the royal hand that was extended to be kissed. (The Queen kept it resolutely to her side for the rest of the day.) Finding her host 'as delightful as the place is beautiful', the Queen graciously left a marble bust of herself by her sculptor (and medallist) in ordinary, Sir Edgar Boehm, as a souvenir. Her heir, a frequent and less formal visitor, later had a still more painful experience, cascading down the spiral west staircase and cracking his kneecap. (Max Beerbohm celebrated the descent in a serial cartoon, Edward loyally proclaiming 'Three sheers for the Queensh!' on the top step: a trifle unjustly – he was found by Daisy Brooke, who was coming to the end of her spell of service as mistress, on her way down to a late Sunday breakfast.)

A widower since 1866, Ferdinand was inclined to be peevish and fretful. Fondly mocking, sometimes mildly malicious, stories circulated about his obsessive observance of an unusually sumptuous style of hospitality with which he regaled the fortunate; it was fear, in fact, that his cousin Alfred would poach his house parties which spurred him to intense competition. Daisy Brooke described Ferdinand, not unreasonably, as a reincarnation of Lorenzo the Magnificent. Waddesdon was indeed truffled with treasures. His father had sensibly recognized that his vocation was artistic and had absolved him from practising the family trade, while leaving him well equipped to follow his natural bent. He graduated into one of the most noted connoisseurs (and collectors) of French eighteenth-century art and English portraits along with early Dutch and Flemish masters. Much of the panelling in his home was of noble origin, from the hôtel of the Maréchal-Duc de Richelieu, or from the château of the Montmorencys; more had been salvaged from the great houses that Baron Haussmann had demolished to make way for the Parisian boulevards designed to provide a clear field of fire in the event of the fickle mob mounting a determined protest against the Empire. Underfoot were superb Savonnerie carpets made for the Louvre and Versailles; Gobelin and Beauvais tapestries from designs by Boucher

---

*Lord Hartington, shortly to become the Duke of Devonshire, recalled 'a horrid nightmare. I dreamed that I was making a speech in the House of Lords – and I woke up and found I was actually doing so.'

graced the walls. One of the two galleries leading from the main entrance was dominated by two views of Venice by Guardi, the largest known paintings by that artist; other rooms sported Gainsboroughs (including his 'Pink Boy'), Romneys and Reynoldses. There was an abundance of rare French furniture, much Meissen, a Sèvres *bleu céleste* dessert service; even arms and armour found their place. In all, the collection filled two dozen catalogues. It was the astute Prince of Wales, surveying these wonders, who urged the British Museum to appoint Ferdinand a trustee, a shrewd choice as it transpired: owners of treasures the museum could not afford for itself were referred to the Baron, in the expectation that they might revert in time.

Ferdinand was a professional bibliophile and a talented amateur littérateur. (The Queen's private secretary, Sir Henry Ponsonby, attended a dinner with Gladstone and Lord Randolph Churchill at which the conversation turned to the sufficiency of books which might be said to constitute a gentleman's library. Ponsonby was amused to see Ferdinand immediately note the company's opinion – 20,000. Mary Gladstone had previously remarked the absence of books at Waddesdon, save for twenty improper French novels.) Ferdinand contributed to *The Nineteenth Century*, had embarked on a novel which he insisted on reading to the ubiquitous Edward Hamilton – 'His pen,' wrote his captive auditor feelingly, 'was fairly ready' – and even composed conceits for private circulation, such as an essay purporting to be an account of a lecture delivered by Baron Rothschild and the Prince of Wales at the Imperial Institute on the subject of 'Copulation, Ancient and Modern'. (This was one treasure not produced for the Queen-Empress's gratification.)

The *Livre d'Or* at Waddesdon boasted contributions from such a mixed galaxy of stars as Robert Browning and Anthony Trollope, Henry James and Matthew Arnold, Guy de Maupassant and Alexandre Dumas fils, the playwright Victorien Sardou and the librettist of Offenbach and Bizet, Ludovic Halévy;[*] even the Prince of Wales tried his hand at composition with an entirely predictable result: 'Le savoir-faire vaut mieux que le savoir'. (Cousin Natty at Tring favoured the audacious Rhoda Broughton and, in improbable Ruritanian mood, Anthony Hope.)

Statesmen, too, came to Waddesdon: no fewer than eight past, present and future prime ministers, spanning an astonishing eighty-five years of intermittent office from Gladstone and Disraeli to Lloyd George and Churchill, stayed there in Waddesdon's brief heyday, as well as one, the

---

[*]This gifted and prolific family, descended from a Bavarian synagogue cantor, took an unusual path. Ludovic Halévy, with a Jewish father, produced one Protestant son, Elie, the historian of the English people, and one Catholic, Daniel, friend of Proust and apologist of Vichy.

Duke of Devonshire, who had three times turned down the office. The Rothschilds, in company with much of British Jewry, had gravitated as a matter of course to the Liberals once they had won their fight for a seat in the House of Commons. This allegiance had been strained by Gladstone's selective indignation over the persecution of the Christians during the Bulgarian atrocities of 1876. They were finally estranged when he declined to utter one word of sympathy for the sufferings of the Jews in Russia, despite the pleas of the loyal Liberal John Simon, the second Jew to be called to the Bar. Edward Levy-Lawson's *Daily Telegraph* cut itself adrift and firmly attached itself to Disraeli's Balkans policy, never to rejoin the Liberal ranks. Nathaniel Rothschild was never more than a nominal Liberal; indeed, by 1879, Natty could refer to Gladstone in a letter to Disraeli as 'that arch-fiend'. When Natty went to the Lords, the Austrian-born Baron Ferdinand, who never lost his accent, took over the Buckinghamshire seat which had been in the family for twenty years (and was to remain so for the best part of another forty).

In 1880, a little over twenty years after their admission to Parliament, twelve Jewish Liberal Members were elected against just one Conservative, Baron Henry de Worms, later Lord Pirbright. Descended from a sister of Nathan Mayer Rothschild, he was the second Jew to serve in government – as Under-Secretary of State for the Colonies under Salisbury – and in the Privy Council. (The honour for this double 'first' had gone to George Jessel, as Solicitor-General, almost ten years before.) A Fellow of the Royal Society, an accomplished speaker (as well as boxer), he was dubbed Baron de Bookworms by the many who found him over-eager to share his obsession with his writings on natural science and current affairs. He was a curious casualty of Edward's accession. A supremely devout man, he resigned his twelve-year-old presidency of the Anglo-Jewish Association when one of his daughters married outside the faith. It was therefore all the more of a shock when after his death it was discovered that, having already reserved for himself a place in the Jewish cemetery at Willesden, he had left instructions to be buried in a Christian churchyard. He was reckoned to have taken offence at his omission from an official deputation of Jews to congratulate the new King. By 1885, when Nathaniel Rothschild received his peerage, it was already respectable to be a Conservative, especially in the City. Another remote Rothschild cousin, the stockbroker Lionel Louis Cohen, vice-president of the National Union of Conservative Associations, was elected for North Paddington and devoted himself to fight 'the domination so long exercised by the so-called Liberal party over the Jews, and [their] monopoly of the Jewish vote'. In the general election of 1885, Cohen spoke on behalf of the Conservative candidate at Tower Hamlets against his nephew and heir, Sir David Lionel Salomons, nephew also of the great champion of Jewish political emancipation. (Salomons won.) Cohen's obstinately orthodox brother-in-law, the over-bearing banker Samuel Montagu, the future Lord Swaythling, took up the gage, branding him as one of 'a few shallow-pated, ignorant people who thought it more respectable to call themselves Conservatives'. Montagu's opponent was armed with a letter of support from the new Lord Rothschild; Montagu retained his Whitechapel seat in a vote of personal loyalty – he was able to address his Jewish supporters, who made up fully half of the constituency, in Yiddish. Then, in 1886, the Liberal party irrevocably split over the issue of Irish Home Rule. Baron Ferdinand formally deserted Gladstone; the alliance between the Unionists, led by Lord Hartington, and Lord Randolph Churchill for the Conservatives, was cemented under his roof. After that date, no Rothschild was again elected to the Commons as a Liberal.

On Saturday, 17 December 1898, Edward Hamilton, who had been planning to visit Mentmore that day with Ferdinand Rothschild to celebrate his birthday, heard 'a horrible rumour', soon confirmed by telegram, of his sudden death at the early age of fifty-nine, apparently from a heart attack following a hot bath. 'I don't think I have ever felt more shocked or upset,' Hamilton wrote. 'There was no-one of late years of whom I have seen more, or from whom I had received greater and more uniform kindness. He always had a room for me at Waddesdon and a cabin on board his yacht.' (The two men had sailed to St Petersburg the previous summer where a Grand Duke had paid them the compliment of a visit.) 'Indeed I have not only lost the best of friends but' – suddenly mindful of a bachelor's comforts – 'a home on shore and at sea . . . There is something rather sublime as well as terribly sad about his dying in solitude as he lived in solitude at Waddesdon, within the walls of his magnificent abode.' The Prince having postponed a dinner that Sunday, to which he had invited himself, Hamilton spent the day at Mentmore with Lord Rosebery and the Arthur Sassoons. Reflecting on Ferdinand's great knowledge of art, Hamilton considered that 'though he presumably had to buy his experience when he was young, I believe he was less "taken in" than almost any other collector. The only times when his taste somewhat failed,' he concluded somewhat sourly, 'was in his choice of presents to others: and the only branch of art which he seemed (like most of his family) to appreciate inadequately was silver plate.' After enumerating his many exceptional qualities, Hamilton reminisced, fondly but frankly, that Ferdinand was not open-handed like other members of the family, for he disliked parting with shillings . . . and had a horror of being *done* . . . He had rather an unfortunate manner, and was not infrequently gauche. He gave and took offence easily; but *au fond* was most kind-hearted and loyal as a friend. No man was more uniformly glad to see one . . . he gave one the heartiest of welcomes. Having lived so much alone, and having at his command everything he wanted, he was rather selfishly disposed, which is not to be wondered at. The spoilt child became the spoilt man . . . His leading characteristic was perhaps his impulsive and impatient nature. He was always in a hurry. He did not eat but devoured. He did not walk but ran . . . He could not wait for anybody or anything . . . There were some curious contradictions about him. He was very nervous about himself and sent for a doctor on the smallest provocation; but he often declined to follow the doctor's advice. He took great care of himself as a rule, and yet he would often commit imprudences. He was proud of his race and of his family; and liked talking about his predecessors as if he had an illustrious ancestry of the bluest of bloods . . . I doubt if he ever was a really happy man. He will be missed by many from the highest in the land who received his hospitality freely to the lowest to whose wants he ministered in the most unostentatious and quiet manner. In my own circle of friends no one could have vanished out of sight who will leave a larger blank.

Waddesdon and the town house in Piccadilly went to Ferdinand's sister, Miss Alice Rothschild, who had long ago followed him to England. Hamilton noted that 'the proceeds of the beautiful *Rona* are to be devoted to sailors institutions' and that the 'cinquecento medieval things said to be worth about a quarter of a million' were bequeathed to the British Museum. (The curator later informed Hamilton that in his opinion the Waddesdon Bequest was worth nearer £400,000.)

Early in the New Year Hamilton was at Sandringham. The Prince, who was 'practically sound again' after his fall down the stairs at Waddesdon, expressed a wish to erect some memorial to 'poor Ferdie', but there was no agreement on the form this might take: 'anything in the village church would', Hamilton thought, 'be incongruous.' 'I think the Prince rather wonders – I certainly do – that Ferdie did not bequeath some little thing to HRH direct.' (Hamilton had himself received £1,000 under the will.) The Prince evidently did not keep such thoughts to himself. Three weeks later, Hamilton, staying with Leopold Rothschild at Ascott, heard that there had been 'a bother about the memento' for the Prince. A member of his suite had hinted at a Romney (perhaps he had his eye on 'Lady

Hamilton'). Miss Alice, whom Francis Knollys described to Edward Hamilton as 'a regular virago', had something more expendable in mind; she 'turned a deaf ear entirely and proposed to make over a Leighton to HRH. She ought never have been put in the position of having to refuse,' wrote Hamilton, who shared the Prince's understandable disappointment. 'Though occasionally she makes handsome presents, she is by nature very close and hates spending money.'

The King was looking to another source for some more generous gesture. At his accession, his Parliamentary income as Prince of Wales had come to a stop; his store of private capital had been largely exhausted and he had no expectation from his mother, whose considerable fortune had been divided among her younger children. There remained little more than £60,000 a year from the Duchy of Lancaster, of which £40,000 went straight out on the upkeep of Sandringham, and he was now saddled with the expense of the other royal residences. For years speculation on the schemes and stratagems to which the Prince had had recourse to keep himself afloat, had exercised minds and tongues. Only hours before the Queen's death, Natty Rothschild had brought some relief to Edward Hamilton at the Treasury with the news that there were no 'affairs' of the Prince to disclose. 'The common impression', wrote Hamilton, 'is that they [Edward and Alexandra] are heavily involved but that is not the case. He has managed to avoid borrowing . . . it is a great relief; and it will be a pleasant surprise to most people. It reflects great credit on him, for the calls upon him have been very heavy.' This was not strictly accurate. Rothschild had also revealed to Hamilton that the Prince had borrowed £160,000 – a sum not significantly less than £5 million in present-day values – on a mortgage of Sandringham. Hamilton, however, did not regard this as of much consequence as it would 'presumably now admit of being liquidated by degrees'. (The King's debts were, in fact, not cleared until three years before his death.) The valiant but ageing Sir Dighton Probyn, who had won his Victoria Cross in the Indian Mutiny, formally the Keeper of the Privy Purse, was excluded from these confidences; he was therefore able honestly to assert that the King had come to the throne 'unencumbered by a single penny of debt'.

Urgent arrangements were at once made to compose a new Civil List for the monarch. A committee was formed with Hamilton and two assistant assessors, the practical and versatile Lord Esher and the diplomat Sir Cecil Spring-Rice, both trusted friends of the King. The conventional courtiers had little notion of house-keeping. Sir Henry Ponsonby, Queen Victoria's private secretary, had informed Francis Knollys that the annual upkeep of Osborne in the Isle of Wight was

£8,000, Balmoral almost £6,000; the real cost, Hamilton's committee learnt, was £17,000 for the former and £20,000 for the Scottish seat. The King took other counsel. Sir Ernest Cassel was on constant call at short notice ('Please could you come and see me *tomorrow* between 3 and 3.30 as I think we have some matters to talk over together'). There was also the newly appointed Master of the Royal Household, the banker-politician Horace Farquhar, rated one of the handsomest and most charming men in London. After three years' otherwise unremarkable service on the Conservative backbenches, he acquired a baronetcy; he then had to content himself for twice that time – a delay occasioned by wariness within his own ranks – before he graduated to a barony, and from there to a viscountcy and an earldom, an ascent he unashamedly attributed to having subscribed more than the 'accepted tariff'. (He not inappropriately chose Castle Rising for his seat.) Farquhar also managed the affairs of the King's son-in-law, the fortunate Duke of Fife, whose income exceeded even his expenditure. It was nevertheless discovered after the Duke's death that £80,000 of trust money from the estate had vanished; a similar sum was found to be missing from the funds of the Conservative party, of which Farquhar was by then Treasurer, although Bonar Law excused the lacuna on the grounds that 'poor old Farquhar' was 'gaga'. Farquhar's own estate, provisionally valued at £400,000 for probate, was discovered to be in worse shape; the Royal Family's expectations under his will could not be met.

Others were tempted to descend into the marketplace. The personal affairs of the King and his Court was mostly treated with discretion by the press, whose proprietors themselves thirsted for honours from that fountainhead. But this demanded that the protected species act with a modicum of restraint. Francis Knollys overstepped this limit and became the centre of a minor City scandal. A Siberian goldmining company, noted the more traditionally high-minded Lord Carrington disapprovingly, 'has been formed by some Jew speculators'. Among the directors of Siberian Proprietary Mines were Lords Knollys, who had by then earned his just reward, and Stanley, future Earl of Derby, whose wife was an Extra Lady of the Bedchamber to Queen Alexandra; the major shareholders, among a crowd of Abrahamses and Nathans, were Lords Farquhar and Michelham, the former Herbert Stern, a Rothschild and Bischoffsheim relation, whose own elevation to baronet and baron within a short six months caused another political scandal (he chose for his motto 'Perseverance Won'). This promotion, along with that of Sir Alfred Harmsworth, subsequently Lord Northcliffe, was urged on the outgoing Prime Minister, Arthur Balfour, by the King; the request was coolly received, but both aspirants were accommodated. Such unaccountable patronage inevitably gave rise to suspicions: Harmsworth and Stern were rumoured to have shown financial favours to Mrs Keppel. (Five years earlier, three months after the Queen's death, Wilfrid Scawen Blunt gathered that the 'King's debts have been paid off privately by his friends, one of whom is said to have lent £100,000, and satisfies himself with £25,000 in repayment plus a knighthood'.) The Siberian enterprise, with an issued capital of £115,000, showed a profit in its first trading year of over £420,000 on the sale of mining options in Russia, a more certain operation than mining proper in the troubled state of that empire; the shares 'were rushed up to £16 . . . [and] have gone down with a rattle'. Farquhar, who was said to have 'netted' £70,000, was supposed to have 'secured all those names, and the papers' – despite the company's cautionary telegraphic address 'Pianissimo' – 'are open-mouthed at this scandal. It is deplorable that the King's private secretary . . . should have been "let in" and mixed up in an affair like this.'

It was as well that the King confided his investments, such as they were, to steadier hands. Six weeks after coming to the throne the King handed to Cassel the last remaining drop of his capital – £26,085. This prospered exceedingly (the special account, designated by a cryptic monogram, that Cassel kept of the King's affairs has perished). By the end of the following year, Edward called on Cassel for £10,000 as he was 'most anxious . . . to pay off an acquisition of property' near Sandringham; he was 'very glad to hear . . . that you will . . . realize sufficient securities to recoup the amount'. And yet, only six weeks later, Cassel had the honour to report that he still held 'upwards of £30,000' in investments, exclusive of Grafton House at Newmarket (formerly the property of Baron Hirsch).

Meanwhile Hamilton submitted his committee's recommendations on the Civil List to the Cabinet before, strangely, he had discussed the question with the King. When he had his first audience, Edward 'took the bull by the horns at once' and declared that 'in view of the way in which he intended to do everything, he did not see how he could get on with less than half a million'. The Chancellor of the Exchequer, Sir Michael Hicks Beach, laid his own proposals before the Cabinet. Hamilton spotted Lord James of Hereford, the Chancellor of the Duchy of Lancaster, coming away from Downing Street, and 'though he said nothing about what had passed at the meeting, I could see by his manner that he was not best pleased . . . I shall always say that this is the most timid Government I have ever had anything to do with.' Contrary to what Hamilton inferred from his manner, however, Lord James's displeasure was directed at the Chancellor: he considered that the sum proposed was too small and that a larger amount could have been carried through Parliament, particularly as there was general satisfaction that no application had been made to discharge any old debts incurred by the King. The Chancellor put his proposals to the King for a Civil List of £450,000, which, after an allowance for the Queen and other items, would leave at his disposal some £400,000. The Cabinet was surprised to be informed that the King had agreed – the Cabinet itself had not done so – and that furthermore the King, following the example of his mother, was prepared to pay income tax on the amount. The day after the Chancellor had secured his assent, the King again sent for Hamilton, this time 'as a friend'. (He was, most unusually, 'My dear Eddy Hamilton' to the King; Sir Ernest, for all his long acquaintance, was never more than 'My dear Cassel'.) It was evident to Hamilton that the King had not followed the Chancellor's high-handed exposition; he intimated that he had not been treated as liberally as he had hoped and seemed 'minded to reject the proposals'. He must have enough, he insisted, to '"do it" handsomely'; he had been told that half a million would not be considered unreasonable and that there could be no difficulty about Parliament passing that amount. Hamilton patiently explained those charges of which the King had been relieved, and proposed an expedient – to prevail on the Duke of York (later George V) to pay £20,000 out of his own pension towards the upkeep of the royal residences whose facilities he shared. 'So there *was* the half million partly in disguise,' Hamilton demonstrated. The King 'fell in at once' with this argument. Hamilton trotted round to York House to put this proposition to the Duke; he found him ready to accept, though not happy with being generally thought to be £20,000 a year better off than he really would be. By now Hamilton was himself unhappy, considering this a 'dodge' which might 'expose the Cabinet to a want of straightforwardness'. He hinted to the King that much would depend on whether he was to be 'sponged off by other members of the Royal Family in the matter of carriages and horses. He will have to be very firm about this; but presumably they will get the better of his good nature.' Hamilton was in a better position than the Cabinet to gauge how the Opposition, Radicals apart, might react to the proposed Civil List: spending the next Sunday at Tring Park with Natty Rothschild, he was able to discuss it with Asquith, who 'on the whole' . . . thought the [proposals] not extravagant'.

By early March the Chancellor had 'practically' agreed to fix the King's pension at £470,000,* £85,000 more than Queen Victoria had received. But as soon as a committee of the House of Commons had been

---

*The Civil List has not kept pace with purchasing power over ninety years; in 1990 it exceeded £7,250,000, of which the Queen received £5,090,000.

appointed to consider this, Hicks Beach informed the Cabinet that the King objected to paying income tax on the sum. To Hamilton, the King expressed himself 'reasonably satisfied' with his portion. That did not last. By the middle of April Knollys informed Hamilton that 'injudicious friends are telling the King that He has not got good enough terms out of the Government. These are very bad friends . . .' This notion festered. At a dinner on Christmas Day in 1902, the King 'harped back on the . . . settlement, and commented on the want of generosity on the part of the Government. He was afraid he would not make ends meet.' The usually resourceful Edward Hamilton unhelpfully replied that time alone would tell. By the next summer, Hamilton observed that the 'Privy Purse is pinching', and one reason, though the King had spared himself the expense of Osborne by presenting it to the nation, was the mortgage on Sandringham. It would have been better, Hamilton now belatedly concluded, if the King had disclosed at his accession the condition of his estate. The Queen was an additional hazard: she had 'no idea of the value of money; nor for that matter has the King'. It would not do, however, 'to "crop" her. Unlike the King, she does not forget or forgive.'

Although Cassel pulled his full weight as financial adviser, he was often called upon to perform humble functions. Reuben Sassoon, who had placed bets for the King, was now slowed down by gout and rheumatism (he died halfway through the reign). Cassel took over the royal book. 'When we meet at Newmarket,' the King requested, 'please hand me in *notes* the result of my investment on Terpsichore'. The Kaiser scorned his uncle as 'a jobber in stocks and shares'. That dealing instinct was indisputably alive and active. One year after Cassel had received the residue of his capital, the King thanked him for carrying out the 'suggestions' so promptly, adding, 'Before Monday or Tuesday I fear no *certain* moves can arise?' One week later, on 1 June 1902, he wrote again: 'You will have doubtless heard that Peace is signed [the Treaty of Vereeniging, ending the Boer War, had been concluded the day before] which is the greatest blessing that has been conferred on this country for a long time! "Consols" are sure to go up tomorrow. Could you not make a large investment for me? It is to be hoped that the Chancellor of the Exchequer may announce on Wednesday not to put the extra pence on the Income Tax . . . I send these lines by hand. Excuse great haste.' Edward Hamilton acted as the horse's mouth for the Chancellor's intentions. For some years he had been in the habit of passing a weekend at Ascott with Leopold Rothschild, sometimes also in the company of Lord Rothschild and the Arthur Sassoons, working on his Budget proposals, of which a résumé was sent to Edward, even when still Prince of Wales, at least twenty-four hours before they were made public by the Chancellor. When in due course a Transvaal loan was mooted to help the Boers and Loyalists restock their land which had been scorched, it was to the same wise heads that Hamilton turned once again for advice on the timing and price, though he would now 'sooner have [Leopold's] advice than Natty's though the elder brother is the cleverer of the two'; in Cassel's opinion both brothers deferred to Alfred, whose nerve often now failed him. City opinion favoured a loan yielding 3 per cent; Lord Rothschild and Cassel, 'certainly a most satisfactory man to do business with', thought the government could get away with 2¾ per cent. The loan was issued at 97½; the underwriters at first demurred, Cassel considered it 'quite right', while Lord Rothschild 'evidently thought we were as usual skinning the City'. The Chancellor had 'practically made up his mind on the side of the majority', but came round to the lower rate. As with Cassel over the war loan, it was now Alfred Rothschild's turn to be 'very angry' over the 'most un-English' decision to cut out the small applications for the loan; he vowed he would gradually surrender his own allotment to be divided among them.

More costly services were expected of Cassel than advice on trimming the margin on government loans; among his privileges was the office of lender, if not donor, of last resort. The King received an impassioned *cri de coeur* from a Mrs Emma Bourke, written in a distraught hand (with minimal punctuation) and addressing him as 'Mon Roi': 'I scarcely know how to tell you but *feel* you will for the sake of your friendship, your strong friendship for me give us great sympathy . . .' She was looking for rather more. She had been through great troubles and, after the 'frightful fall in all Stocks', her husband's firm had 'almost' failed. The Rothschilds and others had come forward to tide them through 'as no one wished so honourable a firm, and such a really good business to go to the wall for want of help . . . Still alas! my husband's capital has *all* been swept away,' and, a sick man of seventy-two, he was 'left without anything'. Mrs Bourke, however, was hardly facing stark ruin: she feared to lose 'my pretty house' in Eaton Square, 'servants, carriage *all* must go . . . it's a cruel calamity'. Slyly she invoked the name of Cassel, who had already once bailed her out and was predictably loath to repeat it: 'Oh, mon Roi – you whose slightest expressed wish would carry such weight, *won't you* for the sake of a friend in great *distress*, use all your influence with Sir E. Cassel to induce him to help us all he can – He has such power, and he could be of such vital help to us did he only choose – He *was* kind to me once *very* at your wish, and I *think* has friendly feeling for us – and if Mon Roi you would convey all this to him it might make *all the difference* to our always being paupers . . .' Emma Bourke was not an altogether deserving case for charity. There is little doubt that she was the author of venomous anonymous letters to the prospective parents-in-law of one of Lord Esher's friends with whom she had once had an affair. Even if Cassel, who knew Esher well, was aware of this, Mrs Bourke was indeed, as the King acknowledged, 'my old friend', and, distressed at this appeal, he passed the missive on to Cassel with the wish that it 'would be more than kind of you if you would be induced to give him a helping hand in their present very serious trouble?' That left little option to a man of sensibility and, as Mrs Bourke did not return to her plight, it is plausible to presume that Cassel once more put his hand in his pocket. (A similar tale is recounted of Baron Hirsch by the entertaining but not famously trustworthy Frank Harris. In that case the lady had need of half a million. Hirsch was prepared to oblige with interest: 'If you would receive me sometimes and regard me as a friend, I would write this cheque for £1 million just to make the figure round, you know, as you say in England.' If there is a faint grain of substance in this, Harris must have confounded pounds sterling with French francs.)

Though usually disobligingly brusque, Sir Ernest melted under an exercise of feminine charm behind a pretty face; the stern principles of a lifetime went by the board. He was known to lend £10,000 to a lady in need on the security of her pearls – on the one condition that she continue to wear them. When the daughter of Cassel's friend Lord Colebrooke was presented with a necklace, pearls again, as a wedding present from King Edward, she at once sold it. Cassel, alerted by the jeweller, bought it back for her. She sold it again. She was less lucky the third time; the purchase price was invested and tied up in trust for her.

Pearls were possibly too practical. This was the age of the exquisitely frivolous wares of Carl Fabergé. The master's London manager had Cassel's measure; silence was the essence of a successful sale. He was left to his own devices, often for the whole morning, piling object after object in front of him. Sonia Keppel, passing each Easter at Cassel's Villa Eugénie at Biarritz, received with agreeable regularity enamelled and bejewelled eggs from 'Kingy' and her host. (When, however, it came to the more serious business of marriage, Sonia received a 'fat cheque' from her mother's lover's friend. Mrs Keppel pronounced this so vulgar that, to Sonia's disappointment, it had to be translated without ado into Canadian sable.)

Leopold Rothschild was less discriminating. Fabergé's workshops in St Petersburg were turned over to mass production; every item that had ever been made was duplicated in the Rothschild racing colours, dark blue and yellow. The consignment was rushed round to New Court to be shown off. 'Splendid!' enthused Leopold. 'I will take the lot.' But after the King's 1896 Derby winner Persimmon had been modelled, Leopold could not be persuaded to have his horse St Frusquin, beaten by a neck in the race, similarly immortalized. 'Such luxury is all very well for the King of England,' he retorted. 'I can't afford it.' (This had as much to do with pique as misplaced modesty. Leopold's horse was the odds-on favourite, while the Prince's had no form and was later beaten by St Frusquin in the Princess of Wales Stakes. Leopold headed the list of winning owners that year with £46,766 in prize money, having also topped it the previous year; he repeated this success in 1898 and won the Derby a second time in 1904.) Mrs Leopold, Mrs Arthur Sassoon's sister, had no such inhibitions. At her command, St Frusquin stood for Fabergé's sculptor. The result was cast in silver, with twelve replicas in bronze for friends. She did not stop there. Favourite staghounds, some prize cattle and the family's French griffon were cut in semi-precious stone. Such drollery was regrettably infectious. The King put Fabergé to work at Sandringham. The modellers started with the royal terrier, Caesar, and the Queen's dogs; they then worked their way through the heifers and bullocks, cocks and hens, turkeys, shire horses and even the pigs in the royal sties.

Following the death of Baron Ferdinand, King Edward graced Rothschild houses less frequently. Perhaps even he hesitated to inflict the Favourite on the forbiddingly strait-laced Lady Rothschild. Emma, after all, steadfastly refused to open her doors to her brother-in-law Alfred's mistress, Marie Boyer, the wife of the auspiciously named Frederick Wombwell. Alfred retaliated; after recounting a scabrous story at dinner one day, he looked around the table and coolly remarked, 'Emma told me that.' (The presumed fruit of this blatant union was, with more loyalty than delicacy, awarded the names of both Victoria and Alexandra. She married the debt-ridden Earl of Carnarvon with a breathtaking £500,000 settlement after Carnarvon's debts had been cleared, and the couple ever after battened on an accommodating Alfred.) Few great ladies were so principled. Hostesses in general took into consideration established liaisons among their house guests; their names were posted on their bedroom doors to avoid potentially embarrassing nocturnal displacements. (Lord Charles Beresford liked to recount how once, taking a wrong turning in the dark, he had mistaken his quarry's room and had leapt into the unwelcoming arms of the Bishop of Chester.)

Another absentee from Rothschild homes was Sir Ernest Cassel. There was an element of jealousy on both sides as much as incompatibility of character and culture. He possessed none of the affability of Leopold, nor the eccentricity (and irresponsibility) of Alfred; an immigrant and self-made millionaire, he was still conscious of being seen as an outsider. And he renounced any role in Jewish community life.

In the summer of 1903 Cassel was offered a seat on the Food Supplies Commission, for which the Prime Minister, A. J. Balfour, wanted 'a good City man' to expose the 'fallacies and absurdities' on the subject. Cassel declined, pleading that his German origin would tell against him on such a contentious issue. All summer Balfour was desperately trying to paper over the gulf in his own party between the devotees of free trade and protection in the guise of Imperial preference as propounded by the restless and ambitious Colonial Secretary, Joe Chamberlain. Edward Hamilton, staying alone with Cassel and his sister at Newmarket, found his host 'decidedly protectionist but fair minded', considering the country should be less dependent on others and that too much thought was given to the consumer. Even Lord Rothschild, a free trader by conviction, was, Hamilton found, 'rather taken' by Chamberlain's plan. Hamilton, sceptical himself, attributed this weakening to the fact that 'city folk have done badly of late; and the people who do badly cast about for some new departure. I am afraid protection will be found to be no remedy.' The public debate waxed acrimonious and emotional. The Chancellor of the Exchequer complained to Hamilton that the King had scolded him in a loud voice at a gala opera that he would never consent to any measure which taxed his people's food. But Cassel had been less than candid with Hamilton. He had already expressed his admiration for Chamberlain's initiative in airing the issue and his hope that he might be of 'some little use'. Little more than three weeks after making a good impression on Hamilton, he sent Chamberlain a massive contribution of £5,000 to provide a war-chest for his Tariff Reform League. This for Cassel was an unprecedented political intervention and he was characteristically discreet about it: anxious lest his contribution become known, for good measure he made his cheque out to 'Bearer'. Three months later Chamberlain resigned in order to have a free hand in his crusade and thereby wrecked the Cabinet.

Cassel's wilful young friend Winston Churchill crossed the floor and joined the Liberals as a 'Free Trader' to cries of 'Rat' from his old colleagues. Cassel, rather than chide him, offered him his hospitality in the Swiss Valais the following August. Winston told his mother that the place produced a 'wholly good' effect on him; he slept like a top in the buoyant air and had never felt in better health. He was gratified to find the Villa Cassel a large, comfortable four-storey house 'complete with baths, a French cook' and other luxuries that would be expected at home. In the afternoons he went for walks on the flat or for a very formidable scramble; the evenings were given over to a statutory four rubbers of bridge. His fellow guest, the ailing Sir Edward Hamilton, who had had to be borne up to the villa upon a *chaise à porteur* by five men, found the paths uneven and settled for sunbathing on the enclosed verandah; mountain air had been prescribed and he thought he might 'as well try the place as a sort of last string to my bow'. (He died four years later after a protracted and painful illness, 'a great loss for all his friends . . . but for him a happy release from a miserable life!' the King judged.) Hamilton found it 'a heavenly spot', in the saddle of the mountains, almost 3,000 metres up, from where he looked down into the Rhône valley on one side and into a great glacier on the other, with the Matterhorn in the distance on a clear day. His host and hostess, Cassel's sister, were 'extraordinarily kind and thoughtful. The power of Cassel', he still had time to consider in these idyllic surroundings, 'much impresses me. He knows his own mind so well on everything, and takes so much trouble about details.' Other guests included Cassel's niece Anna, married to Colonel Edward Jenkins of the Rifle Brigade (he was known in the mess as 'Tiresome Teddy', she as 'Black Maria' on account of her looks), and the daughter of Sir George Lewis, the King's solicitor; among casual callers were Lord Revelstoke, Sir Felix Schuster and the Khedive of Egypt, who, choosing to arrive among snow-clouds, was not easy to entertain as he neither smoked nor played cards.

Cassel's absence from the Rothschild homes was not due solely to want of cordiality. He had his own role as host to play. His elder sister 'Bobbie' kept house for him. Mrs Keppel's daughter Sonia remarked that, though otherwise evidently a woman of some character and charm, Bobbie's docile obedience to her brother had an almost Biblical quality. Although she worshipped her 'bruzzer', her niece Maud's friend the Duchess of Sermoneta thought she was afraid of him. She seems also to have been a Frau Malaprop: she once insisted Cambridge was forty miles away 'as the cock crows'. Cassel was the despair of chefs: he was, in the eyes of one guest, a hopeless dyspeptic. He managed to give the impression that he enjoyed watching other people eating his fine food, heaping their plates with delicacies, while he sadly nibbled a piece of toast. It was surely this prodigious restraint that provoked the sudden flare-ups of temper portended by a clenching of fists on the table top. His sister was not spared, and even friends of his adored daughter received an occasional snubbing. Despite this the Irish Countess of Fingall considered her host 'one of the kindest men I have ever met'.

In contrast with Cassel, 'Mr Alfred' Rothschild was immoderately anxious to shine, although some guests complained that dinner was served at Halton at an uncomfortably late hour in order that the servants might eat at their ease. (One guest was amused to discover that the *poussins Haltonais* on the menu in midsummer were, unseasonably and unsportingly, young pheasants which had had their necks wrung.) Small pony traps with diminutive grooms in blue livery dogged the ladies on their strolls around the grounds in case they tired. In the evening the host would don a frock-coat and bowler in the same colour to act as ringmaster in his private circus where all manner of domestic and farmyard animals were required to perform on the Aubusson. (Not always to great effect: there was a story that after Alfred had been intimidated by a white rabbit which had turned on him, he had every animal drugged before its appearance.) After tea and after dinner, Alfred's private orchestra would entertain the guests, the host exchanging his whip for a baton. The musical Edward Hamilton was granted a rather exceptional treat even by Halton standards. One Sunday in summer the visiting Scala orchestra, forty-five strong, played 'divinely' through the afternoon outside the house, while in the evening Madame Melba 'sang a little'.

Certainly this almost wanton self-indulgence was viewed with irritation and distaste by other members of the family, but it is a tribute to all three Rothschild brothers that the Countess of Warwick, long since seduced by socialism, considered that they were still among the few of all her well-to-do acquaintances who 'could envisage the grim drama of poverty, with its less sensational, but more painful, daily effects'.

A few years later, Hamilton was at Ascott with Leopold Rothschild and Arthur Balfour, then leading his 'Uncle Bob' Salisbury's government in the Commons. Sir Edward was taken over to Halton in the motor car where they came on Alfred conducting his orchestra with an exiguous audience – Arthur Sassoon and one other. Hamilton recorded excitedly that over several timed miles they had reached a rate of thirty miles an hour. (Such 'scorching' was illegal; the speed limit was raised to twenty miles an hour only in 1903.) Two years later, staying along with the Duke of Devonshire at Moulton Paddocks, Hamilton again found himself on the wrong side of the law. He was taken for a spin by Cassel in his new motor, a twenty-five-horsepower Wolseley, and 'got a great pace out of it at times, about 40 miles an hour!' The Wolseley company, named after the recently retired Commander-in-Chief, had been established two years before by Vickers, very much with an eye to its military use. Vickers' financial director, Sigmund Loewe, had been an early fatal victim of the motor car; his place was taken by Cassel's protégé, Sir Vincent Caillard. It was on this same weekend visit that Hamilton came to regard his host, not only as one of the fastest, but 'as the ablest man in the City, he takes a broad and disinterested view . . . a line of his own. His has been a marvellous rise, but he has not had his head turned in the least and is not at all spoilt. I like the man very much.'

King Edward, another determined road-hog, was a more regular visitor to Moulton Paddocks, even in the unavoidable absence of the host. He usually enjoyed a week's fishing and shooting there at the end of the last Newmarket meeting in October, while his son Prince George would come in January to finish off the partridges that were left over. It was noticed that the King never used Cassel's gift, Grafton House, which he was believed locally to have bought, but put up for the races in a suite of apartments in the Jockey Club across the road. Cassel had registered his colours in 1895 (silver grey and light blue, perhaps an intentional contrast with the Rothschilds' dark blue and gold). He then had to wait thirteen years for election to the Jockey Club, owing, it was suggested, to prevailing prejudice. Royal influence was wielded, but was not immediately effective. He was informed in October 1902 by Lord Durham that the Duke of Devonshire would propose him for nomination at the first available opportunity, the Spring meeting the following year, and that he, Durham, would second him if it was desired; Cassel was requested to inform the King of this progress. But despite this patronage, Cassel did not come up for election. There were, in truth, only a few vacancies each year; on the other hand, his sponsors might have been warned privately that he could expect the two blackballs that forever preclude election. He had to wait five more years, being finally admitted in May 1908.

Cassel was unsuccessful as an owner and breeder of racehorses in spite of the fortune he spent on his stud at Moulton Paddocks. He shared the King's racing manager, Lord Marcus Beresford, but it is doubtful if his heart was in the sport; he took to the Turf as a matter of form, a pastime expected of a man of his wealth. The King, indeed, seems to have taken more pleasure in his friend's successes than the owner himself, penning him enthusiastic notes of congratulation whenever he won even a minor race. Cassel might have won the Derby in 1912 with Cylgad, which had already beaten the eventual winner in the Newmarket Stakes; unluckily he broke down before the Epsom meeting. Cassel won just one classic, the Two Thousand Guineas, in 1901. Here he was fortunate. His colt Handicapper, for which he had paid a modest 380 guineas, had won the Richmond Stakes at Goodwood the year before, but began the next season so badly that he started at 33 to 1. He beat sixteen others, but shot his bolt; unplaced in the Derby, he did not run in the St Leger.

It is more certain that Cassel enjoyed the excitements of the chase and the concomitant spills (his seat was never very secure). He hunted with the Quorn, whose members admired more his perverse determination than his skill. In Ireland, he stayed with the famous huntsman Harry Bourke, Lord Mayo's brother, or the brewing Iveaghs. There he was spotted, 'a stout Teutonic gentleman in a pink coat, looking rather uncomfortable in it and on his horse'. This may have prompted him to be generous with his own horseflesh. Margot Asquith received a hunter (that may not have been entirely disinterested; her husband had just become Prime Minister). Less calculated generosity was shown to Felix Semon many years earlier. Staying with Cassel, he admired a hunter he had been lent and asked if his host might be inclined to sell it. Cassel flatly refused. When, however, Semon was taking his leave a few days later, Cassel enquired when he might send him the horse. Semon reminded him that he had already declined to part with it. 'Yes, I did so because I never sell horses,' Cassel replied, 'but I hope you will do me the favour to accept the hack as a small remembrance of your present visit.' When, after nine years' use, the horse, ironically called Free Trade, had to be destroyed, Cassel continued to supply Semon with mounts.

Born the son of Simon Joseph Simon of Danzig, Semon exchanged his medical school at Heidelberg for service in the Prussian Guard in the French war. (He was no mean musician: his regiment returned to Berlin to the strains of a march he had himself composed.) After completing his studies, he settled in London. Five years after taking over the throat department at St Thomas's Hospital, he was urged to take up a similar post at a new University clinic in Berlin, but declined: 'Too vividly I remembered the caste spirit, the religious hatred, the family constraints. I had grown out of all these things.' He soon collected a distinguished clientele in England. Gladstone's doctor sent the old Liberal leader, who was anticipating some wear on his vocal cords in a looming election, to Semon with the resounding admonition 'The future of the Liberal party is in your hands.' Semon tartly retorted, 'I never mix politics and medicine. Moreover, the politics of the Liberal Party are not mine. I need not tell you, however, that I will do my best.' (He prescribed silence.) He cured Nellie Melba, who had strained her voice in the demanding role of Brünnhilde at the Metropolitan Opera House, New York. He examined the old Queen's larynx and, enchanted by her deep contralto, was knighted. He had met the Prince of Wales while treating Lillie Langtry in 1888 and, a witty raconteur, good shot and handy bridge player, became a frequent and popular guest at the royal homes and, later, at Balmoral, where his musical ear was offended by the 'hellish noise' made by the 'deafening tribe of royal pipers' as they ceremonially circled the table whenever game was served. After the accession, Semon took British nationality and was appointed Physician Extraordinary to the sovereign.

Semon enjoyed one other, if inadvertent, knack – the ability to dampen the King's sudden and short-lived rages. (Admiral 'Jackie' Fisher, however, considered that it was a 'pleasure to face his furious anger for the sake of the lovely smile you got later on'.) Hearing that the site for the King Edward VII Sanatorium for tuberculars, the fruit of a £200,000 Coronation gift from Cassel for an object of the King's choice, had been selected at Midhurst where no water supply existed, he turned an alarming shade of imperial purple. He rounded on Sir Felix, charged with the management of the project. 'I'll tell you something,' he ended, cutting short all excuses. 'You doctors are nearly as bad as the lawyers. And, God knows, that will say a great deal!' An uncomfortable silence followed. The discomforted Semon could not suppress a nervous laugh. Surprised at this irreverent reaction, the King too broke into heaving laughter. Edward intended the sanatorium for 'the poorer middle classes'. The rich, he told Semon, could look after themselves, and the poor really ought to be looked after by appropriate institutions; between these there was a seam of educated but indigent patients – teachers, clergymen, governesses, young officers* – who could not afford private treatment yet were too proud to accept public charity. They were to pay a *small* sum so as not to feel demeaned. The rich would not be excluded but would be limited in number and would have to pay much higher fees for greater comforts, partly to subsidize the needy, partly so that other institutions might not complain of unfair competition.

Though grossly overweight – some 225 pounds were packed into 67 inches – the King was favoured with a robust constitution; he had abundant stores of energy and even at sixty was seemingly tireless. As restless and impatient in sickness as in health, he might grudgingly listen to his doctor's advice, but never followed it for long. For over forty years he had been smoking heavily, some twenty cigarettes and twelve huge cigars a day starting before breakfast. He suffered his first serious attack of bronchial catarrh in 1905, but recovered quickly; he rewarded his saviour, Felix Semon, with the KCVO. (Semon at once violated cherished canons: the star of the order, the monarch coldly reminded him, was '*usually* worn on the *left* breast'.) These attacks, more or less grave, recurred in succeeding years until, after a slight affliction in 1908,

*When the War Office suggested that fifty beds, half the planned complement, might be set aside for other ranks, Semon turned down the request on the grounds that to accept the 'lower strata of the population' would seriously imperil 'the social life' of the establishment.

the King left for Biarritz, dismissing Semon with his thanks for a speedy delivery. Semon had sounded the alarm too loudly; his nagging irked his patient, who never again consulted him. Writing to Francis Knollys from Yokohama on the day after the King's death, he was reminded of 'that morning three years ago when . . . I handed you that report, which I strongly felt it my *duty* to make and which has been so sadly justified by the course of events! I don't think anybody will call me an *alarmist* now!' When Semon realized he had been shuffled to one side, shocked and disappointed he handed in his royal warrant, though he withdrew his resignation at the King's request, and sought consolation in travel.

On reflection Edward would have conceded that there was at least one exception to his avowed aversion to lawyers. On her first visit to Sandringham in January 1890, Miss Winifred Sturt, the future Lady Hardinge, thought the solicitor George Lewis odd company to find there. (She also thought it a 'shocking affair' that baccarat, an illegal game, was played every night.) But thirteen years before, her father, Lord Alington, had contributed to a contretemps from which it had taken all Lewis's diplomacy to extricate the Prince. Edward had leased two horses from Lady Stamford, which he undertook to run in his colours and under his name. He then had a change of heart and proposed that Alington and Sir Frederick Johnstone, long since forgiven for having addressed him as 'Tum-Tum' to his face, should take them off his hands. Lord Alington imprudently advised Lady Stamford that as the Prince was wishing to ask the country for more money, the knowledge that he was keeping racehorses might prejudice his chance, though 'all this is confidential between you and me'. Lady Stamford, affecting grievance, threatened sorrowfully that the Prince would be 'a necessary party' to any proceedings to redress her fancied slight. The Prince looked to Lewis for help. He spent five hours with the potential plaintiff – 'I have seldom come across a more capricious woman,' he reported to Knollys – before he managed to persuade her to leave the Prince out of it, and the Prince to eat unaccustomed humble pie.

The famous counsel Charles Russell, Attorney-General and later Lord Chief Justice (the first Roman Catholic to hold that post since the Reformation), whose career Lewis had promoted, judged that Lewis's special qualities were his genius for compromise and his courage. An impressive figure in sablecoat, with deep brown eyes beneath a sweep of prematurely grey hair, he built up a unique practice in Society – divorce, finance, libel or straight scandal. He made his reputation and fortune by keeping his cases, and where possible his clients, out of court. (Oscar Wilde consulted Lewis immediately after his trial, between the verdict and the arrest. 'What is the use of coming to me now?' said Lewis. 'All this trouble was perfectly unnecessary.') In the opinion of the long-time London correspondent of the *New York Tribune*, the solicitor's papers were 'enough to compromize half London and scandalize the other half'. A man of the utmost discretion, he very properly disposed of the contents of his black japanned boxes before his death.

The son of a solicitor, George Lewis was born over the paternal premises and entered the firm in 1856. Within ten years he made his first mark when he appeared, single-handed without the aid of barristers, for the prosecution in the failure of Overend, Gurney. In the Parnell case he appeared for the majority of the Irish nationalists and exposed in open court Richard Piggott's forgery which *The Times* had published in good faith. Two years later, in the notorious Tranby Croft baccarat scandal, Lewis represented the defendants, among them Reuben Sassoon, one of those witnesses to the alleged infraction who signed the solemn declaration of Sir William Gordon-Cumming (who had been accused of cheating) that he would henceforth desist from playing cards. It was hoped that this would close the affair and protect the Prince, who had been present, from public scandal. It was while staying with Baron Hirsch at Wretham Hall, Norfolk, that the Prince heard that the secret was out and that as a result Gordon-Cumming intended to bring an action against his original accusers. The underhand and shabby subterfuges to thwart his efforts to secure an open trial to clear his name were unsuccessful, and the Prince, subpoenaed as a prosecution witness, was roughly handled by Gordon-Cumming's counsel, Sir Edward Clarke. Although Gordon-Cumming lost his case, it is arguable that the Crown suffered more through the light that had been thrown in public on the Prince's private life. Looking for some means to repair his public reputation without appearing too patently hypocritical, he gave it as his opinion to the Archbishop of Canterbury that 'gambling, like intemperance, is one of the greatest curses' (horse-racing was different, a 'manly sport . . . and there is no reason why it should be looked upon as a gambling transaction'). Bridge became suddenly popular in the royal circle.

Daisy Brooke, later Countess of Warwick, the Prince's fellow-guest of Hirsch at Wretham, had herself been a source of scandal only a little more than a year before. At that time enchanting Daisy was enjoying a passionate affair with the Prince's old friend and companion Lord Charles Beresford, the brother of his racing manager. When Daisy learned that he had been unfaithful to her – his wife, the model of rectitude, found herself pregnant – she wrote Lord Charles a furious letter of reproach, insisting on an immediate elopement. Lady Charles opened this in her husband's absence and took it to George Lewis with instructions to ensure that its author caused no more trouble. The contrite correspondent appealed to the Prince. He, gallantly and unwisely, agreed to intercede: 'Suddenly I saw him looking at me in a way all women understand,' Daisy later wrote. He went round to beard George Lewis in the early hours of the same morning. The solicitor allowed him to read the letter, which Edward thought the 'most shocking' he had ever read. He proposed it be destroyed. Lewis insisted that Lady Charles's consent was necessary. Twice the Prince tried to win her over with charm, and when that failed, so the poor lady alleged, menaced her with the most dire social reprisals. Twice she refused, reproaching him instead for his interference; she informed Lewis that she would give the letter up only if Lady Brooke kept away from London for the rest of the Season. The Prince made his disapproval plain by striking Lady Charles's name off the invitation list for Marlborough House and replacing it with that of Lady Brooke. Lord Charles, a fiery Irishman, now turned on the Prince and on George Lewis for his 'lickerish servility', the former narrowly escaping a blow. Lady Charles, facing a social boycott, put her London house up for sale, and her husband, who was now commanding the cruiser *Undaunted* in the Mediterranean, happily recognizing that the days of duelling were past, instead threatened satisfaction by publicity. It took all the tact of the Prime Minister himself, the unworldly Lord Salisbury, to reach a settlement. The Prince, who never conceded his own fault in the affair, vowed that he could never forget or forgive Lord Charles's 'base ingratitude' after twenty years' friendship. He sought consolation in the arms of 'Darling Daisy' or, as she was known to those less besotted, 'Babbling Brooke'.

George Lewis was a regular companion of the Prince at Bad Homburg, where they relaxed in lounging suits, often of a flamboyant colour, and soft hats, grey for day, black for evening. For several weeks in August they would undergo a rigorous regime, taking the waters in the morning and recovering their spirits and strength at one of Reuben Sassoon's famous picnics for as many as seventy ravenous unregenerates. Lewis had received a knighthood from Gladstone in 1893 and a baronetcy from King Edward in 1902 (though he had to wrestle with Lord Salisbury over it); he sponsored the Moneylenders Act to curb usurious extortion and was a principal promoter of the Court of Criminal Appeal, created in the year before he retired in 1908 aged seventy-six. He was succeeded by his son, another George, who was married to the daughter of Baron Hirsch's brother Emil.

The year before the King Edward VII Sanatorium at Midhurst was ready to open its doors, the provider himself prepared to move one step westwards from Grosvenor Square. In 1905 Cassel bought Brook House, incorporating Numbers 28 and 29 Park Lane, to which the owner, Lord Tweedmouth, had added the adjoining property on the corner of Upper Brook Street the previous year. Tweedmouth's wife, Lord Randolph Churchill's sister, had died at the same time, and he had undergone a condition discreetly described as a reversal of fortune. (Despite this, he embarked on a spell of service as an injudicious First Lord of the Admiralty until becoming finally, as Asquith informed the King, 'seriously unhinged'.)

Cassel's new abode was already an overwhelming rather than a welcoming home. 'There is no need for dwellers in Brook House to dream that they dwell in marble halls,' it was said before Cassel took a hand. 'They do dwell in them.' This was not enough for the new owner. It took three years and another 800 tons of marble to transform it; even the six kitchens were said to be covered in it. The grand glass-domed staircase, hall and gallery, itself supported by twenty-foot-high Corinthian pillars, was of white Tuscan marble; it was christened the 'Giant's Lavatory' by his granddaughter Edwina's friends. The outer hall was veneered in a rare blue marble from Ontario; from the wall two portraits regarded guests, one of Edward VII, the other of Ernest Cassel, their likeness 'positively striking' in the dim light. (The marble was popularly believed to be lapis luzuli, and once the myth was made, stories sprang up to corroborate it. A lady related how, showing off a new necklace made of lapis, she asked her host for his opinion. 'Very pretty stuff', Sir Ernest is said to have replied. 'I've got a room made of it.') When Cassel set eyes on his new staircase, he exploded, 'I am not going to pay for this!' The reason for his discontent was that not all the treads were of one piece of stone as he had stipulated. The young designer, Charles Allom, saw his career in ruins. Word of the contretemps reached the King's ears. Wishing to see justice done but not wishing to upset his friend, with exquisite tact and kindliness, he waited until Cassel was out of London. He then called up a maroon Daimler and went round to Brook House. Puffing his way up the staircase, he called for the ubiquitous telegraph pad and wrote a note for the owner: 'Staircase perfect. Don't alter a single stone.' Allom was paid at once and was set to work by Joseph Duveen to devise homes for the art collections of his American millionaire clients, later earning his own royal warrant and a knighthood.

The oak-panelled dining room at Brook House, built out behind across the whole width of the site, with elbow room for 100 eaters, harboured four Van Dycks provided by Duveen at his usual very special price. The thirty rooms beneath the roofs were tended by a staff of thirty-one (the odd man was one of that fast disappearing race, the hall porter), among them the most imposing footmen* resplendent in full livery and powdered hair. Other walls were hung with works by Frans Hals, Romney, Reynolds and Murillo; tables and cabinets (and basement strongroom) were stockpiled with Renaissance bronzes, Dresden china, Chinese jade and old English silver. One who knew the owner of all this treasure judged that he could barely tell one from the other, that he bought anything that was sufficiently expensive and of certified excellence, that he considered the artefacts the appropriate accoutrements of a man of his great wealth. A disappointment to Duveen, Cassel was not a collector, but there is no evidence that he had no spark of artistic sensibility; he was fortunate to be able to pay the top price, and more, to indulge his taste. (At the Tweedmouth sale he acquired the fine Raeburn portrait of the artist's wife for the then unprecedented figure of 8,700 guineas.) Among his friends were the artists Alma Tadema and Burne-Jones *fils*. The latter, who had spotted a 'very fine Gainsborough landscape, also a delightful Romney of a child' under a neighbour's roof, urged Cassel, 'Come and see.' The tone suggests that the appeal was to Cassel's genuine appreciation rather than to his acquisitive streak.

Halfway through the reign, with his move to Brook House, Cassel was at the pinnacle of his power. He had 'gone up wonderfully in the social scale', wrote Sir Edward Hamilton, 'so much so that tongues which were dead against him are now silenced'. A rival for the King's affections, the Portuguese Minister, the Marquis de Soveral, a debonair and gallant bachelor who enchanted the ladies and charmed their husbands, was asked by the King whether he had seen *The Importance of Being Earnest*. 'No, Sir,' replied the diplomat, 'but I have seen the importance of being Ernest Cassel.'

---

*Footmen were paid by the inch. A first footman of 5 foot 6 inches might then earn up to £30 a year; from 5 foot 10 inches upwards from £32 to £40.

9

Turkey: Frustration and Failure

Despite his overcharged social programme, Sir Ernest Cassel found time still to tend, and even to extend, his overseas empire; while keeping a proprietary eye on his interests in Egypt and Sweden, he embarked in December 1904 on a tour of the United States and was received for lunch by President Theodore Roosevelt. He was as ever mainly a one-man bank. The King at the same time was coming to rely less on formal audiences with his ministers to conduct the business of the State. Two days before the Queen's death, Knollys complained to Eddy Hamilton that the Prime Minister Lord Salisbury never showed him any considera-tion; the natural amiability and insouciance of his nephew and successor, Balfour – 'he is "Arthur" to all his colleagues', Hamilton regretted – rendered his condescension the more galling; when it was at last the Liberals turn in office in 1905, the blunt and overweight Scotsman, Sir Henry Campbell-Bannerman, was exasperatingly uncommunicative. He came to count on a coterie of counsellors who made up an informal Cabinet, and a string of informers – diplomats and newspapermen. Among the chosen few was the capable and enigmatic Reginald Brett, who succeeded his father as Viscount Esher in 1899. Affected and abstemious, with a pink-and-white complexion, neatly trimmed moustache and receding hair, he had inherited from his mother elaborate Gallic manners which appeared too smoothly superficial to many of his contemporaries. He chose to perform in the shadows. He had already turned down an offer of a Permanent Under-Secretaryship both at the War Office and at the Colonial Office, and the governorship of the Cape Colony. He was a former confidant of Queen Victoria, and his school friend Lord Rosebery had appointed him Secretary of the Office of Works; King Edward appointed him Deputy Constable and Lieutenant Governor of Windsor Castle. Superficially a curious choice for a post in the City, he was nevertheless bagged by Cassel in December 1901 with the stipulation that the King acquiesce (he did object, but not vehemently).

Cassel made Esher 'really a very handsome offer': an arrangement for three years 'in case we fail to get on' with a guaranteed £5,000 a year and 10 per cent of any profit of a transaction in which he was engaged. Esher accepted principally for the sake of his son, Maurice, whom he smothered with cloying affection and from whom he dreaded being separated if he should have to go to Egypt for a month in the winter. (The boy survived to develop a natural appetite for actresses at an appropriate age.) Esher, who was working on the arrangements for the Coronation as well as sitting on the commission of inquiry into the conduct of the Boer War, took up his post in the following July when his term at the Office of Works ended. Despite these distractions, he found his first day in the City 'interesting and novel'. Cassel was involved in floating a shipping combine to counter the German-American cartel on the Atlantic promoted by J. Pierpont Morgan, and a large steel works in India proposed by the Viceroy, Lord Curzon. Esher had warned Cassel beforehand that he feared he might seem 'dull in perception of great financial and economic problems for a while!'; Esher found Cassel 'very kind and considerate at present. I don't know how long it will last.' His duties were not especially onerous – he put in just half an hour on his third day – though his services were called on for an occasional rubber of bridge. '*I* played pennies,' he told his son, having warned the others, among them Rothschilds' former manager, Carl Meyer, that he was a rotten player; he won two shillings, his employer lost £41.

The Royal Commission on the South African War presented its findings in July 1903. Although War Office reform was not on the agenda, Esher added specific proposals of his own on this score, whereupon Arthur Balfour, assured of the King's support, offered Esher, though Liberal, the post of Secretary of State for War. Still preferring the wings to the stage, he refused. It may have been this perceived dereliction of duty that incurred the King's displeasure. It was not until October that Esher informed Cassel that he had seen the King, was 'scolded a good deal – but in the end, I kissed his hand, and made it up! I am glad it is over!' A committee, reconstituted under Esher's chairmanship, went on to produce early the following year three additional reports on army reform which led to the introduction of the Committee of Imperial Defence and the creation of the General Staff. Balfour thanked Cassel for his 'generous forbearance in allowing Esher to give to the public services which are owed to you', and hoped that the loan might be extended.

Edward Hamilton, who was surprised that Esher could find time to do any work at all for Cassel, concluded that, though he 'was all for getting his full money's worth, [Cassel] may think it better on the whole to have his hold upon a man in such high favour'. Esher, in Paris about Cassel's business, was soon 'bored to death'; though he was kept busy, it was mostly 'uncongenial work with such a lot of tiresome detail'. Three months later he unburdened himself to Lord Revelstoke about the City, 'which I hate, and which I don't think I shall be able to stand', although he wished to prolong the sacrifice so that Maurice would have 'as much money as possible, both now and hereafter'. 'Still,' he added, 'it is not a nice life!' Esher's resolution did not last until the end of the month, and he then amicably severed his association with Cassel. His son judged that he simply could not 'grasp the intricacies of high finance'.

From the City, Esher joined the new-born Committee of Imperial Defence as an unpaid permanent member, but three years later came under attack from the *Standard* for wielding undue influence without constitutional accountability. Whatever his motives – calculation or kindness – Cassel had allowed him to retain directorships in three of his enterprises, the Central London Railway, and the Egyptian Daira Sanieh estates and Agricultural Bank. This association was seen as Esher's one Achilles' heel – Cassel was, after all, a major influence in the great Vickers armaments combine – and he gave the directorships up on the advice of Printing House Square, Downing Street and Buckingham Palace. Esher's part-time place as right-hand man was taken by Sydney Peel, son of the former Speaker and first Viscount, in whom his predecessor ruefully discerned an 'unusual flair' for high finance; indeed, John Morley, Secretary for India, sounded out Esher on the prospect of reversing the tide by tempting Peel to desert Cassel for government service.

The King, who had spent so much of his life fighting to establish his right of access to State papers, had lost none of his appetite for enlightenment. He devised an informal and efficient intelligence service. There was competition for the royal favour. The American journalist, George Smalley, when tardy with some titbit, would be gently chided with an accompanying twinkle in the hooded Hanoverian eye, 'Oh, yes, very interesting but I heard it an hour ago'; when Smalley returned to the United States as correspondent for *The Times*, King Edward gave him his private cipher address with the request to cable news which might interest him. Sir Henry Drummond Wolff, British envoy in Madrid for most of the Nineties, supplemented his official despatches with shrewd and succinct analyses on the Spanish and American attitudes to the Cuban insurrection and its attempted suppression, the Carlist threat and the difficulties of the Queen Regent in maintaining her government. The King's grasp of policies and personalities surprised and impressed foreign statesmen. The most assiduous of all such contributors was Sir Donald Mackenzie Wallace, foreign correspondent of *The Times*, occasional courtier and unofficial emissary. Born in the same year as the King, he had spent five years in Russia, assisted at the Congress of Berlin and passed the next six years at Constantinople before serving two Viceroys of India as private secretary; through the Nineties he had directed the foreign department of *The Times*. Fluent in Russian, he established a rare relationship of trust and friendship with the chronically wary Tsar Nicholas. This was all the more unusual as his name was reputed to conceal a Hebrew origin. On the face of it he was of impeccable descent, the son of an undoubted Wallace of Dunbartonshire, while his mother was the daughter of a Mackenzie. Nonetheless, when staying for protracted spells with his friend Sir Arthur Nicolson* at the Embassy in St Petersburg, he was known to the disrespectful young attachés in the Chancery as 'Mordecai the Jew'. The Kaiser was evidently of the same mind. He described Mackenzie Wallace, then reporting to the King from Algeciras on Germany's ham-fisted efforts to spoil the Anglo-French honeymoon, as 'very intelligent, a friend of King Edward's; a Jew naturally'. (This is by no means conclusive. The Kaiser may have intended this jibe as a malicious reflection on his uncle's social preferences; or he may have been simply unfamiliar with black Highland looks and beaked Stuart nose.) Mackenzie Wallace was regarded generally with favour by the Germans. They imagined he had been sent to Algeciras to mind Nicolson, the British delegate, and at the first sign of a concession the Kaiser noted in the margin of the despatch, 'Wallace is beginning to make himself felt.' The German chargé d'affaires judged that Nicolson, newly arrived in St Petersburg in the immediate aftermath of the revolution, had 'flung himself wholly to the left', and that Wallace, who moved in circles usually closed to diplomats, was responsible for correcting this bias. It was the Russian connection that was of the greatest service to the King. When Japan took up arms against Russia in 1904, there existed a duplicate jumble of alliances. Only two years before, Britain had signed a treaty with Japan designed to restrain Russia's aggressive ambitions in the Far East, while France, nominal ally of Russia, had reached an entente with Britain just two months before the outbreak of hostilities. Russia's unexpected humiliation by Japan set off a violent

---

*His son, Harold Nicolson, drew on Sir Donald Mackenzie Wallace for a composite portrait of Professor Malone in his classic *Some People*.

popular revulsion for the regime, so severe that Nicholas II was obliged to consent to the introduction of a constitution and a parliament, the Duma. (Among the religious and racial minorities elected were Muslims and Armenians, Poles and Ukrainians – and twelve Jews.) Once the Little Father had recovered his nerve, this experiment in 'nonsensical dreams' was to King Edward's private dismay, dissolved. Donald Mackenzie Wallace arrived in St Petersburg the next day and was at once in touch with the new chief minister, Peter Stolypin. (Five years later, Stolypin, the great agrarian reformer, was shot in the theatre at Kiev before the eyes of the Imperial family by a Jewish Socialist Revolutionary – and probable police agent. The threatened pogrom was courageously checked by his successor, Count Kokovtsev.) Mackenzie Wallace was also received in audience by the Tsar. His reception was surprisingly amiable in view of Sir Henry Campbell-Bannerman's recent outburst before a meeting of the Inter-Parliamentary Union, 'The Duma is dead! Long Live the Duma!' which had predictably provoked an official protest. The Tsar, blinkered by sublime certainty, commanded Wallace simply to explain the 'true situation' to the King. Three weeks later Sir Donald was again closeted with Nicholas. After a long discussion of the country's internal affairs, the Tsar, who only a year before had described his uncle to the Kaiser as the arch-intriguer and mischief-maker of Europe, required Sir Donald to take a letter to the King and again explain 'the real state of things here, which is so often misrepresented'; 'anxious to come to an understanding', he would keep in touch with the King, using Wallace and his friend, Alexander Izvolsky, the new Foreign Minister, an arriviste and snob, as a channel. The latter immediately applied himself to removing the outstanding contentious issues between the two countries which led to the Anglo-Russian convention in September of the following year.

Loans followed the pattern of alliances. The savings of the French bourgeoisie shored up the Imperial Russian throne. London was the natural marketplace for the Japanese. When, two months after launching their surprise attack on the Russian fleet at Port Arthur in 1904, they came to London looking for a large war loan, they approached Barings, with whom they were already on borrowing terms. Barings also held valuable Russian government accounts and most reluctantly declined to be publicly associated with the issue. They passed the business to Cassel's old friend Jacob Schiff, on an opportune visit to London; the Russians, ignorant of the ruse, were reassured, while Barings earned the gratitude of the Japanese and a quiet commission for the introduction. The loan, for £10 million at 6 per cent, was brought out in May; Cassel, with among others Horace Farquhar of Parr's Bank (and Master of the Royal

Household), participated. Though Schiff had a personal inducement to undertake the loan – he considered it '*desirable* to admonish the ruling class of Russia by an object lesson' – the Japanese emissary detected a higher hand at work; it was surely not mere chance that King Edward had entertained Ernest Cassel and, to his 'great joy', Jacob Schiff to a private lunch at the conclusion of the negotiations. Cassel did nothing to disabuse him; His Majesty had, he informed the Japanese, expressed his 'gracious appreciation' of Schiff's role in supporting Britain's ally. Further loans to Japan followed; after their victory at Mukden, the rate even came down to 4½ per cent. Schiff subsequently was rewarded with the unprecedented privilege of a meal with the Mikado, Cassel with the Order of the Rising Sun. Russia, its means at home and its credit abroad exhausted, was brought to the peace table.

The British government was not antagonistic to Russia's raising money in the City; it was rather that repugnance to the Tsar's repressive rule and fear of his territorial ambitions were not conducive to a confident investment climate. The Jewish bankers of New York and London held aloof as a matter of principle, but even among them there were varying shades of opinion on the merits of lending. Alfred Rothschild was the most uncompromising: '*No*, on no account,' Lord Salisbury's secretary reported. Alfred's brother Natty was less disinclined; he was loath to bolt the door against Russia, judging that the prospect of a carrot might serve to curb the wildest excesses. Ernest Cassel went further. He considered the favour of a loan would work to the positive benefit of Russia's Jews. The evidence of Jacob Schiff's attitude is equivocal. Russian agents were said to have offered to relax restrictions on Jews in exchange for a loan of $50 million. This was rejected; any improvement should come from recognition of their rights and not as a concession. On the other hand, Theodor Herzl learned on his death bed that Schiff was prepared to negotiate a Russian loan at the desire of Lord Lansdowne, the Foreign Secretary, on condition that something was done to better conditions for the Russian Jews, but 'it would be clearly understood that this good deed would also have to bring him more than the customary rate of interest'. This condition was never met, and Schiff maintained his boycott to the point even of refusing to support later Anglo-French efforts to finance their war effort until their Imperial ally's abdication in March 1917; he then contributed to Kerensky's abortive Liberty Loan. (In fairness to Schiff, he also turned a deaf ear to requests for a wartime German loan from his friends and in-laws, the Warburgs.)

Despite Russia's harsh repression of the revolution and the still unsettled state of the countryside, Campbell-Bannerman's new Liberal administration in London, swimming against the strong tide of public opinion, determined to seek an understanding with the Tsar. King Edward was delighted, but nevertheless resisted an attempt by the new Foreign Secretary, Sir Edward Grey, to convince him to visit Nicholas in Russia: he doubted whether the country would much approve, or whether his nephew would listen to him if he offered any advice. The King told Sir Charles Hardinge, Permanent Under-Secretary at the Foreign Office, that the Russian Finance Minister, Count Witte, hoped 'that by my going I should enable him to float a Loan. What an extraordinary idea! and one that does not appeal to me in any way . . .' Nine months after the signing of the Anglo-Russian convention, the timing was scarcely more propitious. News of the forthcoming visit raised hopes in Paris, fears in Berlin and outrage and suspicion at home. The British government, anticipating the outcry, maintained secrecy until a month before the official meeting; on the eve of the King's departure, a critical motion was put down in the House of Commons in which the Labour leader, Keir Hardie, accused Edward of condoning atrocities. The King, his temper tried, received two gratuitous calls on his goodwill, the one humanitarian, the other flagrantly mercenary.

The Rothschilds, who had neglected their cultivation of ministers that mattered, were not so well served by the new government as they had been under Rosebery and Balfour. (Eddy Hamilton had foreseen as much; Natty, he wrote in the last year of the old century, had 'become so strong a party man, he will now be "out of it" whenever the other side comes in'.) Only a month before he resigned, Balfour, at Natty's instigation, was exhorting the Russian government, still in the throes of revolution, to put an end to 'these atrocious attacks' on the Jews and offering the Rothschilds consular channels for the distribution of aid for the victims. Now, the King was the Rothschilds' strongest card. Three days before he was due to sail, the sporting Leo Rothschild buttonholed His Majesty at Epsom on the subject of the Tsar's Jews. The King, sympathetic, desired a written *aide-mémoire*. This was delivered next day, signed by all three brothers: after dwelling on the sufferings, the memorandum conceded that Jewish anarchists must expect to be dealt with as they deserved, but urged equal rights for the remainder to ensure that they remained 'faithful and devoted subjects'; the alternative was a further effluence of Jewish emigrants to 'disorganize the position and condition of all workmen in many parts of the world' (over half a million had already left for America in the preceding three years). From Cassel, with whom the King dined on the eve of his departure, he received a request of a different nature – a kind word to be dropped in the Tsar's ear on the matter of a loan Cassel was interested in floating. Knollys responded coolly to the Rothschilds the same day: it was 'a very delicate subject' for the King to raise, and it would not be 'constitutionally correct or proper' for him to do so without the full concurrence of Sir Charles Hardinge and Sir Arthur Nicolson. If Knollys had not already himself consulted Hardinge, he anticipated that official enthusiasm for such an initiative would be wanting. The King, however, was not to be fobbed off by the Foreign Office; though the Tsar's sensibilities were spared, Nicolson was deputed to bring it up in a general conversation with Stolypin. Hardinge reported with relief to Knollys that 'it went off all right' and that the Russian Prime Minister contemplated 'legislation for the amelioration of the lot of the Jews in Russia'. The King was prepared to give Stolypin the benefit of the doubt and to leave it at that. Rothschild was sceptical and retorted that he was not prepared to offer up thanks which he did not feel. If the diplomats were reluctant to let the King raise the humanitarian issue, they (as well as Esher) were incensed and scornful at Cassel's effrontery. 'It is a great abuse by Cassel', Hardinge wrote to Knollys, 'of the King's friendliness towards him, to ask His Majesty to mix himself up in any way in a financial transaction of which the King and his Government know nothing . . . It amuses me to see how the Jews, though hating the Russian Government, are always ready to give them money if they themselves can "make a bit"!' Though Hardinge did all he could to discourage the King from endorsing Cassel's scheme, he suspected that when Edward was free of his officials he asked the Tsar to receive his friend if he visited Russia, underlining the fact that he was a Privy Councillor and sweetening Nicholas, who had lost his own navy, by appointing him, without British ministers' approval, an Admiral of the Fleet, to his 'childish delight'. It was this that prompted the Kaiser, who soon learned about Cassel's sly salesmanship, to label his uncle 'a jobber in stocks and shares' who counted on pocketing a 'colossal' personal profit out of any loan. Hardinge himself was agitated lest the news spread and the King's sponsorship be taken as an attempt 'to rig the market' for a Russian loan.

It is not clear whether Cassel's intrusion was crowned with success. He was credited with the launch of a Russian loan of £7.5 million the following year. If so, this would have been for a smaller amount and on joint account with his friend Lord Revelstoke. In March 1906, Barings had been brave enough, once some of the dust of the revolution had settled, to take up £13 million of a massive Russian loan for £89 million (the bulk was left to the French market; the German banks had been ordered not to participate). Lord Rothschild considered this 'a huge responsibility'. 'No doubt', he wrote to his French cousins, 'they are well paid for their trouble and risk, but I must confess that, anxious as I am for business, quite apart from the Jewish question, I should not care much for the responsibility.' This did not prevent speculation in the press that the Rothschilds had covertly taken up a slice of the loan. Enraged, they denied the story. It was the Russians' turn to be enraged when the *Jewish Chronicle*, followed by *The Times*, suggested that their government was responsible for spreading the rumour in the first place so as to enhance their credit. Only three months later, a representative of Count Witte, the Russian Finance Minister, was at New Court with his hand out. 'As far as I understood him,' Natty reported again to his French cousins, 'the remedy is a very simple one. Make a big loan to Russia, and something may be done for the Jews! I told him that he was putting the cart before the horse . . .' There were other unsettling rumours that large amounts of this loan were sitting unsold in the hands of the underwriters, and that as a result Barings were once more in trouble. However, in the changed climate of entente sealed by the King at Reval, a fresh Russian loan was launched in January 1909; Barings, probably in partnership with Cassel, took up just £6 million, Paris again bearing the major burden. 'Opinions', Lord Rothschild noted, 'are absolutely divided whether the public will want it or not.' The issue was a huge success; the lists had to be closed by mid-afternoon of the first day and all applications were scaled down.

Even if the Tsar, under the influence of his uncle's charm, had agreed to receive Privy Councillor Cassel, the financier would have been hard put to it to find the time. He was already instituting yet another, and final, National Bank on the southern borders of the Tsar's empire. This time his field was Turkey, the same pool that Baron Hirsch had paddled in fifteen years and more before.

Three solemn, seasonal engagements in Sir Ernest's year were immutable. Heedless of other calls, he continued his bumpy career in pursuit of the fox; for much of August and September, kings and commoners would have to follow him to the Swiss Alps to seek his services; his winters in Egypt lengthened as his daughter's health declined. His daughter's friend the Duchess of Sermoneta came across him in Cairo in 1908. Cassel, accompanied by Maud and his son-in-law, Wilfrid Ashley, and Jacob Schiff and his wife, insisted she join them. The Duchess found Schiff a charming old man, the soul of honesty and honour, deeply attached to his religion and proud of his American citizenship, though after forty years he spoke as if he had arrived from Frankfurt the day before (Schiff and Cassel conducted most of their correspondence in German). Six weeks were spent in the capital as Cassel's guest before the party proceeded stylishly up the Nile by steamer as far as Wadi Halfa for a further three weeks. There, time running short, the host offered them a choice of Khartoum or Jerusalem. Plumping for the Holy Land, they embarked from Alexandria for Jaffa. Here Cassel, on receipt of a telegram from Mrs Henry Bischoffsheim imploring him to return to London as her husband, Cassel's old employer, was dying, left them in the hands of Jacob Schiff and an impressive dragoman. (On one occasion, their guide, jumping down from the carriage, declared with a dramatic gesture, 'Sir! This is Bethlehem.' Schiff gave the occasion a moment's solemn reflection, then he asked, 'Ach! and vere can ve have our tea?')

Palestine was a poor but peaceful backwater of the Ottoman Empire. Milk and honey, let alone tea, were unfamiliar commodities. A handful of poor Jewish immigrants from eastern Europe scratched a sparse living in a few settlements regulated by the philanthropic French Baron Edmond de Rothschild, younger brother of Alphonse and Gustave. There was nothing here to attract the covetous eyes of the Powers. At the epicentre of the empire, there were pickings aplenty.

Towards the end of 1888, a syndicate led by Georg von Siemens of the Deutsche Bank had won a concession for the Anatolian Railway to build a line from Haidar Pasha, on the Asian shore of Constantinople, inland through Eskishehr to Angora (Ankara) and from Eskishehr south-eastwards to Konya, short of the Taurus range. A little more than a year later, when Baron Hirsch was looking for a buyer for the Vienna –Constantinople Railway, Siemens acquired his controlling share to frustrate a hostile takeover (the Russians were rumoured to be interested) and to ensure that his own Asia Minor lines were not left in the air. Before Konya was reached in 1896, Siemens was already hatching plans to push on to Baghdad and from there to Basra at the top of the Persian Gulf, a distance of 1,800 miles from Constantinople. This grandiose scheme set the alarm bells ringing in London, where hitherto Russia's designs on Constantinople had constituted the major preoccupation; the German drive eastwards might block the Tsar's path to the Mediterranean, but only at the cost of letting the Kaiser into the Persian Gulf, India's backdoor. In January 1893, the British Ambassador to the Porte peremptorily asked Sultan Abdul Hamid to drop negotiations with the Germans. (They retaliated by withdrawing their indispensable diplomatic support for Britain in Egypt.) Political considerations had already persuaded Siemens of the desirability of finding British partners. Cassel, boasting railroad experience and Hirsch's patronage, was the best candidate. He hesitated – Turkish bonds did not sell like hot cakes in the City – and finally balked; perhaps faced with the choice of playing second fiddle to the Deutsche Bank in Turkey, he preferred to be first violin in Egypt. By 1894, the year after Siemens had reached Ankara, the time, if ever propitious, had passed. That summer news trickled through of massacres in Armenia. The British government responded to outraged public opinion by pressing for an inquiry. When the facts came to light, Britain, France and Russia, protesting, again pressed the Sultan to reform his corrupt and callous regime. Germany pointedly dissociated itself from this *démarche*; scenting his advantage, the Sultan, to whom the Kaiser had sent a signed photograph of his family for his birthday, played for time. Four years later the Kaiser, with his wife, made a flamboyant progress from Constantinople to Jerusalem and Damascus, where he provocatively saluted Abdul the Damned as Caliph of 300 million Muslims (a great many of them subjects of the Queen-Empress) and hailed Turkey as Germany's friend and ally. In the last month of the last year of the old century, Abdul Hamid, after lavish expenditure within the palace, signed the convention for the Imperial Ottoman Baghdad Railway, more ominously known as the Berlin to Baghdad Railway. In January 1901, in an attempt to comply with the British wish for some indeterminate participation, strenuously canvassed by Sir Vincent Caillard at the head of the Ottoman Public Debt administration, Dr Siemens sounded out Alfred and Leopold Rothschild. Their opinion was that the scheme had only a political character and was therefore 'not sufficiently matured' for negotiating with the banks. Siemens informed the Foreign Office that he would hold the door open for a British group to enter at a later stage. Despite the cool response he persevered with singular patience and goodwill. Six months later he was back at the Foreign Office to report failure and to reaffirm his readiness to accept British partners. Barings and another London bank had already turned down the chance. Sir Ernest Cassel had proposed two expedients, a London-based corporation which would raise the capital for a 20 per cent holding, or an amalgamation with the old-established Smyrna–Aidin Railway through an exchange of shares at a guaranteed rate of interest; the first had found no favour with investors, the latter had been rejected by the predominantly British shareholders. The Germans instead turned to the French-dominated Imperial Ottoman Bank. Later in the same year Siemens's successor at the Deutsche Bank, Arthur von Gwinne, made a further approach to Cassel and Sir Clinton Dawkins – a former financial adviser under Cromer in Egypt and financial member of the Viceroy's council under Curzon – who had recently been recruited for J. Pierpont Morgan's London house. But public opinion had shifted; the Sultan's sins were forgotten, displaced by bitterness over German sympathy for the Boers.

For several years Alfred Rothschild had been engaged in efforts to cultivate an entente between Germany and Britain by bringing together Joseph Chamberlain and the German diplomat Baron von Eckardstein, the son-in-law of one of Edward's earliest tradesman friends, Sir John Blundell Maple of furnishing fame.* A genial giant who, in his white uniform, spiked helmet and boots, towered above the tallest men, Eckardstein was also a scaremonger, a self-important busybody, and a frustrated careerist, fatally prone to falsification. Edward Hamilton considered his position at the Embassy 'a very nondescript one. He apparently has the right to demand audience of the Emporer, and to act independently of the Ambassador whose health is now very bad. He appears to take all his cues from Alfred Rothschild and to be a sort of unofficial go-between on Anglo-German affairs at the beck and call of the firm of Rothschild!' Little wonder that he did not earn the trust of the incoming Chancellor, Bülow. These and other attempts came to nothing and their failure turned the frustrated Chamberlain into a rabid Germanophobe. There was anyway no common ground between the two sides; the advantages and disadvantages for each were unequal and incompatible; Britain would not concede a quid for a quo, Germany insisted on all or nothing. In December 1901, Lord Lansdowne, Foreign Secretary, informed the new German Ambassador that the state of that perennial pretext, public opinion, ruled out the possibility of any formal alliance.

In London, it came to be recognized at last that the railway would be built with or without a British hand in it. Once completed, it would turn the flank of Britain's traditional trade routes to the East and secure German economic domination of the Ottoman Empire. In the wake of the Kaiser's threatened thrust eastwards – *Drang nach Osten* – there were fears of German colonization along the wayside; neither had it escaped notice that the railway company enjoyed the right to work all mineral resources within a twenty-kilometre band on each side of the track, in all a total of some 45,000 square miles, much of it through oil-bearing Mesopotamia. This concentrated the minds of the Cabinet. In February 1903 Cassel and Clinton Dawkins were again approached, this time on Lansdowne's initiative, in an attempt to reawaken their interest. Simultaneously the new Foreign Secretary enlisted Lord Revelstoke, dangling the lure of a possible grant of a subsidy for the carriage of mails to India and government assistance for the construction of a terminus in Kuwait, with whose ruler the Viceroy, Curzon, had recently concluded a

*He is eponymously commemorated today in the Portuguese *maple*, a commodious easy chair.

treaty. In March the concession for the extension to Basra was confirmed by the Porte. A consortium was quickly put together in which Britain, France and Germany would each take a 25 per cent stake, other countries, principally Switzerland and Austria, a total of 15 per cent and the German Anatolian Railway the remaining 10 per cent. The British government, which was not risking taxpayers' money, had so far expressed a wish for a 'sufficient' or 'equal share'. This was effectively achieved; the slight German preponderance was fair recognition of the fact that they had nine-tenths of the law on their side – the existing track and the concession for the extension. However, it was the bone that came to stick in the throat of the Cabinet and on which it chose to choke.

On 6 April 1903 Lord Esher, still Cassel's aide, was expecting to go to Berlin with his employer and Lord Revelstoke 'some time next month' on railway business. There was no time for such leisurely progress. Newspapers were already attacking the project for its German genesis and urging that Britain withdraw or block it. Esher, noting that this had not prevented the Suez Canal from being dug, commented, 'Stupid fools!' The next day, on the eve of a debate in the Commons, Lord Lansdowne sent for Cassel. 'My instinct', wrote Esher, 'tells me that the Government will flinch. They are very timid just now . . . The Germans will go on just the same and the railway will be made, only we shall be out of it. We never learn by experience.' His suspicion was confirmed the next day. 'The Government are frightened, and run away. In that case Revelstoke and Cassel retire from the scheme, and the Germans and French go on alone. It is a pity', he concluded lamely. Esher's brainchild, the Committee of Imperial Defence, was 'strongly in favour of the line on strategical grounds. Whether they are right or wrong is one question. That the line is sure to be made, and under those circumstances it is well for us to have a joint control, is quite another thing – and upon this point there can be no doubt. But the German Emperor is a Bogey just now in certain quarters; and the English people, led by a foolish half-informed Press, are children in foreign politics. They have always been so, and have often paid dearly.'

There was another influence more baneful than the magisterial disapproval of *The Times*, that of a cuckoo in the Cabinet in the person of the Colonial Secretary, Joseph Chamberlain. 'But for Joe's bile,' Lansdowne wrote to Balfour on 12 April, 'the opposition would not be serious.' On the same day, Easter Sunday, Edward Hamilton, staying at Ascott with Leo Rothschild, understood that Chamberlain was 'in a bad humour, he dislikes the Irish Land Bill, he is sick about the Baghdad Railway, and . . . discontented about the Colonial preference'. The philosophical Premier, struggling to hold his Cabinet together, conceded the advantage to his thrusting colleague.

Balfour had by now sought to placate critics by offering an assurance to the House of Commons that British capital and control would be on the basis of 'absolute equality' with those of the other Powers, a departure from the more flexible arrangement originally foreseen by Lansdowne. The agreement that Cassel and company had reached, secure enough for practical purposes, did not precisely correspond to this new criterion, although it might have been justified by a more robust ministry. Lord Revelstoke, anxious not to close the door irrevocably, requested Lansdowne, an old friend, for an intimation that if the government were unable to support the scheme, they were not in principle opposed to it. Even this was thought to be too much of a committal, and a negative statement, dwelling on the shortcomings, was prepared with the rider that the government would 'not unfavourably view a reconsideration of the question at a later date' if the objections were removed. Ernest Cassel and Clinton Dawkins, who, as the government's surrogates, had secured the best possible terms, refused to subscribe to this paltry obfuscation. The next day Dawkins, writing to Gwinne of the Deutsche Bank, greatly regretted this ignominious ending, 'but', he added, 'I am glad to think, and I feel you will be convinced, that your grievance lies not against the British group but against the British Foreign Office. The fact is that the business has become involved in politics here . . .' He was also, he wrote to Lord Curzon, left 'with a most melancholy impression' of 'the utter incompetence and heedlessness with which the Government managed the whole affair'. He believed that Lansdowne had endeavoured sincerely to convince the Cabinet of his views, but with Balfour intent on appeasing Chamberlain, and the waverers able to shelter behind what Lansdowne described as the 'insensate outcry' of public opinion, he had no chance. Lansdowne himself later put the blame on the financiers who had 'scuttled'; had it not been for them he would have been in favour of 'sticking to our position'. There is no justification for this charge. On the contrary, the financiers had every reason to be thoroughly exasperated; Cassel might have been forgiven for agreeing with the Kaiser's assessment of King Edward's ministers as 'unmitigated noodles'. Germany, watched by Britain, France and Russia, struggled on alone across Asia Minor.

Four years later, during a visit to Windsor Castle at the end of 1907, the Kaiser, after subjecting the new Liberal Foreign Secretary, Sir Edward Grey, to a diatribe against the Jews – 'There are far too many of them in my country. They want stamping out. If I did not restrain my people, there would be a Jew-baiting' – proceeded to the subject of the Baghdad Railway. 'The concession is mine,' he said with his customary bombast. 'You must come in on my terms or stay out. We have plenty of money.' To a fellow guest, Sir Ernest Cassel, he spoke very little of the railway, delivering a monologue on the need for a strong German navy, an opinion Cassel was evidently expected to pass on to his royal friend, who preferred to avoid any political discussion with his volatile nephew. Cassel judged the Kaiser's knowledge to be superficial, his statements unreliable. There was, however, some ground for the Kaiser's neurosis. The Anglo-Russian convention had been signed two months before his visit, against all the confident expectations of the Wilhelmstrasse. (It was after King Edward's meeting with the Tsar in the following summer that the Kaiser himself first raised the spectre of 'encirclement'.) The countries' relations were souring and any form of co-operation was becoming more than ever difficult to sell to the investing (and voting) public. The two nations' newspapers competed in vituperation. 'The Press is dreadful on both sides,' the Kaiser, a master of self-delusion, had conceded a few years earlier, 'but here it has nothing to say, for I am the sole arbiter and master.' (German editors, unfortunately, were inattentive subjects.) In London *The Times* was the most consistently and determinedly hostile to Germany. Paradoxically, four months after Cassel was closeted with the Kaiser, *The Times* approached him for help when £200,000 was needed to buy out fractious shareholders, who had received no dividend for years, and to inject fresh working capital. Cassel's condition was a change of management, the retirement both of the long-serving editor and the chief proprietor, and a reduction in the price to one penny. This surgery was deemed too severe. The paper instead passed surreptitiously to Lord Northcliffe. Less assured than Cassel, he waited five years before bringing the price down to twopence; a final reduction to one penny was only made five months before the outbreak of war in 1914 (the circulation trebled overnight).

In the year after Kaiser Wilhelm had made his abrupt ultimatum to Sir Edward Grey on the Baghdad Railway, Germany's ascendancy in Turkey was checked by a revolt of junior army officers, the Young Turks, against the Sultan's rule. Not least among the factors that spurred them were a generous guarantee by the Porte to the Baghdad Railway at a time when army pay was months in arrears, and fears aroused three months before by King Edward's friendly exchange with the ruler of Russia, Turkey's acquisitive neighbour.

The Young Turks wished to offset the growing influence of Germany, so supportive of the Sultan's regime, by strengthening ties with Britain.

This was not unacceptable to the Foreign Office, which had already been trying to revive British influence in Turkey for political and economic reasons. When Sir Edward Grey had taken office as Foreign Secretary three years before, he had been distressed to find how completely Britain had been ousted by rival Powers: 'We shall make no progress till British capital of a high class takes an energetic interest in Turkey.' The Foreign Office hoped to reverse this decline by bolstering British investment in the French preserve of the Imperial Ottoman Bank. This fanciful conception carried the seeds of subsequent frustration and failure. Each country had a different perception of the four-year-old Entente Cordiale. For the British, it was seen as more of a détente, a device to settle long- standing, often bitter, differences on ostensibly favourable terms. For the French, fired by a fear of Germany and a desire for revenge, it was seen as a step covertly to entangle Britain in a military partnership on the Continent. (Lord Rosebery, one of the few to discern this, was also one of the Entente's rare critics.) France was the friendly lender to the Porte, raising six out of the twelve Turkish loans in the ten years preceding the Great War. These were approved on strict conditions: the award of concessions to French companies for port, railway and other public works, or the purchase of arms. Political ambition and the profit motive were harmoniously married. It is probable that the Foreign Office, with only a vague sense of purpose and unaccustomed to consort in the marketplace, failed totally to appreciate the depth and determination of the French commitment not to surrender any slice of their trade and its dependent political leverage. When the Quai d'Orsay's sharp elbows caused complaints of bruising, the overriding national interest was loftily pleaded; when they met resistance, the 'spirit' of the Entente was piously invoked. It must have delighted as much as astonished the French diplomats that their British colleagues were prepared to abide by these rules. That France should pursue her own perceived interests was natural and legitimate; that her neighbour should lend itself as an accomplice to the detriment of its own interests was stretching charity too far. The Ottoman Bank received the unequivocal support of the French government; the British financiers, though receiving unprecedented support from the Foreign Office, were nonetheless bound by these political considerations. It is arguable at the least that they would have been better off without it. Thus the object desired by the Foreign Office – commercial co-operation with France at Constantinople on at least equal terms while somehow avoiding any conflict and rivalry – was incompatible and unattainable. It is only astonishing, in view of the unhappy antecedent of the Baghdad Railway fiasco, that Cassel even passively condoned such naivety.

Two years before the Young Turks emerged from their barracks, negotiations for collaboration had opened at the highest level in Paris and London. The Ottoman Bank, supported by the Quai d'Orsay, fought a stiff rearguard action against surrendering any part of its near-monopoly. This evasive shuffling was only ended by the Premier, Georges Clemenceau, who feared that any estrangement with Britain would cause that country to drift towards Germany. The London Committee of the Ottoman Bank were, if anything, even more reluctant to share their cake. It was only after eighteen months of energetic trimming that by the middle of 1908, the London Committee was reluctantly brought to the formation of an Anglo-French consortium which included Sir Ernest Cassel and Sir Albert Stern, Mrs Henry Bishoffsheim's nephew (he was to pioneer a bullet-proof 'landship', later known as the tank). By the end of the year Cassel and Stern were informed by the Ottoman Bank that the scheme had been unilaterally 'abandoned'. Cassel had been uncharacteristically patient but, no man's dupe, he had been assembling his own vehicle in anticipation of a breakdown. This direct threat agitated the *pigeonniers* on the Quai d'Orsay.

Notwithstanding the good intentions of the Foreign Office to reinforce British influence, British capital was not eager to oblige. Barings, pressed by the government to offer a loan to the Young Turks, refused. Cassel responded with an immediate advance of £1.5 million on a large loan already contracted with the Ottoman Bank for the following year. This earned him the thanks of the Foreign Office and a promise of 'full diplomatic support' should the Turks renege on the debt. In the same month, November, the formation was announced of the National Bank of Turkey with an initial capital of £3 million and a further £2 million if the concession could be won for a land bank on Cassel's Egyptian model. The bank boasted an impressive Anglo-Turkish board. The local English directors were Sir Adam Block, former consul and attaché at Constantinople, administrator of the Ottoman Public Debt and president of the British Chamber of Commerce; and the head of the leading Levantine merchants, J. W. Whittall & Co. On the Turkish side there was a phalanx of Young Turks and related luminaries: Djemal Pasha, son-in-law of the Empire's spiritual leader, the Sheik of Islam, and subsequently a member of the Young Turks' ruling triumvirate; a rich Egyptian prince, the grandson of Mehemet Ali, former viceroy of Egypt; the Minister of Justice, and Nubar Pasha, a former prime minister of Egypt whom Cromer thought a liar and a rogue, though capable. A seat had also been reserved for Djavid Bey, who, on taking over Turkey's finances, filled the post with his nominee, a newspaper editor. (Djavid, 'a brisk little cock-

226

sparrow of a man' who made devoted friends and bitter enemies, was a Dönme, a descendant of Sephardi Jews who had fled to Salonica from Spain in the fifteenth century and been converted to Islam in the seventeenth.) Cassel nominated three of the six members of the London board, among them Lord Revelstoke of Barings.

Cassel was in Constantinople himself from at least early March 1909 and, despite his distinguished local backing, was meeting heavy weather. He poured his woes into the attentive ear of the King, who was at Biarritz where Cassel's own villa was full of friends. 'You have indeed had many difficulties,' the monarch sympathized, 'and the state of affairs there can hardly be considered satisfactory.' The general situation in the Balkans had given the King 'many dark days', though he hoped matters might yet be settled without going to war, which would really be 'lamentable'. His concern was understated. The sight of the 'Sick Man' stirring from his couch did not suit either Russia or Austria, otherwise rarely in accord. In concert, the one unilaterally declared the Dardanelles open to Russian warships in defiance of international treaty, the other annexed Bosnia and Herzegovina. Prince Ferdinand of Bulgaria profited from this distraction to proclaim his country's complete independence from Turkey; Crete declared its union with Greece. Landlocked Serbia, Russia's friend, was aggrieved by the Austrian action. Germany's loyalties, torn between its ally Austria and its protégé Turkey, declared for the former. The threat of a general war was only averted at the end of March 1908. On 5 April the British Ambassador informed Sir Edward Grey that an Imperial firman had been issued establishing Cassel's National Bank. It was one of the last acts of Abdul the Damned. Such a series of national humiliations had caused popular unrest, whipped up by religious fanatics against the secular Young Turks. The Sultan took advantage of this to stage his own counter-revolution on 12 April. Army units which had mutinied were promptly pardoned by the Sultan, who named a new government. A week elapsed before a relieving army despatched by the Committee of Union and Progress in Salonica encircled the capital and resumed control. Abdul Hamid was forced finally to abdicate in favour of his more amenable brother, a prisoner in the palace for the past thirty years. It was an astonishing feat that Cassel, caught in the midst of this maelstrom, ever managed to put his bank together.

He next cast about for a *genius loci*. He was 'much perplexed', Sir Edward Grey informed the British Ambassador in Constantinople, 'as to getting a good enough man for his Bank. He aims high and I have not so far been able to help him. One cannot urge the best men to leave the public service.' (Grey was evidently unaware that the National Bank had tried to lure Sir Charles Hardinge away from the Foreign Office.) The search took three months before Cassel fixed on Sir Henry Babington Smith, a classical scholar who had replaced Sir Vincent Caillard on the Ottoman Public Debt administration and was currently, aged forty, Secretary of the Post Office. He required 'a good deal of pressure', Hardinge reported, to be persuaded to pitch his tent in Constantinople. When Babington Smith consulted Hardinge, he 'strongly recommended' him to hold out for a salary of not less than £10,000 a year, three times what Hardinge had been offered. Cassel's face was 'a picture of astonishment' when he was faced with this demand, though he came round within twenty-four hours. 'This little transaction', Hardinge recorded, 'gave me great pleasure as a set-off to Cassel's GCB.' For the next two years Cassel spent much of his energy and ingenuity in incessant, sometimes daily, correspondence with Constantinople and in conference with the Foreign Office, which was nervous of his initiative. If faces had changed, old habits persisted in the ancient Byzantine capital. The issue of a £1 million Constantinople municipal loan constituted the National Bank's bizarre baptism. Cassel, who was, courtesy of Djavid, privy to his rivals' offers, was enabled to come up with a more competitive price on condition of immediate acceptance. This was approved. Others, however, with their own sources of information (if not the same), fought back against the interloper. The French Banque de Salonique matched the National Bank's offer and intimated it was prepared to go higher. The National Bank indignantly raised its own offer. (Although taken aback to discover it did not possess the monopoly of inside information, it was decided that there would be difficulty in making this 'a matter of serious reproach'.) Cassel, in placatory mood, proposed that the French take a quarter-share of the issue. This was rejected. An outsider, the London house of Keyser, had already intervened with a bid that had by then spurred the Banque de Salonique to improve its own, a price Cassel judged to be 'quite out of the question'. Pending the arrival of a partner from London, Keyser appointed as its agent the local correspondent of the *Manchester Guardian*. This enterprising journalist, playing for time, spread reports that the Turkish ministers had been bribed, which prompted the Grand Vizier to call in Reuters' man to contradict the calumny. (By a curious coincidence, Lord Revelstoke's youngest brother, Maurice Baring, was the *Morning Post* correspondent in Constantinople at the same time.) Cassel may have made his own displeasure known in the City. Keyser's stockbrokers called on him to excuse their client: they had only taken up the business in the belief that they were not competing for the loan, and that far from having made an offer, the loan had been offered to them at that price. Cassel, in an effort to force a decision, sent a message to Babington Smith to be used in the last extremity. Showing signs of unusual stress, he telegraphed that as there was 'no reasonable prospect of *faire* on lines *satisfaisant . . . nous ferions mieux décider liquider*'. Djavid, armed with this threat, was able to convince the council of ministers to approve the loan on the National Bank's terms. Cassel, considering that Keyser had 'behaved very well towards us', urged Babington Smith that 'we ought not to forget them at the proper time'. The president of the Banque de Salonique also approached him with 'a somewhat delicate task to perform'. The Banque would now very much like to take up the proffered participation. He hinted that they had been previously acting on the instructions of the French government, which had hoped to frustrate the British group by shutting them out of the Paris Bourse. The profits from this business covered the National Bank's expenses for its first year, although Cassel was rumoured to have had the utmost difficulty in placing in London or elsewhere even the fraction for which he had made himself responsible.

Far from being cast down by this inauspicious inauguration, he struck out in another direction, reviving a fifty-year-old dream to open up the route to India from the Mediterranean. Denied a share in the Baghdad Railway by a craven Cabinet, he determined to beard the opposition. He would lease the existing Turkish line from Haifa to Damascus, and thence drive a track 500 miles across the Syrian sands to Baghdad; extensive irrigation schemes would be undertaken to stimulate agriculture, which would in turn generate traffic. From Baghdad he would secure the navigation rights on the Tigris down to Basra, or use this threat to obtain a stake in the projected rail route. He was prepared to offer a share to the Germans, though he expected to face fierce opposition from the French, who had political designs on Syria and had already threatened the Turks that if they were too accommodating to British interests, they would be denied access to the Paris money market. (The Foreign Office had ample evidence from its own sources of this singular interpretation of the Entente Cordiale, but nonetheless never flinched from insisting on sacrifice and self-restraint from the British bankers.) The scheme appealed to Djavid, and was seriously entertained by the Foreign Office at the highest level. Certain solid assurances, however, would be required. Sir Edward Grey jibbed at this prospect and passed the dossier over to the Board of Trade, by now presided over by Winston Churchill, whom Cassel found 'quite uninformed'. Eighteen months later all the detailed plans were completed and Cassel was ready to go ahead, pending only final agreement with the Turkish and British governments on guarantees and subsidies. Cassel had maintained his amicable relations with the Deutsche Bank. In the summer of 1910 Arthur von Gwinne had even offered to share the Baghdad Railway's oil concession in Mesopotamia: he had engaged to give one-quarter to the Paris Rothschilds and the Ottoman Bank; the remaining three-quarters he was prepared to divide equally with the National Bank. (Cassel was not overjoyed at this proposal. He had personal experience of drilling for oil in Mexico, Spain and Egypt and 'in each case I have lost money'.) Cassel had engaged in the race to reach Baghdad before the concession for the final lap to Basra had been awarded; his friend Djavid was also sensible to Britain's strategic concern. When, therefore, the final agreement was signed by the Porte in March 1911, the Deutsche Bank formally declared that a special arrangement would be made to satisfy British interests for the Baghdad–Basra line. Cassel, having attained one end, thereupon shelved his own project.

In July 1910 Djavid Bey arrived in London. Cassel dined him with Winston Churchill, promoted to Home Secretary six months before, and the Chancellor of the Exchequer, David Lloyd George. Winston 'got on swimmingly' with the Turk, the Welshman floundered for want of French. Djavid was nonetheless flattered by the attention he received from the two foremost radical Liberals. Two months later Churchill, with his wife and a party of friends, sailed into Constantinople aboard Baron de Forest's yacht. Djavid and Talaat Bey, the civilian member of the triumvirate of Young Turks, were 'extremely attentive'. Churchill, who came to establish 'amicable relations', needlessly squandered such fruits on his move to the Admiralty in the following year. Turning down a Turkish request for a permanent alliance, the First Lord lectured them imperiously, without an eye for any potential political and strategic advantage, on their need to comport themselves in a proper and fitting manner if they would count on Britain's friendship.

After thirty-three years of the Sultan's capricious rule, Djavid was attempting to introduce a more orthodox management of the precarious economy; he was faced at the same time with the necessity of increased expenditure on the army and navy, more urgent than even the military chiefs could have foreseen. On his way to London he had stopped in Paris to seek a new loan from the Ottoman Bank. The French Foreign Minister insisted on control of Turkey's Treasury as security, as well as recognition of other territorial claims in the Maghreb on the crumbling periphery of the Ottoman Empire; the Finance Minister required that a part of the loan be spent on purchases in France. Djavid refused such conditions. Cassel, who respected Djavid for his tireless application, though considering him highly strung, counselled him to repair his fences with the Ottoman Bank or, if this was impossible, to conclude a contract with another French group. France, he pointed out, with fewer demands for capital from industry, could offer better terms, while the Bourse was used to digesting Turkish debt (some £60 million – or 55 per cent – of Turkish bonds were held in Paris compared to a mere 5 per cent in London). If all else failed, Cassel promised to do what he could to meet Turkey's immediate needs. In Paris, however, Cassel's German ties made him suspect, and he was denounced in the newspapers for conspiring to undermine France's proper interests. (The French government was still unaware that the Ottoman Bank, though denying it, had an arrangement with the Deutsche Bank whereby each offered the other a 30 per cent participation in any Turkish operation.) Djavid obediently returned to Paris and signed a contract with the Crédit Mobilier for an immediate loan of £6 million, with a further £5 million to follow in the spring of 1911. This time the Turks offered as security the revenues of the Constantinople Customs, but the French government was not prepared to forgo its previous conditions. The Foreign Office suddenly woke up and brightly suggested a further proviso. Seven years after preventing Cassel from forging a British link with the Baghdad Railway, disregarding the fact that Cassel had wrested recognition of Britain's interest from the Deutsche Bank and Djavid, it now urged the French to attach the condition of 'a satisfactory settlement' to this issue, without which it offered to restrain London bankers from taking up the loan. Stalemate ensued; the Quai d'Orsay was prepared to give a little, the Finance Ministry, egged on by the Ottoman Bank and the French financial adviser to the Porte, resisted all compromise. The Turks were now represented in Paris by the Grand Vizier, Hakki Pasha, as round as he was tall at five feet, and Cassel's friend Calouste Gulbenkian, the Armenian oil magnate. The press on both sides of the Channel reported that Cassel had ridden to the Turks' rescue with an offer to raise the same amount on their terms in London and Berlin if the French government had not opened the Bourse to the Crédit Mobilier loan by 1 October. The French chargé d'affaires in London, appealing to the Foreign Office's well-tried sense of fair play, cried foul; Sir Edward Grey more mildly considered it would be 'awkward', and Sir Charles Hardinge was deputed to make energetic representations to Cassel to bring him to heel. Cassel denied the rumours and repeated his desire to honour the wishes of the Foreign Office.

It is impossible not to feel a great deal of sympathy for the embattled, and exceptionally forbearing, banker. He was caught between two opponents. In one corner was the Ottoman Bank, enjoying the full support of the French government; in the other, the British government, willing, even eager, to subordinate its aim of reasserting its influence in Turkey for fear of ruffling French feathers. The Young Turks had taken a great step up a steep hill. The Committee of Union and Progress had instituted a programme of public works which introduced European capital to pump blood into the economy (the French had just been awarded the contract for the repair and construction of all roads in Turkey proper). While a German military mission was in charge of the Turkish army, a British admiral had the fleet in hand, and an English inspector-general oversaw the Customs. If German encroachment was feared – a concern originally shared by the Young Turks – the British government had done nothing but discourage Cassel from countering it. The Foreign Office was also at this time singularly ill-served by its Ambassador in Constantinople, Sir Gerard Lowther, of whom even the gentle Sir Edward Grey commented on his remove, 'I cannot say he had done splendidly and been very helpful.' (In all justice to Lowther, he was alone in pointing out to Sir Arthur Nicolson, Hardinge's successor at the Foreign Office, that 'Our position is somewhat ridiculous if we urge Cassel at great expense to establish a bank here and when he wants to do business we oppose him.')

There was, furthermore, a conflict of interest in Paris which may have served to feed the Foreign Office's false optimism. The Foreign Minister, Stephen Pichon, Clemenceau's faithful disciple, who had retained office after his chief's departure in 1909, and who, with the Ambassador Paul Cambon in London, was on the receiving end of mild 'representations', could sincerely agree to the principle of an Anglo-French financial coalition. But the key to the door of the Bourse was held by the Minister of Finance, Georges Cochery, a nonentity but an ardent champion of the Ottoman Bank. After Cassel had cleared the air of misunderstandings, the Foreign Office, as a reward for his restraint, once again pleaded his cause at the Quai d'Orsay. The French protested their good faith. The Foreign Office was exultant, Cassel less credulous. He had already informed Babington Smith that if political considerations arising from the Entente Cordiale were to continue to preclude competition with France, then 'we had better put our shutters down'. He repeated his objections in an interview with Sir Edward Grey and Sir Arthur Nicolson at the Foreign Office. Conditions, he insisted, had rendered it impossible for the National Bank to carry out the promises of support given to Djavid Bey, and would continue to prevent it from assisting the Turkish government in similar circumstances in the future. Furthermore, as a result of false reports in the French press, violent attacks had been directed against him in the papers and, so far as his own personal position was concerned, he had every reason for withdrawing from the connection with Turkey which caused him this annoyance. He informed Grey that the National Bank's London board had met that morning, the last day of September, and resolved to liquidate the bank if the situation did not change. Grey, regretting this, repeated, mantra-like, his conviction that the French were genuinely prepared to welcome British co-operation. Cassel retorted that they were not in the least likely to do so on a basis acceptable to the bank, that French considerations had been directed solely to the protection of French interests, political and commercial. (It took time, and a new ambassador, for the Foreign Office finally to accept that the Ottoman Bank could never 'be anything but a French political and financial instrument with interests often in direct opposition to those of this country'. A welcome recognition of reality, just three years too late.) A few days later Cassel and Babington Smith were informed by Nicolson that 'the maintenance of the *entente*' was 'the bedrock of our policy'. They might have inferred, but were not informed, that in the opinion of the Foreign Office the interests of the British bank were 'a minor consideration'. But the National was a secondary and contingent casualty; there was a greater national interest at stake. Babington Smith, with Cassel's agreement, pointed out to Nicolson that the 'result of the appeal to the *entente cordiale* would have been to efface British financial groups as an independent force' and vitiate the National Bank's object, the regeneration of Turkey in order to secure a stable regime as a means to maintaining the status quo in the Middle East, a policy of exclusive concern to Britain. As long as Britain was seen to be playing a subordinate role to France, a sternly self-serving lender, Cassel forecast that the Turks would be impelled towards financial dependence on Germany and Austria, and thus be drawn into the arms of the Triple Alliance.

Such remonstrations were wasted. While occasionally expressing a sense of obligation (though rarely exercising it) the Foreign Office officials remained distrustful of those financiers whom they had inveigled into an investment with a false prospectus. From his ivory tower overlooking the cloisters of the Foreign Office, Sir Arthur Nicolson set down his disdainful doubts to the British Ambassador in Constantinople: 'We cannot rely on any of these financiers being animated by disinterested and patriotic motives ... It is a matter of perfect indifference to them ... whether the ends which they pursue are or are not in harmony with the interests of this country.' It is less difficult to agree with Cassel's reproach that the Foreign Office, on the contrary, had abdicated its responsibility to represent effectively the interests of the country.

Though he might dissent from the Foreign Office analysis, with its impossible restrictions and consequences, he loyally abided by it. Much of the National Bank's capital had been provided in a 'public and patriotic enterprise', as Babington Smith reminded Nicolson, by Cassel and his two principal partners, Lord Revelstoke and Sir Alexander Henderson. Cassel had all along been pessimistic about the prospects. By July 1910, little more than a year after the National Bank's foundation, they were already discussing the possibility of dissolving it. It says much for his character and his self-denying dedication that, his eyes open, he persevered.

Evidently under pressure from Pichon, the French Foreign Minister, the Crédit Mobilier at last agreed to accept participation by an English group, including Cassel, but in his personal capacity, not as a director of the National Bank. He rejected this rider as improper. It was the accommodating Pichon again who, profiting from the temporary absence of his colleague Cochery, negotiated conditions more acceptable to the Turks. The Finance Minister, affronted, refused his assent. The Crédit Mobilier, its contract about to expire, threatened Cochery with public disclosure of the political pettifogging. The Quai d'Orsay cobbled together a face-saving formula, but it was now the turn of the Turks, their patience exhausted and their pride stung, to take offence. Cassel, awaiting the nod from the Foreign Office, took up the running with Djavid, but before the National Bank could prepare its proposals 'the unexpected and unbelievable happened'. (That, at least, was the view of the Russian Ambassador in Constantinople; Cassel had predicted it.) It was announced that Turkey had secured from a consortium in Berlin led by the Deutsche Bank a loan for £11 million, secured on the Constantinople Customs revenues. The terms were tougher, but there were no political strings attached. German ascendancy was restored at a stroke.

Cassel, sourly aware of the measure of support he could count on from the Foreign Office, had already prepared an audacious counter-stroke. He put it to the Ottoman Bank that if the Entente operated in a negative sense against free competition, it must also operate in a positive sense towards co-operation. He coolly proposed the fusion of the National and Ottoman Banks on terms of equality, with the Ottoman's lightweight London Committee subordinate to the National Bank. (Cassel intended to retire on the completion of this merger, delegating Algernon Mills, of the bankers Glyn, Mills, to represent him.) He had little confidence that the offer would be acceptable; failure, on the other hand, would expose the hollowness of their expressions of willingness to collaborate. This solution commended itself to both Foreign Offices; this time the Turks objected. The Ottoman Bank, once it had recovered from its surprise, protested that the advantages for the National Bank were out of all proportion to its weight. Cassel countered by pointing out that the combined and proven financial muscle of the London directors of the National Bank far outweighed the Ottoman Bank's resources. The Ottoman Bank squirmed and wriggled, but Cassel left them no time to hedge. Two weeks later he informed the Foreign Office that the National Bank had given up any hope of reaching an agreement and the negotiations were now considered closed. Cassel asked for, and reluctantly received, freedom of action. That same day the Turkish loan was signed in Berlin.

The directors of the National Bank, having shaken off the Foreign Office reins and secured the promise of a Baghdad municipal loan from the Grand Vizier, now decided to continue in operation. One year later the Banque de Salonique, an offspring of the Paribas and Société Générale, proposed marriage, with the National Bank as master of the joint household. The Ottoman Bank at once objected and, quite confident of official patronage, contended that the National Bank should first submit to incorporation with the Ottoman Bank on the latter's terms, and only then fuse with the Banque de Salonique to establish a cosy cartel. This option remained as unacceptable as ever to Cassel and company and, as the French government would not sanction the National Bank's prior merger with the Banque de Salonique until it had come to a 'satisfactory' accommodation with the Ottoman Bank, another impasse ensued. The Foreign Office expressed benign approval but, as Cassel wearily wrote to Babington Smith, 'As in other instances so in these negotiations our Government have been content to take the part the French Government has allotted it.' He was sterner with Sir Arthur Nicolson: 'Such evidence we have of the support of our Government brings with it the conviction that, so far from being resolute, it is half-hearted, and that is putting it moderately.' Even the Foreign Office was by now coming to accept that any agreement was out of reach and that the British bank would have to work out its own salvation. By the middle of 1911 a new ministry was formed in Paris under Clemenceau's former Finance Minister, Joseph Caillaux, who retained the finance portfolio for himself. Cassel was informed through a mutual friend that the incoming premier desired to make good 'in the most official manner' the harm done by his predecessor. 'I need not tell you', he wrote to Babington Smith, 'that I have taken this assurance "cum grano salis".' Whatever his intentions, Caillaux had other pressing problems; he spent the rest of the year trying to avoid war with Germany over the Agadir incident; next year he was out of office. By that time Turkey was distracted; after losing Libya to the Italians, it was fighting a war in the Balkans in which it lost all but a toehold in Europe.

By that time, Cassel, looking forward to his sixtieth birthday, and having recently suffered two grievous personal losses – King Edward and his daughter Maud – was preparing to run down his affairs. He was offered a £40,000 participation in the French loan for road construction; he accepted, but passed it on to the National Bank. The bank won a contract for the construction of the Black Sea ports of Trebizond and Samsun in competition with the Ottoman Bank. This encroached on the Russian sphere of influence. A request for Foreign Office support produced a masterpiece of faint commitment and ambiguous circumspection. The Porte was informed that His Majesty's Government 'would certainly do nothing to hamper the Bank and are anxious for its success generally', and 'should in fact be glad if the Bank were successful . . . and, subject to the concurrence of the Russian Government, would be ready to support it officially . . . The Bank, however, has not asked us to approach the Russian Government on their behalf . . .' Cassel had hardly been encouraged to do so. He had pointed out to Sir Arthur Nicolson that 'as we had opened the English market to Russian securities, it was about time that Russia should do something for us if the opportunity arose, but I am sorry to say', he informed Babington Smith, 'that I did not find any enthusiasm or disposition to tackle' the Tsar's ministers. Small wonder that it was widely believed in Constantinople that the British government had abandoned not only the National Bank but any decisive role in Turkey. Cassel was still able to render a last service in another related quarter. On the strength of his financial package as much as on cost and quality, Vickers won the contract for a battleship, the *Reshadieh*, from under the nose of Krupps. The local legal adviser to the National Bank and Vickers, Count Léon Ostrorog,* devised a contract with the power of seizure of the ship if ever the Turks defaulted on the covering Treasury Bonds for £2.5 million. (It would have taken a deft and persuasive bailiff to repossess a 23,000-ton warship with a determined crew.) Two years later the National Bank managed the loan for the contract awarded to Vickers and Armstrongs for the renovation of the arsenal at the Golden Horn and the construction of a naval shipyard with

---

*His son married the adopted daughter of Vickers' principal overseas agent, Sir Basil Zaharoff.

the assurance of a monopoly of orders from the Turkish navy for thirty years. Such confident expectations were, unfortunately, ill-founded.

Cassel made one final, and successful, effort to resolve the contentious issue of the Baghdad Railway. Sir Henry Babington Smith threw in his Turkish towel, no doubt with relief, if not relish; he went on to chair a wartime Royal Commission into the Civil Service, which must have afforded him wry satisfaction, and to become a director of the Bank of England.

10

Buckingham Palace:
End of an Age

Sir Ernest Cassel basked to a unique degree in the public favour and private fellowship of King Edward, an affinity, so seemingly out of keeping with their characters, which waxed as the reign waned. This may have been one crucial consideration which influenced him to bow to the dictates of the Foreign Office over Turkey with such meek resignation, and to continue to do so after the King's death in 1910. Cassel was already unjustly vilified in Paris as 'the scourge of the Entente', itself a testament to Edward's tact and charm. His German and Jewish roots made him an ideal whipping-boy for the stridently chauvinistic French press; if he could with more reason be represented as a wilful obstruction, the predictable escalation of vituperation would have proved an added annoyance to him, but a positive and political embarrassment to the King's ministers. At home he would have been accused by many who would have delighted in his discomfiture of compromising Britain's foreign relations through personal greed. To defend themselves, the directors of the National Bank, if they had had the stomach for controversy, would have needed to expose the Foreign Office's vacillation and pusillanimity. The inevitable outcry, centred on the late King's friend, would have reflected on the throne.

The year 1908 witnessed a remarkable demonstration of the confidence the King placed in Cassel. Campbell-Bannerman's ill-health forced him to resign as Prime Minister in early April, though the King had hoped this might be avoided while he was on holiday in Biarritz. With an uncharacteristic lapse of his strong sense of duty he summoned Campbell-Bannerman's successor to France formally to kiss hands. Asquith packed his frock-coat and set off, reaching his destination twenty-four hours later on 7 April, looking, as even the King noticed 'very tired'. After a night's rest, the appointments were considered over lunch:

the King, Asquith wrote his wife, 'made no objection to any of them and discussed the various men very freely and with a good deal of shrewdness'. Edward did, however, have reservations about two of the proposed ministers' fitness for office, and expressed these to Cassel's sister, Bobbie, with whom he and Asquith dined that night at her brother's villa. The King was ill at ease with Asquith. Although neither he nor his predecessor had come from the traditional ruling caste, the more congenially earthy Campbell-Bannerman had a respectable Glaswegian merchant fortune; Asquith, who earned his way at the Bar, had none. The King's temper was not improved by a leader in *The Times* that day which sarcastically interpreted their transaction of most important constitutional business on French soil as 'a picturesque and graceful tribute to the reality of the "Entente"', expressing the hope that the precedent would not be followed. (The prospect had briefly been worse. To Knollys's dismay, the King had had it in mind to summon the members of the new Cabinet to Paris to receive their seals of office in the Hôtel Crillon.) Bobbie Cassel passed on the King's message, which concerned his disquiet over the appointment of Lloyd George as Chancellor of the Exchequer, an office Asquith had informed the King at his last audience he intended to keep for himself, and Winston Churchill as President of the Board of Trade. Cassel, acting the self-appointed royal surrogate, at once sought an interview with Asquith at the earliest opportunity on his return to London (he had to wait three days as the Prime Minister was still putting his Cabinet together). Cassel knew Asquith well enough, but it was still, even as one Privy Councillor to another, a significant trespass on prerogative. Much of the lengthy conversation concentrated on the fancied misfits in the Cabinet. Cassel did his best to reassure his sovereign: 'I believe that from the materials at his disposal he could not have made a better choice and I told him so. Lloyd George has been an unqualified success at the Board of Trade and that is a strong indication that when he assumes the reins as Chancellor of Exchequer his actions will be less violent and more prudent than his speeches have been. The assumption of power and responsibility has a most sobering effect upon radical tendencies . . . To follow him at the Board of Trade will be no easy matter but I am confident that Winston Churchill will do well – all the more so as the post he holds removes him . . . from any violent political controversy . . .'

It was the King's foreboding rather than Cassel's forecast which was justified. By the summer both ministers had shown evidence of an unwelcome propensity to open their minds and mouths in public on foreign affairs, a choice of subject which raised hackles at Buckingham Palace. Lloyd George, who had never set foot abroad before, was the principal offender by a narrow margin. Clemenceau, invited by the King to relieve his cure at Marienbad, expressed his amazement at the Chancellor's 'crass ignorance' of this field. The canny Welshman struck up a friendship with the Favourite, Mrs Keppel, which did much to repair his reputation. The liberal Knollys, whose poor health at this time might excuse him, was more incensed at Cassel's friend: the 'very idea', he confided to Esher, of Churchill's acting 'from conviction or principle . . . is enough to make anyone laugh'. The King forgave Churchill, partly out of fondness for his mother, partly out of hope that he might ripen. When Winston telegraphed the King with news of his engagement in September 1908, the latter expressed his hope to Cassel that wedlock would have 'a calming influence on him' – and serve incidentally to cut down the number of his public utterances. Cassel had continued to keep a kindly eye on his protégé. Three years before, he had furnished a small library for Churchill, with his mother's approval; he now most handsomely provided a £500 cheque as a wedding present for the still indebted, but now salaried, groom.

Asquith's new government had a strong reforming streak; the radical Lloyd George and the wayward Winston Churchill stole the scheme and much of the thunder. Lord Rothschild, the embodiment of laissez-faire liberalism, roused himself. He opposed a scheme for non-contributory old age pensions as 'profligate'; a fanatical opponent of votes for women, he financed the Anti-Suffrage Society (its colours were rather unfortunately chosen – black and blue); he led the 'beerage', opposed by the bishops, in the House of Lords, to kill the Licensing Bill on the grounds not only that it would 'restrict the comforts and amusements of the public' – or that part of it which was not the Liberal Nonconformist constituency – but that the principle, once conceded, would point the way to the expropriation of all property for the benefit of the State, and without compensation. His taste for controversy whetted, he limbered up for the big fight: Lloyd George's 'People's Budget' of 1909.

The accelerating shipbuilding programme of the German navy was for the first time seen to pose a threat to Britannia's undisputed rule of the waves. Lord Rothschild topped the bill with Arthur Balfour at a mass meeting at the Guildhall in late March 1909 to urge the government to match this challenge by laying down more Dreadnoughts. The new First Lord of the Admiralty, Reginald McKenna, whose appointment the King, fearing him to be penny-pinching, had only approved on condition that Admiral Fisher be kept on as First Sea Lord, proposed to provide for six that year and six in each of the two years following; this was violently opposed by Lloyd George and Churchill, who argued that four were sufficient. A compromise was countered by a popular clamour to the music-hall refrain of 'We want eight, And we won't wait' – the equivalent of fourpence on income tax. The King was much comforted on learning Sir Edward Grey had threatened to resign unless this number was produced. The government buckled. Unemployment was high, the party's fortunes were low and required restoring with some partisan spirit. Forced to find the money for defence, the Chancellor determined to retaliate by raising further funds for the Liberals' full programme of social reform, lately so emasculated by the Lords, some £15 million in all, a call on the Treasury without even wartime precedent. With calculated provocation, he shrouded his counter-offensive in his Budget. He raised the income tax to 1s 2d, introduced a super-tax of a maximum of sixpence on incomes over £5,000 (an arbitrary threshold which was conveniently the salary of a minister of the Crown) and imposed an increase in death duties. But the most contentious features were new levies on the value of land, the valuation of which was seen as a sinister and inquisitorial trespass by the State on private property. This aroused proportionate passions. The Duke of Buccleuch complained that the imposition would prevent him from paying his subscription to his local football club (which doubtless leased its pitch on some corner of his 450,000-odd acres). Lloyd George retorted in east London's Limehouse that 'a fully equipped duke costs as much to keep up as two Dreadnoughts; and they are just as great a terror and they last longer'. Lord Rosebery, the former Liberal leader, denounced the packet as not so much a budget as a revolution. His kinsman by marriage Lord Rothschild sent a petition to the Prime Minister signed by the principals of most of the City's leading banks, and in June, the following month, took the chair at a protest meeting of agitated financial magnates. (A notable omission from this august company was the signature and presence of Sir Ernest Cassel. Later in the year he emphasized to Wilfred Ashley, his son-in-law and a Conservative Member of Parliament, his 'absolute loyalty to whatever government I happen to be serving, and if whoever happened to be in power could not be certain of this he would not give me, and I certainly should not wish, his confidence'. But there was another reason why his signature would have been superfluous, even specious. Two years before, he had told Lord Esher that the current panic in the United States was the most interesting financial situation within his experience; that he had no belief in an immediate revival and that it would, he thought, take two years for confidence and trade to recover. J. Pierpont Morgan had averted a crash by a massive intervention in the market, and Cassel removed the bulk of his assets to America in time to avoid Lloyd George's exactions.)

The Chancellor responded to these interventions by the head of the house of Rothschild with rhetorical relish: 'I think we are having too much Lord Rothschild. We are not to have temperance reform in this country. Why not? Because Lord Rothschild has sent a circular to the peers to say so. We must have more Dreadnoughts. Why? Because Lord Rothschild said so at a meeting in the City. We must not pay for them when we have them. Why? Because Lord Rothschild said so at another meeting. You must not have estate duties and a super-tax. Why? Because Lord Rothschild signed a protest on behalf of the bankers to say he would not stand it . . . You ought not to have old age pensions. Why? Because Lord Rothschild was a member of a committee that said it could not be done. Now, really, I should like to know, is Lord Rothschild the dictator of this country? Are we really to have all the ways of reform, financial and social, blocked simply by a notice-board, "No thoroughfare. By order of Lord Rothschild"?' (This was a gross misrepresentation, as the Chancellor was well aware. Natty Rothschild did not question the ends, merely the means.)

Such clamour dismayed and depressed King Edward. He protested 'in the most vigorous terms against one of his Ministers making such a speech', which 'would not have been tolerated by any Prime Minister until within the last few years' and which he 'regards as being in the highest degree improper, and which he almost looks upon as an insult to the Sovereign . . .' Asquith's excuses he dismissed as 'pitiful', though he equally deplored the 'foolish and *mean* speeches and sayings' of the Chancellor's antagonists. (Churchill, boisterous conductor of the Budget League, was, indeed, formally rebuked by the Cabinet for overstepping the bounds, but then the Cabinet was itself divided between the radicals and the Whigs.) By the middle of the summer it was evident that the Conservative and Unionist majority in the House of Lords was set on a collision course with the Commons. Mr Balfour's 'poodle', as Lloyd George scornfully described the Upper House, began to bark and growl. Backwoodsmen and 'Diehards', in a closed season for other blood sports, took up arms, spurred on by Lord Northcliffe's *The Times* and *Daily Mail*. The King, with Esher often at his elbow, sought to cool tempers and counsel moderation, but never having been on cordial terms with the Conservative leaders, Balfour and Lansdowne, he had no influence with them. He confided despairingly to Knollys that in his opinion the 'Peers were mad'. Surprisingly for one whom the King regarded as having the wisest head in England, Cassel lined up with the Diehards, considering that if the Lords let the Commons get away with the Budget there was no further use for them and they had better hang up their coronets and head home. The issue was no longer the Budget, but the Lords' power of veto. By constitutional convention they had no power over the purse; they could only reject, and not amend, a finance bill. The Budget passed the Commons after a long-drawn-out debate by 379 votes to 149. Eyes now turned to the Lords. They obliged their antagonists by rejecting the same Budget by 350 votes, among them Lord Rothschild, to 75 (the King had properly restrained Lord Knollys, as he considered doing, from voting with the minority). The Lower House at once resolved that the action of the Lords was 'a breach of the Constitution and a usurpation of the rights of the Commons'. The King accordingly was obliged to dissolve Parliament. He informed his guests that night at Sandringham that he had never spent a more miserable day. (He had had a tooth extracted that same afternoon: such pain, he announced stoically, he could tolerate.)

In the ensuing general election campaign Lloyd George returned to the charge at the top of his demagogic form. 'Who clamoured for additional Dreadnoughts?' he asked at the Elephant and Castle. He remembered a great meeting in the City, presided over by Lord Rothschild (hisses), who demanded that eight Dreadnoughts should be instantly laid down. The government had ordered four, and Lord Rothschild would not pay. (Laughter.) There was a very cruel King in the past who ordered Lord Rothschild's ancestors to make bricks without straw. (Loud laughter.) That was a much easier job than making Dreadnoughts without money . . . Such drollery apart, the real issue of the election was 'Peers against People' (the People themselves were disappointingly cool about such a paramount issue). In the highest turn-out in election history – 86.8 per cent – the Conservatives regained some of the seats they had lost four years before, while the reduced Liberal ranks relied for a majority on the Socialists and the unaccountable Irish Nationalists, who had a particular grouse of their own, the new duty on whisky (or, more specifically, whiskey).

As soon as the campaign had ended, Asquith had hurried off to Cannes, overlooking in his haste an engagement to dine and sleep at Windsor. For such an unaccustomed impropriety, the King was obliged to accept Asquith's excuse that he was 'completely knocked up' by the election. The King, in sight of seventy, was as much, if not more, knocked up. The popular triumph of his third Derby win in the previous year, when the assembled crowds on Epsom Downs had sung 'God Save the King' and then broken into cries of 'Good old Teddy! Teddy boy! Hurrah! Hurrah!', was forgotten. His health had worsened that winter. In moments of depression he began to talk of abdication. He was additionally anxious about the impression Asquith had given that he had agreed to create several hundred Liberal peers, if necessary, to pack the House of Lords. When the election, spread over two weeks, had begun in mid-January, he decided to escape to the Arthur Sassoons' at King's Gardens, on the front at Hove. The King had developed an addiction to Brighton since his accession, believing the air suited him. On his first visit he had put up with his son-in-law, the Duke of Fife, though slipping off to dine with the Sassoons. Thereafter he abandoned all pretence of familial preference. Arthur and Louise were some of the last survivors of his old intimate circle; Reuben Sassoon and the Duke of Devonshire were dead; he saw less of the Rothschilds. He would stroll on the sea front, arm in arm with 'dear Arthur', now quite bald and plumper than ever, or go shopping with the elegant Louise. Eddy Hamilton, staying with her in Brighton, judged her (as great an angel as ever. Her nature is such that she would in old days have been canonized). The Sassoon establishment, though, was modest, and any gentlemen-in-waiting had to lodge at a neighbouring hotel, though boarding at the house. On the whole the King's privacy was respected; when the crowds threatened to become a nuisance the mayor had the seats and railings around the Sassoon residence freshly painted to discourage people from loitering. In the first week of February, before the State opening of the new Parliament, the King, a glum guest, paid his last visit to Brighton.

When Parliament reconvened, Asquith told his surprised supporters that he had never received, nor even requested, a guarantee from the King that he would create the necessary number of Liberal peers to ensure the passage of the Budget through the Lords. The Prime Minister made it clear that this alone would not be enough, the issue was now the limitation of the peers' powers: they were, firstly, to be divested of their veto on any money bills. This Parliament Bill was introduced on 14 April; two weeks later the Budget again passed the Commons, and the next day, in accordance with Lord Lansdowne's pledge that the Lords would respect a mandate from the electorate, the Upper Chamber let it through. Parliament took a short break.

The King's doctors, concerned for his health, had been urging him to take his routine rest in Biarritz, but he had only agreed at five days' notice to leave England on 6 March once he was satisfied that no immediate crisis loomed. His appetite at least was unimpaired. On the eve of his departure he worked his way through turtle soup, salmon, chicken, mutton, before tackling his favourite snipe stuffed with foie gras, asparagus, ices and a savoury. On his way through Paris he caught a chill in an overheated theatre and collapsed on arrival at the Hôtel du Palais in a rain-swept Biarritz with Mrs Keppel and her children. Cassel's grandchildren, the King's god-daughter Edwina and her sister Mary Ashley, were already in residence; his villa was 'looking very bright and cheerful', the King assured Cassel, 'and I must honestly say that we miss you and your sister very much'. Cassel had been tempted by Jacob Schiff to tour Alaska as an investment prospect, but, anxious about his daughter Maud's health – she was, like her mother, consumptive – he had chosen instead another extreme of climate. He had taken Maud, his sister and her daughter Anna Jenkins, up the Nile to Aswan where, to ensure that his daughter was not disturbed by noise, he engaged three floors of the hotel. Unaware of the King's failing health, Cassel did not spare him detailed medical bulletins on Maud's condition. Edward, his own lungs in little better shape, and overburdened moreover with political anxieties, did not neglect to respond with courteous concern. 'Let me express how deeply I sympathise with you', he wrote to Cassel, 'at the long and tedious illness which your daughter is suffering from. Your anxiety during the many months has been intense and I wish you would give me a more favourable account . . . When you reach Cairo please let me have a telegram saying how Mrs Ashley took the journey . . . Trusting', the King ended, 'that I may receive more satisfactory accounts of your daughter's health.' Cassel sent his sister and niece back to England while he remained in Cairo with Maud. He duly obliged with a further communiqué. The King diligently acknowledged the 'welcome news of [her] excellent progress . . . I feel sure that this year she should be very careful to avoid the fatigues and excitement of a London Season' (he was not to experience them himself). The weather promising a smooth passage, Cassel chartered a steamer to take Maud home; they sailed on 25 April. The King wrote to him on the same day from Biarritz: 'My stay here is now drawing to a close. I trust we may see you back in England next week and I am looking forward to talking over many matters with you' (it was the time for the annual rendering of accounts). He left by train the next day. The Basques bade him a fond and rowdy farewell with fireworks and bands playing, it is hoped, tactful tunes – popular republican anthems caused him pain. The King had some premonition. 'I shall be sorry to leave Biarritz,' he declared sadly next morning. 'Perhaps it will be for ever.' He arrived back at Buckingham Palace on 27 April. Braving the chill east winds, he passed the weekend at Sandringham. He returned to London on Monday to dine quietly with 'Sister Agnes', playing bridge with Mrs Keppel and the two Misses Keyser. As he was palpably sickening for another bronchial attack, the Favourite packed him off to the Palace for an early bed. He would not leave it again alive. Queen Alexandra, summoned from Corfu, arrived on the evening of 5 May. The country was formally informed of the state of the monarch's health. Throughout that same day he had continued to conduct business and to give audiences, exclaiming at intervals, 'I must fight this!' Next morning, a Friday, the King's condition had worsened. Impatiently rejecting the informal clothes laid out for him, he called for a frock-coat. Incorrigibly, he lit one of his huge cigars, but did not appear to enjoy it. Sir Ernest Cassel, alone in Brook House, was waiting to be received by his old friend. At eleven o'clock the Palace telephoned to inform him that the King was too unwell to see him. Half an hour later there was a message from Knollys that he should come at once. Sir Francis Laking, the King's doctor, caught Cassel first at the Palace and urged him to let the King speak as little as possible. The Queen repeated the admonition. Both she and the Prince of Wales, whom Cassel met on the stairs, with extraordinary courtesy and consideration in the circumstances asked after Maud's health. 'Finally,' he wrote to his 'own and dearest' Maud later that sad day, 'I was ushered in and found the King dressed as usual, in his sitting room, rising from his chair to shake hands with me. He looked as if he had suffered great pain, and spoke indistinctly. His kindly smile came out as he congratulated me on having brought you home so much improved in health. He said, "I am very seedy, but I wanted to see you. Tell your daughter how glad I am that she has safely got home and that I hope she will be careful and patient so as to recover complete health". He then talked about other matters, and I had to ask his leave to go as I felt it was not good for him to go on speaking . . . Sir James Reid told me he had dressed on purpose to receive me, and they could not stop him . . .' After Cassel's departure, the King took a light luncheon in his bedroom. He collapsed a little later, suffering a series of heart attacks. Late in the afternoon, in a brief lucid interval, his son brought news that his horse had just won a race at Kempton Park 'Yes. I have heard it,' replied the King, as well served as ever. 'I am very glad.' Lapsing into a coma, he died peacefully at a quarter to midnight.

The King in his last hours had sent for Mrs Keppel and attempted an awkward reconciliation between his wife and his mistress. Mrs Keppel, usually so composed and discreet, was with difficulty led away from the death-bed on the verge of hysteria, lamenting at the top of her voice, 'What is to become of me?' She falsely bruited it abroad that she had been summoned by the Queen and had received a forgiving kiss with a promise that the Royal Family 'would look after her'. This was, indeed, as much a major preoccupation with the King as with the somewhat rapacious but genuinely affectionate favourite. The 'looking after', however, was to fall on other, more tried and trusty shoulders.

Five weeks before his death, King Edward, writing to Cassel from Biarritz, had thanked him for the advice that 'the matter you generally report to me at this time of the year is as satisfactory as the preceding ones'. There was an extraordinary sequel. Five days later Cassel received a letter with an enclosure from the Palace. In an envelope Cassel had left beside the King, the Queen had found a bundle of banknotes. Knollys returned them with an almost audible sniff of distaste: 'I presume they belong to you and are not the result of any speculation which you went into for him.' (Knollys was not above accepting favours for himself. Thanking Cassel eighteen months before for his kindness in allotting him shares in an Egyptian bank, he wrote: 'I think it would perhaps be wise were I to take at once the profit which I should now get.') Cassel explained that the money represented an 'interest I gave to the King in financial matters I am undertaking' and handed it back. It was £10,000, the equivalent in present-day purchasing power of a quarter of a million, an exceptional sum to handle in banknotes; it may be conjectured that it had been intended for Mrs Keppel. If this grand total was 'interest', it was the fruit of a quite exceptionally lucrative investment. In 1901 Cassel had received from the King £20,685 to cherish; this had risen, after the King had drawn £10,000, to £30,000 by 1903. There is unfortunately no surviving record of the nature of this investment as a tribute to Cassel's talent for making money multiply at such a prodigious rate; all the King's personal and private correspondence was scrupulously burnt by the zealous Lords Knollys and Esher after his death, a 'lamentable combustion' in the eyes of one of Edward VII's biographers.

The day after King Edward's death, the Privy Council was sworn in. The Jews, George Wyndham remarked, took their oaths on the Old Testament, the Catholics separately. Amongst the latter, to the general surprise, was Cassel, whose conversion had remained a closely guarded secret. Afterwards, Cassel went to see Margot Asquith; 'we cried together on the sofa,' she recalled.

The question which intrigued others besides Max Beerbohm was 'Are we as welcome as ever?' (His cartoon of this title depicts Sir Ernest Cassel, Alfred Rothschild, Lord Burnham, Arthur Sassoon and Leopold Rothschild, creeping apprehensively along a Palace corridor under the new regime.) A lady confidently predicted to Wilfrid Scawen Blunt that 'There will be a regular sweep of the people who used to be about the Court, the Jews and the second-rate women that the King preferred to his aristocracy because they amused him. The Prince of Wales [George V] hates all these and would have nothing to do with them.' Mrs Keppel was a predictable casualty. Rebuffed when she tried to sign her name in the book at Marlborough House, she grudgingly admitted defeat and took her family off to the East for two years. With Cassel the courtesies were continued. 'My dear Father had a great regard for you,' the new King acknowledged. 'Perhaps the remembrance that you were one of the last to see Him on that terrible Friday will be a sad satisfaction to you.' He continued to shoot with Cassel at Moulton Paddocks and with Lord Burnham at Hall Barn, Beaconsfield, though uneasy in his conscience over the high toll of game. Neither was Cassel's Midas-touch an inappreciable quality to be lightly waived. He evidently continued to oversee the royal portfolio, though undoubtedly with more plausibly realistic results, and he bought from King George Baron Hirsch's Grafton House at Newmarket, which had been made over as a gift to the late King. (Cassel offered it to the local authorities; it was demolished to make way for the King Edward VII Memorial Hall and gardens for the use of the people of Newmarket.)

Cassel continued his dispensations to charities for the ill or underprivileged. Encouraged by King Edward, whose sister Victoria, the Empress Frederick, had died of cancer, he had given £46,000 as his half-share (with Lord Iveagh) to found the Radium Institute; and in the late King's memory he created the British-German Foundation with a donation of £210,000 to aid destitute Britons in Germany and Germans in Britain; and a further £50,000 for the relief of the sick and poor in his home town of Cologne.

In the aftermath of the King's death a party truce was called in the constitutional controversy. As no behind-the-scenes compromise could be agreed, a further general election was called for December. The result left the state of the parties virtually unchanged. Lord Knollys, who had stayed on to provide continuity in the crisis, had advised King George to accept Asquith's request before the election that he should give a secret pledge to create a sufficient number of Liberal peers to pass the Parliament Bill through the Lords. The threat sufficed to persuade the peers, by a narrow margin, to drop their opposition. The Prime Minister had up his sleeve a list of 249 possible peers of Liberal bent. It has been assumed that the absence of Cassel's name was solely accounted for by persistent animosity and envy. The list included the solicitor Sir George Lewis, the banker Sir Edgar Speyer, Sir 'Tom Tea' Lipton and other brand names – Coleman, Rowntree, Dewar – plutocrats of lesser eminence. It was Cassel's politics that set him apart. Though a non-party man, he was by conviction a conservative and protectionist; and unlike the majority of his fellows, he had never contributed to Liberal party funds, the usual route to the House of Lords. There was, indeed, only one candidate that the King warned Asquith he would resolutely refuse to consider: Baron de Forest, Hirsch's heir. Forest had recently been elected Liberal Member of Parliament (after vigorous lobbying of the Chief Whip by Winston Churchill to find him a winnable seat) – in the same year that he sued his mother-in-law for slander. His inherited blend of extreme riches and radicalism was deemed insupportable, and not only in more conservative circles; his contributions to Lloyd George's land inquiry earned him the animus of the respectable Whig landowning oligarchy. At the end of the next year his name appeared on the candidates' book of the Liberal stronghold, the Reform Club. As an MP, he was moved to the top of the list of fifteen aspirants; the other fourteen were elected, 'Tuty' was blackballed. Winston Churchill, his proposer, resigned in protest, never to return; Lloyd George followed him out of sympathy.

In December 1910, Cassel, still wrestling with the Foreign Office over its submissive attitude to the French in Turkey, retired, an event which was celebrated with a respectful eulogy in *The Times*. He moved out of the City into premises in Green Street, a short walk from Brook House, but otherwise retirement was relative. He had just added another iron to the fire: a watchful and wide-awake sleeping partnership in the bank S. Japhet & Company. An agreement with a previous partner, the Darmstädter Bank, was due to expire and Saemy Japhet, a Frankfurter, wished to replace its stake with indigenous capital. 'I looked about,' wrote Japhet, 'but in reality in one direction only: Sir Ernest Cassel!' The money to repurchase the Darmstädter holding had to be found at once. Curiously, Japhet turned for a bridging loan to Basil Zaharoff, Vickers' overseas agent; he agreed in three minutes to put up £100,000 on no more security than Japhet's confidence in his ability to sell the proposition to Cassel. Japhets, Saemy informed Cassel, could mobilize £200,000; he wanted to find another similar sum. The transaction affords an illuminating insight into Sir Ernest Cassel's succinct and incisive manner. Though Cassel was a good listener, Japhet was careful not to say one word more than was absolutely necessary, and remained silent after delivering his short declaration. 'I have always heard nothing but good of you and your firm,' Cassel responded, 'and I am prepared to accept your offer.' Reassured that the books were properly audited, he went on, 'My chief secretary Kritzler will call on you; he will go through the list of your clients and will report to me. If his report is satisfactory and I have no doubt it will be, we will discuss details and conditions. And now tell me something about your business.' Satisfied in due course, he signed. (He later admitted that he had obtained additional information on Japhet from Berlin.) Lord Rothschild sent his flattering congratulations to Japhet on his good fortune. Over the next few years, however, the bank's results were disappointing; trade inflated, but not profit. 'This kind of business', Japhet diffidently excused himself to Cassel, 'can hardly be interesting to you?' Saemy Japhet's problem was, unusually, too great a diffidence. It was this that caused him to turn down the offer of a share in an issue proposed by Robert Fleming. 'You made a mistake and missed an opportunity,' Cassel admonished him. 'If Mr Fleming himself talked to you in the way he did, prudence demanded that you should ask for a participation. It will be a long time before he will ask you again.' On Japhet remonstrating that he could not have resold the stock, Cassel retorted simply, 'You forgot that I was still there.'

Having lost the pleasure, indeed happiness, of his royal friend's company, Cassel had his daughter's health to worry about. On their return from Egypt, Cassel had left Maud at Broadlands in Hampshire, her husband's family seat, 'a charming place for her to stop at' in the late King's opinion. Every care and attention that money could buy was lavished on the patient; helpless, her father heaped propitiatory presents on her. Maud, showing off the expensive gifts to her friend the Duchess of Sermoneta, murmured, 'And all I need now are a few nightgowns.' Among the offerings was a Pekinese, which took such a dislike to her that he had to be chained up to the bedposts whenever her father visited her for fear of hurting his feelings. (Cassel later adopted the dog, taking it on his regular early morning constitutional around Hyde Park. Absent-mindedly, he took it abroad; the perverse Peke pined to death in quarantine.) In early February 1911, tuberculosis claimed Maud, as it had her mother thirty years before. Although he might tell the Duchess with his hand on his heart that 'Money never brought me any happiness,' he responded in the only way that was familiar to him – a donation of £50,000 to King Edward VII's Hospital Fund.

'Bobbie' Cassel's health was also frequently a matter of concern, although she survived her younger brother. She soon retired to the bracing air of Bournemouth, where her brother bought her a house at Branksome Dene. (He bought himself another one at Six Mile Bottom, Newmarket.) Her son Felix, who had also kept the name of Cassel, had in 1908 married Lady Helen Grimston, daughter of the Earl of Verulam – 'such a nice family', King Edward had assured Cassel. The wedding, in the family tradition, had had to wait until the King completed his cure at Marienbad.

11

Berlin: Bid for Peace

The Edwardian age, imbued with so much of the King's own character, seems in retrospect the serene and confident Indian summer of the old European order. Its ageing survivors were still Victorians in their attitudes and assurance. But the public pomp and private ceremony obscured increasing doubt, scientists and sociologists excepted, in the certainty of 'progress'. At home, it was a period of bitter political controversy, restless social pressures and continuing, if still relative, erosion of industrial primacy. Abroad there were slow-burning tensions and abrupt confrontations which more than once threatened a major war.

Cultural and artistic tastes too were changing. Ostentation was giving way to comfort. Brook House was fast becoming an anachronism five years after it was refurbished at such expense. Elsewhere, the potted palms were being thrown out, sombre wallpaper being replaced by plain paint, extraneous clutter jettisoned. The hourglass figure of bustle, accentuated bosom and pinched whalebone waist was abandoned for looser vertical lines, pastel shades were exchanged for bright colours, ankles peeped out. The conservative Cassel, brooding in the solitary confinement of his marble halls, could only have shaken his head in mute disapproval.

But the most acute misgiving of the age had been triggered by the Kaiser's provocative challenge: 'Our future lies upon the ocean.'

In June 1897 Admiral Tirpitz became Secretary of State for the Imperial Navy and proceeded at once to flesh out in steel his Emperor's ambition. An adroit political navigator (and publicist) on land, he won the unreserved and unwavering support of the capricious Kaiser and his strong-willed wife, who regarded liberalism and England as similar unnecessary evils. The already substantial increase in shipbuilding envisaged by Tirpitz's first Navy Law was doubled in the Law of 1900 –

and its author ennobled. The Kaiser was infatuated with this prospect: a disciple of the American advocate of sea power Alfred Mahan, and a partisan of the bellicose Boy Scout Theodore Roosevelt, he professed a childhood admiration for the Royal Navy which he attributed quaintly to 'kind aunts and friendly admirals'. Threatened by short-range battlefleets in the North Sea, the Royal Navy, signally unmoved by such flattery, was forced to reply in kind; by 1902 the Lords of the Admiralty for the first time began to consider the German *Flotte* as a potential foe. Then, Admiral 'Jackie' Fisher unveiled his scoop which achieved the ultimate military success – surprise. HMS *Dreadnought*, laid down at the end of 1905 in the greatest secrecy, was ready for trials within a year and a day. The first all-big-gun ship, with the first steam turbine from Vickers, she made all existing fleets obsolete at a stroke. It was a considerable time before the Germans were able to discover enough about her design to lay down their own counter-weapon; they were at the same time obliged to undertake the widening of the Kiel Canal to allow the new monsters to pass between the main naval bases in the North Sea and the Baltic (the work was only completed, not coincidentally, six weeks before the outbreak of the Great War). This unmatchable lead, however, was thrown away by Campbell-Bannerman's new Liberal government, which spurred the Germans to renew their efforts to close the gap.

Against this background of souring rivalry, the relationship of the two Powers' sovereigns was critical. Each, between moments of exasperation with the other, earnestly desired national reconciliation – on his own terms; each was equally sceptical of its likely success; each condoned any initiative towards this end in the belief that its failure would expose the other's bad faith. Kaiser Wilhelm was excitable, condescending, tactless and a self-anointed moralist; ill at ease with his uncle, he was driven to compensate by being over-assertive. In the face of such an uncongenial and unpredictable temperament, King Edward shied away from ever raising any contentious political issue with his nephew. And of all the sensitive issues, the Kaiser's maritime ambitions were the least tractable. During his visit to Windsor at the end of 1907 the Kaiser had preached to Cassel on Germany's need for an enlarged High Seas Fleet, words which were certainly intended for the King's ear. To maintain the pressure, the Kaiser set one of his closest confidants on to Cassel. Albert Ballin, the head of the Hamburg–Amerika Line, was dismissed by Chaim Weizmann as 'the usual type of "Kaiser-Juden", more German than the Germans, obsequious, superpatriotic, eagerly anticipating the wishes and plans of the masters of Germany'; but he was one of the few who could criticize the Kaiser and count on a cool hearing. An original advocate of Tirpitz's big navy, he opposed it as soon as its consequences on Anglo-German relations were evident; more practically, he considered that Britain was always destined to win a naval race, whereas the Kaiser and the admiral were certain that Britain would be the first to crack under internal political pressures. Ballin also rode high in the esteem of Chancellor Bülow: few, he reckoned, had 'done so much good all their lives'; his failing was 'a certain tendency to wish to please everyone'. This and his natural optimism led him to mislead the Kaiser – only too eager not to credit the opinion of his ambassador in London, Count Paul von Metternich – into a dangerously false impression of the King's personal authority. In July 1908 Ballin was in London to discuss his anxieties with Cassel. The latter assured him that he would do all in his power to persuade the 'English royal pair' to visit Berlin. The Kaiser retorted that he would not be back from the Baltic if the King might happen to pass through Germany to Marienbad. This moment of petulance passed, and in August King and Kaiser met at Cronberg for a long tête-à-tête, 'but the subject of the Navy', the King informed Cassel, 'was *not* broached'. Early in the next year, on a last visit to Berlin marred (but enlivened for the onlookers) by a succession of comic mishaps, King Edward did finally steel himself to broach the awkward subject, but in such an uncharacteristically hesitant, even apologetic manner at the last minute before his departure, that he cannot have convinced the Kaiser of the true measure of his and Great Britain's concern.

Cassel and Ballin resumed their efforts. They proposed that the two navy chiefs, Tirpitz and Fisher, meet in Switzerland to hammer out an understanding; Ballin estimated that Tirpitz, if given a positive role, would prove more conciliatory than if confined to criticism from the side lines. In July Bülow resigned. His successor, Theobald von Bethmann Hollweg, the Kaiser's reluctant choice (he had considered Ballin, among others, for the post), though 'timid and hesitating', in his predecessor's not unprejudiced opinion, and lacking any experience of foreign affairs, was jealous of his prerogatives. His sulking persuaded the Kaiser to drop the idea. It was decided instead – to the relief of the ambassadors on each side – to revert to official channels, a recipe for inaction. The unofficial Cassel–Ballin channel, chosen by the Kaiser and acquiesced in by the British, had one overriding advantage. Neither Power wished to be the one seen to have opened overtures. Bülow had recognized that anti-British feeling in Germany, born of jealousy and nationalist assertiveness, was stronger than anti-German feeling in Britain. The German leaders could not therefore afford, as the lesser Power, to be accused of truckling to Britannia. There was also less sense of urgency in Berlin, where it was never seriously believed that the cement of the Anglo-French entente would hold under applied pressure. The British government considered that any initiative on their part would be construed as a sign of weakness.

After King Edward's death, Cassel's British-German Foundation, of which the Kaiser and Kaiserin were patrons, took him often to Berlin (Ballin was one of the administrators of the German end). In May 1911 he was honoured with one of the Kaiser's harangues. Cassel pencilled notes in German – what remains legible is occult: the conversation ranged over the whole spectrum of foreign and commercial affairs; it touched on Grey, Bismarck, Holstein and Delcassé, the French architect of the Entente Cordiale. There was one more ominous note – 'Morocco [two words illegible] if necessary.' That country's virtual session to France under the Entente was disputed by Germany (and the Turkish Sultan). Just over a month later the German gunboat *Panther* arrived off Agadir in a show of strength and intimidation, ostensibly to protect German commercial interests on which France was accused of encroaching. This crisis lasted until November. War was averted, but the adventure served to reinforce Britain's suspicions of Germany's aggressive ambitions. In October, Winston Churchill had become First Lord of the Admiralty. The fierce advocate of domestic economy over rearmament had undergone a metamorphosis; it had not escaped his attention that in the two elections in the previous year the Liberal pacifist wing, the 'Lambs' (League of Liberals against Aggression and Militarism), had been decimated. Once his friend had found his sea legs, Cassel, without any apparent authority, struck. As a sop to sensibilities, it was decided that Cassel would inform the British government that the Kaiser had expressed a desire to receive a British Cabinet minister in Berlin; Ballin would formally inform the Kaiser, who was aware of the plan, that the British government had expressed a desire to send a special representative to Berlin to discuss an accommodation. Cassel was due to return to Berlin for the Kaiser's birthday celebrations at the end of January 1912. He invited Winston Churchill to accompany him.

The time was riper than it ever had been before, or would ever be again. A final supplement to the Navy Law had been laid on the German Chancellor's desk by Tirpitz. The strength of the active fleet was to be strengthened; the projected building of an additional battleship every second year for six years would alone have resulted in an increase in naval expenditure of over one-quarter. This prospect alarmed the Chancellor and the army chiefs, who feared a dilution of their budget; the Minister of Finance, faced with another large deficit as the Reichstag was not expected to approve extra taxation, resigned. Rumours of this multiplication reached London and Churchill's first reaction was to approve of a visit to Berlin. In his enthusiasm to do 'anything in my power to terminate' the 'insensate' antagonism, he had overlooked the Parliamentary calendar: Sir Edward Grey and the Prime Minister, whose sanction he belatedly recognized as necessary, were out of town for the Christmas recess. He cautiously advised Cassel on 8 January that he did not consider it wise at that juncture 'to have any parley with y[ou]r august friend' and begged him to disengage him with the greatest respect. The Kaiser replied through Ballin that Churchill's difficulties were appreciated but that he could nonetheless count on a very good reception in Berlin.

Churchill had expressed to Cassel his doubts about whether Germany would be prepared to take the one step that would lead to *détente* by dropping her naval challenge. Indeed, it is probable that the Kaiser had already determined on an uncompromising line on the assumption that he could force a shift of foreign policy on the British government. Cassel, meanwhile, buoyed by Ballin's false confidence, took himself off to Cannes for a breath of fresh air. On 23 January he was recalled by Churchill, who had by then had a chance to discuss the project with Grey; the 'matter', he urged, 'is sufficiently weighty and urgent to justify my trespassing on your holiday. I know that you are always ready to sacrifice your convenience where public interests are concerned.' Three days later Cassel was back in London where, on the morrow, he received his instructions from Sir Edward Grey (who had returned specially from the country), Churchill and Lloyd George. He was to put it that German naval expenditure was not to be increased, but if possible retarded and reduced; that Britain was prepared to discuss Germany's colonial aspirations; and that Britain would welcome proposals for reciprocal assurances debarring either Power from joining in aggressive combinations against the other.

Cassel arrived in Berlin on 29 January. (The ostensible purpose of his visit was to receive from the Kaiser the Order of the Red Eagle to add to his Crown of Prussia, awarded four years before.) He revealed his three points to Ballin, Ballin repeated them to the Chancellor, who pronounced his 'complete agreement'. This was doubtless Ballin's own spurious gloss. Bethmann Hollweg had one reservation of paramount importance: the naval increases already planned could not be repealed. Both Ballin, the optimist, and Bethmann Hollweg, the emollient, made light of the effect of these clauses, and Cassel, ignorant of naval matters, accepted their interpretation. Ballin was called to the Kaiser's side from lunch at two o'clock, Cassel over an hour later. The German Emperor was the model of affability. He slyly chose to treat the go-between as an official envoy, and his message therefore as a symptom of a weakening of the British position (Grey was meanwhile emphasizing that the choice of channel was the Kaiser's). He did not foresee any difficulty in arriving at 'a complete and thorough understanding'; Britain would be surprised at how modest were Germany's colonial ambitions (it had just acquired a large slice of the French Congo as a result of the Agadir imbroglio). The Kaiser and his Chancellor drafted a reply for Cassel to take home, which Ballin copied down. Both sought again to reassure Cassel over the implications of the provisions of the new Navy Bill; he replied that as he had received Ballin's assurance that the estimates were not 'material', he supposed there would be no real objection at home. There was further obfuscating talk of crew levels and reserves, which Cassel could not follow. He was on terra firma over costs: the £2.5 million additional annual expenditure was, he insisted, 'a very material matter'. The Kaiser ended by issuing an invitation to Sir Edward Grey to visit him in Berlin – he 'had made up his mind that there should be no failure'. Cassel and Ballin were dismissed from the Imperial presence, the former nursing 'considerable anxiety'. Again, notwithstanding the Chancellor's insistence that the naval estimates could not be withdrawn, the fatefully bullish Ballin nevertheless sought to encourage Cassel to believe that some modification might still be achieved. If Grey made this a condition of his visit, Ballin said when pressed, he had no doubt that the answer would be that the matter should be open to discussion.

Cassel returned to London next morning with a résumé of the Navy Bill, prepared by the Chancellor, in his pocket. Churchill came round hotfoot that same evening: 'the temper is good', he recorded, 'but the facts are grim'. Cassel repeated Ballin's unwarranted supposition that it was susceptible of amendment. Lloyd George by then being in bed, the three, in the absence of Grey, arranged to meet at Brook House the next morning for breakfast. Over the coffee and croissants, Churchill expounded on the undesirability of the tension being allowed to continue and both ministers agreed that Cassel should forthwith telegraph to Ballin in an effort to keep the dialogue open. Later in the day, Churchill telephoned Cassel. He had received 'rather a stiff letter' from Grey and now wished Cassel to make it clear that he had telegraphed nothing but his personal view.

Within a few days of his return to London, Cassel was the centre of a pertinent incident. He found himself, along with Prince Louis of Battenberg, the First Sea Lord, at a dinner with the British-born Princess of Pless, sister of Winston Churchill's stepfather, George Cornwallis-West. Daisy Pless was a tiresome mischief-maker (she claimed that she was responsible for the award of the Red Eagle as she had impressed on Berlin that Cassel was dangerous and needed 'a little plaster'.) 'You seem to have all gone mad in your country,' Cassel reproached her. 'I suppose you mean in *your* country,' she replied hotly. Then he added quietly, 'Well, I feel certain there will be war in the spring.' Daisy Pless, though she felt like throwing a knife at him, kept her temper and managed a smile. She duly reported the incident to the Kaiser, begging him not to trust Sir Ernest; if the Princess is to be believed, he replied that he did not, but was most surprised all the same. Doubtless, aware of her sympathies, Cassel hoped by his plain-spoken prophecy to induce the Kaiser to take a more reasonable and realistic attitude by applying a dash of cold water to his complacency.

The Berlin business now went to the Cabinet. On 3 February Cassel was authorized by Sir Edward Grey, Winston Churchill and Richard Haldane to reopen his line to Ballin. If the tempo of the new German shipbuilding programme could be slowed so as to render increases in British naval expenditure unnecessary, the government would be prepared to pursue negotiations on the understanding that this point was open to discussion and that there was a fair prospect of settling it favourably. Berlin apparently did not demur at this understanding, though Cassel should by now have been made aware that Germany's terms had hardened: before Berlin would consider a compromise on the naval question, Britain would be required to agree to a 'strongly enunciated neutrality' in place of the empty declaration of 'reciprocal assurances'. In place of Grey – 'this would never do' – the Cabinet chose Haldane, Secretary of State for War, to go to Berlin on a private and unofficial visit to engage in 'a very frank exchange of views'; he was accompanied by his brother, a professor and physiologist, to lend colour to the official explanation that he was enquiring into scientific education in Germany. Cassel was to make up the party, but to keep at a discreet distance in a different hotel.

A cerebral Scot, Haldane was a big, burly lawyer and a German-speaking philosopher (he had been code-named 'Schopenhauer' by his late chief, Campbell-Bannerman). Appointed at the wish of Edward VII, he had brilliantly (and thriftily) reorganized the British Army, founded the Territorials and created a general staff; he was altogether at sea on naval affairs. (He was a friend both of the English and French Rothschilds; Natty always had a room reserved for him at Tring.) Haldane arrived in Berlin early on 8 February 1912. Only the day before, the Kaiser, with either calculated malice or tactless ill-timing, had announced to the Reichstag his intention to introduce the controversial Navy Bill; two days later Churchill stirred the embers in a speech asserting that 'The British Navy is to us a necessity and . . . the German Navy is to them more in the nature of a luxury.' This caused an outcry in Germany and was even branded as provocative by the Liberal press in England. Cassel and Ballin were also now getting under the feet of the diplomats and politicians. Bethmann Hollweg strongly denied to the British Ambassador, Sir Edward Goschen, that he or the Kaiser had had anything to do with Ballin's initiative and said that, for his part, he had been most surprised that Cassel had been chosen by the British as an intermediary in such an important matter when there was a German Ambassador in London. Goschen commented to Sir Arthur Nicolson that the Chancellor's remarks were 'queer and there must be some – we'll call it misunderstanding – somewhere'; and, as he had similarly been bypassed, what about *his* face? Bethmann Hollweg determined that the twin unofficial channels should depart. Haldane energetically objected. The Kaiser deferred to Haldane's wishes, but gave Ballin his gracious permission to retire. Cassel prudently followed suit, with Haldane's thanks for his 'great work'.

Haldane first spent an hour and a half with the Chancellor after a lunch at the Embassy. Bethmann Hollweg convinced Haldane of his 'absolute sincerity and goodwill', but his problem, as he admitted, was that 'My admirals are very difficult.' (This was the root of the problem; they were not 'his' admirals.) Haldane sympathized and, counting on convincing the Germans that they could not win if they persisted in entering a naval race, warned that Britain would respond by laying down two keels for every one addition to the German fleet in order to maintain superiority at sea. Goschen considered that even a concession such as spreading construction over a period of twelve instead of the planned six years would prove 'gall and wormwood' to Tirpitz, who would choose to resign. The loss of '*mein* Tirpitz', who was not only irreplaceable but had the predictable backing of Krupp and 'the whole "armour-plated" crew', the pan-German lobby and much of public opinion, was unthinkable; the Kaiser was himself nervously aware that if the military oligarchy sensed any wavering in his purpose, his own throne would be in danger. Haldane got very little further the next day with the Kaiser and Tirpitz. The German leaders now revealed their change of tack. They intimated they might be brought to consider a minor concession on condition that this was preceded by a declaration of Britain's absolute neutrality in the event of war; the British were prepared to go no further than to consider neutrality only in the case of Germany as victim, not aggressor. This did not go far enough to satisfy the Germans. Haldane returned home without an olive branch. Cassel, to commemorate their mission, commissioned a consolatory portrait of him for the Privy Council office.

Haldane could not have been expected to read the mind of the Kaiser and the warlords, but he should, more than any other British minister, have been more aware of the fatal dualism at the heart of the German system of government. However sincere the Chancellor in his desire for peace, it was not in his power to combine the exercise of foreign and military policy. The latter was the preserve of the Kaiser; even military and naval attachés abroad reported directly to him over the heads of their diplomatic missions. It is the more surprising that, as Haldane had attended German army manoeuvres as an observer, he was not more sensible to the intensity of public opinion in support of Tirpitz's naval dreams.

A new and troublesome factor emerged. The Admiralty had been studying the Navy Law that Cassel had brought back. It turned out to mean, as Haldane explained to him, 'much more in men and money and craft' (including submarines, a field in which the German navy were latecomers) than Bethmann Hollweg had originally suggested. This in turn would require an increase in expenditure on the Royal Navy of £18 million over five years. In spite of these unpromising developments and the failure to find any common ground, both sides continued to express their earnest desire to conclude an agreement – on their own mutually irreconcilable terms. Bethmann Hollweg entreated Ballin, now forgiven, to do what he could 'through discreet private support' to keep the exchange open. Urging Cassel to return from the South of France, he himself made for London, as sanguine and credulous as ever. (Ballin's confidence was only once shaken. 'I am absolutely shattered, of course,' he wrote to Cassel in the middle of April, 'by the disaster of the *Titanic*.' His distress was of a practical nature. 'If the ship is really lost, then all our assumptions and technical calculations are wrong and an insuperable uncertainty is introduced into our business.') In the middle of March he dined with Churchill at Brook House and by the end of the evening had deluded himself that Britain would be willing to declare unconditional neutrality, and that, moreover, before the contentious naval points were settled. Ballin, it is said, light-headed with euphoria, returned to Berlin. He went straight to the Kaiser and announced, 'Your Majesty, I bring the alliance with England!' promising that the formal proposal would arrive that afternoon. The German Ambassador instead telegraphed Grey's correction: Britain could not accept the increases in naval personnel in the new Navy Law and could offer no more than a declaration that it would not make or join in any unprovoked attack on

Germany, which was indeed the extent of its obligations towards Russia and France.

This gaffe certainly (if curiously) did not affect the Kaiser's personal regard for Ballin, neither did it in the least diminish Ballin's noble but foolish hopes. He implored Cassel to persuade Churchill to atone for his unflattering references to Germany's 'luxury fleet' in the speech introducing his own naval budget in March. The result, as it happened, unfortunately 'made a very bad impression in Berlin. It does sound very provocative,' Ballin admonished Cassel, 'and is totally lacking in warmth. The Emperor is very unfavourably impressed.' Cassel, back in Grasse, countered in a draft which he did not send, that on the contrary he considered the speech 'an accurate and masterly analysis of the facts. Whether it is good politics to put your cards on the table with such openness can be questioned, but it is honest politics. I cannot see any trace of provocation.' Moreover, he was, he had intended to say, 'rather offended' that Ballin had taken no notice of an earlier despatch which seemed to him 'much more important than the hullabaloo in the newspapers and passing public opinion (I use an expression of the Kaiser's which has stuck in my mind)'. (Cassel, after much discussion with Grey, Haldane and Lord Morley, judged that the British government was 'ready to carry matters through' as soon as public opinion had grown accustomed to the German naval increase, a matter of several months at the latest. Given the state of Liberal opinion at least, this might have been an accurate assessment.) Ballin came round. He accepted that 'such openness and honesty' on Churchill's part 'is unusual which dumbfounded the whole world and, above all, the authorities here and created a furious storm in the press. After this eternal secretiveness, it is not easy to accustom oneself to such a complete reversal.' He suggested that 'a few friendly lines' from Churchill to Cassel would have 'a very fortunate effect' in the right royal circles. Churchill obliged on 14 April, in respectful and conciliatory terms, emphasizing Britain's preoccupation with 'the steady and remorseless development of a rival naval power of the highest efficiency' and proclaiming the innocence of any offensive design on Britain's part. He ended on a hopeful note: 'Patience, however, and good temper accomplish much: and as the years pass many difficulties seem to settle themselves peacefully.' He had already proposed a 'naval holiday' between the two Powers to the German naval attaché in London. The attaché was officially instructed by Tirpitz to portray Churchill's offer as a weakening of will to maintain the hot pace of competition, thus confirming the Kaiser's expectations and ensuring his continued intransigence. Bethmann Hollweg was himself coming under fire from the war party for allowing himself to become the dupe of the English; the Kaiser, demonstrating the strength of his commitment to rapprochement, recalled and retired Metternich from London. Debilitated by the degenerate air of St James's, he had been tactless enough to preach the inevitability of war within three years unless Germany reduced the pace of naval rearmament. On 21 May 1912, the supplementary Navy Bill passed into law.

The Kaiser still did not let go of Ballin; it was most likely his unquenchable optimism which appealed to wayward Wilhelm. Within months of the Navy Law's adoption, Ballin urged Cassel to join them for breakfast. By January 1913 he was astonishingly still insisting that 'the opportunity for reaching an understanding is more favourable than ever before. Feelings towards Grey are very friendly. Everything is working in favour, except Churchill, who keeps pouring oil on the flames.' Nonetheless, even Ballin's nerves were by now in 'a fairly bad way'. But he remained determined and tireless. Early in 1914 he floated another balloon. Churchill, he persuaded Cassel, should get together with Tirpitz. Ballin suggested to the Kaiser that the First Lord, who, despite Grey's scepticism, was not unsympathetic, should be invited to attend Kiel Week, the annual naval show of strength. The Kaiser insisted that he first formally request an invitation. The British, and even Ballin, cooled. Two weeks after the assassination of Archduke Franz Ferdinand at Sarajevo, Ballin was sent secretly to London – at the prompting of the Kaiser, Churchill thought – to probe Britain's likely response if the crisis with Serbia led to a general war. (The new German Ambassador, Prince Lichnowsky, sent to London to charm the English with his attractive personality and his agreeably pacific convictions, did not learn of it until the following year.) On the day that Austria served its ultimatum on Serbia, Ballin dined with the Foreign Secretary and Lord Morley, one of the chief doves in the Cabinet, at Lord Haldane's home (he had been translated to the Woolsack two years before). Haldane, among the minority of Liberal imperialists distrusted by their radical colleagues, would not go further than to impress on his guest that in the case of a German attack on France, the aggressor could not count on British neutrality. That was, in a negative fashion, reassuring. Ballin himself was persuaded that Britain would only be moved to act if the balance of power were to be upset by Germany's annexation of French territory. He doubtless fed his optimism by sounding opinion in the City during the next two days. He would have found Germanophile influence uppermost, led by bankers and financiers who were mostly of German origin or descent (and often Jewish). There was widespread objection to intervention on the Continent. This attitude was not unrepresentative of public opinion throughout the country. Most thoughtful Liberals, whose voice was the *Manchester Guardian*, were, if interested in foreign affairs at all, seduced by the impracticable ideal of isolationism; the rank and file indulged in raw national prejudice against the objects of their entanglement – Russia and France. On 24 July Ballin dined again with Churchill at Brook House. He revealed just part of his hand. What difference would it make to England's attitude, he asked, if Germany gave a guarantee beforehand not to take an inch of territory, save some colonies as an indemnification? Churchill was guarded. Repeating Haldane's warning, he admitted that he did not know what Britain's decision would be, the Cabinet 'would judge events as they arose'. Churchill taking his leave of Ballin, so a colleague recalled, 'implored him, almost with tears in his eyes, not to go to war!' Churchill was justifiably non-committal. That same day Asquith, with Ulster worries on his mind, himself had said that 'we are within measurable . . . distance of a real Armageddon. Happily there seems no reason why we should be more than spectators'; Lloyd George was to be yet blunter. Ballin returned to Berlin the day before Austria declared war on Serbia. Two days later, on 29 July, Bethmann Hollweg made a last bid for British neutrality on the lines of Ballin's offer, with one desperate and dishonest inducement, that 'when the war was over Belgian integrity would be respected, if she had not sided against Germany', that is, if Belgium refused passage for the German armies, the ultimatum for which was already in the Chancellor's drawer and which he well knew to be unacceptable. Three days later Ballin followed this up with a letter to Haldane in which he hoped it would still be 'possible for England to preserve a friendly neutrality in return for certain guarantees'. Extraordinarily, the Cabinet had never till then considered the question of Belgium's neutrality, of which Britain was one of the three guarantors. The majority was still opposed to any involvement. It was only on 3 August, the day before the violation of Belgium by Germany, that opposition in the Cabinet crumbled. Grey, assured of Conservative support, swung Parliament behind him in a memorable speech. (Lord Hugh Cecil, commending 'its great dignity, warm emotion and perfect taste', paid his respects to the 'extraordinary dexterity with which he dealt with the weak spot of his argument . . . the nature of our obligation to France, under the Entente'.)

Ballin, a wise and good man, had one fatal flaw. His ardent hopes led him to mislead himself and others, not least the Kaiser, who was confirmed in his conviction that he held all the high cards. Ballin also seemed unconsciously to have regarded Cassel as a fellow spirit, that is, at best a disinterested partisan of peace, at worst a German patriot. (This view was not untypical, as Cassel was to learn to his cost. Lord Esher, in an earlier Anglo-German dispute, wrote: 'Of course he takes the German and Semitic point of view of it all. This is only natural. After all, *we* are fighting for our lives . . . The Cassels are at home in all lands – equally rich, equally composed.') Of Metternich, who had consistently warned that a failure to reduce the pace of naval armament would lead ineluctably to war, Ballin could only bring himself to tell Cassel that 'his ill-humour is now such that one could not expect much pleasure from his company'. Both Ballin and, less plausibly, the Kaiser were dismayed and incredulous when this prophecy was fulfilled. 'I only wish', the Kaiser whined at Imperial headquarters, 'someone had told me beforehand that England would take up arms against us.' A quiet whisper of 'Metternich' was heard; the conversation was hastily diverted. (The Kaiser was either forgetful or deceitful. His own General Staff had taken British intervention for granted ever since the Schlieffen plan, which hinged on infringement of Belgian neutrality, had been drawn up almost ten years before.) Ballin himself recorded: 'My ships did not need the protection of a German fleet and I should have emphatically said so to the Kaiser. But I could never summon the courage to do so . . . We were all too weak towards the Kaiser. No one wished to disturb his childlike, happy optimism, which could shift at once into an almost helpless depression if anyone criticized one of his pet projects. And among these, the fleet was the greatest. Now we have the result of our lack of courage!'

Among the peripheral points Haldane had raised on his abortive mission to Berlin was the Baghdad Railway, or rather, more pertinently, its extension to Basra. The concession for this last leg was still in the gift of the Porte, subject to the condition that Germany was to have a share at least equal to that of any other country. The British government itself, Turkey having now formally recognized Britain's special position in the Persian Gulf, would have been content with shared international control. (Ballin's ships had already carved out a presence in the Gulf, undercutting the prices of the British shipping monopoly by as much as 50 per cent.) By June 1914 Britain and Germany concluded an agreement which was shortly frustrated by matters of greater moment, although on much less favourable terms than Cassel had negotiated years before, only to be spurned by the Cabinet.

Cassel had acquired another, related interest, more in a despairing effort to stave off insolvency for the National Bank. He prepared, despite earlier misgivings, a foothold in Mesopotamian oil; the Turkish Petroleum Company was formed with an issue of capital of 40,000 £1 shares, of which only one shilling was called up. Cassel's was not the only rod on the river; one disappointed claimant to the concession was Calouste Gulbenkian, the Turks' own economic counsellor, who had teamed up with the Royal Dutch Shell group. Emboldened by his recent amicable exchanges with the Kaiser and the German Chancellor, Cassel suggested to Gulbenkian that if he took a substantial stake with him, he, Cassel, would put Sir Henry Babington Smith in touch with his friend Gwinne of the Deutsche Bank, which held the trackside concession for minerals. The Germans responded positively. In 1912 Turkish Petroleum's capital was doubled; the Deutsche Bank received 20,000 shares in exchange for pooling its rights; Cassel acquired for cash 28,000, and Gulbenkian 32,000 of the remaining shares. The National Bank then sought diplomatic assistance to soften the Turks towards its claims for a concession, only to discover that the Foreign Office, under Admiralty pressure, favoured the all-British Anglo-Persian Oil Company. Such competition was counter-productive, allowing the Turks to avoid any commitment by playing off one national interest against the other. To break the stalemate, the British and German governments pressured their protégés to compromise and consolidate so as to present a united front. In March 1914 Anglo-Persian obtained 50 per cent of the reorganized Turkish Petroleum Company, Royal Dutch Shell and the Deutsche Bank getting a quarter-share each. Gulbenkian settled for 5 per cent interest. Cassel was less fortunate; he and his associates were prevailed upon by the British government to cede their holding to Anglo-Persian, later to become British Petroleum. At the end of June 1914 the Porte informed the British and German ambassadors that the concession would be awarded to the Turkish Petroleum Company. A wiser and an appreciably poorer man, Cassel decided to pull out of Turkey. He arranged to sell out to the Banque de Salonique, he and the other shareholders of the National Bank retaining just a quarter-stake in the new group. This arrangement too was overtaken by war, and the National Bank floundered in limbo, though it survived its founder by ten years.

Cassel could be forgiven if, after these repeated reverses, he had finally laid down his arms a saddened, even embittered, man. (There were sorrows still in store.) In the course of the London Season in the year before the outbreak of war he was spotted (admittedly somewhat out of his element) by Sir Almeric Fitzroy, Clerk of the Privy Council, at a dinner party for the fancy-dress Versailles Ball at the Albert Hall. Fitzroy found him 'a dejected and pathetic figure – a sermon, if you like, on the vanity of great wealth; nothing seems to rouse his interests except a reference to his grandchildren'.

Talking of Turkey, Winston Churchill later admitted that 'the Germans had got the better of our diplomacy there'. He had done little to improve the position himself, giving the thumbs-down to the Turks' request for an alliance, admonishing them instead to mind their conduct. He now compounded his sins of omission by one of commission. On the eve of the rape of Belgium, the First Lord snatched from under the noses of the Turkish crews standing by, the battleships *Reshadieh* and the *Sultan Osman I*,* completing at Vickers' and Armstrongs' yards, respectively. This seizure caused the Turkish Navy Minister, Djemal Pasha, a founder-director of the National Bank, 'mental anguish', an emotion certainly shared by Cassel and his other colleagues, who were left with the bad debt, now worthless Turkish treasury bills; in Turkey, still smarting from the humiliations suffered by Turkish arms in the last Balkan wars, it aroused bitter anger. It was to prove a major factor in precipitating a temporizing Turkey into the arms of Germany. The want of one soft word of justification and regret with the offer, or even the prospect, of compensation, fatally weakened the peace party; Djavid, the Finance Minister, was isolated and had no choice but to resign. (He was later hanged by Atatürk after a rigged treason trial.)

When Cassel had entertained Albert Ballin and Churchill at Brook House on 24 July, he had staying with him King Edward's former physician, Sir Felix Semon. Next morning he and Semon calmly left for Switzerland for a fortnight's breath of Alpine air. Accustomed as the world was to recurring crises in the Balkans, it was less remarkable that Cassel, normally so coolly calculating, had allowed himself to be lulled into undue confidence, against his instincts and better judgement, by Ballin with his wishful thinking and the well-meaning but weak Bethmann Hollweg, than that he missed the portents: the massive increase in the intake of army conscripts and the colossal capital levy of some £50 million on an already over-taxed and not over-rich country for once-and-for-all military purposes. But what was still more remarkable was that the unusual fluctuations of the money markets and the flow of funds to Berlin escaped his attention, or at least gave him no inkling of the impending disaster. He was ideally, perhaps uniquely, placed to feel the

---

*The *Sultan Osman I* was laid down for Brazil as the *Rio de Janeiro*. With fourteen 12-inch guns, she was 70 per cent more powerful than the original Dreadnought, and the Admiralty was not happy at the prospect of such a behemoth passing into foreign hands, least of all in the Mediterranean. There was, however, no budget for such a contingency. It was natural, if unorthodox, that Churchill should turn to the antagonist of the Chancellor's naval cheese-paring. 'Secret. Would you let me know', he wrote to Lord Rothschild on 3 December 1913, 'whether you would be prepared to buy the ship from Brazil and hold her till her transference.' Natty evidently balked at taking such a bulky and illiquid asset onto his books. After her seizure, she was commissioned as HMS *Agincourt*.

pulse of the international exchanges; he enjoyed amicable relations with the Deutsche Bank; Japhets operated a joint account with the Berlin Commerz und Privat-Bank; he was a major shareholder of the Anglo-Austrian Bank; he had an intimate association with Kuhn, Leob in New York and with Max Warburg of Hamburg, who had served his apprenticeship with him in London, quite apart from his own banking operations in Turkey and Egypt. And yet he missed two major German tricks. In order to forestall a financial crash on the German exchange such as the Agadir crisis had provoked, the government set about amassing a substantial gold and silver reserve. Simultaneously, German companies began to call in their overseas debts, which caused the discount rate on the London market to bob up and down; by the outbreak of war Germany's trading partners among her potential enemies found that they had paid everything out and received nothing back. Japhet was among those so discomfited.

His faith in the future undisturbed, Cassel spent 1914 unconcernedly undertaking additions to his sumptuous racing establishment at Moulton Paddocks; the year before, he had intended to supply himself with a winter retreat in Algeria, the Garden of Allah at Biskra. At the Villa Cassel, Semon was the first to succumb to forebodings. His host remained serenely confident that the clouds would pass; he promised the fidgety Sir Felix that he would prepare for his departure if France mobilized. Early on the Saturday morning of 1 August 1914, Cassel awoke Semon with the news that the previous night a neighbouring mayor had come to warn him that Switzerland had mobilized and that therefore most of Cassel's staff, including the chef, would join their units on Monday. That was decisive. The wires to Brig and Lausanne started imperiously humming to reserve sleeping-car accommodation for Paris or Calais – in such straitened times the privilege of private carriages might have to be forgone. It was too late. The station-master at Brig promised to do what he could to find seats, but could not even guarantee that much. At four o'clock on a glorious sunny afternoon the glum little party set off on foot down the valley. At Brig there were too many others in the same plight; every seat on the Simplon Express had been taken by earlier birds. The station-master advised them to take the new line to Paris by Belfort. This passed behind the French frontier fortresses, and Semon was anxious military traffic would take priority over them; but there was no alternative way out. A mile short of the frontier they were obliged to alight and cross into France on foot. One of Cassel's staff managed to find seats on a long, crowded train, whose destination and hour of departure were unknown. They arrived in Paris after a twenty-hour journey and then had to walk most of the way to Cassel's flat, in the Rue du Cirque, so often the refuge of Mrs Keppel on her way to and from Biarritz. Cassel, the multi-millionaire, had the greatest difficulty in raising the 400 gold francs needed to pay for their journey to London.

12

Hostilities

In the balmy heyday of Marienbad, Cassel had told an Austrian journalist, 'I hope I shall be spared the necessity of ever siding with my new country against my old.' He was not spared, and the choice he had made was not universally appreciated. Alongside the wave of patriotism which led young men to flock to the recruiting offices for fear of missing the fighting, another, much less creditable emotion swept the country – war hysteria. Any remote Teutonic taint was the cause of unpleasant insinuations. Had not the German Cassel had the poor taste to come within a nose of winning the Derby in that same year with the provocatively named Habsburg? Spy mania was excited by a host of newspapers. Society ladies, when they were not handing out white feathers, considered that they could contribute most successfully (and enjoyably) to the war effort by disseminating alarmist rumours of collaboration to enliven their bridge parties. (Few had the wit and stout assurance of G. K. Chesterton, who, when asked 'Why are you not out at the Front?' replied, 'Madam, if you go round to the side, you will find that I am.') The novelist E. F. Benson, son of the late Archbishop of Canterbury, was informed in all seriousness that as long as Cassel was in residence at Brook House, London was safe from the Zeppelin raids: he harboured a wireless apparatus of secret design on his roof with which he would signal the news of his movements to German headquarters. (Benson maliciously replied that Cassel's loyalty was as firm as that of the Royal House of Hanover, which itself belatedly rectified the anomaly by taking the name of Windsor and relinquishing its German titles.) There was one concrete cause for recrimination which escaped the good gossips of Grosvenor Square. Cassel's Swedish combine of iron ore mines, railways and shipping was undeniably trading with England's enemy, whose navy was now able to slip through the Kiel Canal to dominate the Baltic. Cassel was powerless to prevent it, but it would have been still less desirable to dispose of shares in a strategic monopoly in a profitably neutral country.

There was also the awkward matter, if it had occurred to anyone, of Cassel's old accomplice the Khedive of Egypt. Deposed by the British four months after the opening of hostilities, he offered his services to the Germans and was used to subvert French newspapers, which he had formerly subsidized to whip up nationalist feeling against the English in Egypt, through generous subventions to their proprietors. (Most of these funds were embezzled by a colourful confidence trickster, Bolo Pasha, the son of a Marseilles café owner, who, under Clemenceau, ended up before a firing squad, as did the proprietor of *Le Journal*, with one of the largest circulations in Paris.)

While many who had battened on Cassel's hospitality turned their backs, the Churchills and Asquiths, who might have suffered most from such an association, remained staunchly and defiantly loyal. Clementine Churchill, eighteen months into war, put on 'three layers of armour' – Winston had been made the scapegoat for the Dardanelles disaster – and went to lunch with Reginald McKenna, a former Home Secretary, First Lord of the Admiralty, and currently Chancellor of the Exchequer. Sir Ernest Cassel was another guest. Mrs Churchill reported to her husband that she had been 'tickled by the contrast in his attitude to the war, the red-hot patriotism of the German and tepid counter-jumping calculating of the Englishman', who, if he had the power, would reduce the size of the army and pay the allies to do all the fighting while Britain provided their arms. 'Sir Ernest and I walked away from the house much depressed.'

Cassel was not the sole sacrificial victim of blinkered bigotry. Lord Haldane, who, as a philosopher, had incautiously referred to Germany as his spiritual home, was hounded from public life within ten months of ordering the mobilization of the expeditionary force he had created, in what Asquith described as 'one of those fanatical and malignant outcries which from time to time disgrace our national character'. (He was rewarded with the Order of Merit.) King George's cousin, Prince Louis of Battenberg, who had left Germany at the same time as his contemporary Cassel and had become a naturalized British subject a decade before him, was forced to resign as First Sea Lord by press agitation within two months of mobilizing the Grand Fleet. The British-born Sir Felix Schuster, for whom Sir Edward Hamilton had had such a high regard, the Governor of the Union Bank, a member of the Council of India, and who worked with the Bank of England on various essential commissions during the war, was similarly reviled.

A less undeserving whipping-boy was the rich, rogue radical Baron de Forest. He was accused, as a newly gazetted lieutenant commander, of disparaging a successful British naval engagement off Heligoland, and was denounced before the Public Prosecutor on the grounds that his sympathies were 'entirely with the Germans' as befitted an owner of vast estates in Moravia, part of the Hirsch inheritance. Forest appealed to Churchill, pointing out that he had placed the castle of Eichhorn at the disposal of the Red Cross (it would otherwise certainly have been sequestrated); that he had offered his new house at Coombe both to the Red Cross and the War Office; and that he had proposed his yacht as a hospital ship as well as putting his own name forward for active service 'in spite of my not very robust health'. (*Crise de foie* was the most probable diagnosis of this otherwise fit thirty-five-year-old.) Churchill absolved him of disloyalty, 'tho' it is clear', he wrote to the Public Prosecutor, 'at times he has talked loosely and argumentatively . . . He has been ordered to join at Dunkirk on next Saturday.'

The Rothschilds, British to their boots, were the object of no such unpleasantness. Soon after the outbreak of hostilities, Lloyd George summoned the leading lights of the City to the Treasury to discuss the financing of the war effort. The Chancellor, who five years before had had too much of Lord Rothschild, now fell back on him. 'We shook hands,' Lloyd George recollected. 'I said: "Lord Rothschild, we have had some political unpleasantness . . ." He interrupted me: "Mr Lloyd George, this is no time to recall these things. What can I do to help?" I told him. He undertook to do it at once. It was done.' 'Only the old Jew made sense,' Lloyd George later remarked to his private secretary. The essence of Lord Rothschild's advice was 'Tax the rich, and tax them heavily.' Already in his 1914 Budget, Lloyd George had raised income tax by two pence to 1s 4d, lowered the threshold for super-tax and increased death duties. This provoked the banker Lord Michelham, the former Herbert Stern, whose immediate family boasted two new-born baronies and a baronetcy, to protest publicly at the Chancellor's grave error: such unwarranted despoliation must result in the flight of foreign investors and native rich – a loss to charity as much as to the Exchequer. Stern's rapid promotion from baronet to baron within six months had caused a scandal; though his peerage was unquestionably pressed on Balfour by King Edward – not implausibly an object of such charity on his own or Alice Keppel's account – if there was ever any written record of their relationship, it was destroyed by that industrious weeder Lord Knollys. (All that remains as a token of Stern's gratitude is the bronze quadriga crowning the Wellington Arch at Hyde Park Corner, which he presented as 'a mark of deepest loyalty and respect to King Edward'.) Baron de Forest, an enthusiastic supporter of Lloyd George's land duties – his own Austrian estates were out of reach of the English Exchequer – likewise violently opposed the 1914 Budget increases; such opposition of rich Liberals moved the government to reduce the new rate of tax on unearned income by a penny. Further wails from the rich went up over Lloyd George's succeeding Budget. Cassel, more measured in his reactions than the excitable Michelham, retired to his study for one whole morning. He emerged at lunch with the reassuring words 'It is not so bad after all.' Severe economy was nonetheless exercised at home. When the price of starch and laundry wages began to pinch, white waistcoats were abandoned for evening wear. One of Cassel's guests at Bournemouth was served partridge for dinner. The keen-eyed host spied that one bird had been taken away uneaten. Next day at lunch he abruptly enquired, 'What has become of that other partridge?' (Luckily it was discovered among the cold dishes on the sideboard.) And Cassel continued to give the lie to Lord Michelham's jeremiad. He gave more generously than ever. He donated a further £50,000 in War Loan stock to the King Edward VII Hospital Fund, some £100,000 to the British Red Cross and Order of St John and over £200,000 to a broad band of charities and agencies for the relief of the families of servicemen.

None of this open-handedness served to abate to any degree the dark mutterings about Sir Ernest's origins. In May 1915 he was provoked into taking the extreme step of protesting his unswerving allegiance and patriotism, lest his 'silence might be misunderstood'. For nearly half a century, he pleaded, all his interests – family, business and social – had been centred in England; all his male relations of military age were serving with the King's forces. (The only apparent Cassel bearing arms was his nephew, Felix. A Member of Parliament, he enlisted in the London Regiment until, in 1916, he was appointed Judge Advocate-General. It is unlikely that there were no German cousins serving their country.) 'My unfailing loyalty and devotion to this country', Sir Ernest ended, 'have never varied or been questioned and while affirming this I desire also to express my deep sense of horror at the manner in which the War is being conducted by the German Government'. (He no doubt had the recent sinking of the *Lusitania* in mind. He was shortly to cross the Atlantic himself.)

This declaration may only have served to draw unwelcome attention to himself. His position as a Privy Councillor was now challenged, despite his naturalization, on the grounds of his alien birth. Sir Edgar Speyer, born in New York, was also singled out. The Speyers, descended from the richest Jewish family in Frankfurt, had set up house in America in 1837 and by the end of the century had grown into one of the three greatest investment banks alongside J. P. Morgan and Kuhn, Loeb. The London branch had been opened in 1861 and took a leading role in financing London's underground railways. Edgar Speyer, who contributed to his share of good works, was musically inclined; he made good the annual deficits incurred by Sir Henry Wood's Promenade Concerts for the less well-to-do (a season ticket worked out at fourpence a night); Richard Strauss dedicated his *Salomé* to him. Unluckily, Edgar's brother James, who ran the New York house, was notoriously Anglophobe, and the London bank itself had retained close ties with Germany. Speyer himself, in a variation of the rumours surrounding Ernest Cassel, was supposed to signal to German submarines from his house at Overstrand, near Cromer in Norfolk. Once their trials started, Lady Speyer, a spirited violinist of German-American birth, and not one to offer either cheek, over-reacted. She railed against the ingratitude and perfidy of her former friends who now ostracized her, and goaded her husband to respond. At the time Cassel was stating his case to *The Times*'s readers, Speyer instead wrote to his friend Asquith, the Prime Minister. Although 'not a man who can be driven or drummed by threats or abuse into an attitude of justification', he said, he considered it 'due to my honour as a loyal British subject and my personal dignity' to ask Asquith to accept his resignation from the Privy Council and to revoke his baronetcy. This was delicately and sympathetically refused by the Prime Minister on behalf of the King. (Asquith was already suspected of being under a financial obligation to Speyer.) By December 1915, however, both Cassel and Speyer were required to defend their membership of the Privy Council after legal proceedings had been instituted by an obscure Scottish baronet. The case was heard by the Lord Chief Justice, Lord Reading (the former Isaac Rufus), who upheld Cassel's and Speyer's rights. Sir Almeric Fitzroy, the Clerk to the Council, later quizzed Reading on the reason for differentiating in such a marked manner between the two parties' costs: Cassel, he explained, had respectfully submitted an affidavit attesting in earnest language his loyalty to the King, and to the country of his adoption; Speyer had in effect 'told the King and Privy Council to go hang'. Speyer wound up his affairs and took himself off to the United States even before the verdict was known. There he consorted with the pro-German party, to the subsequent embarrassment of Lord Reading when he was appointed British Ambassador in Washington. (After the war, Speyer was held to have been, by act and speech, 'disaffected and disloyal'; his naturalization was revoked and his name was removed from the roll of the Privy Council. He died in Berlin.) Cassel took the badgering more meekly and settled down to a dignified retirement in Bournemouth with his sister, leaving the German Zeppelins a free hand over London (Brook House was spared).

It was seemingly unorthodox that Reading did not excuse himself from sitting in judgement on Cassel. Just three months before, the respondent, a personal friend, had accompanied him, at the invitation of the Chancellor of the Exchequer, on the mission to the United States which resulted in the flotation of the first $500 million war loan. (Another member was Sir Henry Babington Smith.) Cassel set an example to laggards by subscribing a substantial sum to it. Scrupulous as ever in sharing his news, he informed King George of his errand and of the health of the royal portfolio. The King congratulated him on the government's good fortune in securing his services; he was beginning to feel the strain of 'this terrible war', but was happy at the same time to hear that Cassel had managed to realize a small profit on some oil certificates in his charge. Cassel, with consummate lack of tact in the circumstances, had let fall that his own fortune was out of reach of adversity. 'It is indeed a blessing', the King replied with unexpected (or unintended) sarcasm, 'that most of your fortune is invested in America and therefore safe.' Once Cassel himself was safe at home again, King George expressed a wish to hear Cassel's impressions of the United States; in particular he was 'very glad to hear about the Ore Certificates, everything seems to be going up in the States now'. Cassel's impressions would have been interesting. He had had a hot reception across the Atlantic, the mirror of the animus heaped on him in England. He was vilified as doubly disloyal by the well-organized and vociferous legions of German-Americans, fertile ground for the Central Powers' agents and saboteurs, as well as by the millions of Jewish refugees from Tsarist oppression. (Their hostility, allied to Germany's efforts to woo the Zionists with an offer of a homeland in Palestine under her protection, was not a little responsible for the Balfour Declaration in November 1917.) Even Cassel's old friend Jacob Schiff held aloof from extending any aid to the Allies; a courageous exception was his partner, Otto Kahn, who, though a German and a Jew, donated St Dunstan's for blinded soldiers and was largely instrumental in barring access to the American capital market to the Central Powers. Although hypersensitive beneath that stiff exterior, Cassel's reserve was such that he himself never so much as referred to his troubles. The Chancellor of the Exchequer, Reginald McKenna, who had seen him at the Treasury on his return, only learned about it from Reading's reports. He at once offered his regrets to Cassel that 'you had to meet most unfortunate and unpleasant opposition which you bore with great dignity and admirable patience and restraint . . . [Reading] says that you have done all that was possible to help the Commission, and his letter gives me the impression that he is much distressed by the want of consideration shown to you. His feelings are mine. With exemplary public spirit you spared no effort to assist this Government in obtaining a loan without which we should have been seriously embarrassed and I trust I may be allowed to express my warm personal appreciation . . . and my very profound regret . . .' It must also be regretted that the government did not feel that he had earned the entitlement to some public recognition of his services; it might not have stilled malicious tongues, but it would have consoled Cassel.

His tribulations had not yet ended. In early August 1918, shortly after the German reverse in the second battle of the Marne and six days before the German army met its 'Black Day', Cassel again found himself the centre of unwelcome attantion. In a maiden speech in the House of Lords, an amendment was proposed to strip him and Speyer of their membership of the Privy Council as 'men whose allegiance is claimed by Germany'; the new peer, carried away by his sense of the occasion, called for the cleansing of the Augean stables. Cassel was defended by Lord Verulam, Felix Cassel's father-in-law, and by another noble Lord who vehemently urged that Cassel, 'one of the most benevolent subjects of the King in every walk of life . . . should not be subjected to what I call the insult proposed . . . against all ideas of British justice'. The Marquis of Lincolnshire, the former Lord Carrington, one of the late King's early favourites, next rose. Although he protested that it pained him to utter a word against anybody, his intervention was evidence of malice or mental decline. He pointed out that the amendment regarding 'aliens' applied to only two men, 'leaving out the Royal Family – as I believe we ought to leave it out', Cassel and Sir Edgar Speyer, who 'has fortunately taken himself off to the United States, where I hope he will remain'. He invoked 'a great principle', which had once already been overset by the Lord Chief Justice; he conceded that Sir Ernest had 'in the language of the Foreign Office . . . behaved in a very correct manner', but 'What, after all,' he asked, 'are the special services' he was said to have rendered? There was no person better fitted to administer a magisterial set-down than Lord Curzon, and the Lord President of the Council obliged. After a due encomium of such services, he singled out the 'regeneration of Egypt [which] has been largely contributed to by his generosity and public spirit. There are few aspects of public life', Curzon pronounced, 'in which Sir Ernest Cassel has not played a large, magnanimous, generous and patriotic part, and for your Lordships to take any action now which would single this gentleman out for the slur that would arise . . . would be an action which, upon whomever it might inflict pain, would inflict nothing but discredit upon your Lordships' House.' He was seconded by Lord Willoughby de Broke, whose father had introduced Cassel to King Edward thirty years before, and by Lord Chaplin, the late King's old Cambridge friend, both of whom had had the privilege of Cassel's intimate friendship. The débutant Lord, having misjudged the mood of the House, immediately withdrew the amendment. Lord Esher, who had sat through the proceedings in abject silence, wrote to congratulate Cassel that the House had 'behaved with decency and showed, for once, a little sense and courage . . . I loathe cant, cowardice and bullying to such an extent that it was difficult', he protested feebly, 'to refrain' from speaking. 'When I think of the services you have rendered this country and how the King trusted you – he, the best of judges of character – and how gallantly you sustained our nation's interest in all that Baghdad affair, you can imagine how one's gorge rises at the nonsense talked by these fools.'

Cassel resurfaced only five days after the Armistice, writing to the King: 'Will Your Majesty permit me to convey to you my heartfelt congratulations on the wonderful victory . . . It is a long time since I had the honour of seeing Your Majesty and I am sure you understand that in view of the attacks made in the press against me ['owing to the unfortunate accident of my birth' – omitted from draft] I did not consider it right to approach Your Majesty. This year is the 50th anniversary of my life in England and I desire to commemorate the occasion by creating some institutions for the public benefit. If it would interest you, Sir, I shall be only too pleased to lay my plans before you and to secure your approval before I take any definite action.' There is no evidence that King George had any such interest; neither did Cassel himself have any plans. A month or two later, Lord Haldane found him alone in Brook House, plainly out of sorts. He surprised his visitor by suddenly announcing that he wanted to spend a million on bettering the condition of the poor. Haldane replied that this amount, 'if applied thus at large, would do little more good than if he were to throw a drop of water into a bucket'. He advised him to spend it on a definite object such as the higher education of the less blessed. Cassel characteristically reflected for a minute. He would, he then announced, spend half the million on such an aim if Haldane would undertake to chair a body of wise men; the other half he would donate for the treatment of the mentally afflicted. (He achieved some economy in this case; the hospital for functional nervous disorders was set up for just £225,000 in eighty acres near Penshurst in Kent four months before his death.) His Educational Trust was under way by February 1919 with

£500,000 of War Loan. Among the original trustees were Arthur Balfour, Asquith, the historian H. A. L. Fisher and Sidney Webb. The Workers Education Association received a large grant, and donations were made towards the higher education of women (Newnham, Girton and Somerville Colleges received £25,000 each, St Hilda's £15,000); further sums went to promote the teaching of foreign languages at five universities; £150,000 went to establish a faculty of commerce at London University with professorial posts in banking and currency, foreign trade, accountancy and business methods, transport and shipping, industrial organization and commercial law; Sir William Beveridge's research at the London School of Economics was supported.

Cassel's generosity was not always so acceptable. When in 1917 the Marlborough Club threatened to sink under its debts, Sir Ernest offered to rescue it out of his own pocket. The other members refused his money. They turned to the founder's son; George V produced the necessary £7,000 (Lord Revelstoke was now the principal overseer of the royal finances; Edward VII would have needed Cassel's assistance in raising a similar sum). Very occasionally the King's sons Prince Albert, Duke of York (later King George VI), and Henry, Duke of Gloucester, shot with Cassel. Society in general was less accommodating. It was too soon in the first year of peace for passions, let alone prejudices, to have cooled. Margot Asquith was deemed not to have been a hot enough patriot; even Mrs Keppel was denounced as a German spy. Cassel offered a chance for a gratuitous humiliation. A Knight Grand Cross of the Order of St Michael and St George, he insisted on attending a service for that Order. Like many sensitive people, he was indifferent to the sensibilities of others and, considering that he had the right, was determined to exercise it. The result was not happy. The Marquis de Soveral, longtime Portuguese Ambassador to the Edwardian court, who had abhorred everything German since overhearing the Kaiser refer to him as the 'Blue Monkey', was angry at having to process alongside him; worse, the Marquis of Lincolnshire, abashed, perhaps, after his churlish performance in the House of Lords, turned his back on him.

One who was not too proud or prejudiced to accept his hand to bail him out was John Maynard Keynes. Charged with foreign exchange dealings for the British government during the war, he set out in its aftermath to speculate on his faith that the dollar would rise against the European currencies on his own behalf and that of relations and friends from the Bloomsbury set, who pledged a fund of £30,000. At first his trust was vindicated, but then the market turned, and in 1920 he came within an ace of losing not only his previous profits but his entire stake. He was rescued by an advance on royalties for his recently published and opportune book, *The Economic Consequences of the Peace* and an equal amount of £15,000 on loan from Cassel.

In the summer of the same year a wild and unsavoury libel must have come to Cassel's ears, to be dismissed as contemptuously as it deserved. An obscure but scurrilous journal, *Plain English*, edited by the vituperative paranoiac Lord Alfred Douglas, accused Winston Churchill of having conspired with Cassel to issue a false report of the result of the battle of Jutland in 1916 in order to make a killing on the Stock Exchange. Cassel was alleged to have profited by £18 million while Churchill was said to have been presented with a mere several thousand pounds' worth of furniture. No further notice was taken in Cassel's lifetime. Unhappily publication coincided with, and contributed to, an upsurge in anti-Semitism, stoked by the publication of *The Protocols of the Elders of Zion*, which, though soon exposed as a clumsy plagiarism, purported to expound the Jewish plan for world domination. Then, in the spring of 1922, the signing of the Russo-German treaty at Rapallo, which ended the two countries' isolation after revolution and defeat, caused disquiet and discomfiture to the former Western Allies. On the one hand, the architect was the German Foreign Minister, Walter Rathenau, the Jewish polymath and boyhood friend of Albert Ballin; on the other were the Bolsheviks, synonymous in many minds with the arm of the Jewish international revolution. (A few months later Rathenau, who had presided over the German economy in war and revived it in peace, was assassinated by nationalist terrorists.) Douglas had not ceased his muck-raking, and in April 1922 he was accused by the right-wing *Morning Post* of inventing 'vile insults against the Jews'. Douglas thereupon sued for libel. He charged that Churchill, 'short of money and eager for power, was trapped by the Jews' to whom he was financially indebted, but that 'the Jewish plotters never paid him properly': Cassel and his syndicate, Douglas claimed, cleared £48 million – the profit was mounting – while Churchill was fobbed off with £40,000. Balfour, the First Lord of the Admiralty at the time of Jutland, and Churchill were called by the defendants; Cassel's secretary also appeared to deny that his late employer had transacted any share deals over the period. The jury found in favour of Douglas on the ground that, although the accusations were not held to be true, neither were they deliberately fabricated. He was awarded a farthing's damages. Douglas continued and intensified his vendetta until he was finally arrested in November 1923 and charged with publishing 'a malicious and defamatory' libel against Churchill. The latter did not come quite clean in court over his financial dealings with Cassel: he admitted only that Cassel had furnished him with a library with his mother's approval in 1905 and had sent him a cheque of £500 for a wedding present three years later, 'which I spent'. Cassel's own character and career came in for some gratuitous (and posthumous) disparagement, though some of it was closer to comedy. His German background was the subject of some irrelevant speculation.

'You know he started in the City of London as a clerk at £2 a week?' asked the counsel for the defence.

'Is that very much against him?' replied Churchill.

Cassel would have been obliged to agree that his seat on a horse was never too safe; this was somehow attributed to his German accent which was enough to have disqualified him from becoming Master of the Quorn. 'A naturalized German!' counsel asked with affected shock and disbelief. 'You remember how he used to speak. A full-blown German naturalized in England. Do you remember what he looked like on a horse?' Having indulged himself, counsel tried to point to some obligation on Churchill's behalf by emphasizing his 'close terms of friendship'; Churchill insisted that the terms were those of 'honourable friendship'. Fortunately for Churchill's reputation, Douglas was this time sentenced to six months' imprisonment and bound over to keep the peace for a further six.

Cassel's widowed son-in-law, Wilfrid Ashley, had remarried in 1914. (Cassel had attended the wedding, which, in view of the poignancy of the occasion for him, Sir Almeric Fitzroy deemed 'a generous act'.) A hard-bitten and ambitious divorcee, Mrs Muriel Forbes-Sempill made life intolerable for her stepdaughter, whom Cassel invited to come and live with him at Brook House. There Edwina made her debut at a magnificent ball in the spring of 1920, wearing a pale gold dress, and was at once acclaimed by the Society journals, with little exaggeration, as the 'Richest Heiress in England'. That autumn Sir Ernest's doctors ordered him to the South of France; as bronchial and overweight as King Edward, it was feared that London's fogs would finish him. Edwina dutifully went with him. His grim and taciturn personality melted under his granddaughter's charm, vivacity and enthusiasm. Miss Stella Underhill, who had been with him as secretary since 1913, did not remember being thanked more than three times. Now his staff noticed that, normally so distant and demanding, he was suddenly solicitous of their welfare and personal affairs.

On 19 August 1921, he completed the purchase for £88,000 of a permanent winter retreat, the glorious Villa des Cèdres in forty of the choicest acres at Cap Ferrat, which had belonged to Queen Victoria's cousin, King Leopold of the Belgians. Edwina had spent the first week of

August at Cowes. It did not pass unnoticed by anxious mothers of other débutantes that in her wake she drew Lieutenant Lord Louis Mountbatten, RN, whom she had met for the first time at a ball given by Mrs Cornelius Vanderbilt at Claridge's Hotel in the autumn of the previous year. After the racing was over, the Vanderbilts invited the couple for a ten-day Channel cruise on their yacht. Tongues wagged more furiously when it was learned that Edwina had been invited to meet Lord Louis's parents. (Prince Louis of Battenburg had, at the King's request, relinquished his German titles in 1917 and been created Marquess of Milford Haven.) They next found themselves, Queen Victoria's last godchild and one of King Edward's first, together under the battlemented roof of the Sutherlands in the north-east corner of Scotland. Mountbatten, waiting for the most propitious opportunity to propose marriage, received a telegram on 11 September announcing that his father had suddenly and unexpectedly died. He hurried to London for the funeral, Edwina following him ten days later. She was met at the station by Stella Underhill with yet more tragic news: 'dear Grandpapa' had died the previous evening, 21 September, alone at his desk in the great empty house on Park Lane, his hand next to the three bell buttons with which he could summon particular members of his staff. On the eve of his death he had cancelled a dinner party, at which the Asquiths were expected, as he was feeling poorly. Next day Miss Underhill had left him at half past five after finishing the day's correspondence. She was telephoned at her flat an hour and a half later by the butler. A footman, bringing Sir Ernest a telegram, had found him, his head in his papers, his heart stopped. He was six months short of his seventieth birthday. To the surprise of some, this secretive man's funeral was held five days later at the Jesuit church in Farm Street, Mayfair. Sir Almeric Fitzroy estimated that 'so large and varied a congregation was testimony enough to the esteem in which the dead man had come to be held, in spite of all the prejudices to the contrary'. Queen Alexandra's wreath bore the valediction: 'In sorrowing memory of Sir Ernest Cassel, the kindest and most generous of men, and a great personal friend of my beloved husband, King Edward. Now Comes Rest.' 'I do not know that his claims to the hospitality of the Catholic Church had been conspicuous since he joined it,' Fitzroy reflected, 'until he entrusted himself to its supreme services.' It may be presumed that Sir Ernest's attachment to the Church, to which he had been converted at the wish of his dying wife, was perfunctory. He complained to an Irish lady, 'I did everything that your Church told me. I obeyed all the rules . . . I subscribed to their charities. But when she [his daughter

Maud] died I said, "The Lord has not treated me fairly".' He was buried in Kensal Green cemetery.

There was as great an interest in certain circles in what he left behind him as in the manner of his departure. His estate was worth £7,333,000, which, with the more than £2 million he had given away in his lifetime, represented one of the largest fortunes ever amassed in one generation. The figure had only once been surpassed in England twelve years before, and it stood as a record for another six years.* It exceeded the total proven estates of the three Rothschild brothers, who, of course, had male heirs with a family business to perpetuate. Cassel's former employer, Henry Bischoffsheim, had left £1.6 million, pretty much the mean average for British millionaires. True, J. Pierpont Morgan had left £13.5 million in 1913, excluding his art treasures, but he had inherited a fortune from his father.

Brook House, Moulton Paddocks and £30,000 a year went to Cassel's sister for life – she died within three years – and then passed to Edwina, who also received the lion's share of the residual capital, over £2.5 million. His niece and nephew, Anna Jenkins and Felix Cassel, were also provided for. 'Old and valued friends' were left small tokens in remembrance; Winston Churchill received his watch and chain.

The protean brilliance and material pomp of the public figure contrasted with the pathos of the private man. At an early age Cassel had rejected his German and Jewish birthright but never won general acceptance in exchange in his chosen world. Married for a bare three years, he subordinated everything to the pursuit of riches and power. He exercised great influence and gave shrewd, loyal and discreet service to the country of his adoption, its King and his friends. Yet, with his unaccommodating manner, unforgiving and over-sensitive, few managed to penetrate his reserve. His munificence was scrupulously recorded by the obituarists, but even his generosity was impersonal, often even offhand, lacking all spontaneity, piety or warmth. 'At heart', wrote one who had observed him, he was 'the saddest of millionaires'. The knowledge that his granddaughter was to marry Queen Victoria's great-grandson would have brought him final happiness, but even that reward eluded him. Winston Churchill condoled with Edwina 'at this solemn time'. 'Your grandfather was a great man and he made a mark on his generation and on the world which will last long. He was also a good and just man who was trusted, respected and honoured by all who knew him.

*Charles Morrison, financier and warehouseman, the wealthiest Briton after the Duke of Westminster, left £10,939,000 in 1909, the first eight-figure fortune; Edward Guinness, 1st Earl of Iveagh, left £13,486,000 in 1927.

He was a valued friend of my father's and I have taken up that friendship and have held it all my grown-up life. I had the knowledge that he was very fond of me and believed in me at all times – especially in bad times. I had a real and deep affection for him . . . The last talk we had, almost six weeks ago, he told me that he hoped he would live to see me at the head of Affairs. I could see how great his interest was in my doings and fortunes . . . I have lost a good friend whose like I shall never see again.' Sir Ernest Cassel pronounced his own more poignant and melancholic epitaph: 'I have had everything in the world that I did not want, and nothing that I did.'

Epilogue

Sir Ernest Cassel outlived the oldest members of King Edward's Jewish court circle. He had lost other old friends of his own. Albert Ballin, following the failure of the German offensives on the Western Front in the spring of 1918, and hoped to persuade the Kaiser to face the ineluctable facts which the General Staff were equally determined to keep from him. He was cautioned not to indulge in defeatist talk in front of his master as it served only to make him lose his nerve; the Kaiserin and other minders ensured that they were never left alone. On 8 November 1918, the offices of his shipping line in Hamburg were occupied by a Soldiers' and Workers' Soviet. Ballin walked home and took a fatal, possibly accidental, overdose of sleeping tablets. Jacob Schiff died eight months before Cassel. 'One of the things in my life of which I am proudest and upon which I look back with the greatest satisfaction is our true and devoted friendship', he wrote to his widow, closing a correspondence which had begun over forty years before.

Cassel's crown prince, Felix, came down from Oxford with academic laurels, took silk and was appointed Judge Advocate General. He was at the same time a member of the London County Council and, for six years, Conservative Member of Parliament for a London constituency. He came to represent his uncle on his many educational and medical charities and, fittingly in view of Cassel's own reputed aptitude for the violin in his youth, was elected Master of the Musicians Company (his own son developed into a talented pianist). He became High Sheriff of Hertfordshire, a baronet and Privy Councillor. He married the Earl of Verulam's daughter, Cassel's niece, Marjorie Jenkins, the Countess of Brecknock.

Arthur Sassoon had died two years before the outbreak of the war while staying with his brother-in-law, Leopold Rothschild. Childless, he left the principal residuary interest in his estate, a little over half a modest million, to his brother Reuben's children. The head of the senior branch of the family, his nephew Sir Edward Sassoon, died the same year of 1912: his wife Aline, daughter of the French Baron Gustave de Rothschild, had predeceased him by three years. An ineffective Unionist Member of Parliament (though an early advocate, through his wife, of the Channel Tunnel) for the Hythe seat previously held by Baron Mayer Rothschild in the Liberal interest, he gradually withdrew from the City, neglected his splendid properties in Bombay and Poona and let his faith lapse. Judging death duties to be radically wrong, he left not a penny to charity in protest. His son, Philip, third and last baronet of that line, inherited his father's seat and although scathing about the company he felt occasionally obliged to keep in the House, held it for over a quarter of a century. He served Field Marshal Haig as military, and Lloyd George as Parliamentary, private secretary, and was twice Under Secretary of State for Air for a total of ten years. The beneficiary of the confluent riches of Sassoon and Rothschild, he was the richest of the clan – and died a bachelor; inheriting his mother's artistic tastes, he became Chairman of the National Gallery and a trustee of the Wallace Collection. He lived surrounded by art treasures in solitary splendour at Trent Park and Port Lympne where he cut a 'strange, lonely, un-English little figure'; he 'always seemed to me', thought Harold Nicolson, 'the most unreal creature I have known'. The alembic of assimilation had distilled too fine and rare a spirit. As swarthy as his father, he put it about that he was of Parsee extraction; nonetheless, a Jewish historian suggested that it was the knowledge of his true descent that caused his demotion in Chamberlain's administration in 1937 to First Commissioner of Works out of consideration for German susceptibilities. His sister Sybil married the Earl of Rocksavage, future Marquess of Cholmondeley, Joint Hereditary Lord Great Chamberlain and bearer of the Royal Standard at the Coronation of King George VI. A great beauty, she served in the Great War in the new-born WRNS, to whose foundation she had contributed, and died only in 1990.

Baron de Forest, wearying at last of the sport as the greying *enfant terrible* of radicalism, moved to Liechtenstein soon after the war. He was created, in exchange for the bequest of his art treasures to the Principality, Count de Bendern and a Councillor of State. He later presented the ruins of Baron Hirsch's once proud château de Beauregard to the city of Paris; nothing today remains but the portico.

Lord Rothschild, the eldest of the three brothers, was the first to go. In 1915 Lord Haldane, in temporary charge of the Foreign Office in Grey's absence on holiday, found him at his Piccadilly house, recumbent and obviously unwell. Before his visitor could say anything, Rothschild put up his hand: 'Haldane, I do not know what you are come for except to see me, but I have said to myself that if Haldane asks me to write a cheque for him for £25,000 and to ask no questions, I will do it on the spot.' Haldane denied that any such presumptuous interest had occurred to him; he had come instead to ask whether Rothschild could arrange for a neutral ship from South America, suspected of carrying material for the Germans, to be stopped. Rothschild roused himself and issued the necessary orders. He succumbed to a surgical operation that March, to well-earned encomiums and mourning crowds of thousands of the humble and high. The great influence he had wielded was ascribed not so much to his wealth and the magic of his name, but 'in much greater measure to his high personal character' which put the public interest above any consideration of private profit. His passing was mourned as the loss of a great national asset. Leopold followed in May 1917. Six months later, Evelyn, the son of Leo and Marie, an implacable opponent of Zionism, was killed in Palestine. In the same month, his cousin, Neil Primrose, son of Lord Rosebery and Hannah Rothschild, a recent Under Secretary of State for Foreign Affairs and joint Parliamentary Secretary to the Treasury, also fell in action; his sister married the Liberal politician, the first and last Marquess of Crewe.

At the end of January 1918, Alfred, a joyless, lonely bachelor, joined his brothers. Perverse to the last, it was discovered with consternation – the partnership was burdened already with double death duties – that he had bequeathed a great part of his £2,500,000 estate outside the family. The principal beneficiaries were the importunate and extravagant Almina, daughter of his mistress Marie Wombwell, and her husband, the Earl of Carnarvon. They were also left the sumptuous house in Seymour Place, Piccadilly; Halton, a headache which Alfred had abandoned to the War Office during the war, was left to Leopold's son Lionel; with his brother Anthony, he also received £25,000, the same amount willed to Carnarvon and each of his two children. In similarly mischievous vein he left to Emma, Natty's widow, Greuze's 'Le Baiser Envoyé' featuring an inadequately covered nymph, which he knew would not be to her severe taste. (She averted her eyes and passed it to her daughter-in-law.) There was an unusual dénouement to this windfall. The Earl was now able to afford to resume his excavations in the Valley of the Kings, which resulted in the discovery of Tutankhamen's tomb. He died in the following year from an infected insect bite, a fate popularly ascribed to the curse of the Pharaohs.

It did not prove to be a corresponding blessing for the N. M. Rothschild & Sons. Over a dozen years before, Sir Edward Hamilton had mused on the relative strength of the pillars on which the Treasury relied in the City: 'The man in whom I have the greatest confidence for his judgement is Cassel. The others are Felix Schuster, Revelstoke, E[verard] Hambro and C[harles] Goschen . . . I say nothing of the Rothschilds who I consider have a sort of prescriptive right to be consulted by the Government but who are rather left behind in the great race.' (By the turn of the century, the Frankfurt and Naples houses had foundered for want of Rothschild male heirs.) Postwar conditions were even less propitious for the new generation of untried partners. The empires, dynasties and institutions in which the Rothschilds had established such ascendancy had been swept away by the war. The weight in the balance of financial power had substantially shifted. The United States, the greatest debtor nation in the heyday of Cassel and the earlier Rothschilds, had now become the world's greatest creditor and overseas investor. At home, the economy drained of foreign assets by the imperatives of war, the Rothschild role was diminished by the rise of the joint-stock banks and the growing authority of government and the Bank of England.

The succession at New Court itself was troubled. The first Lord Rothschild had long abandoned all hope for his heir Walter as a responsible banker, let alone a suitable senior partner, though he was thought fit to inherit the Rothschild seat in the Commons, which he adorned in his white top hat. An awkward 300-pounder, eccentric, secretive, with a grave speech impediment, a covert and, more unforgivably, hapless speculator (and unknown to his family, a victim of systematic blackmail by some unscrupulous peeress), he was put out to grass amidst his specimens at his Natural History Museum at Tring, where he also dedicated himself to Jewish affairs. All the responsibility of the bank devolved on his brother Charles, who would himself have preferred to devote himself to the study of butterflies and fleas. A natural melancholic, he took his own life in 1923 after his health had broken down. Leopold's two sons, Lionel and Anthony, took up the reins. The elder married a Beer, a distant relation of the Sassoons, the younger a Cahen d'Anvers, descended through marriage from the Bischoffsheims, Baron Hirsch's in-laws, Sir Ernest Cassel's erstwhile employers. The world was still a small circle.

Edward's 'warm human kindness' and his freedom from prejudice, as much as his blatant self-interest, had combined to offer an outlet to the philanthropic energies and social aspirations of the creators of new money, English or immigrant, Jewish and Gentile. His wishes in such matters, if not welcomed by society at large, were nonetheless observed. The King's death was the occasion to which many envious and resentful members of the old order had been looking forward for a purge of those whom even Margot Asquith labelled the 'Court Pests'. Their style, indeed, was not to the taste of the new King. 'It might be a dull court', Sir Edward Hamilton had foreseen, 'but it will certainly be a respectable one.' For the conspicuously rich, those that had crossed the blurred borderline between acceptable and unseemly riches, their pocket books had provided them with a passport to the short cut into Society. But as sudden as had been their ascension, their acceptance had not extended far beyond the immediate entourage of their prince and patron, though the City was understandably more reverent than Society towards its own sons. However, with prosperity percolating down from Cassel's marble halls in Park Lane to Pooter's modest villa in Brickfield Terrace, Holloway, those values which Queen Victoria had earlier discerned and deplored in the aristocracy – 'frivolity, the love of pleasure, self-indulgence, luxury and idleness' – were no longer the sole prerogative of the affluent; twenty years later such savoury dissipations were increasingly within the reach not only of the professional middle classes but of shopkeepers and clerks, an achievement owing not a little to the enterprise of a later wave of resourceful Jews who fashioned a new niche in catering (Lyons, Salmon and Gluckstein), tailoring (Burton) and 'bazaar stores' (Marks, Sieff and Cohen).

The consequence, subsequently severely diagnosed by a contemporary analyst of the Victorian age and its 'flash Edwardian epilogue', was a discernible diminution of 'intelligence, character and purpose'. Religious indifference had largely succeeded the sectarian animosity of the early Victorian years. Though nationalist prejudices were sporadically stirred and sustained by the press, former fears of immigration of 'alien paupers', the great majority Jewish, had largely subsided; industrious and provident, they were concentrated in close-knit kindred and politically assertive communities. The scions of the pioneering plutocrats themselves wore their money more modestly, its mint condition muted and its rough edges worn smooth by use. The native-born effortlessly integrated with their peers, often through intermarriage, and were otherwise indistinguishable in education and culture, with only their names, and sometimes faith, to remind others of their origins; when the salvage operation for Barings was mounted in 1890 it was notable that only a handful of the City's leading lights bore English names.

England's Jews were fortunate in the personal characters and professional ethics of their champions. They never abused the power of their deep pockets. There was no breath of scandal or hint of sharp practice. This set them apart. If any had failed to keep to this path of rectitude, as did too many who also darkened the doors of Marlborough House and Sandringham, then tolerance might have turned into hatred, ridicule and contempt. The first Lord Rothschild's obituarist hailed him as, 'at once a Prince in Israel and an Englishman of whom all England could be proud'. He was not an exception, rather *primus inter pares*.

The phenomenon was viewed rather differently from the other side. If all civic and political disabilities under which the Jews had laboured had long been removed, social restraint and vestigial prejudice lingered on in salons and smoking rooms. The success of the Jewish money magnates, quite disproportionate to their numbers in the population, had an effect on their entire community. There was pride, certainly, in their worldly rank and material achievement, more than a tithe of which rubbed off on the needy. Undoubtedly, too, their example served to instil into the newly arrived immigrants toiling in the sweatshops of Whitechapel, racial pride and the resolution to escape from poverty. But the price of this successful assimilation was, to the dismay of the orthodox, a dissipation of faith more telling than any results of the proselytizing Christian societies for the conversion of Jews. In the long run, a liberal Jewish historian considered, the adverse effects of their close association with the throne were greater by far; 'this royal recognition resulted in hastening a process of disintegration among the upper classes of English Jewry – sometimes more discernible in the younger generation' who demanded their place in the forefront of Jewish affairs in which they were 'barely and perfunctorily' interested. Furthermore, through the example of the few, their religion was identified with riches in the popular imagination, arousing envy and resentment for which their poorer brethren, particularly in London's East End, often suffered.

It was doubtless sensitivity to their presence which, among other considerations, persuaded Sir Sidney Lee, born Solomon Lazarus Levi, the son of Hungarian Jewish immigrants, when invited by King George V to write his father's biography, to consign King Edward's Jewish friends to the wings. He gave the game away with a defensive disclaimer tucked into the text that, though there was, 'some criticism at the time of the prominence in the King's circle of his Jewish friends . . . they were more than balanced by friends of British aristocratic descent . . . fairly representative of the flower of the peerage'. This was, at the least, uncommonly naive of the man who had been editor of the *Dictionary of National Biography*. The role of the Rothschilds, Sassoons, Hirsch and

Cassel was watered down; among lesser figures Sir Felix Semon, who engaged in a long uphill battle to tend the royal tubes ravaged by cigar smoke, was credited with his German, but not his Jewish, descent; Sir George Lewis, of whom another Jewish historian wrote that he was, 'one of the most quoted figures in the chronicles and the biographies of the time', did not once figure in the monumental two-volume work.

If such circumspection be judged otiose today, like partisan passions, both racial and religious, have, leaving aside the performance of the aberrant twin agencies of fascism and communism, been rekindled some one hundred years later. Though the Balkans may no longer feature as a theatre for inter-Power rivalry, from the old Pale of Settlement to the Black Sea, age-old animosities towards ethnic minorities are once again raising their heads to tax the ingenuity of a new race of raw statesmen; fears of renewed anti-Semitic agitation have not been effectively dispelled in the precarious patchwork of the Russian Empire. Within (and beyond) the southernmost confines of the former Ottoman domains another faction-ridden Semitic faith is undergoing a fundamentalist resurgence clothed in clerical xenophobia; Zionism itself has betrayed its founders' ideals of a secular and socialist homeland founded on conciliatory co-existence. Western Europe, engaged in sublimating its own ancient conflicting ambitions, is assailed by fresh anxieties for finding itself again the refuge for the destitute and downtrodden from the East; Britain, France and even Germany are already home to large foreign-born communities, distinct and indigestible, where superficial harmony is uneasily preserved by regulation. Despite the present-day insistence on rights, too often to the detriment of responsibilities, their predecessors, sturdily optimistic and self-reliant fugitives from religious persecution, would with hindsight perhaps have regarded themselves as exceptionally blessed. King Edward's friends had set them a precedent – and a worthy pattern.

Source References

Source references are prefaced by the number of the page on which the source is quoted, followed by the catch-phrase with which to identify the passage. Where the sources are books listed in the Select Bibliography, they are referred to simply by the surname of the authors, followed by the volume numbers (where appropriate) in Roman numerals, and the page numbers; where more than one book by the same author is listed in the Bibliography, a brief indication of the title is added, i.e. Paul H. Emden's *Jews of Britain* is rendered as Emden, *Jews*.

The following abbreviations have been used to refer to other sources:

Bdlds   The Papers of Sir Ernest Cassel, Broadlands, Hampshire
EH   The Diaries of Sir Edward Hamilton, British Library
HBS   The Papers of Sir Henry Babington Smith, Trinity College, Cambridge
PRO   Foreign Office, General Correspondence, Public Record Office
RA   Royal Archives, Windsor Castle

I have not thought it necessary to give all the references relating to Edward VII's early life and education, which are all available in the standard biographies.

Introduction
p. 3 'horrid Russians'. St Aubyn, 66.
p. 4 'more sense'. Gwynn, I, 501–2.
   'undisputed authority'. Viscount Esher, *The Influence of King Edward & Other Essays* (1915), 42.
   'combining bonhomie'. Viscount Grey of Fallodon, *Twenty-Five Years* (1925), II, 206.
p. 5 'Queen invisible'. Magnus, 111.
p. 6 'inexorable necessities'. Tuchman, 12.

p. 7 'best day's shooting'. Hibbert, 226.
p. 8 'fishmonger's account'. Rothschild, 30.
p. 14 'innate sense'. Benson, *Are*, 239.

Chapter 1 – Rothschilds: Breaking Down the Barriers
p. 18 'work the Court': Davis, 75–6.
   '*a gentleman*': Emden, *Jews*, 204.

p. 19 'sufficient force': ibid. 213.

p. 20 'a glorious day': Shaftesbury to Gladstone, 2 December 1862. Roth, 'Court Jews', 358.

p. 21 'not very robust': Davis, 78–9.
'select sheepfold': E. F. Benson, *King Edward VII: An Appreciation* (1933), 151.
'little harm': Roth, *Rothschilds*, 83.
'15 per cent': Leonore Davidoff. *The Best Circles* (1973), 60.

p. 22 'his private character': James Bryce, *The American Commonwealth* (New York, 1910) II, 815.
'Certainly *money*': Dowager Countess Cowper to Earl Cowper, October 1874. *Memoir of Earl Cowper* by his wife (privately printed 1913).
'conspicuous consumption': Thorstein Veblen, *The Theory of the Leisure Class* (1899).
'marked predilection': Bülow, II, 183.

p. 23 'moneyed associates': EH, LI, 5 November 1902.
'not but feel': EH, XLII, 19 June 1897.

p. 24 'financial matters': Bdlds, X1, E VII to Cassel, 15 August, 1908.
'makes it impossible': St Aubyn, 84.

p. 25 'unable to do much': Magnus, 63.
'Thank God': St Aubyn, 117–18.
'long as capital lasts': Knollys Papers, 20 March, 1865.
'postponed much longer': Hibbert, 200.

p. 26 Oxford Street dealer: S. N. Behrman, *Duveen* (1952), 42.

p. 27 'nice young Court': Emily Eden to Lord Clarendon, 1866. St Aubyn, 135.
'curious mixture': H. E. Wortham, *Delightful Profession* (1931), 190.

'*absolutely* necessary': Davis, 112.
'perfectly *safe*': ibid., 132.
'commonplace and slow': ibid., 113–14.

p. 28 'cordiality and frankness': ibid., 110.
£20,000 for capital: ibid., Lord Rothschild, *The Shadow of a Great Man*. 23.
60,000 sovereigns: Lord Rothschild, *The Shadow of a Great Man* (1982), 41–7.

p. 29 Rothschild capital: Davis, 33.
'uncouth': Roth, 'Court Jews', 357.
'everything to business': Davis, 21.
'marry a Christian': ibid., 59–60.
Thomas Baring: Ziegler, 170–1.

p. 30 Disraeli humbug: M. Rothschild, 26.
'Though very eloquent': ibid., 31.
'snug': Gladstone, 21 April 1879, 154.
'much as a romp': Wilson, 221–2.

p. 31 'agitation and': ibid., 222.
Russian commoner: J. O. Field, 165.
'great outcry': Spencer to Knollys, St Aubyn, 128.

p. 32 'two chairs': Emden, *Jews*, 284.
'Natty's death': B. E. C. Dugdale, *Arthur James Balfour* (1936), II, 35.

p. 33 'good heart but': M. Rothschild, 11n.
'positive greed': Roth, *Rothschilds*, 172.
'all his life': Crewe, II, 653.
'dear old duck': Davis, 126.
'effete': Lady Walpurga Paget, *In My Tower* (1924), 109–10.
promised £2,000: Roth, *Rothschilds*, 172.

p. 34 'need his help': Sykes, 309.

p. 35 'the Medici': Roth, *Rothschilds*, 217.
'large, fat': Davis, 165.
moral wrench: Crewe, I, 117.

'with force': James, 84.

'poignant grief': *Jewish Chronicle*, 5 October 1877. Ibid., 84.

p. 36 'am Jewish': M. Rothschild, 3.

'weird and wonderful':
M. Rothschild, 7.

'fairy-land':, ibid., 6.

'old red': Asquith, *Memories*, 98.

'glorified old': Algernon West, 313.

'exaggerated nightmare': ibid., 84.

'wonderful brightness': EH, XLI, 27 October 1896.

'extreme gorgeousness': Gladstone, 21 April 1879, 154.

p. 37 'bottomless purses': Warwick, *Afterthoughts*, 258.

Ortolans farcis: Davis, 99–100.

'know exactly': Roth, *Rothschilds*, 214.

p. 38 'extraordinarily uninteresting': Gwynn, I, 435.

'titbits': Hibbert, 146.

'magnificent supply': St Aubyn, 232.

p. 39 'judicious indiscretion': ibid., 204.

'completely informed': Viscount Esher, *Cloud Capp'd Towers* (1927), 173–4.

'Quite right': Davis, 123–4.

p. 40 Pall Mall club: Blunt, *Diaries*, I, 96.

Natty in London: John Morley, *Life of W. E. Gladstone* (1903), II, 325.

p. 41 'pheasants at Ferrières': Wilson, 209.

p. 42 'flirtations': Countess of Warwick, *Life's Ebb and Flow* (1929), 74.

'only Jew': Painter, I, 92.

'never heard': ibid., I, 161–2.

p. 43 'most thoroughly': Benson, *Were*, 237.

'little Bohemian': Blunt, *Diaries*, I, 721–2.

'very unsatisfactory': Magnus, 128.

'horrible fright': Rosebery Papers. Hibbert, 305 n. 118.

La Barucci: Allen Andrews, *The Follies of King Edward VII* (1975), 92.

p. 44 'make my début': Janet Flanner, *Paris was Yesterday* (New York, 1973), 13–14.

p. 45 'shameless character': Lady Frederick Cavendish, *Diary*, ed. John Bailey (1927), II, 235.

'deaf and disinclined': Gwynn, I, 414.

'Vive': Hibbert, 255.

'one not likely': Magnus, 155.

p. 46 'merry supper': X. Paoli, *My Royal Clients* (1911), 206.

'no little delicacy': Magnus, 155.

Chapter 2 – Sassoons: Baghdad to Belgravia

p. 48 'pig-sticking': Hibbert, 127.

'creatures': Magnus, 133.

'*never* would': Hibbert, 126.

p. 49 'monks': Lincolnshire Papers. Ibid., 129.

'Tell Mama': ibid., 130.

p. 51 'sending a son': *Illustrated London News*, 5 December 1863.

p. 52 'malign influence': Hibbert, 135.

p. 53 'most delightful': Asquith, *Memories*, 221.

p. 55 'opened his mouth': Cornwallis-West, 103.

Reuben Chancellor: Fitzroy, II, 193.

'impudent Semite': J. O. Field, 330.

p. 56 Burmarsh Farm: Lord Rothschild, *The Shadow of a Great Man*, 32.

bowstrung: Nevill, 208–9.

p. 57 'most beautiful': Chauncey M. Depew, *My Memories of Eighty Years* (1922), 195.

'corrupt constituency': Hardinge to Lansdowne. McLean, 'Informal Empire', 298.

p. 58 'are snops': Nevill, 200.

p. 59 'undertook, if possible': H. Drummond Wolff, *Rambling Recollections* October 1889, II, 371.

p. 60 'blood of Abraham': Nevill, 115–17. Ralph Nevill was a cousin of Lady Georgina Wolff and served under her husband, Sir Henry, as attaché and private secretary in Tehran and Madrid.

p. 61 'scrap of morals': Paget, I, 213.

p. 62 'Notre Dame': Hans Tietze, *Die Juden Wiens* (1932), 231.

p. 64 'most beautiful': Corti, II, 167.
'All the brothers': ibid., 135.

p. 65 'devil fetches': ibid., 276.
'peace of the world': J. A. Froude, *The Earl of Beaconsfield* (1890), 186.

p. 67 Footnote: 'am astonished': Davis, 227.
'27 Archdukes': Lady Bloomfield to Queen Victoria, 26 January 1869. Magnus, 101.
Pope for permission: RA Z.280/53, Sir Edward Malet to Sir Henry Ponsonby, 9 February, 1889.

p. 68 Rudolf's mother: E. Corti, *Elizabeth: Empress of Austria* (1936), 456–93.
60,000 gulden: Count Carl Lonyay, *Rudolf: The Tragedy of Mayerling* (1950), 143.

p. 69 'probably Hirsch': Salisbury Papers 3M/Class E, Lytton to Salisbury, 14 November 1889.
Westminster Gazette, 30 April 1896.
fifteen million francs: Paul Cambon, 23 February 1901. French Documentary Series, 2, Vol. I, 100.
Grunwald, *Türkenhirsch*, 94.

Chapter 3 – Türkenhirsch: A Bavarian in the Balkans

p. 71 'loyalty': Adler-Rudel, 7.
£70,000: ibid., 8.
'selfless devotion': ibid., 9.

p. 72 'not without risk': Weizmann, 14.

p. 73 'think Rothschild': Grunwalk, *Türkenhirsch*, 16.

p. 74 diplomat's wife: Baroness Ainis de Wilmar. Ibid., 18.

'sceptical of you': ibid., 21.
'Croesus': ibid., 22.

p. 75 'authentic documents': Stock Exchange Loan and Company Prospectuses, 1864. Guildhall Library MSS 18,000.
sickly shares: M. Rothschild, 9.

p. 76 'cunning, force': G. W. F. Hallgarten, *Imperialismus vor 1914*, I, 212, Munich 1951.
'the pivot': *The Times*, 21 August 1888.

p. 78 plans leaked: PRO Domestic various, Vienna, 6 December 1867.
'hold Count Beust': Jenks, 269.
Wodianer: Sigmund Mayer, *Wiener Juden* (1930), 292.

p. 81 'mon métier': Prince Chlodwig von Hohenlohe-Schillingsfürst, *Memoirs* (1906), II, 173.

p. 82 *The Times*, 21 August 1888.
German newspaper: Grunwald, *Türkenhirsch*, 33.
'handsome commission': EH, XLIV, 19 June 1898.
'second thoughts': ibid., 22 June 1898.

p. 83 'evidently fears': ibid., 27 July 1898.
Mahmud confessed: Radoslav M. Dimchov, *Das Eisenbahnwesen auf der Balkan-Halbinsel* (Bamberg, 1894), 35.

p. 84 'Japanese ivories': Graves, 40.
Philip Graves, *The Times* correspondent in Constantinople for many years, was the first to expose *The Protocols of the Elders of Zion* as forgeries.

p. 85 Veneziani: *The Times*, 15 October 1877.
£40,000: *Jewish Chronicle*, 24 April 1896.
Belgian traveller: Emil de Lavelaye, *The Balkan Peninsula* (1887), 265.

p. 86 'intimacy': Grunwald, *Türkenhirsch*, 44.

strongly seconded: The *Times*, 21
August 1888.

'always busy': Grunwald,
Türkenhirsch, 46.

distributed charity: £10,000 for the
Austrian Patriotic Fund for war
veterans; an endowment for the maintenance of the Jewish girls' orphanage
in Budapest.

p. 88 informed Dilke: Gwynn, I, 435.

p. 89 onerous specification: *The Times*,
21 August 1888.

advanced £1 million: Grunwald,
Türkenhirsch, 58.

p. 90 Clara paid: Oscar Straus, *Under
Four Administrations* (Boston, Mass.,
1925), 95.

'Any transaction': ibid., 94.

'I may proceed': Gneist to Hirsch.
Kohler Papers, American Jewish
Historical Society. Grunwald,
Türkenhirsch, 59.

p.92 bright young men: Karl Morawitz,
Les Finances de la Turquie (Paris,
1902), 422. Morawitz, a former correspondent of Hirsch's brother-in-law,
Heinrich Bamberger, of Paribas,
joined the Ottoman Bank in 1870;
financial director of the Orient
Railway 1871; director (1885) and
president (1906), Anglo-Austrian
Bank.

Jewish Chronicle, 24 April 1896.

'my principles': Eckardstein, 53–4.

p. 93 'never flattering': *Neues Wiener
Tageblatt*, 22 April 1896.

'humanity is my heir':
Adler-Rudel, 15.

secretary testified: Gustav Held, 15
March 1910. Kohler Papers,
American Jewish Historical Society.

p. 94 four pictures: Weizmann, 24.

'fat Edward': Smalley (1912), 258.

$100 million: Oscar Straus, *Jewish
Encyclopaedia*.

'knew thoroughly': Martin, I, 270.

p. 95 'all these people': Drumont, II, 87.

p.   Footnote: 'lackey': A. Netch-
vollodow, *L'Empereur Nicolas II et les
Juifs* (1924), 125.

'painfully impressed': Grunwald,
Türkenhirsch, 66.

p. 96 Liveliest satisfaction: *Jewish
Chronicle*, 24 April 1896.

p. 97 later biographer: Gordon
Brook-Shepherd, 49.

Chapter 4 – Dangerous Liaisons

p. 98 'human weaknesses': Emden,
Money Powers, 323.

'sturdy radicalism': *Jewish Chronicle*, 24 April 1896.

'agree with every word': ibid.

p. 99 'unpretentious': RA Geo V
AA.18/32, E VII to Prince George,
12 October 1890.

'good one or not': Magnus, 219.

Lucien Wolf: *Jewish Chronicle*, 8
May 1896, 'Glimpses of Baron
Hirsch'. Wolf was one of the found-
ers of the Jewish Historical Society of
England.

p. 100 'simple, natural': Herzl, 19.

'sanguine and': Jenks, 269.

dreadfully annoyed: Knollys to
Ponsonby, 26 June 1890. Magnus,
219.

p. 101 'couldn't afford': Grunwald,
Türkenhirsch, 105.

'archdukes gasped': Magnus,
221.

'simple and healthy': Mrs
George Cornwallis-West, *The Re-
miniscences of Lady Randolph Churchill*
(1908), 218.

'amaze you': RA Geo V
AA.18/32, E VII to Prince George of
York, 12 October 1890.

'beats everything': RA Geo V
AA.18/33, E VII to Prince George of
York, 19 October 1890.

persistent practice: Portland,
230–1.

'rich, vulgar': Andrews, 13–14.

p. 102 pointedly excluded: Roth, 'Court Jews', 363.

'glad to receive': White, 73.

'Three cheers': John Porter, *An Autobiography* (1919), 330.

name to the animal: Sewell, 161–5.

p. 103 'property of a German': ibid., 171–2.

'London hospitals': The *Times*, 22 April 1896.

'Come 'ungry': Nevill, 95.

'not on account': Eckardstein, 54.

p. 104 'nature distrustful': Münz, 250.

'throw good money': Nellie Melba, *Melodies and Memories* (1925), 190–1.

'intellectual energy': Drumont, II, 5 eme Livre.

p. 105 'slightest idea': Asquith, Autobiography, I, 95–9.

p. 106 'career of own': ibid., I, 162.

'Take this cigar': Drumont, I 200.

inexpensive melons: Emden, *Money Powers*, 320.

p. 107 'chaque scrupule': Drumont, II, 85–6.

compromising letter: Joachim von Kuremberg, *His Excellency the Spectre: The Life of Fritz von Holstein* (1933), 24.

'worked the market': Stern, 238.

p. 108 honourable successor: Prince Chlodwig von Hohenlohe Schillingsfürst, *Memoirs* (1906), II, 121, 172, 206, 293.

taken to be Jewish: Lonergan, 159.

p. 109 'France for Frenchmen': Herzl, Introduction.

'none of the pride': Drumont, II 85.

caught in the neck: Lonergan, 87.

p. 110 'Hirsch was not averse': Grunwald, *Türkenhirsch*, 88.

'knees shook': Martin, II, 269–70.

'three Macabres': R. Churchill, I,

174–5. 13 January 1892.

ears of Foreign Office: PRO Calendar of Letters, 6 January 1889.

'poor creature': Martin, II, 166.

'A bientôt': Nevill, 276–7.

p. 111 'thousand-franc notes': Drumont, II, 85.

'swallowed insults': Sewell, 161–5.

'half a Jew': Herzl, 191.

'faithful friend': Münz, 100.

The Times, 22 April 1896.

'typical Orleans': R. von Kühlmann, *Erinnerungen* (1948), 443.

p. 112 'especially his nose': Sir Valentine Chirol, *Fifty Years in a Changing World* (1927), 127.

'felt so uncomfortable': Portland, 136.

'Dear Baron': Philippe Jullian, *Edward and the Edwardians* (1967), 195.

Chapter 5 – Philanthropy in the Pampas

p. 114 'rather strange': E. J. Bing (ed.), *The Letters of the Tsar Nicholas II and the Empress Marie* (1937), 84.

p. 115 £50. Litvinoff, 220.

'are socialists': Davis, 234.

passionate obscurantist: Crankshaw, 279.

£70 million: Davis, 156.

p. 116 'anti-Semitic backlash': Zoza Szajkowsji, 'How the Mass Migration to America Began', *Jewish Social Studies*, Vol. IV, No. 4 (October 1942), 291ff.

p. 117 'wild men': Weizmann, 58.

'worst element': Szajkowsji, op. cit.

p. 118 650,000 Jews: Litvinoff, 226.

'poor boy': Paul F. Boller and Ronald L. Davis, *Hollywood Anecdotes* (1987).

burning a hole: Norman, 19.

encouraged by Prince: Roth,

'Court Jews', 365.

p. 119 'undesirable aliens': White, 5.
'international capitalists': Searle, 26, 120, 133.
'work out': EH, XLIII, St Petersburg, undated.
'typical Jew': White, Appendix, 294–301.
Samson and Delilah: Elaine Brody, *Paris: The Musical Kaleidoscope 1870–1925* (1988).

p. 120 Weizmann: Litvinoff, 232.
unrealistically rosy: Adler-Rudel, 24.

p. 121 seven other: In addition to Lord Rothschild and Sir Ernest Cassel, these were: Sir Julian Goldsmid, PC, MP, President Anglo-Jewish Association, and Chairman, Russo-Jewish Committee; S. H. Goldschmidt, President, and Salomon Reinach, Alliance Israélite Universelle, Paris; Benjamin L. Cohen, President, Jewish Board of Guardians; and F. D. Mocatta, scholar and bibliophile.

p. 122 estate duty: Norman M. Bentwich, 'More Anglo-Jewish Leading Cases', *Jewish Historical Society*, Vol. XVI (1932), 160.
'form of idolatry': Weizmann, 230.
Lowenthall packed back: Norman, 22ff.
white slave: ibid., 309, n. 4.

p. 123 flew into a rage: ibid., 24.
'my difficulty': *Jewish Chronicle*, 24 July 1891. Adler-Rudel, 30.
Albert Goldsmid: Emden, *Jews*, 146–7.

p. 124 'Michael': Theodor Herzl, *Yearbook* (Vienna, 1937), 203.
'idea is great': Adler-Rudel, 32.
optimistic paper: *Report on Baron Hirsch's Jewish Colonisation Scheme*, HMSO, No. 323, March 1894.

p. 125 'keenly sensible': White, 131–5.

family's debt: Norman, 32.

p. 126 'root and branch': ibid., 35.
'German hausfrau': Lady Augusta Fane, *Chit-Chat* (1926), 282.
'sown wheat': Norman, 39.
lost confidence: Adler-Rudel, 41.
'first-class British': Herzl Diaries, 18.

p. 127 'filthy abuse': EH XLVI, 3 December 1899.
'French beans': Nevill, 289.
'Jewish-political': Herzl Diaries, 13–28.

p. 130 'few millions': ibid., 109.
agent Veneziani: Adler-Rudel, 38–40.
'no government': EH, XLI, 17 September, 1896.
always reckoned: Herzl Diaries, 133.

p. 131 'universal heiress': *Jewish Chronicle*, 15 May 1896.
'myself decide': Tuchman, 327.

p. 132 legitimate children: Verwaltungsarchiv, Vienna.
Maurice Arnold's son: Count John de Bendern to author.
Austrian descendants: Donald Freiherr von Hirsch to Dr Dorothea McEwan.

p. 133 'satisfaction of knowing': Herzl Diaries, 439.
street disappeared: Adler-Rudel, 45n.
Jacob Schiff: letter to *New York Times*, 11 May 1900. Grunwald Türkenhirsch. 75.

Chapter 6 – Cassel: American Apprenticeship

p. 135 unlimited confidence: Hirsch's will: *Jewish Chronicle*, 15 May 1896.
'Visit Emperor': Magnus, 247.
'fat man': Lincolnshire Papers. Ibid., 247.

p. 136 'handle all that money': Painter, I, 156.

'thought to economize': Stanley Weintraub, *Victoria* (1987), 591.

Hirsch left instructions: Count John de Bendern to author.

Viennese journalist: Münz, 243–4.

p. 137 'renewal of your offer': Bdlds, X1, E VII to Cassel, 21 April 1901.

'exclusive of Grafton': Bdlds, X3, Cassel to E VII, 5 February 1903.

'man who can commit': *The Times*, 23 September 1921.

'not had his head turned': EH, LIII, 29 December 1904.

'whenever he wanted': Japhet, 127.

'make for happiness': Bdlds, A.1000a, Cassel to Stella Underhill.

'strange and barren': Benson, *Ave*, 239.

p. 138 'superfluous urbanity': *The Times*, 23 September 1921.

'friends for life': Lee, 60.

'not self-evident': EH, LIII, 29 December 1904.

'greatly . . . always interests': Bdlds, E VII to Cassel, Isle of Wight, 1906, Marienbad, 3 September 1908.

'cleverest head': H. E. Wortham, *Delightful Profession* (1931), 371.

p. 139 'striking nor': Semon, 235.

'indefinable tang': Harris, III, 160.

'illegitimate grandson': Blunt Papers, Fitzwilliam Museum. Longford, 376.

p. 140 'gilt-edged security': Keppel, 23.

long-time colleague: Japhet, 125.

'much happier': Bdlds, A.1000a, Cassel to Stella Underhill.

another version: Connell, 56.

'200,000 marks': Japhet, 130.

p. 141 Edward VII's biographer: Lee, 60.

p. 142 'financial vultures': Report of the Select Committee on Loans to Foreign States, Vol. IX, Parliamentary Papers, 1875.

Footnote: 'Jew's a harp': Jenks, 254.

'mean £5,000': Emden, *Jews*, 335.

'never got less': *The Times*, 23 September 1921.

'hard work': ibid.

p. 143 'Better a lean': Connell, 60.

left £4,500: Pat Thane, *Dictionary of Business Biography*, I, 605.

Privy Councillor: Fitzroy, I, 97.

dying wish: Benson, *Are*, 236.

p. 145 capital of £150,000: *Dictionary of National Biography*. The entry was based on private information supplied by a Mr Geddes, who joined Cassel as an office junior in 1893.

'brokerage connection': Adler, I, 14. Schiff to Cassel, 28 May 1883.

p. 146 'aggressively ambitious': *New York Times*, Kuhn, Loeb Centenary, 1 February 1967.

Mer de Glace: Adler, II, 322.

'Frieda is standing': ibid., 333.

'most faithful friend': ibid., 329. Schiff to Cassel, Vienna, 15 April 1894.

p. 147 'your kindness': ibid., 331. Schiff to Cassel, 8 October 1886.

'there is nothing': ibid., 331. Schiff to Cassel, 30 December 1889.

'I shall answer': ibid., I, 30. Schiff to Cassel, 14 May 1884.

p. 148 'not share at all': ibid, 152.

'personally can remain': ibid., 60.

'promising enterprise': ibid., 83–6.

'shocking experience': Andrews, 188.

p. 149 'no one in Europe': Adler, I, 113.

'Here I am': ibid., 116.

p. 150 large issue direct: Ziegler, 294.

'now both direct': Adler, I, 157.

'permanent check': ibid., 200.

p. 151 never again entered: Emden, *Jews*, 336.

'commission': Stern, 427.

'only possible conclusion': Adler, I, 205.

'much to be regretted': ibid. Schiff to Albert Ballin, 13 January 1914.

Chapter 7 – Eastern Enterprise

p. 154 'power, power': Sebastian Haffner, *Germany's Self-Destruction* (1989), 4.

'only one master': Tuchman, 240.

'hot-headed': *Letters of Queen Victoria*, 3rd Series, I, 440–1. Balfour, 123.

'all there': Lady Gwendoline Cecil, *Life of Robert, Marquis of Salisbury* (4 vols, 1932), IV, 367.

Maurice Baring, *The Puppet Show of Memory* (Cassell, 1987), 129, 173–5.

Rothschild vengeful: Ziegler, 247.

p. 155 'greatest effort': ibid., 248.

'Still pondering': Thane, *Business History*. Schiff to Cassel 25 November 1890.

'call that rich': Benson, *Are*, 240.

'considerable excitement': EH, XLIII, 12 December 1897.

p. 156 'had one trump': Stanley F. Wright, *Hart and the Chinese Customs*, (1950).

'Bank could answer': McLean, 'Foreign Office', 303–21.

p. 157 'conceal his hope': ibid., 319.

The *Times*, 26 September 1895.

'great mortification': EH, XLIII, 6 January 1898.

'so bellicose': ibid., 27 January 1898.

p. 158 'scored in China': ibid., 25 February 1898.

'excluded from China': ibid., XLIV, 9 March 1898.

'have bungled': ibid., 1 May 1898.

'clever move': ibid., 19 March 1898.

Secretary of State: John W. Foster. Adler, 243.

p. 159 'Chinese transaction': Thane, *Business History*, 97 n. 28.

'feels obliged': Esher, II, 266.

'demands were exorbitant': Fairbank et al., II, 972.

'Cassel affair': ibid., 974.

'knocked on the head': ibid., 983.

'absolutely sacred': EH, XLVII, 24 July 1900.

'close privacy': PRO, August 1906, 10 28793 and 5489, FO 371.27.

p. 161 'It's lovely': Bdlds, X19, Fisher to Cassel, 19 November.

'pleasantest features': Ziegler, 289.

moving spirit: T. C. Barker and M. Robbins, *A History of London Transport* (2 vols, 1974), I, 39–41.

p. 163 'right people': Grunwald, 'Windsor-Cassel', 132.

p. 164 'borrowing at 30 per cent': David S. Landes, *Bankers and Pashas* (Harvard, 1958), 338ff.

Rivers Wilson: Blunt, *Secret History*, 241.

p. 165 £4,000 a year: ibid., 334.

'arrogant altruism': Lutfi al-Sayyid, 139.

'found themselves': Alfred Duff Cooper. Anthony Nutting, *The Arabs* (1964), 372.

'sound financial': Viscount d'Abernon, *Portraits and Appreciations* (1931), 14. As Sir Edgar Vincent, d'Abernon was for many years adviser to the Egyptian Ministry of Finance.

p. 116 'extreme delicacy': Crewe, I, 212.

advanced £1 million: Roth, *Rothschilds*, 110.

'heartily wish': Salisbury Papers, Salisbury to H. Drummond Wolff, 23 February 1887. Lutfi al-Sayyid, 47.

'European capital': PRO FO 633/8, 18 December 1895. Thane, *Business History*, 90.

'French are mad': Magnus, 254.

p. 167 considering selling: EH XLI, 25 October 1896.

Treasury was proposing: ibid., XLIII, 13 and 16 December 1897.

Alfred Rothschild: ibid., XLVII, 28 April 1900.

'never submitted': R. K. Middlemas, *The Master Builders* (1963), 145.

'Mind you try': R. S. Churchill, I, 426.

p. 168 'best investment': Middlemas, op. cit., 145.

'now express': ibid., 147.

4,000 per cent: Longford, 358.

'know nothing': Grunwald, 'Windsor Cassel', 135.

p. 169 over £13 million: A. B.Guernville, *New Egypt* (1905), 52–3.

German capital: Middlemas, op. cit., 146.

p. 170 below £20: Bdlds, X3, Cassel to E VII, 29 November 1902.

'we rejoice': Adler, 334.

Rumbold: Brook-Shepherd, 133.

p. 171 'very pleasant': EH, LIII, 23 August 1904.

'I should hardly': Bdlds, X3, E VII to Cassel, 30 December 1902.

'ill and aged': ibid., 17 February 1903.

'King's millionaire': Blunt, *Diaries*, 63, 25 June 1903.

p. 172 retire Cromer: ibid., 90, 10 March 1904.

his predecessor: Sir Clinton Dawkins: Milner Papers. Al-Sayyid, 81.

'hardened opportunist': Clara Boyle, *A Servant of the Empire: Memoir of Harry Boyle* (1938), 113. Al-Sayyid, 82.

Cromer disapproved: Blunt, *Diaries*, 97, 5 April 1904.

Cassel intervened: Bdlds, X17, Gorst to Cassel, 26 February 1904.

'very vigilant': Ziegler, 276.

p. 173 '*so* cheap': Storrs, 82.

The Times correspondent: Graves, 148–9.

'am happy': Blunt, *Diaries*, 276, 19 August 1909.

'seems to take': Storrs, 52.

'actual determining': Lord Sanderson, Permanent Under-Secretary of State for Foreign Affairs. Al-Sayyid, 135.

'upon considerations': HBS, 30, 102.

p. 174 'oblige the Government': EH, Add MS 48680–3, 22 April 1903.

'mainly a difference': ibid., 21 May 1903.

'Moorish loan': ibid., 30 December 1903.

Mufti revealed: Blunt, *Diaries*, 98, 10 April 1904.

Footnote: Gavin Maxwell, *Lords of the Atlas* (Century, 1983), 27.

p. 175 King displeased: Hardinge, 164.

verbal approval: Asquith MSS, Bodleian, 83, folio 33.

'loss of time': ibid., folio 107/8, Knollys to Nash, 18 December 1908.

Whip was selling: Searle, 147.

'childish desire': Vansittart, 61.

Chapter 8 – Jews at Court

p. 176 'see Baron Hirsch': R. S. Churchill, I, 169.

his new clothes: ibid., 170.

p. 177 'something very good': ibid., 182.

'communicated everything': Rosebery MSS 10176. Foster, 311n.

'spending his weekends': *Sunday Sun*, 3 July 1904. Searle, 50.

first consulting: Davis, 205.

'trouble might': Rosebery MSS 10032. Foster, 331.

'damned dots': Shane Leslie, *The End of a Chapter* (1916), 30.

'make a little money': Stanley Jackson, *The Great Barnato* (1970), 136.

p. 178 'sown the seed': M. Rothschild, 47n.

£65,000: Davis, 202.

'Cornwallis-Wests': EH, xlviii, 6 December 1900.

'short on brains': Martin, ii, 144.

'Not the City?': Cornwallis-West, 123.

'measures words': Fitzroy, ii, 516.

p. 179 'little present': Cornwallis-West, 159–60.

Winston guest: W. S. Churchill, *Early Life*, 247.

unusually sued: R. S. Churchill, *Lord Derby: 'King of Lancashire'* (1959), 112.

p. 180 Footnote: M. Rothschild, 80.

'Feed my sheep': W. S.-Churchill, *Early Life*, 376.

'war was almost over': Martin, ii, 245.

'Cassel ready': ibid., 246.

p. 181 'behind the scenes': EH, xlvii, 12 February 1900.

called on to defend: *The Times*, 28 February 1901.

'Cassel and Schuster': EH, xlvii, 7 March 1900.

'don't think': ibid., 11 March 1900.

'Magersfontein': ibid., 13 March 1900.

'very agreeable': ibid., xlvi, 23 May 1899.

'small guy': ibid., xlvii, 16 March 1900.

p. 182 'nob friends': Anita Leslie, *Edwardians in Love* (1974), 238.

Sister Agnes: King Edward VII's Hospital for Officers: Historical Record, 1952.

p. 183 'delightful companion': Sermoneta, 136.

crown of diamonds: Hough, 24.

'fill throne': EH, xlviii, 22 January 1901.

p. 184 importuned by temptation: *The Times* 23 January 1901.

'shows how easy': EH, xlix, 13 May 1901.

'dining about': ibid., 15 May 1901.

'going round': ibid., 9 June 1901.

'sensible of the honour': ibid., 22 July 1901.

'fact is': ibid., 3 August 1901.

p. 185 'some indiscretion': ibid., lii, 11 November 1903.

'continuously surrounded': ibid., liv, 3 May 1905.

peerage for Cassel: Searle, 90.

'nobody here': EH, xlix, 29 April 1901.

'share the same': James Pope-Hennessy (ed.), *Livre d'Or* (1957).

p. 186 'horrid nightmare': Portland, 187.

p. 187 gentleman's library: Arthur Ponsonby, 261.

'fairly ready': EH, xlv, 18 December 1898.

'Copulation': James, 80.

p. 188 'arch-fiend': Davis, 179.

'domination so long exercised': *Jewish Chronicle*, 1 July 1887. Alderman, 40.

p. 189 'shallow-pated': *Jewish Chronicle*, 13 November 1885. Alderman, 45–6.

'more shocked': EH, xlv, 17 December 1898.

'though he presumably': ibid., 18 December 1898.

p. 190 'beautiful *Rona*': ibid., 26 December 1898.

'Prince rather wonders': ibid., 6 January 1899.

p. 191 'regular virago': EH, BM Add MS 48606, 17 January 1899.

'deaf ear': EH, xlv, 28 January 1899.

no 'affairs': EH, XLVIII, 22 January 1901.

'unencumbered': Emden, *Jews*, 340.

p. 192 'see me *tomorrow*': Bdlds, X3, E VII to Cassel, Monday 1902.

'accepted tariff': Searle, 90.

£80,000 of trust: Rose, 279.

'gaga': Searle, 389.

Carrington disapprovingly: Lincolnshire Papers. Magnus, 389.

urged on Balfour: Searle, 93.

p. 193 'paid off privately': Blunt, *Diaries*, II, 8, 21 April 1901.

£26,085: Bdlds, X3, Cassel to E VII, 7 March 1901.

'glad to hear': ibid., E VII to Cassel, 23 November 1902.

'upwards of £30,000': ibid., Cassel to E VII, 5 February 1903.

'bull by horns': EH, XLVIII, 10 February 1901.

'said nothing': ibid., 13 February 1901.

sum too small: Lord Askwith, *Lord James of Hereford* (1930), 264.

p. 194 'minded to reject': EH, XLVIII, 20 February 1901.

'dodge': ibid., 28 February 1901.

'not extravagant': ibid., 8 March 1901.

'practically': ibid., 3 March 1901.

p. 195 'injudicious friends': ibid., XLIX, 15 April 1901.

'harped back': ibid., LI, 25 December 1902.

'Privy Purse': ibid., LII, 2 August 1903.

'meet at Newmarket': Bdlds, X3, E VII to Cassel, 6 October 1903.

"Consols": ibid., E VII to Cassel, 1 June 1902.

p. 196 'sooner have': EH, LI, 14 September 1902.

'quite right': ibid., LIII, June 1904.

'practically made up': ibid., LI, 4 May 1903.

'very angry': ibid., 15 May 1903.

'Mon Roi': Bdlds, X1, Bourke to E VII, undated.

p. 197 similar tale: Harris, III, 171.

daughter of Cassel's friend: Hon. Bridget Colebrooke, married in 1922 Lord Victor Paget. Nicholas Paget to author.

Cassel's measure: Bainbridge, 84–5.

bejewelled eggs: Keppel, 201.

'fat cheque': ibid., 45.

p. 198 'Such luxury': Bainbridge, 89.

'King put Fabergé: ibid., 102–3.

Alfred's mistress: Davis, 225.

'Emma told': M. Rothschild, 11n.

Lord Charles Beresford: Hibbert, 155.

p. 199 'City man': EH, LI, 2 April 1903.

'decidedly protectionist': ibid., LII, 5 July 1903.

'rather taken': ibid., 3 July 1903.

King had scolded: ibid., 8 July 1903.

'Bearer': J. L. Garvin, *Life of Joseph Chamberlain* (6 vols, 1932–9), V, 301.

'wholly good': R. S. Churchill, II, 88, 22 August 1904.

p. 200 'last string': EH, LIII, 22 July 1904.

'great loss': Bdlds, X3, E VII to Cassel, Marienbad, 3 September 1908.

'heavenly spot': EH, LIII, 6 August 1904.

'extraordinarily': ibid., 14 August 1904.

'Tiresome Teddy': Hough, 29.

Biblical quality: Keppel, 44.

'cock crows': Sermoneta, 140.

'kindest man': Fingall, 189.

p. 201 uncomfortably late: Algernon West, 313.

ringmaster: Cornwallis-West, 135–6.

scared by rabbit: Sermoneta, 74.
'divinely': EH, xLIV, 31 July 1898.
'could envisage': Warwick, 56.
'great pace': EH, xLIX, 11 March
1901.
p. 202 'the ablest': ibid., LI, 22 March
1903.
    informed in October: Bdlds, X17,
Durham to Devonshire 22 October
1902.
p. 203 'stout Teutonic': Fingall, 362.
    'never sell': Semon, 182.
    'Too vividly': Emden, *Jews*,
286–90.
    'hellish noise': Hibbert, 203.
p. 204 'Jackie' Fisher: ibid., 295.
    'tell you something': ibid., 295–6.
    'poorer middle': Lee, 400.
    Footnote: 'lower strata': RA
X.39/6, Semon to Knollys, 30 January
1902.
    '*usually* worn': Hibbert, 194.
p. 205 '*alarmist* now': St Aubyn, 474–5.
    'shocking affair': Hardinge
Papers. Magnus, 222–3.
    'necessary party': St Aubyn,
132–3.
p. 206 'All this trouble': Emden, *Jews*,
293.
    'enough to compromise': Smalley,
268.
    'greatest curses': Benson, *Were*,
218–9.
p. 207 'Suddenly I saw': Hibbert, 156.
    'lickerish': Magnus, 232.
    'base ingratitude': ibid., 236.
p. 208 'do dwell': *Survey of London*
(1980), xL, 281.
    'positively striking': Warwick, 92.
    'Very pretty': Alden Hatch, *The
Mountbattens* (1066), 190.
    'pay for this': Stewart Perowne to
author.
p. 209 knew the owner: Benson, *Are*, 238.
    'Come & see': Bdlds, X19, Sir
Philip Burne-Jones to Cassel, 1 April
1914.

    Footnote: Charles Booth, *Life and
Labour of the People of London*
(1891–1902). Frank Victor Dawes,
Not in Front of the Servants (Century,
1989), 127.
    'gone up wonderfully': EH, LII, 8
June 1904.
    'importance of being': Virginia
Cowles, *Edward VII and His Circle*
(1956), 283.

**Chapter 9 – Turkey: Frustration and
Failure**
p. 210 "Arthur": EH, LIII, 4 March,
1904.
p. 211 'very handsome': Esher, I, 322.
    'dull in perception': Bdlds, X1,
Esher to Cassel, 17 May 1902.
    'very kind': Esher, I, 339.
    'played pennies': ibid., 396.
    'scolded': Bdlds, X17, Esher to
Cassel, 12 October 1903.
    'generous forbearance': ibid.,
Balfour to Cassel, 15 February 1904.
p. 212 'money's worth': EH, LIII, 4
March 1904.
    'uncongenial work': Esher, II, 58.
    'intricacies': ibid., 60.
    'unusual flair': ibid., 175.
    'very interesting': Smalley, 377.
p. 213 'Mordecai': Harold Nicolson, *Sir
Arthur Nicolson, Lord Carnock*, (1930),
212.
    'Jew naturally': ibid., 171.
    'flung himself': ibid., 224.
p. 214 courageously checked:
Crankshaw, 387.
    'real state': Lee, II, 568–70.
    approached Barings: Ziegler,
312.
p. 215 '*desirable* to': Adler, 213.
    'great joy': ibid., 336.
    '*No*, on no account': Davis, 231.
    loan of $50 million: Cyrus Adler,
Jacob S. Schiff, A Biographical Sketch
(New York, 1921), 16–7.
    'clearly understood': Herzl

Diaries, 439.

p. 216 'enable him to float': RA
W.48/97.

"out of it": EH, xlvi, 23 May
1899.

'atrocious attacks': Balfour to
Rothschild, 6 November 1905.
M. Rothschild, 325 n. 54.

memorandum conceded: RA
W.53/98, 3 June 1908.

p. 217 Knollys responded: RA
W.53/99, 3 June 1908.

'off all right': Hardinge Papers.
Magnus, 407.

'great abuse': Hardinge Papers.
Ibid., 406.

'jobber in stocks': Bülow, iii,
309.

'huge responsibility': Ziegler,
314.

p. 218 'remedy simple': Davis, 229–30.

'absolutely divided': Ziegler, 315.
Duchess found: Sermoneta, 137.

p. 219 'have our tea': ibid., 139.

Siemens sounded: HBS, 29, Sir
Neil O'Conor and Dr von Siemens,
FO, 4 June 1901.

p. 221 'very nondescript': EH, xlvi, 21
October 1899.

enlisted Lord Revelstoke:
Ziegler, 316.

p. 222 'equal share': Francis, 169.

'Stupid fools': Esher, ii, 396.

'Joe's bile': Balfour MSS,
Lansdowne to Balfour, 12 April
1903. Francis, 172.

'bad humour': EH, li, 12 April
1903.

p. 223 'not unfavourably': Francis,
173–4.

'glad to think': Dawkins to
Gwinne, 23 April 1903. Gwinne,
1090.

'most melancholy': Dawkins to
Curzon, 26 April 1903. Francis, 177.

'sticking to our position':
Grunwald, 'Windsor Castle', 145.

'unmitigated noodles': Balfour,
233.

'stamping out': Esher, ii, 255.

p. 224 'Press dreadful': Balfour, 234.

£200,000: Esher, ii, 254–6.

p. 225 'energetic interest': McLean, 'Informal Empire' 294.

p. 226 'abandoned': Kent, 371.

Barings, pressed: Ziegler, 310.

'full diplomatic': Kent, 373.

p. 227 'many difficulties': Bdlds, X3, E
VII to Cassel, 19 March 1909.

'much perplexed': Kent, 372.

p. 228 'deal of pressure': McLean, 'Informal Empire' 295.

'strongly recommended': Hardinge, 165.

p. 229 'lines *satisfaisant*': HBS, 28, 18
October 1909.

'behaved very well': ibid., 19
October 1909.

difficulty in placing: *The Times*,
22 September 1910.

p. 230 Gwinne offered: HBS, 29, 20
July 1910.

'not overjoyed': ibid., 30, 3 April
1911.

'swimmingly': ibid., 29, 28 July
1910.

'amicable relations': W. S.
Churchill, *World Crisis, The Aftermath*,
iv, 374.

p. 231 'satisfactory settlement': Kent,
376.

p. 232 'done splendidly': ibid., 387
n. 71.

'position ridiculous': ibid., 378
n. 40.

'shutters down': HBS, 30, 21
September 1910.

repeated objections: ibid., Memo
30 September 1910.

p. 233 'direct opposition': McLean, 'Informal Empire', 297.

'bedrock': Kent, 377.

'result of the appeal': HBS, 30, 7
October 1910.

'cannot rely': Kent, 384.

'none keen': Ziegler, 310.

p. 235 'content to take part': HBS, 30, Cassel to Smith, undated.

'Such evidence': ibid., Cassel to Nicolson, undated.

'most official': ibid., Cassel to Smith, undated.

p. 236 'nothing to hamper': Kent, 385.

'had opened': HBS, 30, Cassel to Smith, undated.

Chapter 10 – Buckingham Palace: End of an Age

p. 238 'very tired': Magnus, 403.

p. 239 'made no objection': Jenkins, 180.

Crillon: ibid., 179.

'I believe': Bdlds, X1, Cassel to E VII, 13 April 1908.

p. 240 *'crass ignorance'*: Hardinge Papers, Magnus, 412.

'very idea': Esher Papers, ibid., 413.

'calming influence': Bdlds, X1, E VII to Cassel, undated.

'restrict the comforts': Davis, 239.

p. 241 'absolute loyalty': Bdlds, X6, Cassel to Ashley, 18 November 1909.

interesting financial: Esher, II, 266.

p. 242 'I think we': M. Rothschild, 41–2.

'vigorous terms': Knollys to Crewe, 1 August 1909. Magnus, 430–1.

'and *mean*': Knollys to Esher, 25 October 1909. Ibid., 431.

'Peers were mad': Hibbert, 285.

no further use: Lees-Milne, 200.

p. 243 informed guests: Viscount Knutsford, *In Black and White* (1926), 245.

'Who clamoured': *The Times*, 18 December 1909.

'knocked up': Jenkins, 199–200.

p. 244 crowds threatened: Frederic Ponsonby, 207.

p. 245 'looking very bright': Bdlds, X1, E VII to Cassel, 28 March 1910.

'welcome news': ibid., E VII to Cassel, 25 April 1910.

'sorry to leave': Hibbert, 288.

p. 246 'ushered in': Lee, II, 716–7.

'heard it': Hibbert, 291.

'look after': Lees-Milne, 206.

p. 247 'presume they belong': Bdlds, X19, Knollys to Cassel, 11 May 1910.

'perhaps be wise': ibid., X17, Knollys to Cassel, 29 November 1908.

'lamentable combustion': Magnus, 461.

Wyndham remarked: Blunt, *Diaries*, II, 316.

'cried together': Asquith, *Autobiography*, 103.

'regular sweep': Blunt, *Diaries*, II, 314.

p. 248 admitted defeat: Aronson, 253.

'dear Father': Bdlds, X11, G V to Cassel, 28 May 1910.

p. 249 resolutely refuse: Rose, 129.

'Tuty' blackballed: George Wadbridge, *The Reform Club 1836–1978* (1978), 91.

'heard nothing but': Japhet, 104–5.

p. 250 'made a mistake': ibid., 113.

'few nightgowns': Sermoneta, 141.

p. 251 'nice family': Bdlds, X1 E VII to Cassel, 23 September 1908.

Chapter 11 – Berlin: Bid for Peace

p. 253 'kind aunts': Tuchman, 275.

"Kaiser-Juden": Weizmann, 184.

p. 254 'so much good': Bülow, III, 275.

false impression: Frederic Whyte (trans.), *Letters of Prince von Bülow* (1931–2), 246, Kaiser to Bülow, 6 July 1908.

'*not* broached': Bdlds, X1, E VII to Cassel, 15 August 1908.

'timid': Bülow, 127.

p. 255 pencilled notes: Bdlds, X4

p. 256 'have any parley': Gooch, 666,
No. 492

'sufficiently weighty': Bdlds, X4,
Doc. 30, Churchill to Cassel, 23
January 1912.

naval expenditure: ibid., Docs. 35
and 36.

'complete agreement': ibid.,
Doc. 44.

p. 257 'temper is good': ibid., Doc. 53,
Churchill to Cassel, 31 January 1912.

'stiff letter': ibid., Doc. 45, Cassel
Memo, 30 January 1912.

p. 258 'suppose you mean': Desmond
Chapman-Huston (ed.), *Daisy,
Princess of Pless by Herself* (1928), 252.

Cassel authorized: W. S.-
Churchill, *Crisis*, I, 75.

'never do': Gooch, 670, No. 499.

p. 259 'nature of a luxury':
W. S. Churchill, *Crisis*, I, 76.

'queer and': Gooch, 674, No. 504.

'absolute sincerity': ibid., 678,
No. 506.

'gall and': ibid., 673, No. 502.

p. 260 'more in men': Bdlds, XX,
Haldane to Cassel, 25 February 1912.

'discreet private': Cecil, 192.

'absolutely shattered': Bdlds, X4,
Ballin to Cassel, 16 April 1912.

'bring the alliance': Cecil, 195.

p. 261 'bad impression': Bdlds, X4,
Ballin to Cassel, 20 March 1912.
(Ballin's letters translated by Dr
Dorothea McEwan).

'masterly analysis': ibid., Cassel to
Ballin, 22 March 1912.

'openness and honesty': ibid.,
Ballin to Cassel, 22 April 1912.

'steady and remorseless':
R. S. Churchill, II, 569.

p. 262 'opportunity for reaching': Bdlds,
X4, Ballin to Cassel, 19 January 1913.

further than to impress: Haldane,
288.

p. 263 'judge events': R. S. Churchill II,
Companion part 3, 1988.

'almost with tears': Bernard
Huldermann, *Albert Ballin* (Berlin,
1922), 302.

'possible for England': Cecil, 211.

p. 264 'takes the German': Esher, II,
295, 14 March 1908.

'ill-humour': Bdlds, X4, Ballin to
Cassel, 26 May 1912.

'only wish': Huldermann, op. cit.,
212.

'My ships': Cecil, 212.

p. 265 one shilling: Nubar Gulbenkian,
Pantaraxia: An Autobiography (1965),
82.

Banque de Salonique: Kent, 387.

p. 266 Footnote: Churchill to
Rothschild. M. Rothschild, 42n.

p. 267 succumb to forebodings: Semon,
295–8.

Chapter 12 – Hostilities

p. 269 'shall be spared': Münz, 244.

contribute most successfully:
Benson, *Are*, 57.

p. 270 'three layers': Gilbert, III, 693.

p. 271 Baron de Forest: R. S. Churchill,
II, 158.

'We shook hands': David Lloyd
George, *War Memoirs* (1933–6), I, 70.

'old Jew': M. Rothschild,
326–n. 15.

provoked Lord Michelham: *The
Times*, 29 May 1914.

p. 272 Forest opposed: John Grigg,
Lloyd George, From Peace to War
(1985), 105.

'not so bad': Benson, *Are*, 240.

p. 273 'driven or drummed': Emden,
Jews, 345.

obscure Scottish baronet:
H. Montgomery Hyde, *Lord Reading*
(1967), 171–2.

'go hang': Fitzroy, 613–4.

p. 274 'indeed a blessing': Bdlds, X11, G
V to Cassel, 27 August, 1915.

'up in the States': ibid., G V to
Cassel, 13 October 1915.

'most unfortunate': Bdlds, X19, McKenna to Cassel, 18 October 1915.

p. 275 House of Lords: British Nationality and State of Aliens Bill. Amendment re Privy Councillors being English moved by Lord Wittenham, 2 August 1918.

p. 276 'loathe cant': Bdlds, X18, Esher to Cassel, 4 August 1918.

'Majesty permit': ibid., X1, Cassel to G V, 16 November 1918.

spend a million: Haldane, 297–8.

p. 277 necessary £7,000: Lincolnshire Papers. Hibbert, 305 n. 97.

turned his back: Lincolnshire Papers. Rose, 230.

p. 278 Douglas sued: *The Times* Law Report, 18 July 1923. Rabinowicz, 175–184.

p. 279 'naturalized German': ibid., 12 December 1923. Ibid.,

'generous act': Fitzroy, 228.

thanked three times: Stella Underhill, Bdlds, A.1000a.

p. 280 'large and varied': Fitzroy, II, 762.

'Now Comes Rest': Madeleine Masson, *Edwina* (1958), 17.

'Church told me'. Fingall, 188.

p. 281 Footnote: Rubinstein, 472.

'At heart': Vansittart, 61.

'a great man': Bdlds, X19,

Churchill to Edwina Ashley, 25 September 1921.

p. 282 'everything in the world': Fingall, 188.

Epilogue

p. 283 'am proudest': Bdlds, X19, Cassel to Mrs Schiff, 15 January 1921.

p. 284 'most unreal': Harold Nicolson, *Diaries and Letters 1945–62*, ed. Nigel Nicolson (1968), 76, 1 June 1931.

historian suggested: Roth, *Sassoon*, 254.

p. 285 'Haldane asks': Haldane, 163.

'greater measure': *Daily Chronicle*, 8 April 1915. M. Rothschild, 46.

'principal beneficiaries': Wilson, 343.

p. 286 'greatest confidence': EH, LIV, 5 September 1905.

'human kindness': Viscount Grey of Fallodon, *Twenty-Five Years* (1925), II, 206.

p. 287 'dull court'. EH, LI, 5 November 1902.

'character and purpose': G. M. Young, *Victorian England: Portrait of an Age* (1936), 187.

p. 288 'barely and perfunctorily'. Roth. 'Court Jews', 365.

'more than balanced': Lee, II, 63.

Select Bibliography

Adler, Cyrus, *Jacob H. Schiff: His Life and Letters*, 2 vols, 1929.

Adler-Rudel, S. 'Moritz Baron Hirsch: Profile of a Great Philanthropist', *Year Book* VIII, Leo Baeck Institute, 1963.

Alderman, Geoffrey, *The Jewish Community in British Politics*, 1983.

Andrews, Allen, *The Splendid Pauper*, New York, 1968.

Aronson, Theo, *The King in Love: Edward VII's Mistresses*, 1988.

Asquith, Margot, *More Memories*, 1933.

Asquith, Margot, *Autobiography*, 2 vols, 1922.

Bainbridge, H. C., *Peter Carl Fabergé: His Life and Work*, 1949.

Balfour, Michael, *The Kaiser and His Times*, 1964.

Benson, E. F., *As We Are*, 1932.

Benson, E. F., *As We Were*, 1930.

Blunt, W. S., *My Diaries 1881–1914*, 2 vols, 1919-20.

Blunt, W. S., *The Secret History of the English Occupation of Egypt*, 1907.

Brook-Shepherd, Gordon, *Uncle of Europe*, 1975.

Bülow, Prince von, *Memoirs*, trans. F. A. Voigt, 4 vols, 1931–2.

Camplin, Jamie, *The Rise of the Plutocrats*, 1978.

Cecil, Lamar, *Business and Politics in Imperial Germany 1888–1918*, Princeton, 1967.

Churchill, Randolph S., *Winston S. Churchill*, Vols I and II, 1966–67

Churchill, Winston S., *My Early Life*, 1930.

Churchill, Winston S., *The World Crisis*, Vols I and IV, 1923–9.

Connell, Brian, *Manifest Destiny*, 1953.

Cornwallis-West, George, *Edwardian Hey-days*, 1930.

Corti, Egon, *The Reign of the House of Rothschild*, trans. Brian and Beatrix Lunn, 1928.

Crankshaw, Edward, *The Shadow of the Winter Palace*, 1976.

Crewe, Marquis of, *Lord Rosebery*, 2 vols, 1931.

Davis, Richard, *The English Rothschilds*, 1983.

Drumont, E., *La France juive*, Paris, 2 vols, 1886.

Eckardstein, Baron von, *Ten Years at the Court of St James's 1895–1905*, 1921.

Emden, Paul H., *Jews of Britain*, 1944.

Emden, Paul H., *Money Powers of Europe*, 1934.

Esher, Viscount, *Letters and Journals*, ed. M. V. Brett, 4 vols, 1934–8.

Fairbank, J. K., Bruner, K. F., and Matheson, E. M. (eds), *The I.G. in Peking: Letters of Robert Hart, Chinese Maritime Customs 1868–1907*, 1975.

Field, Geoffrey G., 'Anti-Semitism with the Boots Off', *Wiener Library Bulletin*, Special Issue.

Field, J. O., *Uncensored Recollections*, 1924.

Fingall, Elizabeth, Countess of, *Seventy Years Young*, 1937.

Fitzroy, Sir Almeric, *Memoirs*, 2 vols, 1925.

Foster, R. F., *Lord Randolph Churchill: A Political Life*, 1988.

Francis, R. M., 'The British Withdrawal from the Baghdad Railway Project in April 1903', *Historical Journal*, Vol. XVI, No. 1, 1973.

Gaillard, Gaston, *The Turks and Europe*, 1921.

Gilbert, Martin, *Winston S. Churchill*, Vol. III, 1969

Gladstone, Mary, *Her Diaries and Letters*, ed. Lucy Masterman, 1930.

Gooch, G. P., and Temperley, H. W. V. *British Documents on the Origins of the War 1898–1914*, Vol. VI

Graves, Philip, *Briton and Turk*, 1941.

Grunwald, Kurt, *Türkenhirsch*, Jerusalem, 1966.

Grunwald, Kurt, ' "Windsor Cassel": The Last Court Jew', *Year Book XIV*, Leo Baeck Institute, 1969.

Gwinne, Arthur von, 'The Baghdad Railway and the Question of British Cooperation', *The Nineteenth Century and After*, No. 388, 1909.

Gwynn, Stephen, and Tuckwell, Gertrude M., *Life of the Rt Hon. Sir Charles Dilke*, 2 vols, 1918.

Haldane, Viscount, *Autobiography*, 1929.

Hardinge of Penshurst, Lord, *Old Diplomacy*, 1947.

Harris, Frank, *My Life and Loves*, 4 vols, 1922–7.

Herzl, Theodor, *Diaries*, trans. and ed. Marvin Lowenthal, 1958.

Hibbert, Christopher, *Edward VII: A Portrait*, 1976.

Hough, Richard, *Edwina*, 1983.

Huldermann, Bernard, *Albert Ballin*, 1922.

James, Robert Rhodes, *Rosebery*, 1963.

Japhet, S., *Recollections*, 1931.

Jenkins, Roy, *Asquith*, 1964.

Jenks, L. H., *Migration of British Capital to 1875*, 1927.

Kent, Marian, 'Agent of Empire? The National Bank of Turkey and British Foreign Policy', *Historical Journal*, Vol. XVIII, No. 2, 1975.

Keppel, Sonia, *Edwardian Daughter*, 1958.

Lee, Sir Sidney, *King Edward VII*, 2 vols, 1925–7.

Lees-Milne, James, *The Enigmatic Edwardian*, 1986.

Litvinoff, Barnet, *The Burning Bush: Anti-Semitism and World History*, 1988.

Lonergan, W. F., *Forty Years of Paris*, 1907.

Longford, Elizabeth, *A Pilgrimage of Passion*, 1979.

Lufti, al-Sayyid, Afaf, *Egypt and Cromer*, 1968.

McLean, D., 'Finance and "Informal Empire" before the First World War', *Economic History Review*, Vol. 29, Series 2, 1976.

McLean, D., 'The Foreign Office and the First Chinese Indemnity Loan', *Historical Journal*, Vol. 16, No. 1, 1973.

Magnus, Sir Philip, *King Edward the Seventh*, 1964.

Martin, Ralph G., *Jennie: The Life of Lady Randolph Churchill*, 2 vols, 1971.

Münz, Sigmund, *King Edward VII at Marienbad*, 1934.

Nevill, Ralph, *Unconventional Memories*, 1923.

Norman, Theodore, *An Outstretched Arm: A History of the Jewish Colonization Association*, 1985.

Paget, Walpurga, Lady, *Embassies of Other Days*, 2 vols, 1923.

Painter, George D., *Marcel Proust*, 2 vols, 1967.

Ponsonby, Arthur, *Henry Ponsonby, Queen Victoria's Private Secretary: His Life from His Letters*, 1942.

Ponsonby, Sir Frederic, *Recollections of Three Reigns*, 1951.

Portland, Duke of, *Men, Women and Things*, 1937.

Rabinowicz, Oskar K., *Winston Churchill on Jewish Problems*, New York, 1960.

Rose, Kenneth, *George V*, 1983.

Roth, Cecil, 'The Court Jews of Edwardian England', *Jewish Social Studies*, Vol. V, No. 4, 1943.

Roth, Cecil, *The Magnificent Rothschilds*, 1939.

Roth, Cecil, *The Sassoon Dynasty*, 1941.

Rothschild, Miriam, *Dear Lord Rothschild: Birds, Butterflies and History*, 1983.

Rubinstein, W. D., 'British Millionaires 1809–1949', *Bulletin of the Institute of Historical Research*, Vol. XLVII, No. 116, 1974.

St Aubyn, Giles, *Edward VII: Prince and King*, 1979.

Searle, G. R., *Corruption in British Politics 1895–1930*, 1987.

Semon, Sir Felix, *Autobiography*, 1926.

Sermoneta, Duchess of, *Things Past*, 1929.

Sewell, J. P. C. (ed.), *Personal Letters of King Edward VII*, 1931.

Smalley, George W., *Anglo-American Memories*, 1911 and 1912.

Stern, Fritz, *Gold and Iron: Bismarck, Bleichröder and the Building of the German Empire*, New York, 1977.

Storrs, Sir Ronald, *Orientations*, 1937.

Sykes, Christopher Simon, *Private Palaces: Life in the Great London Houses*, 1985.

Szajkowski, Zoza, 'How the Mass Migration to America Began', *Jewish Social Studies*, Vol. IV, No. 4, 1942.

Thane, Pat, 'Financiers and the British State: The Case of Sir Ernest Cassel', *Business History*, Vol. XXVIII, No. 1, 1986.

Tuchman, Barbara, *The Proud Tower*, 1966.

Vansittart, Lord, *The Mist Procession*, 1938.

Warwick, Countess of, *Afterthoughts*, 1931.

Weizmann, Chaim, *Trial and Error*, 1949.

West, Sir Algernon, *Private Diaries*, ed. H. Hutchinson, 1922.

White, Arnold, *The Modern Jew*, 1899.

Wilson, Derek, *Rothschild*, 1988.

Wolf, Lucien, *Essays in Jewish History*, ed. Cecil Roth, Jewish Historical Society, 1934.

Ziegler, Philip, *The Sixth Great Power: Barings 1762–1929*, 1988.

Miscellaneous
Jewish Encyclopaedia.
Semi-Gotha, Munich, 1912–14.

Unpublished Sources
Babington Smith Papers (Trinity College, Cambridge).
Cassel Ledger (Bank of England).
Cassel Papers (Broadlands).
Foreign Office, general correspondence (Public Record Office).
Hamilton Diaries (British Library).
Knollys Papers (Kent Archives, Maidstone).
Royal Archives (Windsor Castle).
Salisbury Papers (Hatfield House).
Sublime Porte, Archive of the Office of the Grand Vizier (Istanbul).
Verwaltungsarchiv (Vienna).
Vickers Archives (University Library, Cambridge).

Index